To Madelyn and Bob

Table of Contents

Acknowledgments

I have many people to thank for helping make this book a reality. First, I thank Leonard Allen and his staff at Abilene Christian University Press. I have received full support and assistance from Leonard and ACUP. I also owe a debt of gratitude to the staff of the Marion E. Wade Center, particularly Laura Schmidt, Heidi Truty, Christopher W. Mitchell, and Marjorie L. Mead who encouraged my research and provided invaluable assistance during my many visits to the Wade Center.

I am grateful to the C. S. Lewis Society of Oxford for inviting me on several occasions to speak on Lewis, Ruth Pitter, and Joy Davidman, and for the helpful criticism and discussion by those in attendance. I thank also the C. S. Lewis Foundation for permitting me to lead two, two-week seminars at the Kilns in the summers of 2004 and 2009 where I floated many of my ideas with those in attendance. Elizabeth Pearson, the library director at Montreat College, and her staff have been endlessly patient and helpful in securing materials, especially Nathan King and Sue Diehl. I owe debts of gratitude to Dan Struble, president of Montreat College, for granting me a sabbatical to work on this book, and the Appalachian College Association for awarding me two summer research grants. Thanks are due as well to Corrie Greene, my research assistant Alyssa Klaus, and Joanna King-Yost who provided the initial ideas for the cover design. Finally, I owe my wife Jeanine a great debt since I spent so many hours away from her while working on this book.

In many of my original essays and reviews I made reference to unpublished sources; since most of those sources have since been published, I have updated the essays and reviews to reflect citations to the now published sources. Essays and reviews appearing in this collection were first published in and are used by the permission of *Books & Culture*, *Christianity and Literature*,

Christian Scholar's Review, The Chronicle of the Oxford C. S. Lewis Society, CSL: Bulletin of the New York C. S. Lewis Society, HIS, The Lamp-Post of the Southern California C. S. Lewis Society, Mythlore, Studies in the Literary Imagination, SEVEN: An Anglo-American Literary Review, and *World*. I cite the original publication information at the beginning of each essay and review.

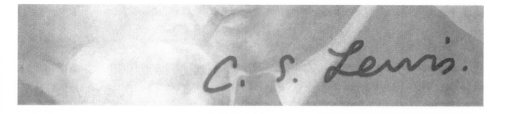

Introduction

May I seize this occasion to trot out a hobby-horse and a grievance? There is today far too little straightforward interpretative criticism. Everybody insists on doing "creative" criticism—which means that the critic simply uses his author as a spring-board from which to leap off into an exposition of his own views about the universe . . . . There is no doubt a place for this kind of thing. But I still think we need the pure interpreter, who will sit down before a poem, or whatever it is, with humility to it and charity to the reader, and begin by finding out and explaining what the author actually did say, before he starts to explain what the author ought to have said and would have said if he had been as enlightened a person as his critic. A friend of mine, after toiling through unintelligible books about modern poetry, said plaintively, "I want a critic who will say: 'This is a poem about a bus; this is what the poem says about the bus; this is the conclusion the writer draws from his observation about the bus; I think he has said it well (beautifully, badly, etc.) for the following reasons.' After that he can say what he likes, and I shall know where I am." (Letter from Dorothy L. Sayers to C. S. Lewis, Oct. 22, 1948)[1]

When I first read this passage I was struck by how similar Sayers and Lewis were in their perspectives on literary crit-icism. Saying essentially the same thing, Lewis put it this way in his poem "*Spartan Nactus*": "I am so coarse, the things the poets see / Are obstinately invisible to me . . . / I am like that odd man Wordsworth knew, to whom / a primrose was a yellow primrose."[2] As interpretative critics Sayers and

Lewis model well her admonition that literary critics should "sit down before a poem, or whatever it is, with humility to it and charity to the reader, and begin by finding out and explaining what the author actually did say." *Plain to the Inward Eye: Selected Essays on C. S. Lewis* has been written in that spirit, and while I make no claim to be the equal of either Sayers or Lewis, my own approach to literary criticism, and thus this collection of essays and reviews, follows the same critical perspective.

The genesis for this collection coalesced around the fiftieth anniversary of the death of Lewis and the realization that for the last forty years I have been reading, thinking, and writing about Lewis. Realizing these two facts led me to think it might be time to harvest some of the essays I have written during that time period and bring them together in one volume. These essays—arranged more or less chronologically—concern four aspects of my writing about Lewis. The first deals mainly with what will perhaps be Lewis's longest lasting legacy—his Chronicles of Narnia. The second focuses upon Lewis's poetry, an area of his work that I believe has been neglected for too long. The third shifts attention to Lewis and the two women poets with whom he had lasting relationships: Ruth Pitter and Joy Davidman. This group of essays is necessarily biographical but not exclusively so; that is, I try to examine the nature of Lewis's relationship with Pitter and Davidman via their poetry, in the process committing what Lewis might call the "personal heresy." The fourth gleans some of my reviews and review essays of key books on Lewis, offering a perspective on the ways in which scholarly interest in Lewis has developed over the last thirty years and concluding with a new review essay that covers several of the most important recent books written on Lewis.

A fair question at this point might be why readers should bother with my essays on Lewis. I am, of course, only one among a number of literary scholars who take Lewis's work seriously. An initial reply to this concern is that if longitude is important then I am among a group of less than a dozen Lewis scholars who have kept an eye on Lewis studies for four decades. Longevity, however, is no guarantee of literary acumen. One can offer bad literary criticism over forty years much easier than good literary criticism. So having watched the development of Lewis criticism for a long time is important but that is not enough. A more telling reply is that I have surveyed with a critical eye the way in which Lewis's work has become increasingly popular over this time period. For instance, the Chronicles of Narnia sell over a million copies annually, and since 2005 they have become even more popular because of major film adaptations of the first three Narnian books. During this period I have seen a distinct shift in the nature of Lewis criticism. When I first started writing about Lewis in the early 1980s, most critical writing about him was hagiography, focusing primarily upon Lewis as one who wrote winsomely and effectively about Christianity. Writers saw in Lewis an intellectual who could think, argue, and write—broadly speaking—in defense of Christianity.

However, there was a small group of scholars who focused attention on Lewis as literary craftsman—on his even-handed use of rhetoric, the depth of his formal education, his intellectual range, his quick mind, his good humor, his debt to other writers and thinkers, his stylistic achievements, his apt use of language, his use of figurative devices (especially analogy and metaphor), his fine ear for the sound of words, his turn of the phrase, and, finally, his intuitive ability to write clear, lucid prose. These critics saw Lewis primarily as a writer, not as a Christian writer. Having watched this body of critics do their work, I believe I have a perspective on the nature of Lewis studies that is unique and potentially helpful to those interested in viewing this work through a focusing lens. At the same time I do not offer my perspective as authoritative; there are other compelling critical perspectives on Lewis, and throughout the book I will be directing readers to other Lewis scholars from whom they can learn much.

Plain to the Inward Eye attempts to continue the tradition of literary criticism modeled by Sayers and Lewis. It is not offered as a refutation of other critical perspectives popular in the last fifty years, including post-structuralism and deconstruction; instead it is offered as a viable alternative. That this kind of literary criticism is still important finds support in Lewis's poem "The Country of the Blind" where he suggests that language—and by implication meaning—is under attack by persons "Whose blind mouths would abuse words that belonged to their / Great-grandsires, unabashed, talking of *light* in some / Eunuch'd, etiolated, / Fungoid sense." If one doubts such is the case, Lewis ends the poem by saying:

> Go then about among
> Men now famous; attempt speech on the truths that once,
> Opaque, carved in divine forms, irremovable,
> Dread but dear as a mountain-
> Mass, stood plain to the inward eye.[3]

My hope is that the essays in this collection illustrate the principles of literary criticism advocated by Sayers, Lewis, and other like-minded scholars who have shaped and inspired my journey.

August 2012
Montreat College
Montreat, North Carolina

Introduction Notes

1. *The Letters of Dorothy L. Sayers, Vol. 3, 1944–1950: A Noble Daring*, ed. Barbara Reynolds (Cambridge: The Dorothy L. Sayers Society, 1998), 401.

2. *Punch* 227 (December 1, 1954): 685 (subsequent references in the text). The title means "Spartan having obtained." Revised and titled "A Confession" in *Poems*, ed. Walter Hooper (New York: Harcourt, Brace Jovanovich, 1964), 1.

3. "The Country of the Blind," *Punch* 221 (September 12, 1951): 303 (emphasis Lewis). Revised and reprinted in *Poems*, 33.

Narnia and the Seven Deadly Sins[1]

Several years ago while teaching a fantasy literature course, I thought I saw an interesting relationship between the seven deadly sins and C. S. Lewis's Chronicles of Narnia; it struck me that Lewis, a medieval scholar, had an intimate knowledge of the seven deadly sins. In this essay I briefly summarize the history of the seven deadly sins, illustrate Lewis's knowledge of them by referring to several non-Narnian works, and conclude by suggesting how each sin may connect to a particular book in the Chronicles.

The development of a list of seven especially damning sins is shadowy. Early church fathers (Hermas, Tertullian, Augustine), while never actually listing specific "deadly" sins, did suggest some sins were worse than others, perhaps with 1 John 5:16–17 in mind: "If anyone sees his brother committing a sin not leading to death, he shall ask and God will for him give life to those who commit sin not leading to death. There is a sin leading to death; I do not say that he should make request for this. All unrighteousness is sin, and there is a sin not leading to death." What eventually resulted were numerous lists of especially harmful sins. However, the list that came to be most influential in the church was the one developed by Gregory the Great (540–605 A.D.) characterized by its Latin acronym, *saligia*: *superbia* (pride), *avaritia* (greed), *luxuria* (luxury, later lust), *invidia* (envy), *gula* (gluttony), *ira* (anger), and *acedia* (sloth).[2] Medieval texts such as William Langland's *Piers Plowman*, Dante's *Divine Comedia*, Chaucer's "The Parson's Tale," and Spenser's *Faerie Queen* all devote serious attention to these seven sins.

It is not surprising then that Lewis often discusses the seven deadly sins. For instance, throughout his *The Allegory of Love* Lewis refers to the seven deadly sins. While commenting on Langland, Lewis says that his "excellent satiric comedy, as displayed in the behavior of the seven Deadly Sins belongs to a tradition as old as the *Ancren Riwle*."[3] Elsewhere he refers to specific sins on the list. In *Mere Christianity* he saves an entire chapter for pride ("the great sin"); in *The Screwtape Letters* he devotes letters to lust (IX, XVII), gluttony (XVII), and pride (XXIV); in *The Great Divorce* he pictures sinners unwilling to enter heaven because of greed, sloth, and envy; and finally, in *Poems* an entire poem, "Deadly Sins," focuses on each one of the seven deadly sins. Since Lewis so readily refers to the seven deadly sins in many of his other works, he may either consciously or subconsciously have emphasized one of the seven deadly sins in each of the seven Narnian books.[4] Let me add here that it is certain Lewis deals with multiple sins in Narnia; in fact, each book reflects this. Nonetheless, each book does seem to portray one particular deadly sin above the others.[5]

In *The Lion, the Witch and the Wardrobe*, Edmund Pevensie personifies *gula*, the sin of excessively using things, in themselves legitimate, but associated with over-indulging the appetite; in effect, he makes his belly the god he serves (Phil. 3:19). Jadis, the White Witch, exploits Edmund's gluttony when she meets him in a snowy woods, offering him a warm drink and Turkish Delight, his favorite candy. From the first bite, he is hooked, for each "piece was sweet and light to the very centre and Edmund had never tasted anything more delicious."[6] As she pumps him for information regarding his brother and sisters, he readily replies, driven by an insatiable hunger for more and more Turkish Delight: "At first Edmund tried to remember that it is rude to speak with one's mouth full, but soon he forgot about this and thought only of trying to shovel down as much Turkish Delight as he could, and the more he ate, the more he wanted to eat, and he never asked himself why the Queen should be so inquisitive" (28–29). This scene recalls Eve's gluttonous indulgence in Milton's *Paradise Lost* when she first eats the forbidden fruit:

> . . . . for Eve
> Intent now wholly on her taste, naught else

Regarded, such delight till then, as seem'd
In fruit she never tasted, whether true
Or fancied so, through expectation high
Of knowledge, nor was God-head from her thought,
Greedily she ingorged without restraint,
And knew not eating Death. (IX, 785–92)[7]

Like Eve's, Edmund's gluttonous desire has deadly ramifications, for later in the tale, after he has betrayed his brother and sisters in order to obtain more and more Turkish Delight (which, ironically, he does not receive), Jadis demands his life by invoking Deep Magic: an ancient Narnian law that entitles her to the blood of any traitor. And while Edmund is saved by the intervention and intercession of Aslan, the cost is deadly to the latter. Lewis's point in emphasizing Edmund's gluttony is to illustrate vividly the effects of sins in general and this sin in particular; over indulgence blinds us to the truth, turning us inward, making us slaves to our own insatiable desires.

In *Prince Caspian* Lewis emphasizes the deadly sin of luxury. Some explanation is necessary here regarding the meaning of *luxuria*. Many early lists of the seven deadly sins substitute for *luxuria* the terms *fornicatio*, *sodomita*, or *libido*, all suggesting sexual immorality or unchecked physical passion. I believe, however, that Lewis chose to use *luxuria* in the sense of lust for things in general. I base my reasoning on his analysis of a medieval poem by Prudentius, "Psychomachia," recorded in *The Allegory of Love*. There Lewis comments: "It should be noticed that Prudentius' seven champions do not exactly correspond with the familiar list of the seven deadly sins in later writers. *Luxuria*, . . . is, in fact, something very like 'luxury' in the modern meaning of the word—the sin of the profiteer" (70). That Lewis would choose the use *luxuria* in this sense is not surprising, considering that the bulk of his audience, young children, would be more likely to understand it rather than sexual lust.[8]

In the tale Prince Caspian's uncle, King Miraz, is guilty of profiteering in his desire to gain power, wealth, and position. After Caspian's father died, Miraz initially ruled as "Lord Protector" for his young nephew. However, after the lords who were loyal to Caspian's father died, Miraz allowed himself to be proclaimed king by planted flatterers. Dr. Cornelius, Caspian's tutor, neatly describes this lusty grab for power:

And then, one by one, all the great lords who had known your father, died or disappeared. Not by accident, either. Miraz weeded them out. Belisar and Uvilas were shot with arrows on a hunting party: by chance, it was pretended. All the great houses of the Passarids he sent to fight giants on the Northern frontier till one by one they fell. Arlian and Eriman and a dozen more he executed for treason on a false charge. The two brothers of Beaversdam he shut up as madmen. And finally he persuaded the seven noble lords, who alone among all the Telmarines did not fear the sea, to sail away and look for new lands beyond the Eastern Ocean, and, as he intended, they never came back.[9]

Later the truth of Miraz' lust for power becomes crystallized for Caspian when he learns that Miraz had murdered Caspian's father; furthermore, Caspian discovers that to establish himself permanently as the rightful ruler and guarantee his line, Miraz plans to kill him on the night the queen gives birth to a son.

I think Lewis intends to demonstrate through Miraz the effect that *luxuria* can have on a society when embodied in its rulers. While Miraz rules, truth is suppressed; talking Narnian creatures are outlawed as well as tales about them. There is little trust between the members of society, including native born Narnians. For instance, at one point a leader of the Black Dwarves is willing to call up the spirit of Jadis to fight Miraz: "'I'll believe in anyone or anything,' said Nikabrik, 'that'll batter these cursed Telmarines barbarians to pieces or drive them out of Narnia. Anyone or anything. Aslan *or* the White Witch, do you understand?'" (63; emphasis Lewis). Such a disintegration of society is to be expected when government becomes primarily concerned with consolidating its own power and authority instead of promoting the welfare of its people.

In *The Voyage of the Dawn Treader* Lewis emphasizes *avaritia*, pictured in the thoroughly obnoxious Eustace Clarence Scrubb. Eustace, besides being entirely egocentric and totally selfish, is greedy beyond bounds. His greed and its consequences provide the central episode of the tale. After an exhausting storm drives Eustace and his shipmates to an island where they intend to replenish their supplies, Eustace, feeling picked on, slinks away to the center of the island where, to his shock, he encounters a dying dragon. He watches the dragon breathe its last gasp and begins "to feel as if he had fought and killed the dragon instead of merely seeing it die."[10] Eustace is then driven by a fierce rainstorm into the dragon's lair where he discovers its rich hoard. Delighted with his find, Eustace greedily stuffs his pockets with diamonds and slips a large diamond bracelet above his elbow. Once he realizes he can carry no more, he falls asleep on a pile of golden coins.

When Eustace awakens because of a pain in his arm, he sees before him a dragon's claw. Much to his consternation he notices that whenever he moves, the claw moves. At first he thinks the dead dragon's mate has come to avenge its death, but soon he realizes the truth: "He had turned into a dragon while he was asleep. Sleeping on a dragon's hoard with greedy thoughts in his heart, he had become a dragon himself" (87). His transformation, of course, explains the pain in his arm: "the bracelet which fitted very nicely on the upper arm of a boy was far too small for the thick, stumpy foreleg of a dragon" (87). The pain this causes serves as an appropriate reminder to Eustace of his greed. In him Lewis illustrates the negative, egocentric effect greed has upon an individual. Eustace is "useless" both to himself and to society. The greedy person is only interested in elevation of self and is more than willing to use others for his own advantage. Fortunately Eustace has an encounter with Aslan and is re-transformed, though only through an extremely painful experience. Unable to shed his dragon skin himself, Eustace submits to the fierce claws of Aslan and is reborn a new, whole person.

The Silver Chair portrays the dangerous effects of *acedia*, a disgust with the spiritual because of the physical effort involved. Jill Pole is confronted by Aslan early in the tale and is commanded to set to memory four important signs that will aid her and Eustace as they quest for a lost prince of Narnia. The importance of remembering the signs is paramount as Aslan indicates:

> Remember, remember, remember the Signs. Say them to yourself when you wake in the morning and when you lie down at night. And whatever strange things may happen to you, let nothing turn your mind from following the Signs . . . . Take great care [the Narnian air] does not confuse your mind. And the Signs which you have learned here will not look at all as you expect them to look, when you meet them there. This is why it is so important to know them by heart and

pay no attention to appearances. Remember the Signs and believe the Signs. Nothing else matters.[11]

Here Lewis is echoing Deuteronomy 6:6–9:

> And these words, which I am commanding you today, shall be on your heart; and you shall teach them diligently to your sons and shall talk of them when you sit in your house and when you walk by the way and when you lie down and when you rise up. And you shall bind them as a sign on your hand and they shall be as frontals on your forehead. And you shall write them on the door posts of your house and gates.

The thrust of this parallel is clear: just as God gives humankind certain rules, commands, and signs to live by, so Aslan gives his followers similar rules. The emphasis in each case is on binding or remembering the signs in order that life be lived in direct accord with the Creator.

Jill fails, as do many of us, because of sloth. That is, her sloth is not so much overt laziness or reckless disregard as it is a gradual erosion of devotion—an ever creeping numbness regarding the spiritual tasks set before her. Indeed, at first she is keenly aware of the signs and tells Eustace about them; however, within a matter of hours after her arrival in Narnia "she had forgotten all about the Signs and the lost prince for the moment" (35). Consequently, she and her companions stumble along on their quest and as the going gets rougher, her diligence in remembering the signs fades: "They never talked about Aslan, or even about the lost prince now. And Jill gave up her habit of repeating the Signs over to herself every night and morning. She said to herself, at first, that she was too tired, but she soon forgot all about it" (78).

Jill's lack of diligence turns to irritability when she is called upon to remember the signs; for instance, during a snow storm (that blinds them all to one of the signs) Jill is asked which sign they should be looking for: "Oh come on! Bother the signs . . . . Something about someone mentioning Aslan's name I think but I'm jolly well not going to give a recitation here" (85). Lewis points out:

> She had got the order wrong. That was because she had given up saying the signs over every night. She still really knew them, if she

troubled to think: but she was no longer so "pat" in her lesson as to be sure of reeling them off in the right order at a moment's notice and without thinking. [The] question annoyed her because deep down inside her, she was already annoyed with herself for not knowing the Lion's lesson quite so well as she felt she ought to have known it. (85)

Fortunately for Jill, however, Aslan intervenes by means of a dream and re-awakens her faithfulness. As a result, later on after having failed to recognize the first three signs because of sloth, she does recognize the fourth, and she acts to follow it, even though the risk is enormous. In Jill, Lewis portrays all who fail to persevere, who fail to keep the vision. Like Jill, many are susceptible to the weary grind, the dull repetition of routine, the easy slide into self-fulfillment at the cost of spirituality. Yet Lewis suggests that we, like Jill, can break the chains of *acedia*; we too can regain a spiritual vision.

Pride characterizes three key characters in *The Horse and His Boy*. Bree, a talking Narnian war horse, is acutely conscious of how he looks; as he travels towards Narnia, he does all he can to make sure he acts and looks the part. Aravis, an escaped princess of Calormene, holds an extremely high opinion of herself and her position; she is royalty and demands respect, in spite of her runaway status. Most indicative of her pride is her tendency to use others regardless of the consequences for them. However, Prince Rabadash, the evil heir of Calormene, is Lewis's supreme example of pride. And in him Lewis creates a comic episode appropriate to the sin of *superbia*.

Rabadash, after having let a Narnian princess he wants to marry slip through his fingers at sea, rushes an armed sortie to attack Narnia overland. During the ensuing battle, Rabadash is captured in a most embarrassing way. Hemmed in at the top of a wall, he decides to jump down into the midst of the battle raging below:

And he meant to look and sound—no doubt for a moment he did look and sound—very grand and very dreadful as he jumped, crying "the bolt of Tash fall from above." But he had to jump sideways because the crowd in front of him left him no landing place in that direction. And then, in the neatest way you could wish, [a] tear in the back of his hauberk caught on a hook in the wall . . . . And there he found himself, like a piece of washing hung up to dry, with everyone laughing at him.[12]

Lewis's use of humor to attack pride is, of course, traditional. Elsewhere he quotes both Thomas More's "the devil . . . the prowde spirit . . . cannot endure to be mocked" and Martin Luther's "the best way to drive out the devil, if he will not yield to the texts of Scripture, is to jeer and flount him, for he cannot bear scorn."[13]

Lewis continues the humiliation of Rabadash's pride with comedy. When he later arrogantly refuses surrender terms, Aslan appears and says to him: "Forget your pride (what have you to be proud of?) and your anger (who has done you wrong?) and accept the mercy of these good kings" (*HHB*, 192). Unfortunately, Rabadash lashes out at Aslan, calling him a demon, a foul fiend, and enemy of his own gods. Furthermore, he invokes the aid of his own god, Tash. Aslan warns him calmly to "have a care . . . . Thy doom is nearer now: it is at the door: it has lifted the latch" (193). Still Rabadash abuses Aslan until he turns Rabadash into an ass: "'Oh, not a Donkey! Mercy! If it were even a horse—even a horse—e'en—a—hor—eeh—auh, eeh-auh.' And so the words died away into a donkey's bray. . . . Of course the Donkey twitched its ears forward—and that also was so funny that everybody laughed all the more. They tried not to, but they tried in vain" (194). So, just as Eustace's greed turned him into a dragon, Rabadash, whose pride makes him act like an ass, gets turned into one. In Rabadash, Lewis reminds us that "pride goes before destruction, and a haughty spirit before stumbling" (Proverbs 16:18).

The sixth Narnian tale, *The Magician's Nephew*, portrays the deadly sin of *ira*. The tale, which reveals both how Narnia was created and how evil first entered it, revolves around the adventures of Polly Plummer, Digory Ketterley, and Digory's Uncle Andrew, a somewhat ludicrous black magician who Digory thinks "mad," an obvious pun used for effect throughout the story. Uncle Andrew's madness is concerned with diabolical experiments (he develops rings that whisk people out of this world and into others); however, his madness is also concerned with anger. Digory, too, evidences a quick temper. An episode early on provides a typical example of how wrath works in this tale. After Uncle Andrew has tricked Polly into trying on one of the rings and she has disappeared, Digory confronts him with cheeks that "were flaming with anger."[14] Not to be frightened, his uncle, "bringing his hand down on the table," said: "I will not be talked to like that by a little dirty schoolboy. You don't understand. I am the great scholar, the magician, the adept, who is *doing* the experiment" (20; emphasis Lewis). Digory replies by shouting at him, telling him to "shut up," speaking fiercely at him, and wishing he was "big enough to punch [his uncle's] head!" Later, when Digory and Polly are attempting to enter another world, they argue: "And Polly gave him a pretty sharp answer and he said something even nastier in reply. The quarrel lasted for several minutes" (33–34).

Soon they discover a world inhabited by people who are standing perfectly still, apparently in some kind of suspended animation. They find an inscription directing the reader to "strike a bell and bide the danger" or wonder "till it drives you mad." Digory, impulsive and brash, wants to strike the bell while Polly does not. Once again their anger surfaces. After he insults her timidity as childish, she "who was now in a real rage," threatens to leave him, calling him a "beastly, stuck-up obstinate pig!" (45). Digory, responding "in a voice even nastier than he meant it to be," struck the bell before she could disappear; his act, motivated primarily by anger at Polly, unintentionally set into motion the process whereby evil, in the person of Jadis, eventually entered Narnia.

Once Jadis enters the story, the focus of *ira* shifts from the others to her. For instance, while she is in London for a short time, she is so angered by Digory's Aunt Letty's lack of respect that she "caught Aunt Letty round the neck and the knees, raised her high above her head as if she had been no heavier than a doll, and threw her across the room" (71). Later, she comes riding down the street on the top of a hansom: "Her teeth were bared, her eyes shone like fire, and her long hair streamed out behind her like a comet's tail. She was flogging the horse without mercy" (76). Before she can do more damage, Digory grabs her (and inadvertently several others) and transports her into a brand new world. They all hear the song of creation and witness the making of Narnia. But for Jadis it is a hateful experience: "She hated it. She would have smashed that whole world, or all worlds, to pieces, if it would only stop singing" (89). When she comes face to face with the singer, Aslan, the highest irony of the tale occurs. In her wrath and rage, she takes an iron bar and throws it at Aslan, striking him "fair between the eyes." Instead of hurting him it glances off and, because of the land's creative fecundity, it begins to grow into a "perfect little model of a lamp-post." From here Jadis goes skulking off, determined to thwart Aslan, to get her own way. And for a while she does get her way, a way that causes Narnia to be winter always, but "never Christmas." The frozen landscapes and hushed streams her way brings are appropriate emblems of the effect *ira* can have; it brings about a coldness in relationships and life that penetrates deeply, freezing to the roots the necessary interplay of human affection.

The pettiness of wrath, the demand that all others must agree and consent to "my way," is at the same time both comic and tragic—comic in that those on the outside can so easily see the ludicrous position of the angry person, and tragic in that those same people can do very little to assuage the violent passion that this sin evokes. That the focusing sin in *The Magician's Nephew* is wrath is finally underscored in the last lines of the tale where we read Uncle Andrew's evaluation of Jadis: "'A devilish temper she had,' he would say. 'But she was a dem fine woman, sir, a dem fine woman'" (167). In these words Lewis hints at the key problem of wrath: it is of the devil. Jadis's "devilish temper" is emphasized time and time again in the story; at one point she even mimics Milton's Satan in the temptation scene of *Paradise Lost*. Lewis would have us see that *ira*, uncontrolled rage, is another form of blindness. It turns us away from a right and whole vision of the truth, and instead leads us towards egoism, expressed by choler and revenge.

In *The Last Battle* Lewis displays the devastating power of *invidia*. Envy, the inordinate desire for someone else's possessions or position, is unique in the list of seven deadly sins since it is the only one also mentioned in the Ten Commandments: "You shall not covet your neighbor's wife or his male servant or his female servant or his ox or his donkey or anything that belongs to your neighbor" (Exodus 20:17). The focus of envy in this tale centers upon the attempt of the ape, Shift, to usurp the position and authority of Aslan by having his dim-witted donkey friend, Puzzle, impersonate Aslan while being manipulated by Shift. Fashioning a make-shift lion's skin for Puzzle to wear, Shift hopes to pass the ass off as Aslan: "No one who had ever seen a real lion would have been taken in for a moment. But if someone who had never seen a lion looked at Puzzle in his lionskin, he just might mistake him for a lion, if he didn't come too close, and if the light was not too good, and if Puzzle didn't let out a bray and didn't make any noise with his hoofs."[15] When Puzzle protests against the presumption of pretending to be Aslan, Shift counters with clever words arguing that together they could do much good, promising "to advise you, you know. I'd think of sensible orders for you to give. And everyone would have to obey us, even the King himself. We would set everything right in Narnia" (10).

Shift's desire to take Aslan's place is urged on because of his infrequent appearance in recent Narnian history. Indeed, Shift does not believe in Aslan, for when Puzzle wonders what will happen if the real Aslan shows up while they are impersonating him, Shift replies: "I expect he'd be very pleased . . . . Probably he sent us the lion skin on purpose, so that we could set things to right. Anyway, he never *does* turn up, you know. Not now-a-days" (10; emphasis Lewis). In effect, then, Shift's desire to become Aslan is a kind of cynical envy; that is, while denying the reality of an Aslan, he deliberately sets about to appropriate the honor and authority associated with Aslan's name.

The impact of Shift's envy is catastrophic to Narnia in two distinct ways: socially and spiritually. First, Shift's envy of Aslan's power leads to break-downs in the social fabric of Narnian society. For instance, he adopts a policy of selling Narnian timber to Calormene speculators; this would be innocuous except the timber is made up of talking Narnian trees. This policy is, in effect, murder, as King Tirian exclaims: "What? . . . . Murdering the talking trees?" (16). In addition, the environment is ravaged and stripped: "Right through the middle of that ancient forest—that forest where the trees of gold and of silver had once grown. . .—a broad land had already been opened. It was a hideous land like a raw-gash in the land, full of muddy ruts where felled trees had been dragged down to the river" (20).

Furthermore, the rightful inhabitants of Narnia are confused by the old stories about Aslan's goodness and the contradictory commands and demands made by Shift, the so-called "mouthpiece of Aslan." For example, a mouse explains: "It would have been better if we'd died before all this began. But there's no doubt about it. Everyone says it is Aslan's orders, and we've seen him. We didn't think Aslan would be like that" (37). It is germane here to mention as well that there are destructive political ramifications of Shift's actions since the authority of Tirian is wrested away by Shift. At one point, Tirian is dragged before Shift, who "wore what seemed to be a paper crown on his head" (27). And although the king still enjoys the loyalty and love of most true Narnian subjects, he eventually loses all real political power to Shift.

However, much more debilitating is the spiritual upheaval caused by Shift's envious power grab. Motivated by selfishness, expressed most often by demands of tribute nuts, oranges, and bananas, Shift uses Aslan's name to force the Narnians to placate his palate: "Now attend to me. I want—I mean, Aslan wants—some more nuts. These you've brought aren't anything near enough. You must bring . . . twice as many . . . by sunset tomorrow, and there mustn't be any bad ones or any small ones among them" (27–28). In fact Shift substitutes his will for Aslan's. He claims that "I'm the only one Aslan is ever going to speak to . . . . He'll tell me what you've got to do, and I'll tell the rest of you" (29).

All this leads to a kind of spiritual heresy, for when the animals question Shift, he associates Aslan with Tash, the cruel god of the Calormenes: "Tash is only another name for Aslan . . .Tash and Aslan are only two different names for you know who . . . . Tash is Aslan: Aslan is Tash" (31). The impact of Shift's lie is terrible: "You know how sad your own dog's face can look sometimes. Think of that and then think of all the faces of those Talking Beasts—all those honest, humble, bewildered birds, bears, badgers, rabbits, moles, and mice— all far sadder than that. Every tail was down, every whisker drooped. It would have broken your heart with very pity to see their faces" (31–32). The eventual result of Shift's envy is the physical destruction of Narnia. The Narnians are defeated in battle with the Calormenes, although the end of the tale is far from tragic as Aslan intervenes once more. Nonetheless, the envy of Shift does much disservice to Aslan and the cause of truth. Innocent lives are taken and a world is destroyed. Once more, Lewis illustrates the destructive power of a deadly sin in the context of a Narnian tale.

The thrust of my argument has been simple: that Lewis consciously or unconsciously emphasized one particular deadly sin in each of the seven Chronicles of Narnia. The evidence I have presented is only indicative of a good deal more. What Lewis would have us draw out of all this is a clear moral vision of right and wrong, good and evil. That is, while the Chronicles exist in their own right as imaginative vehicles of Lewis's creative energy, they are not works set in a moral vacuum. Lewis would agree with George MacDonald at this point:

> In the moral world . . . a man may clothe in new forms, and for this employ his imagination freely, but he must invent nothing. He may not, for any purpose, turn its laws upside down . . . . The laws of the spirit of man must hold, alike in this world and in any world he may invent. It were no offence to suppose a world in which everything repelled instead of attracted the things around it; it would be wicked to write a tale representing a man it called good as always doing bad things, or a man it called bad as always doing good things: the notion itself is absolutely lawless. In physical things a man may invent; in

moral things he must obey—and take their laws with him into his invented world as well.[16]

Lewis has done just this in his Chronicles of Narnia. He has taken the seven deadly sins into Narnia, shown their destructive power, and set before us examples to avoid. Although each book highlights a particular sin and illustrates its specific effect on characters, the message in each case is the same: sin is deadly.

Chapter 1 Notes

1. A version of this essay first appeared in *Mythlore* 10 (Spring 1984): 14–19. It was reprinted in *Pilgrimage: The Newsletter of the Toronto C. S. Lewis Society* 10, no. 1 (Nov. 2002): 1–8.

2. The best study of the seven deadly sins is found in Morton W. Bloomfield, *The Seven Deadly Sins: An Introduction to the History of a Religious Concept, with Special Reference to Medieval English Literature* (East Lansing, MI: Michigan State University, 1952).

3. C. S. Lewis, *The Allegory of Love: A Study in Medieval Tradition* (London: Oxford University Press, 1936), 159–60 (subsequent references in the text).

4. At the same time I am not arguing that the entire series is framed around the seven deadly sins, nor am I claiming that Lewis intended the seven deadly sins as the organizing principle of chronicles. Instead, I am simply pointing out that Lewis may have used each book to explore the ramifications of the seven deadly sins.

5. Since this essay first appeared, much excellent scholarship on the Chronicles of Narnia has been published. Of particular note is Michael Ward's magisterial *Planet Narnia: The Seven Heavens in the Imagination of C. S. Lewis* (Oxford: Oxford University Press, 2008); see a review of this book later in the collection.

6. *The Lion, the Witch and the Wardrobe* (New York: Macmillan, 1950), 28 (hereafter *LWW* and subsequent references in the text).

7. *Paradise Lost*, in *Complete Poems and Major Prose*, ed. Merritt Y. Hughes (New York: Odyssey Press, 1957).

8. Lewis may also have had in mind the concept of the pride of life as found in I John 2:15–16: "Do not love the world, nor the things in the world. If anyone loves the world, the love of the Father is not in him. For all that is in the world, the lust of the flesh and the lust of the eyes and the boastful pride of life, is not from the Father, but is from the world."

9. *Prince Caspian* (New York: Macmillan, 1951), 55–56 (hereafter *PC* and subsequent references in the text).

10. *The Voyage of the Dawn Treader* (London: Bles, 1952), 83 (hereafter *VDT* and subsequent references in the text).

11. *The Silver Chair* (New York: Macmillan, 1953), 20–21 (hereafter *SC* and subsequent references in the text).

12. *The Horse and His Boy* (London: Bles, 1954), 172–73 (hereafter *HHB* and subsequent references in the text).

13. *The Screwtape Letters* (New York: Macmillan, 1943), 5 (hereafter *SL* and subsequent references in the text).

14. *The Magician's Nephew* (New York: Macmillan, 1955), 20 (hereafter *MN* and subsequent references in the text).

15. *The Last Battle* (New York: Macmillan, 1956), 9 (hereafter *LB* and subsequent references in the text).

16. George MacDonald, *The Gifts of the Child Christ*, ed. Glenn Edward Sadler (Grand Rapids, MI: Eerdmans, 1973), 1:24–25.

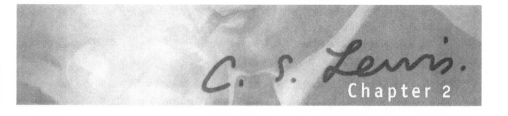

The Childlike in George MacDonald and C. S. Lewis[1]

**It is a curious fact that two writers who are frequently iden-
tified with children's literature, George MacDonald and C. S.**
Lewis, go out of their ways to claim that they did not write their stories primarily for children. Lewis, reviewing some of the books he read in his childhood, says that "I never met *The Wind in the Willows* or the Bastable books till
I was in my late twenties, and I do not think I have enjoyed them any the less
on that account. I am almost inclined to set it up as a canon that a children's
story which is enjoyed only by children is a bad children's story. The good ones
last."[2] He also notes that "it certainly is my opinion that a book worth reading
only in childhood is not worth reading even then."[3] MacDonald, commenting
on those who try to find specific meanings in fairy-tales, claims that "children
are not likely to trouble you about meaning. They find what they are capable
of finding, and more would be too much. For my part, I do not write for children, but for the childlike, whether of five, or fifty, or seventy-five."[4] In effect,
both Lewis and MacDonald argue that it is the childlike attitude, not age,
that marks his readers; at the same time, however, neither ever states what
childlike means. The focus of this essay, then, is two-fold. First, I describe
what I believe are the childlike attitudes of their readers. Second, I explore the
relationship between childlike readers and fictional characters, especially the
children, within each writer's stories.

In order to discover the attributes of the childlike audience, we must begin by answering the following: "What does each writer mean by childlike?" For MacDonald, the answer to this question was a life-long quest. That is, although he intuitively understood what childlike meant to him, he never succinctly described it. Even in his most direct efforts, he remains imprecise. For example, he often deals with the idea of the childlike in his sermons; yet his explanations are less than definitive. A case in point is his commentary on Mark 9:33–37 and Matthew 18:1–5, passages that recount an argument Jesus' disciples have over who will be the greatest in the kingdom of God. Christ resolves the argument by calling a child to himself and saying: "If anyone wants to be first, he shall be last of all, and servant of all" (Mark 9:35), and "Truly I say to you, unless you are converted and become like children, you shall not enter the kingdom of heaven. Whoever then humbles himself as this child, he is the greatest in the kingdom of heaven" (Matthew 18:3–4). The Lord's paradoxical answer is not lost on MacDonald: "[Jesus told his disciples] they could not enter into the kingdom save by becoming little children—by humbling themselves. For the idea of ruling was excluded where childlikeness was the one essential quality."[5]

However, beyond this clear linking of humility with childlikeness, MacDonald's other attempts to define the childlike are enigmatic. He claims that "the childlike is the divine" (30), and that "to receive a child in the name of Jesus is to receive Jesus; to receive Jesus is to receive God; therefore, to receive the child is to receive God Himself" (32). Later MacDonald attempts to explain the relationship between childlikeness and God: "To receive a child in the name of God is to receive God Himself. How to receive Him? As alone He can be received—by knowing Him as He is. To know Him is to have Him in us" (32). To understand what the childlike means, he tells us to look within. Thoughtful readers are unconvinced by such circular reasoning. Even though we may intuitively understand what he means when he says that "to exist . . . is to be a child of God; and to know it, to feel it, is to rejoice evermore" (*Gifts of the Child Christ*, 19), we want to know more precisely what childlike means.

Thus far we have established that humility is an attribute MacDonald associates with the childlike. If we explore what he means by this, we will see that he ties humility directly to selflessness: "To be rid of self is to have the heart bare to God and to the neighbour—to have all life ours, and possess all things. I see, in my mind's eye, the little children clambering up to sit on the throne with Jesus" (19). The humility of a childlike personality is also characterized by unpretentiousness: "He who will be a man, and will not be a child, must—he cannot help himself—become a little man, that is, a dwarf. He will, however, need no consolation, for he is sure to think himself a very large creature indeed" (28). As one critic has noted: "The self of the ego MacDonald sees as the source of evil; 'the one principle,' he declares, 'is—"I am my own."'"6

How does MacDonald's emphasis on the childlike characteristic of humility relate to his appeal to the childlike reader? Perhaps if we substitute the word "innocence" for "humility" we can draw nearer to grasping the appeal his stories make to the childlike reader. That is, his tales speak to childlike readers on a level that does not immediately raise "adult" objections to the improbable. His stories ask us to leave open for the moment that this or that thing could happen, regardless of how loudly our adult voices, nurtured by realism and the scientific method, speak against such an improbability. However, the kind of innocence MacDonald assumes of his audience is not to be confused with gullibility; he is not addressing readers who lack discernment. Instead, his childlike readers are those who are willing, even eager, to "exercise a willing suspension of disbelief."

Although I could at this point posit what I believe are the other elements of the childlike in MacDonald, I think a better approach will be to turn to Lewis's comments on the childlike. Since Lewis was by training a literary critic, we can expect to find more discussion about the childlike in Lewis's writings than in MacDonald's. Additionally, because MacDonald's influence upon Lewis was overwhelming, we should not be surprised that he appeals to the same kind of audience as his "master": "I have never concealed the fact that I regarded him [MacDonald] as my master; indeed I fancy I have never written a book in which I did not quote from him."7 In a number of different essays Lewis discusses his ideas about writing for children. In one he declares: "I put in [my children's stories] what I would have liked to read when I was a child and what I still like reading now that I am in my fifties" ("On Three Ways," 22). Elsewhere he says he writes "'for children' only in the sense that I excluded what I thought they would not like or understand; not in the sense of writing what I intended to be below adult attention" ("Sometimes Fairy Stories," 37–38). In another essay he says that the best children's writers "work from the common, universally human, ground they share with the children, and indeed with countless adults."8 Perhaps the most interesting point he makes is that childlike readers should not be patronized: "The child as reader is neither to be patronized nor idolized: we talk to him as man to man" ("On Three Ways," 33). This no nonsense approach to communicating with childlike readers does not spare them scenes of "death, violence, wounds, adventure, heroism and cowardice, good and evil" (31). To do less than this, Lewis claims, is "to give children a false impression and feed them on escapism" (31).

What comes through in these comments is Lewis's insistence that he "speaks to the adult, the child, and the child within the adult. He speaks to everyone, except to those ossified grown-ups who have stifled the child within."[9] More importantly, Lewis indirectly suggests in these essays other characteristics of the childlike reader besides innocence. The first of these is a sense of awe. In "On Stories," Lewis reflects on how *Oedipus Rex*, *The Man Who Would Be King*, and *The Hobbit* produce such an effect upon him: "Such stories produce . . . a feeling of awe, coupled with a certain sort of bewilderment such as one often feels in looking at a complex pattern of lines that pass over and under one another."[10] Another way of saying this is that the child within, our childlike self, enables us to see, even if momentarily, that there is more to life than the physical reality about us. Such knowledge is both terrifying and refreshing—terrifying in that we are left to ponder the possibility of unperceived dimensions of life, yet refreshing because we are exposed to the unexpected flash of hope that the banality of our own world is not all there is.

As a part of the childlike reader's sense of awe, Lewis includes the enthusiastic delight in surprise. In "On Stories" he notes that no story can be fully enjoyed on an initial reading. Instead, we have to get past our curiosities about plot, theme, and character until "we are at leisure to savour the real beauties." Children, he goes on, "understand this well when they ask for the same story over and over again, and in the same words. They want to have again the 'surprise' of discovering that what seemed Little-Red-Riding Hood's grandmother is really the wolf" (18). The pleasure of the surprise draws the childlike reader back time and again to a well-worn story. Could we really enter another world through the back of a wardrobe, fly on the back of a giant eagle, or converse with a talking raven? As we encounter such unlooked-for experiences, our surprise and awe intensify even more.

In "On Three Ways of Writing for Children" Lewis suggests another aspect of the childlike reader's awe: limitless imagination. In defending his own love of fantasy, Lewis takes issue with how "the modern critical world uses 'adult' as a term of approval. It is hostile to what it calls 'nostalgia' and contemptuous of what it calls 'Peter Pantheism.' Hence, a man who admits that dwarfs and giants and talking beasts and witches are still dear to him in his fifty-third year is now less likely to be praised for his perennial youth than scorned and pitied for arrested development" (25). The childlike reader is not offended by the seeming impossible; indeed, as I have already suggested, the childlike reader is delighted instead. J. R. R. Tolkien's description of the fairy tale makes a similar point: "The magic of Faerie is not an end in itself, its virtue is in its operations: among these are the satisfaction of certain primordial human desires. One of these desires is to survey the depths of space and time. Another is . . . to hold communion with other living things."[11] The childlike reader's imagination can soar as far as the story can take it, and in some cases return to the physical world energized and refreshed.

The sense of awe is also intimately linked to the third characteristic of the childlike reader: a romantic yearning for something more. Corbin Scott Carnell, in his book *Bright Shadow of Reality: C. S. Lewis and the Feeling Intellect*, concentrates exclusively on this notion as it runs through Lewis's work. Carnell uses the German word *Sehnsucht* to denote "an underlying sense of displacement or alienation from what is desired."[12] The childlike reader is attracted to MacDonald and Lewis because of his or her own longing for a deeper, more meaningful experience than is available in the daily march of time. Yet this longing is not to be viewed as morbid. Lewis makes this clear when he writes that a schoolboy who reads about enchanted woods does not then become depressed about his own world: "He does not despise real woods because he has read of enchanted woods: the reading makes all real woods a little enchanted. This is a special kind of longing . . . . The boy reading the fairy-tale desires and is happy in the very fact of desiring" ("On Three Ways," 29–30). He argues elsewhere that a sense of longing is the central strength of MacDonald's myth-making: "[MacDonald's myths arouse] in us sensations we have never had before, never anticipated having, as though we had broken out of our normal mode of consciousness and 'possessed joys not promised to our birth.' It gets under our skin, hits us at a level deeper than our thoughts or even our passions, troubles oldest certainties till all questions are re-opened, and in general shocks us more fully awake than we are for most of our lives" (*George MacDonald: An Anthology*, 16–17).

Innocence, awe, and longing—all are basic elements of the childlike reader that are tapped by Lewis and MacDonald. These attributes of the childlike reader are not all inclusive—good arguments can be made for justice, honesty, faith, earnestness, loyalty, discretion and so on—but I believe these three comprise the core of the appeal to childlike readers. What also should be clear is the overlap and intrinsic relationship that each attribute has with the others; none exists in isolation, but combines with the others, heightening our pleasure as readers. The next focus of this essay, therefore, concerns the relationship between the childlike reader and the youthful characters who appear in the stories of Lewis and MacDonald.

At the risk of appearing simplistic, it seems to me that the childlike reader generally encounters two kinds of youthful characters in the stories of Lewis and MacDonald. The first is the childish one who is characterized primarily by egocentricity. The childish character is overly concerned with himself or herself and only relates to his or her surroundings in terms of self-aggrandizement. Others are important only because of what the childish character can get from them. Edmund Pevensie from *The Lion, the Witch and the Wardrobe* and Eustace Clarence Scrubb from *The Voyage of the Dawn Treader* are memorable examples of childish characters. Both view the world as revolving about themselves, as Edmund's gluttony and traitorous behavior and Eustace's whining megalomania and greed illustrate. In *Lilith* MacDonald adds an ironic twist to the notion of the childish character, for we encounter young, relatively uncorrupted children who become more childish as they grow older. As one character says: "If a Little One doesn't care, he grows greedy, and then lazy, and then big, and then stupid and then bad."[13]

In addition to egocentricity, other attributes of childishness are dishonesty, spite, pettiness, cruelty, and pseudo-sophistication. MacDonald comments in particular upon this last point: "For it must be confessed that there are children who are not childlike. One of the saddest and not least common sights in the world is the face of a child whose mind is so brimful of worldly wisdom that the human childishness has vanished from it" (*Creation in Christ*, 29–30). Yet, interestingly, both Lewis and MacDonald take pains to move the childish character toward the childlike. Indeed, the childish character plays a pivotal role in the great recurring theme of their stories—the search for redemption. Both writers frequently present "unwhole," childish characters who gradually mature into "whole," childlike characters.

In Lewis this pattern is seen in a number of children: Shasta and Aravis from *The Horse and His Boy*, Jill from *The Silver Chair*, and Digory and Polly from *The Magician's Nephew*. However, Edmund and Eustace provide us with the best examples; both begin as thoroughly obnoxious, childish little creatures, devolve into spiritually damnable children, and, after profound personal experiences with Aslan that lead to self-realization, emerge as redeemed, "whole" creatures. Although each is blind to his unwhole nature at the beginning, each eventually sees the truth about himself and evolves into a fruitful, productive, whole person. In MacDonald, more often than not, it is an adult who is childish and thus in need of being made childlike. Mr. Vane (his name is an obvious pun) in *Lilith* is a striking example. Throughout most of the story he is vain, short-sighted, egocentric, conceited, stubborn, and over-confident. It is only through his relationship with Mr. Raven and after a series of misadventures that almost lead to a catastrophe for the innocent children who inhabit Lilith's world that Vane finally comes to see his shortcomings; and, in the end, after he gains a childlike attitude toward life, he experiences a kind of inner healing.

The second kind of character the childlike reader meets is the child (or, less often, an adult) who is much like the childlike reader; that is, this character may evidence innocence, awe, and longing within the story itself. Such characters, of course, are of crucial importance because by identifying with them, we vicariously enter the stories. If we cannot see ourselves in the characters of any tale, whether it be by Lewis, MacDonald, Joseph Conrad, Fyodor Dostoyevsky, or William Faulkner, our attention is not likely to be held nor will we be drawn into their fictional worlds. We must see ourselves in these worlds or we will care little for the stories. Our ability to identify with childlike characters depends to a great degree upon how these characters are portrayed. Significantly, childlike characters are not perfect; though they avoid the extremes of the childish character, they are fallible. They err, they make mistakes, they fall short. Two characters who best illustrate childlikeness are Lucy from the Chronicles of Narnia and Irene from MacDonald's *The Princess and the Goblin*. Both are attractive yet not without fault; in them the childlike reader finds his or her own reflection.

Lucy is one of Lewis's most endearing childlike characters. We follow her from her initial entry into Narnia and share her wonder and excitement as she encounters the Narnian world. Later, when she meets abuse from Edmund and skepticism from Peter and Susan, we sympathize with her. When all the children eventually make their way into Narnia, Peter and Susan apologize to Lucy and ask her to lead the way. Paradoxically, it is in this role as leader that we see Lucy exercising the childlike attributes of innocence, awe, and longing as she encourages the children to follow a robin who appears to want to help them. Throughout *The Lion, the Witch and the Wardrobe* Lucy maintains a childlike attitude, perhaps peaking during Aslan's passion when she and Susan accompany the great Lion towards his humiliating death. And when Aslan re-appears after his death, it is Lucy, not Susan, who cries: "Oh, you're real, you're real! Oh, Aslan!" (*LWW*, 132).

In *Prince Caspian* Lucy's childlikeness is again emphasized, although her susceptibility to failure is underscored. In this story the children have been literally called back into Narnia by Prince Caspian, but they are disoriented and unsure of the best way to reach him. Unable to sleep one night, Lucy wanders away from the camp hoping to regain her earlier experiences of pleasure in Narnian nature: "Oh, Trees, Trees, Trees. . . . Oh Trees, wake, wake, wake. Don't you remember it? Don't you remember me? Dryads and Hamadryads, come out, come out to me" (*PC*, 96–97). Yet just as she feels about to make contact with them, the moment passes. Lucy "had the feeling . . . that she had just missed something: as if she had spoken to the trees a split second too soon or a split second too late, or used all the right words except one; or put in one word that was just wrong" (97).

Lucy's inability to recapture her intuitive relationship with nature foreshadows a failure of obedience the next day. When the children eventually find themselves lost, Lucy sees Aslan off in the distance. However, no one else can see Aslan. In fact, when Susan asks Lucy "where do you think you saw him," Lucy says: "Don't talk like a grown-up . . . . I didn't think I saw him. I saw him" (104). The others, however, (except, ironically, Edmund) refuse to believe her, and Lucy, instead of following Aslan on her own and what she knows to be the truth, goes along with the others, sad and depressed. Not surprisingly the group bumbles along that day and endures an ambush before collapsing with fatigue in the evening. Once again Lucy wanders off into the forest, this time successfully communing with the tree spirits; more importantly, she sees and talks with Aslan who firmly but gently points out her failure and commissions her to go convince the others that he will lead them. Lucy does this in spite of the others' scorn and disbelief. That Aslan appears only to Lucy is significant because it underscores her humility and great capacity for faith. At the same time, her initial failure to obey Aslan reminds us of our own capacity for failure. However, Lucy's subsequent affirmation of Aslan and determination to do as he asks brings us encouragement.

Her childlike nature culminates in *The Voyage of the Dawn Treader*. Several times in the story her childlikeness is emphasized. The first time we see this is when Eustace returns to his shipmates after his metamorphosis into a dragon. While the others hold back in fear, Lucy runs up to Eustace and discovers who he is; she even consoles him and "screwed up her courage to kiss the scaly face" (*VDT*, 95). A second illustration occurs later after Eustace's dream encounter with Aslan and re-transformation back into his human form. Edmund explains to Eustace who Aslan is and indicates Lucy's close relationship to Aslan: "He is the great Lion, the son of the Emperor over the Sea, who saved me and saved Narnia. We've all seen him. Lucy sees him most often" (104). Lucy's childlikeness and close tie to Aslan is re-emphasized still later when he appears to her while she is reading a magic book and discovering spells that can give her great power. For instance, she reads of spells that can give her money, knowledge, power, and advantage. She is tempted most by a spell that will *"make beautiful her that uttereth beyond the lot of mortals"* (141; emphasis Lewis). As she begins to say the spell, Aslan appears in the text itself, and "he was growling and you could see most of his teeth. She became horribly afraid and turned over the page at once" (142).

When we last see her in this tale, her childlikeness is again highlighted as she speaks with Aslan for the final time. She asks him: "Oh, Aslan . . . . Will you tell us how to get into your country from our world?" (221). When she learns that she can never return, she says: "It isn't Narnia, you know . . . . It's you. We shan't meet you there. And how can we live, never meeting you?" (222). Lucy has to be content with Aslan's promise that she will meet him in her own world under another name. The centrality of Lucy's childlike character in the first three Narnia books is significant. Indeed, even though Lewis employs an omniscient narrator, much of what we learn about Narnia comes to us through Lucy's eyes. Furthermore, she is the first one to enter Narnia, she is the one who sees Aslan most often, and she is the one who longs most fiercely to remain in Narnia. Lucy's longing for and sensitivity to Aslan's guidance, her humility, and her willingness to submit her own desires to a force higher than herself mark her as an attractive childlike character.

In MacDonald's *The Princess and the Goblin*, we encounter another little girl, Irene, the childlike character after whom I believe Lewis patterned Lucy. I say this based both upon Lewis's aforementioned salute to MacDonald and upon the obvious similarities between Lucy and Irene. Irene is also a childlike character who exercises innocence, awe, and longing. For instance, her first adventure occurs because she is bored by her toys on a rainy day and longs for something more. When left alone for a moment by her nurse, Irene opens a door to a stairway she has never seen before, and makes her way, after a long climb, to an unfamiliar room inhabited by a mysterious old woman who identifies herself as Irene's great-great-grandmother. During this meeting the old woman promises to be Irene's caretaker and does so throughout the story, serving as a kind of fairy godmother. When Irene returns to her own room, she, like Lucy, has a hard time convincing others of the reality of her experience.

In later visits to her grandmother, Irene's childlike character is further explored. When she next sees her grandmother, she tells Irene that she must endure a test: "But I must put you to one trial—not a very hard one, I hope. This night week you must come back to me. If you don't, I do not know when you may find me again, and you will soon want me very much."[14] Of course the real test is to discover whether or not Irene believes in the old lady: "The only question is whether you will believe I am anywhere—whether you will believe I am anything but a dream" (86). This test of Irene's imagination and allegiance is very similar to Lucy's test of obedience to Aslan in *Prince Caspian*.

During the week that follows, Irene tries to maintain her belief although at times "she could not feel quite sure that she had not been dreaming" (95). Nonetheless, she determines to seek her out, and, when the week is up, Irene does make her way back to the old lady's room. Once there, the grandmother commends Irene and shows her various mysterious objects, including pigeons, burning roses, a bright mobile globe, a spinning wheel, a fire-opal ring, and an invisible thread. Irene's childlike innocence is underlined as she reaches out to touch the thread: "Oh! I do feel it! . . . But I can't see it" (107). The old lady explains the value of this invisible thread: "If ever you find yourself in any danger . . . you must take off your ring and put it under the pillow of you bed. Then you must lay your forefinger, the same that wore the ring, upon the thread, and follow the thread wherever it leads you" (107–108). Then she adds: "But, remember, it may seem to you a very roundabout way indeed, and you must not doubt the thread" (108).

Irene's faithfulness to her grandmother and her childlike sense of awe and wonder regarding the old lady form the basis for much of the action in the story, especially when Irene meets Curdie, another childlike character. Curdie, a young miner, discovers a plot by underworld goblins against Irene and her father. Unfortunately, Curdie is captured and would have remained so had not Irene's grandmother intervened by means of the invisible thread. Irene is led by the thread directly to where Curdie is imprisoned; their encounter brings into focus the difference between her childlikeness and Curdie's. Curious as to how she found him, Curdie asks for an explanation; to her comments about following an invisible thread, Curdie says: "What nonsense the child talks! . . . I must follow her, though, and see that she comes to no harm" (144). Curdie's inability to "see" or "feel" the thread parallels closely the problem Lucy's brothers and sister have in *Prince Caspian*. Like them, Curdie is overly influenced by adult perceptions rather than by childlike instincts.

The contrast between Irene's childlike nature and Curdie's adult perception peaks when Irene takes him to see her grandmother. When Irene expresses frustration at Curdie's lack of belief, her grandmother says: "People must believe what they can, and those who believe more must not be hard upon those who believe less" (153). If Irene "sees" easily, Curdie does not. When she asks him what he sees, he says: "I see a big, bare, garret-room . . . . I see a tub, and a heap of musty straw, and a withered apple." Then he adds: "I think you had better drop it, princess, and go down to the nursery, like a good girl" (154–155). Curdie's pomposity here has an uncomfortable yet familiar adult ring to it, and prefigures a scene in Lewis's *The Last Battle* where a group of dwarves have the same problem; that is, instead of seeing and enjoying a feast provided by Aslan in a stable, the dwarves "thought they were eating and drinking only the sorts of things you might find in a Stable. One said he was trying to eat hay and another said he had got a bit of an old turnip and a third said he found a raw cabbage leaf" (*LB*, 139). Like them, Curdie only sees with his adult eyes, not with childlike innocence and awe.

He remains unconvinced until his mother shares a mysterious incident from her early married life as a way of showing him that all is not always what it seems. Prefacing her story with "perhaps some people can see things other people can't see" (162), Curdie's mother relates how she was once saved from the goblins by what sounds like the grandmother's mobile globe and one of her pigeons. To the goblins, however, the grandmother's objects, especially the pigeon, appeared much different: "It looked to me just like a white pigeon. But whatever it was, when the cobs [goblins] caught sight of it coming straight down upon them, they took to their heels and scampered away across the mountain" (164). When Curdie reacts by saying that her story sounds strange, his mother responds with: "Yes, it was strange; but I can't help believing it, whether you do or not" (164).

Curdie's mother, like Irene, has the childlike ability to see, and her story does influence Curdie although it is only later, after Curdie has been wounded by the goblins, that he gains his childlike eyes. As he lies in bed unable to move so as to alert everyone of the goblin's forthcoming attack, he sees "a lady with white hair, carrying a silver box in her hand, enter the room. She came to his bed, he thought, stroked his head and face with cool, soft hands, took the dressing from his leg, rubbed it with something that smelt like roses, and then waved her hands over him three times" (182). Still later, when he is trying to decide how to find Irene in order to protect her from the goblins, "something touched his hand. It was the slightest touch, and when he looked he could see nothing. Feeling and peering about in the grey of the dawn, his fingers came upon a tight thread" (188). He follows the thread he cannot see and had earlier doubted and is led to Irene's hiding place.

In Curdie, MacDonald pictures the character who has the capacity for childlike innocence even if temporarily hobbled by adult perceptions. Earlier the grandmother assures Irene that Curdie will one day see the truth, although it will take some time: "You must give him time . . . and you must be content not to be believed for a while" (155). Indeed, she further reveals that Curdie cannot see her because she "did not mean to show myself. Curdie is not yet able to believe some things. Seeing is not believing—it is only seeing" (156). Here MacDonald underscores the idea that childlikeness is a quality of the soul or spirit, characterized by attributes immeasurable by empirical methods. It is only when Curdie learns that truth may involve more than what can be seen and tested that he gains the insight to see and to understand. He is on the same pilgrimage as many of us.

Within the stories of Lewis and MacDonald we can find many childlike characters. They abound in the Chronicles of Narnia: Reepicheep, Mr. and Mrs. Beaver, Jewel, Tirian, Dr. Cornelius, Caspian, Emeth, Hwin, Strawberry-Fledge, King Frank and Queen Helen, and many others. In MacDonald's tales we find Phosy from "The Gifts of the Child Christ," Diamond from *At the Back of the North Wind*, Mossy and Tangle from "The Golden Key," Mr. and Mrs. Raven, Lona, and the Little Ones from *Lilith*, and scores of others. Regardless the name, childlike characters evidence innocence, awe, and longing—all attributes linking them to childlike readers.

In conclusion, Lewis and MacDonald write for the child within the adult. Often they contrast childish characters with childlike characters, perhaps in order to remind us that "there are only two kinds of people in the end: those who say to God, 'Thy will be done,' and those to whom God says, in the end, '*Thy* will be done.'"[15] In the childish characters we see our own capacities for conceit, cruelty, deceit, vanity, and egocentricity; on the other hand, in the childlike characters we see a more constructive side of ourselves—self-sacrifice, wonder at life's mysteries, and longing for a world cleaner and more alive than our own. Because of our vicarious experiences with the childlike characters we meet in Lewis and MacDonald, we may be able to ask with Lucy: "Will you tell us how to get into your country from our world?"

Chapter 2 Notes

1. A version of this essay first appeared in *Mythlore* 12 (Summer 1986): 17–22, 26.

2. "On Three Ways of Writing for Children," in *Of Other Worlds: Essays and Stories*, ed. Walter Hooper (New York: Harcourt, Brace, Jovanovich, 1966), 24 (subsequent references in the text).

3. "Sometimes Fairy Stories May Say Best What's To Be Said," in *Of Other Worlds*, 38 (subsequent references in the text).

4. *The Gifts of the Child Christ: Fairytales and Stories for the Childlike*, ed. Glenn Edward Sadler (Grand Rapids, MI: Eerdmans,1973), 1:25 (subsequent references in the text).

5. *Creation in Christ: Unspoken Sermons*, ed. Rolland Hein (Wheaton, Ill.: Harold Shaw, 1976), 30 (subsequent references in the text).

6. Colin Manlove, *Modern Fantasy: Five Studies* (Cambridge: Cambridge University Press, 1975), 60.

7. *George MacDonald: An Anthology*, ed. C. S. Lewis (London: Bles, 1946), 20 (subsequent references in the text).

8. "On Juvenile Tastes," in *Of Other Worlds*, 41 (subsequent references in the text).

9. Chad Walsh, *The Literary Legacy of C. S. Lewis* (New York: Harcourt, Brace, Jovanovich, 1979), 157.

10. "On Stories," in *Of Other Worlds*, 15 (subsequent references in the text).

11. J. R. R. Tolkien, "On Fairy-Stories," in *Tree and Leaf*; reprinted in *The Tolkien Reader* (New York: Ballantine, 1972), 13.

12. Corbin Scott Carnell, *Bright Shadow of Reality: C. S. Lewis and the Feeling Intellect* (Grand Rapids: Eerdmans, 1974), 15.

13. *Phantastes and Lilith* (Grand Rapids: Eerdmans, 1964), 244 (subsequent references in the text).

14. George MacDonald, *The Princess and the Goblin* (London: Puffin, 1976), 86 (subsequent references in the text).

15. C. S. Lewis, *The Great Divorce* (New York: MacMillan, 1946), 72; emphasis Lewis.

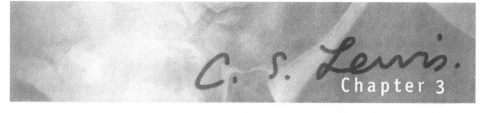

The Door as Christian Metaphor in the Chronicles of Narnia[1]

One outstanding characteristic of C. S. Lewis's non-fiction prose is his use of metaphor.[2] Regardless of the work, examples of metaphor abound as Lewis uses word pictures to clarify his arguments and ideas.[3] For instance, in *The Abolition of Man* Lewis notes that "the task of the modern educator is not to cut down jungles but to irrigate deserts."[4] In *Surprised by Joy*, referring to the numerous books available to him as a child, he writes: "I had always the same certainty of finding a book that was new to me as a man who walks into a field has of finding a new blade of grass."[5] And in the preface to *Mere Christianity* he includes a disclaimer that cautions the reader against regarding his mere Christianity "as an alternative to the creeds of the existing communions—as if a man would adopt it in preference to Congregationalism or Greek Orthodoxy or anything else."[6] To make his point clearer, Lewis creates a helpful metaphor:

> It is more like a hall out of which doors open into several rooms. If I can bring anyone into that hall I shall have done what I attempted. But it is in the rooms, not in the hall, that there are fires and chairs and meals. The hall is a place to wait in, a place from which to try the various doors, not a place to live in. (xi)

Lewis's use of the door metaphor recalls how frequently it also appears in the New Testament. References are made to "striving to enter [heaven] by the narrow door" (Luke 13:24), to "the door of faith" (Acts 14:27), to "a wide door for effective service [being] opened" (1 Cor. 16:9), to "a door [being] opened for me [Paul] in the Lord" (2 Cor. 2:12), and to God opening "up to us a door for the word" (Col. 4:3). Jesus himself is often associated with a door. For example, after Jesus relates to his disciples some of the signs of the end times, he says: "When you see all these things, recognize that He [God] is near, right at the door" (Matt. 24:33). Better known perhaps is Christ's famous statement in Revelation 3:20: "Behold, I stand at the door and knock; if anyone hears my voice and opens the door, I will come in to him, and will dine with him, and he with me."

However, it is the passages where Jesus claims to be the door to communion with God that we see the fullest operation of this metaphor. In John 10 we find the best example of this. In verses 1–5 Jesus uses the parable of the shepherd whose sheep will only respond to his voice to indicate his own relationship to his disciples. St. John notes that because the disciples did not understand "this figure of speech," Jesus has to go on and make explicit his meaning: "Truly, truly, I say to you, I am the door of the sheep . . . . I am the door; if anyone enters through me, he shall be saved, and shall go in and out, and find pasture" (7, 9). Later he finalizes the metaphor by answering Thomas' question regarding how they would find Christ after his crucifixion: "I am the way, and the truth, and the life; no one comes to the Father, but through me" (John 14:6).

Lewis's knowledge of this New Testament metaphor is put to work throughout the Chronicles of Narnia. Four specific points about Lewis's use of doors are explored in this essay: 1) physical doors lead to the Door, Aslan; 2) Aslan is a two-way Door; 3) passage through the different doors into Narnia is always unplanned; and 4) all who enter the doors are called into Narnia, but none are compelled to stay; indeed, some who are called do not seem to belong. First, in every instance the physical doors leading into Narnia eventually lead to the Door, Aslan. The doors themselves take on different forms, from the wardrobe door in *The Lion, the Witch and the Wardrobe* to the railway station in *Prince Caspian* to the framed picture in *The Voyage of the Dawn Treader* to the magic rings and the Wood Between the Worlds in *The Magician's Nephew* and to another train station in *The Last Battle*.[7] The doors take the children out of their world and into a new world; that is, the doors move them from a mundane, everyday experience to a new world, a new reality, a new life. More importantly, the doors inexorably lead to Aslan who offers the children an additional "new life" experience. Edmund, for instance, in *The Lion, the Witch and the Wardrobe* confers with Aslan after betraying his brother and sisters and after being rescued by Aslan's forces. Of their conversation "there is no need to tell you (and no one ever heard) what Aslan was saying but it was a conversation which Edmund never forgot" (*LWW*, 112). From this point on Edmund, though far from perfect, is a "new creature" with Aslan confirming this by becoming the sacrificial door to Edmund's new life.

Second, the children become aware of Jesus Christ in their own world after meeting Aslan in Narnia; Aslan, then, serves as a two-way door—both to new life in Narnia and in the world of the children. The best example of this occurs in *The Voyage of the Dawn Treader*. At the end of the book, Lucy and Edmund meet Aslan in the form of a lamb. To Lucy's question about how to enter Aslan's country, the lamb replies: "For you the door into Aslan's country is from your own world" (*VDT*, 221). That the children fail to make the immediate connection between Aslan and Jesus Christ is clear when, after the lamb is transfigured into Aslan, Edmund asks: "Are—are you there [in our world] too, Sir?" In Aslan's response we see Lewis's use of one of the biblical names of God: "I am . . . . But there I have another name. You must learn to know me by that name. This was the very reason why you were brought to Narnia, that by knowing me here for a little, you may know me better there" (222). Aslan explains that the childrens' experiences in Narnia have been preparation for the more important event of meeting him in their own world. In addition, Aslan promises to "open the door in the sky and send you to your own land" (222). We see that Aslan functions here, as in Scripture, as both the agent (who opens the door) of new life and the object (he is the door) of new life. He is the two-way door to new life. In an episode from *The Horse and His Boy* a variation on this idea occurs. After King Lune and his twins sons, Cor and Corin, have been re-united and the Calormenes defeated, Prince Rabadash is brought before them for judgment. In spite of Lune's goodness towards Rabadash, he mocks and scorns the king: "I hear no conditions from barbarians and sorcerers. . . . The bolt of Tash falls from above!" (*HHB*, 191–92). In the midst of this Aslan suddenly appears and warns Rabadash to forget his pride and to accept the mercy of Lune. When Rabadash sees Aslan, however, he calls him "demon," "the foul fiend of Narnia," and "the enemy of the gods." He curses Aslan and calls for "lightning in the shape of scorpions [to rain on Him]" (193). Aslan gently warns the prince: "Have a care, Rabadash. . . . The doom is nearer now: it is at the door: it has lifted the latch " (193). Then, because Rabadash rejects Aslan's warning, he is turned into an ass. The use of the door here is to show that not everyone who meets Aslan in Narnia makes the appropriate connection—that he is God—and, furthermore, that those who scornfully reject him will be judged. The two-way door leads to judgment since Rabadash rejects mercy.

Another variation on this theme takes place at the stable door near the end of *The Last Battle*. Once the children and the others are thrust through the door, they are surprised to find themselves not in a dark, damp stable, but "on grass, the deep blue was overhead, and the air which blew gently on their faces was that of a day in early summer" (*LB*, 128). Actually they have entered Aslan's country through the stable door. As if to emphasize the metaphorical function of the door in terms of the Christian doctrine of regeneration, Lewis includes the story of Emeth, the devout Calormene. In a passage that disturbs some because of its suggestion of universalism, Lewis makes this clear: "If any man swear by Tash and keep his oath for the oath's sake, it is by me that he has truly sworn. . . . Unless thy desire had been for me thou wouldst not have sought so long and so truly. For all find what they truly seek" (156). Aslan is the two-way door into new life. In still another place we see this idea. At the end of *Prince Caspian* Aslan is revealed as the door out of Narnia and back into the real world. There he "caused to be set up two stakes of wood, higher than a man's head and about three feet apart. A third, and lighter, piece of wood was bound across them at the top uniting them, so that the whole thing looked like a doorway from nowhere into nowhere" (*PC*, 179–80). In order for the children and the older Telemarine men to return to their world, they must pass through this "door in the air."

Third, entry through the various doors is almost always unplanned by those who enter. In *The Lion, the Witch and the Wardrobe*, the children, individually and collectively, stumble through the wardrobe door, seemingly by accident. In *Prince Caspian* the four children are unexpectedly jerked from a railway platform and thrust into Narnian life 400 years after they had left. In *The Voyage of the Dawn Treader* a picture of a sailing vessel on a wall suddenly comes alive and Lucy, Edmund, and Eustace tumble into the waves and are hauled on board by Caspian and the men of the Dawn Treader. In *The Magician's Nephew* Polly and Digory are used by Digory's mad uncle to experiment with magic rings that send them to the Wood Between the Worlds where they eventually make their way into Narnia. In each case the children are not consciously seeking to enter Narnia; when they find themselves there, they are surprised.

Only in *The Silver Chair* and *The Last Battle* do we find instances of the children trying to get into Narnia; these cases, however, bear qualification. In *The Silver Chair* Eustace and his classmate, Jill Pole, do ask to be taken into Narnia. Yet their initial request appears to be unheeded; instead, after they are chased by bullying schoolmates, in desperation they try to flee through a locked door in a garden wall. This time the previously locked door opens and they unexpectedly enter Narnia. And in *The Last Battle* the children, although actively seeking to use the magic rings again in order to respond to the mysterious apparition of Tirian who calls upon them for help, actually enter Narnia for the final time as a result of a train crash that has killed all of them, a fact they do not initially comprehend.

That the entries tend to be unplanned suggests two things. On the one hand, the unexpected entries parallel Lewis's realization about his life-long quest for joy. As he records in *Surprised by Joy*, finding joy became an obsession, yet its occurrence was always unexpected. If he tried to seek it or find it or produce it, he never had success; it had to occur spontaneously. Eventually the experience of joy itself came to have a slightly different meaning for him: "I believe. . . that the old stab [of joy], the old bittersweet, has come to me as often and as sharply since my conversion as at any time of my life whatever. But I now know that the experience . . . was valuable only as a pointer to something other and outer" (*SJ*, 238). In a similar vein, Lewis arranges the unexpected entries into Narnia so that the children will experience the awe and wonder of Narnia not at their own bidding, which could become cheap and worn out, but at the bidding of Another. To underline this point, Lewis has the Professor at the end of *The Lion, the Witch and the Wardrobe* answer the children's question about their possible return to Narnia: "Of course you'll get back to Narnia again some day. . . . But don't go trying to use the same route twice. Indeed, don't try to get there at all. It'll happen when you're not looking for it" (153).

On the other hand, a second reason the entries appear to be accidental parallels the process by which some people experience spiritual regeneration.

That is, some people come into a saving knowledge of Jesus Christ in an unplanned way. Faith in Christ may have been the furtherest thing from their minds—indeed they may have been openly hostile to the Christian message—and yet, for whatever reason, they were suddenly struck by the beauty and truth of Christ's call and found themselves irresistibly drawn to faith in him. The unexpected surprise by joy that the children experience when they tumble through Narnian doors is an apt parallel to the joy a new believer in Christ often experiences.

The final significant use of doors as a metaphor concerns those who enter. Specifically, all who enter Narnia are, in one way or another, called to be there. This point may seem to contradict my previous argument that characters enter Narnia unexpectedly, but, of course it does not. Just because the characters may have not been planning to enter Narnia does not mean that they were not called. The evidence that characters are called into Narnia is overwhelming. In *The Lion, the Witch and the Wardrobe* the children have been called into Narnia at the exact time that they are in order to fulfill several prophecies and to coincide with the precise return of Aslan; their entry through the wardrobe door may have surprised them, but it was planned and predetermined by Aslan. In *Prince Caspian* the children are called into Narnia when Caspian, in desperation, blows Susan's magic horn. In *The Voyage of the Dawn Treader* the children are called into Narnia in order that they can discover, as has already been mentioned, that Aslan exists in their own world as Jesus Christ.

In *The Silver Chair* Eustace and Jill only think they are calling Aslan; actually, he has called them. After Jill passes through the previously locked garden door, she meets Aslan and has a conversation with him. After he rebukes her for having caused Eustace to fall over the Narnian cliff, he says that "the task [to help find the lost Prince Rilian] for which I called you and him here out of your own world" would be harder now (*SC*, 18). When she tries to correct Aslan by saying that she and Eustace had been calling to a "Somebody," Aslan replies: "You would not have called to me unless I had been calling to you" (19). Lewis is paralleling here the biblical notion of God calling to himself all those who are willing to come to him. In the John 10 passage referred to earlier we see this: "He who enters by the door is a shepherd of the sheep . . . and the sheep hear his voice, and he calls his own sheep by name, and leads them out. . . . And the sheep follow him because they know his voice" (2–4).

In *The Magician's Nephew* Digory is called into Narnia so that he can be the agent of both death and life. Because of his pride he causes Jadis and evil to enter Narnia at its creation; yet, Aslan uses him to bring back the seeds from the silver apple tree that are planted and bring forth the tree of protection. In passing it is worth noting that Lewis again alludes to the John 10 passage, for when Digory approaches the place where the tree is, he encounters a high wall and door. Above the door is the following inscription: "Come in by the gold gate or not at all, / Take of my fruit for others or forbear. / For those who steal or those who climb my wall / Shall find their heart's desire and find despair" (*MN*, 141). In John 10:1 we read: "Truly, truly, I say to you, he who does not enter by the door into the fold of the sheep, but climbs up some other way, he is a thief and a robber."

Finally, in *The Last Battle* the children are called into Narnia both to help Tirian in the final defense of Narnia and to be taken into Aslan's country. Yet not all who are called decide to stay in Narnia, the most notable being Susan, who, we learn in *The Last Battle*, is "interested in nothing now-a-days except nylons and lipstick and invitations" (*LB*, 127). Others, however, refuse to stay in Narnia once they have entered through the door because they are unable or unwilling to see what Narnia is all about ("They have eyes but see not; they have ears but do not hear"). Eustace might have been like this had he not been transformed into a dragon and seen himself for what he really was; as a result, he changed and later enters Aslan's country. Conversely, there is Digory's Uncle Andrew. Although his entry into the pre-Narnian world appears to be accidental, he is called by Aslan so that he might be given the chance to re-focus his life away from black magic and egocentricity and towards righteousness and selflessness. Yet Uncle Andrew does not respond because his sensibilities have been deadened. For example, while Aslan sings his song of creation, Uncle Andrew "was not liking the Voice." Later, all he could hear was "nothing but roaring in Aslan's song": "And when at last the Lion spoke and said 'Narnia, awake,' he [Uncle Andrew] didn't hear any words: he heard only a snarl. And when the Beasts spoke in answer, he heard only barkings, growlings, bayings and howlings. And when they laughed . . . such a horrid, bloodthirsty din of hungry and angry brutes he had never heard in his life" (113). Aslan himself sums up Uncle Andrew's problem later in response to Polly's request that Aslan remove the old man's fear: "I cannot tell [the meaning of His song of creation] to this old sinner, and I cannot comfort him either; he has made himself unable to hear my voice. If I spoke to him, he would hear only growlings and roarings. Oh Adam's sons, how cleverly you defend yourselves against all that might do you good!" (153). Uncle Andrew's failure to heed Aslan's call is reminiscent of those in Jesus' parable who failed to respond properly to a wedding invitation: "For many are called, but few are chosen" (Matt. 22:14).

Lewis's frequent use of the door as a metaphor having to do with Christian themes and ideas is both subtle and clear. The literal doors lead to the Door, Aslan; Aslan functions as a two-way door; entry through the doors is unplanned; and all who enter are called but not compelled to stay. In his sermon "The Weight of Glory," Lewis employs this same metaphor, and it is appropriate to conclude by quoting him:

> The sense that in this universe we are treated as strangers, the longing to be acknowledged, to meet with some response, to bridge some chasm that yawns between us and reality, is part of our inconsolable secret. And surely, from this point of view, the promise of glory, in the sense described, becomes highly relevant to our deep desire. For glory meant good report with God, acceptance by God, response, acknowledgment, and welcome into the heart of things. The door on which we have been knocking all our lives will open at last. . . . Apparently, then, our lifelong nostalgia, our longing to be reunited with something in the universe from which we now feel cut off, to be on the inside of some door which we have always seen from the outside, is no mere neurotic fancy, but the truest index of our real situation.[8]

Chapter 3 Notes

1. A version of this essay first appeared in *Mythlore* 14 (Autumn 1987): 25–27, 33.

2. For a thoughtful discussion of Lewis's use of metaphor in his fiction, see Kath Filmer, "The Polemic Image: The Role of Metaphor and Symbol in the Fiction of C. S. Lewis," *SEVEN: An Anglo-American Review* 7 (1986): 61–76.

3. Chad Walsh has some helpful general comments on Lewis's use of metaphor in his *The Literary Legacy of C. S. Lewis* (New York: Harcourt Brace Jovanovich, 1979), 203–205.

4. C. S. Lewis, *The Abolition of Man* (New York: Macmillan, 1947), 9 (subsequent references in the text).

5. *Surprised by Joy: The Shape of My Early Life* (New York: Harcourt, Brace & World, 1955), 10 (hereafter *SJ* and subsequent references in the text).

6. C. S. Lewis, *Mere Christianity* (New York: Macmillan, 1960), xi (subsequent references in the text).

7. Michael Murrin offers an indepth analysis of the Platonic nature of the doors into Narnia in "The Dialectic of Multiple Worlds: An Analysis of C. S. Lewis's Narnia Stories," *SEVEN: An Anglo-American Review*, 3 (1982): 93–112.

8. C. S. Lewis, *The Weight of Glory and Other Addresses* (Grand Rapids: Eerdmans, 1965), 11–12.

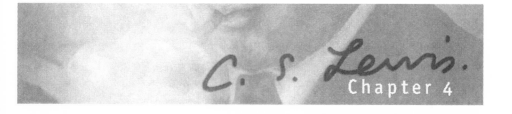

The Rhetorical Similarities of C. S. Lewis and Bertrand Russell[1]

Everything, real or imagined, can be appraised by us [humankind], and there is no outside standard to show that our valuation is wrong. We are ourselves the ultimate and irrefutable arbiters of value . . . It is we who create value and our desires which confer value.[2] (Bertrand Russell)

[The Tao] is the reality beyond all predicates, the abyss that was before the Creator Himself . . . . It is the Way in which the universe goes on, the Way in which things everlastingly emerge, stilly and tranquilly, into space and time . . . . It is the doctrine of objective value, the belief that certain attitudes are really true, and others really false.[3] (C. S. Lewis)

As these two quotes suggest, Bertrand Russell and C. S. Lewis are on opposite sides of the philosophical coin; indeed, on almost every issue they are at odds. Nevertheless, in spite of not sharing philosophical predilections, they often "sound" alike. That is, the tone of their popular works is very similar. The reason for this is that both employ time-tested rhetorical devices. The focus of this essay, therefore, will be to examine briefly how Russell and Lewis use rhetoric and, by implication, to suggest that this application accounts for the similarity of tone in their popular essays and books.

Rhetoric, according to Aristotle, is the "art of persuasion" and most often finds expression in deliberative (advocacy), forensic (legal), and epideictic (praise or blame) contexts. In this essay I am going to focus on examples of Russell's and Lewis's deliberative writing. In the development of any argument one must make certain appeals. In short, one can make an appeal to *ethos* (to the speaker's or writer's own moral character), to *pathos* (to the audience's emotions), and/or to *logos* (to reason and logic). While all of these come into play in any rhetorical situation, *ethos*, says Aristotle, is the most effective. His point may be expressed as follows: "If you can convince your audience that you are someone to be trusted, that you are fair-minded, that you have examined the issue from all sides, that you are not completely closed to the other person's argument, then you stand a very good chance of persuading the audience to your point of view" (note, by the way, that the speaker or writer may not be trustworthy or fair-minded, although for Aristotle himself it was important that this be the case). The writer's *ethos* or persona, as it is called today, is central to effective argumentation.

Russell and Lewis are old hands when it comes to projecting a winsome persona. For instance, in Russell's seminal essay, "Why I Am Not a Christian," he avoids a shrill, strident, offensive persona and instead adopts one that appears to be tolerant, generous, and, if bemused, at least sympathetic. He begins by debunking what are to him watered down definitions of the word Christian. A Christian, says Russell, is not someone who lives a good life nor is he someone who lives in a certain geographic location:

> I think . . . that there are two different items which are essential to anybody calling himself a Christian. The first is one of a dogmatic nature—namely, that you must believe in God and immortality . . . . Then further than that, as the name implies, you must have some kind of belief about Christ . . . at the very lowest the belief that Christ was, if not divine, at least the best and wisest of men. If you are not going to believe that much about Christ, I do not think you have any right to call yourself a Christian. (13–14)

In making this preliminary remark Russell shows himself to be informed, certain of his object of argumentation, and enlightened. He does not begin his attack on Christianity by bashing the entire Christian faith with a verbal club. His persona comes across as someone worth listening to, regardless of the audience's own stand.

In like fashion, Lewis adopts a persona that comes across as knowledgeable, friendly, cultured, unpretentious, and buoyed up by good humor; indeed, he often sounds like a jovial yet serious elder brother trying to get a problem sibling to "straighten up a bit and stop worrying mum and dad." For example, in the preface to *Mere Christianity* Lewis considers the meaning of the word Christian. For Lewis Christian means "one who accepts the common doctrines of Christianity."[4] He anticipates then the objections of some who would fault him for judging who and who is not a Christian. May not many who cannot accept such doctrines "be far more truly a Christian, far closer to the spirit of Christ, than some who do?" Lewis counters with a friendly yet determined voice: "Now this objection is in one sense very right, very charitable, very spiritual, very sensitive. It has every amiable quality except that of being useful" (ix). To spiritualize the word Christian, says Lewis, will only serve to make it meaningless. At the same time, he recognizes the intent of the objection, so he adds: "It is not for us to say who, in the deepest sense, is or is not close to the spirit of Christ. We do not see into men's hearts. We cannot judge, and are indeed forbidden to judge" (x). But in order for the word to have any real use in language, Lewis says "we must therefore stick to the original, obvious meaning . . . to those who accepted the teaching of the apostles" (xi). Both Russell and Lewis make careful use of persona for their own rhetorical ends. It does no good in an argument to pontificate, harass, or browbeat an audience. To avoid this, both men adopt personas that reflect intellectual honesty, openness, and curiosity while maintaining their own strongly held views. This mixture of candor and urbane confidence works well; in fact, many in their audience who would not share their philosophical positions might at least for the moment grant each man a thoughtful hearing.

Audience awareness, not coincidentally, is the second rhetorical element consistently used to advantage by Russell and Lewis. Once again Aristotle is instructive. While an attractive *ethos* or persona is the most effective appeal an arguer can make, *pathos* or an appeal to the audience's emotion is the most efficient. The reason for this is that an appeal to emotion can be volatile. In order to argue effectively, a writer must possess an intimate knowledge of who the audience is—its attitudes, beliefs, longings, prejudices, and tolerances. Here any honest rhetorician must strike a delicate balance between the desire to convince and a respect for the audience. Failure to do so leads at best to paternalism and at worst to manipulation. The phrases "God Save the King" or "Shoot the Capitalist Pigs" are different sides of the propagandist's coin. For the most part both Russell and Lewis maintain this balance. They use what they know of their audience to full advantage, yet avoid dishonest manipulation.

Before I provide some examples of how each man uses his awareness of audience to his advantage, a word on how any effective writer must approach his or her audience. In "The Writer's Audience Is Always a Fiction," Walter Ong notes that writing is addressed almost exclusively to a non-present person. The implications of this are contradictory. First, the act of writing itself is a kind of withdrawal; one can hardly imagine a writer sitting at his or her desk madly engaged in the writing process while the audience calmly sits before him or her—patiently waiting, perhaps humming a bit, even smoking a cigarette and drinking a cup of coffee. Second, and paradoxically, in spite of this necessary withdrawal, this forced isolation, the writer must attempt to write to or for a non-present person; writing for the wall, the chair, or even for oneself in the context of deliberation is fruitless. In order to be successful, therefore, a writer must "fictionalize in his imagination an audience he has learned to know not from daily life."[5] The upshot of this is that a writer must develop in his or her imagination an audience to which he or she ascribes some kind of role; the writer may view the audience as entertainment seekers, sports enthusiasts, or fantasy aficionados. In this regard I believe Russell and Lewis are most successful. The typical audience they "fictionalize" in their popular books and essays may be described as "common"—decently though not extravagantly educated, pragmatic, sharp, able to "smell a rat," and not terribly patient. For such an audience rhetoric must be clear, cogent, concise, and convincing; otherwise, the audience will lose interest quickly.

Russell, a mathematician and philosopher, writes, like Lewis, both academic and popular books. Of the seventy odd books and pamphlets he wrote, more than half were addressed to the common man or woman. Consider the following titles: *The Problems of Philosophy* (1912)—according to many this little book published in the Home University Library series is still the best introduction of the subject published in English—*Sceptical Essays* (1928), *The Conquest of Happiness* (1930), *A History of Western Philosophy* (1945), *Why I*

Am Not a Christian (1957), and *My Philosophical Development* (1959). In each Russell earnestly attempts to persuade his audience of his way of thinking; yet he is fair and even-handed.

For example, in the preface to *The Conquest of Happiness* Russell writes:

> This book is not addressed to highbrows, or to those who regard a practical problem merely as something to be talked about. No profound philosophy or deep erudition will be found in the following pages. I have aimed only at putting together some remarks which are inspired by what I hope is common sense. All that I claim for the recipes offered to the reader is that they are such as are confirmed by my own experience and observation, and that they have increased my own happiness whenever I have acted in accordance with them. On this ground I venture to hope that some among those multitudes of men and women who suffer unhappiness without enjoying, it may find their situation diagnosed and a method of escape suggested. It is in the belief that many people who are unhappy could become happy by well-directed effort that I have written this book.[6]

A number of things in this passage are noteworthy. First, Russell establishes that his audience is not the intellectual elite but those guided by "common sense." In this way he underlines that he is "one of them," a chum, a mate, one of the crowd. Second, his advice to this audience is not based on theory or hypothesis but on his "own experience and observation" acted upon; that is, his is practical, pragmatic, and utilitarian advice. Third, he is addressing an audience not content to simmer in its misery, but one willing to utilize his "method of escape." He is aiming at an audience that is willing to act, to change, to grow. The overall tone of this appeal, consequently, is no-nonsense yet benevolent, grounded in personal conviction yet tolerant, gregarious yet individualistic. Russell aims squarely for an audience that may be described as a cross between Everyman and Sam Gamgee.

Examples from Lewis's works that illustrate his awareness of audience and its particularities are too numerous to mention. In essay after essay he addresses his common sense readers. In *The Problem of Pain*, for instance, he wastes no time in appealing to his audience's conventional wisdom regarding the practical implications of pain. Assuming that the primary responsibility of each human being is to "surrender itself to its Creator,"[7] Lewis goes on to suggest that pain is sometimes used to remind us of this responsibility: "The human spirit will not even begin to try to surrender self-will as long as all seems to be well with it. Now error and sin both have this property, that the deeper they are the less their victim suspects their existence; they are masked evil. Pain is unmasked, unmistakable evil; every man knows that something is wrong when he is being hurt" (80). Like Russell, Lewis speaks directly and sympathetically to his audience; every man, says Lewis, including himself, knows that pain is the least common denominator, the mathematical reduction that puts all of us on the same existential level. He adds later that pain is "impossible to ignore" (81). This forthright candor goes straight to the heart of the audience so that even those not in philosophical agreement with Lewis can appreciate his point; after all, who among them has not suffered pain?

In *The Four Loves* Lewis again treats his audience as an equal, an intimate. About friendship or *phileo* he tells us: "You become a man's Friend without knowing or caring whether he is married or single or how he earns his living. What have all these with the real question, *Do you see the same truth?*"[8] Throughout this book, and indeed in many others, Lewis speaks to his audience as if in confidence. It is as if he says: "Here, I've something to share with you that makes sense to me. Sit down, lean back; put off your shoes and take up a glass of wine. Let's work on this thing together." In fact, Lewis's use of the second person "you" throughout *The Four Loves* reinforces the familiarity he is trying to create between himself and his audience. Making a bridge to the audience for Lewis is all important; what good is the writer's persona or even his arguments if he ignores his audience's character?

The third kind of appeal a rhetorician can make is that of *logos*; that is, an appeal to reason. Aristotle notes that while *ethos* is the most effective and *pathos* the most efficient rhetorical appeals, he says that the rational appeal is the most compelling and convincing. Aristotle has a long list of specific *topoi* or heuristic probes that produce reasoned appeals: arguments based on definition, comparison, contrast, cause and effect, contradictions, paradox, irony, and analogy. Russell and Lewis, of course, use all these kinds of arguments. We have already seen, for example, how each uses the argument from definition in their concern with the word Christian. Both employ paradox extensively. About God's mercy Lewis writes: "The hardness of God is kinder than the softness of men, and His compulsion is our liberation" (*SJ*, 229).

About "good" and "bad" Russell says: "A thing is 'good,' as I wish to use the term, if it is valued for its own sake, and not only for its effects. We take medicines because we hope they will have desirable effects, but a gouty connoisseur drinks old wine for its own sake, in spite of possible disagreeable effects. The medicine is useful but not good, the wine is good but not useful."[9]

However the *topoi* used most effectively by each writer is the argument by metaphor or analogy. Indeed, it is their facility in creating startling metaphors and analogies that make them so powerful as deliberative writers. Metaphors and analogies take difficult or unusual ideas and try to make them understandable by comparing them to something the audience will be able to comprehend. Consider the following examples from Russell's writings:

1. I regard [religion] as a disease born of fear (*Why I Am Not a Christian*, 27).

2. Our memories and habits are bound up with the structure of the brain, in much the same way in which a river is connected with the river-bed. The water in the river is always changing but it keeps to the same course because previous rains have worn a channel. In like manner, previous events have worn a channel in the brain and our thoughts flow along this channel (71).

3. It has become clear that, while the individual may have difficulty in deliberately altering his character, the scientific psychologist, if allowed a free run with children, can manipulate human nature as freely as Californians manipulate the desert (108).

4. Dealing with children is a specialized activity requiring specialized knowledge and a suitable environment. The rearing of children in the home is of a piece with the spinning wheel, and is equally uneconomic (109).

5. Mathematics, rightly viewed, possesses not only truth but supreme beauty—a beauty cold and austere, like that of sculpture.[10]

6. Every man, wherever he goes, is encompassed by a cloud of comforting convictions, which move with him like flies on a summer day.[11]

Selecting a series of Russell's metaphors and analogies is not as difficult as selecting a list of Lewis's; here I offer the following as only a representative list, impartial and personal:

1. The task of the modern educator is not to cut down jungles but to irrigate deserts (*The Abolition of Man*, 9).
2. The Divine "goodness" differs from ours, but it is not sheerly different: it differs from ours not as white from black but as a perfect circle from a child's first attempt to draw a wheel. But when the child has learned to draw, it will know that the circle it then makes is what it was trying to make from the very beginning (*Problem of Pain*, 27)
3. [God's love for man is] persistent as the artist's love for his work and despotic as a man's love for his dog, provident and venerable as a father's love for a child, jealous, inexorable, exacting as love between the sexes (35).
4. [Pain] plants the flag of truth within the fortress of a rebel soul (83).
5. God made us: invented us as a man invents an engine. A car is made to run on gasoline, and it would not run properly on anything else. Now God designed the human machine to run on Himself. He Himself is the fuel our spirits were designed to burn, or the food our spirits were designed to feed on (*MC*, 39).
6. Pride is spiritual cancer: it eats up the possibility of love, or contentment, or even common sense (*MC*, 97).
7. The safest road to Hell is the gradual one—the gentle slope, soft underfoot, without sudden turnings, without milestones, without signposts (*SL*, 65).

To do each writer justice regarding his use of metaphor and analogy would obviously take much more space than this essay allows. My point is that Russell and Lewis rely on this kind of appeal to reason because of their audience; to an audience of common sense people it is wise to create comparisons and mental pictures when the subject under discussion begins to get weighty. The advantage of the metaphor or analogy is that it creates an immediate mental image in the audience's mind that helps hold and focus the argument being considered.

The thrust of this essay has been upon the rhetorical similarities in the popular books and essays of Russell and Lewis. Of their opposite philosophical positions little has been said. Russell, a materialist and atheist, argues for the centrality of scientific progress and human potential. He believes that the future is solely in the hands of humankind. Science, says Russell, should replace religion as the arbiter of human behavior, especially with regard to child development and human sexuality. Lewis, on the other hand, an idealist and Christian, argues for the necessity of natural law and human obedience. He believes the future is solely in the hands of an omniscient, personal God. Science, for Lewis, has its function as a tool of humankind, but it can never take the place of religion; it speaks only to the physical world while religion speaks to the spiritual. It is hard to find two men more out of philosophical sympathy with one another; *Why I Am Not a Christian* is as far from *Mere Christianity* as Pluto is from the Sun.

My reticence at addressing in more detail their philosophical differences is not because I want to avoid the rather volatile nature of their opposing views; indeed, when I began writing this essay I realized that an understanding of Russell's and Lewis's rhetorical skills would enhance an understanding of their philosophical views. What I have come to suspect as a result of writing this essay is that Lewis may have been using many of Russell's arguments as a springboard for his own counter arguments. Earlier in this paper I spoke of the need for every writer to fictionalize an audience. I now believe that in many of Lewis's popular books and essays he may have been actually fictionalizing not only his "common-sense" audience, but also Bertrand Russell; an interesting follow-up essay to this one might explore how Lewis had specific passages from Russell's work in mind as he considered a number of philosophical issues upon which he and Russell disagreed. Lewis's responses might have been specifically targeted to contravene ones Russell had made to their common "fictionalized" audience.[12]

I conclude by noting that each writer demands from us a fair hearing regardless of our philosophical predilections. Each, through a careful application of rhetorical principles, manages to capture our attention and hold us for the moments we read their works. Each challenges us to pause, to consider, to cogitate, and to respond. However, in the end their success in persuading turns both upon the force with which they communicate their ideas and our own "cloud of comforting convictions."

Chapter 4 Notes

1. A version of this essay first appeared in *Mythlore* 15 (Autumn 1988): 28–31.

2. "Why I Am Not a Christian," in *Why I Am Not a Christian* (London: Allen and Unwin, 1957), 48 (subsequent references in the text).

3. *The Abolition of Man* (New York: Macmillan, 1947), 12 (subsequent references in the text).

4. *Mere Christianity* (New York: Macmillan, 1952), xii (hereafter *MC* and subsequent references in the text).

5. "The Writer's Audience Is Always a Fiction." *PMLA* 90 (1975): 9–22.

6. *The Conquest of Happiness* (London: Allen & Unwin, 1930), ix.

7. *The Problem of Pain* (New York: Macmillan, 1943), 78 (subsequent references in the text).

8. *The Four Loves* (London: Bles, 1960), 78 (emphasis Lewis).

9. *Human Society in Ethics and Politics* (New York: Simon and Schuster, 1955), 31 (subsequent references in the text).

10. From Chapter Four of *Mysticism and Logic* (New York: Longmans, 1918), 75.

11. *Sceptical Essays* (New York: Norton, 1928), 28 (subsequent references in the text).

12. Some evidence for this argument exists in Lewis's diary, *All My Road before Me: The Diary of C. S. Lewis, 1922–1927.* Edited by Walter Hooper (London: Harper Collins, 1991). In his entry of January 5, 1924, Lewis writes: "In [Bertrand Russell's] "Worship of a Free Man" I found a very clear and noble statement of what I myself believed a few years ago. But he does not face the real difficulty—that our beliefs are after all a natural product, facts with a relation to all other facts, and cannot survive the condemnation of the fact as a whole. The Promethean attitude would be tenable only if we were really members of some other whole outside the real whole: wh. we're not" (281). A few days later he adds: "I decided to try and write . . . an answer to Bertrand Russell's "Worship of a Free Man" (January 8, 1924; 282). Written well before Lewis's conversion, these two diary entries show Lewis's early desire to engage Russell philosophically.

The Distant Voice in C. S. Lewis's *Poems*[1]

C. S. Lewis's popularity as a writer rests squarely on a prose style that is clear, lucid, and engaging. Lewis's attractive prose is not limited to one or two genres, but instead is apparent in his literary criticism as well as his children stories, in his devotional works as well as his science fiction, in his apologetics as well as his letters. It is commonplace, then, to underscore the enormous success his prose brought him. Yet Lewis began his publishing career as a poet with *Spirits in Bondage* (1919), a volume of lyrical poems, and followed this with *Dymer* (1926), a long narrative poem in rhyme royal (both published under the pseudonym, Clive Hamilton, using his own first name and his mother's maiden name). Moreover, throughout his life Lewis continued to write poetry; some poems were included in prose works like *The Pilgrim's Regress*, the Chronicles of Narnia, and the Ransom Space trilogy, and others were published independently in magazines, journals, and newspapers. Many were collected by Walter Hooper and published in 1964 as *Poems*.

Although *Spirits in Bondage* and *Dymer* merit further study, *Poems*, according to Tom Howard, "the best—the glorious best—of Lewis," is of special interest because some of these poems offer an insight into an aspect of Lewis's work that is infrequently seen in his prose.[2] On the one hand, there are a number of striking features about this collection that will delight rather than disturb: its heavy emphasis upon pagan and Christian allusion, its sense of play, its antimodernist bias, and its range of subject. However, on the other hand, these poems also reveal a disturbing "voice" not often heard in Lewis's prose; that is, a distant voice—uncertain, unsure, and ambivalent toward matters of life and meaning—surfaces in *Poems* that challenges a too facile understanding of Lewis. The focus of this essay is to identify the specific characteristics of this voice and to identify the specific poems where it is present.

In approaching the task of identifying which poems express this distant voice, it is necessary to review what Walter Hooper says in the preface to *Poems* about his editing and ordering of this volume. Hooper notes that Lewis had been collecting his poems over the years for a volume to be called "Young King Cole and Other Pieces."[3] In addition to this manuscript and to a number of already published poems, Hooper found among Lewis's papers a number of handwritten, undated, and unfinished poems. Thus, when Hooper began the task of editing Lewis's poems, he followed his "judgment as to what should be printed." He found poems "scribbled on scraps of paper or in the flyleaves of books." Others were in notebooks "at least as old as the poems in *The Pilgrim's Regress*," and almost all were untitled. As a consequence, Hooper chose "to arrange the poems more or less topically rather than attempt a chronological ordering."[4] Hooper faced a challenging job as editor, and his decision to organize the book topically is justified. However, I have approached the study of the distant voice by considering the poems in chronological order whenever possible. Such an approach offers evidence of the lifelong presence of this distant voice in Lewis's poetry.[5]

What are the characteristics of the distant voice in *Poems*? There are two: the first considers the human condition as deeply melancholic, tending towards nihilism, and spiritually skeptical concerning the benevolent nature of God, while the second focuses on personal isolation, most often expressed through terminated relationships—often terminated friendships. Of course, not every poem incorporates both characteristics, but at least one dominates enough so that the distant voice is distinctly heard. Specifically, then, which poems in *Poems* reflect this distant voice? While I could choose from dozens, for purposes of this essay I have selected two small groups of dated and undated poems. Although the presence of the distant voice is more pronounced in some of these poems than in others, each is strikingly different from other poems in *Poems*.

Representative poems where the distant voice communicates religious skepticism and a deep melancholy for the human condition include "Caught" (1933), "To a Friend" (October 1942), "The Salamander" (June 1945), "To Charles Williams" (August 1945), and "A Confession" (December 1954). In "Caught," first published in *The Pilgrim's Regress* (1933), we find a persona who is struggling to come to grips with a fierce omnipotence, much as a dog would strain at the leash of an unyielding master. The poem begins with the persona noting that he feels like a person trapped in a burning desert bathed by unrelenting, suffocating light and heat. God, like the sun, is the "inevitable Eye" that confines a desert traveler in a smothering tent and "hammers the rocks with light." He is an unyielding, unrelenting, uncompromising force. In desperation the persona longs for "one cool breath in seven / One air from northern climes / The changing and the castle-clouded heaven / Of my old Pagan times" (115). It is difficult to read these lines and not recall Lewis's professed affection for "northerness" in terms of both its religious and metaphorical influences on his youth and young adulthood. In addition, these lines suggest a powerful longing for freedom from the "heat" of God's eye; he is ready to retreat from the demands of an unyielding God toward the comfort and security of his pagan days. Such an option is denied him: "But you have seized all in your rage / Of Oneness. Round about / Beating my wings, all ways, within your cage, / I flutter, but not out." Here God is pictured as possessive, angry, and intent on his prey. At the same time the persona pictures himself as a bird trapped in a cage, straining earnestly to wing his way out, but to no avail.

This poem leaves two impressions. The first, of course, is of a "convert" who yearns for his preconversion days where, rightly or wrongly, he believes life held more freedom, more satisfaction. Indeed, the tone of this poem is similar to George Herbert's "The Collar" where the persona advises himself to "leave thy cold dispute / Of what is fit and not. Forsake thy cage, / Thy ropes of sands, / Which petty thoughts have made."[6] As in Herbert's poem, the persona in "Caught" is frustrated ("beating my wings") yet thwarted ("I flutter, but not out"). The second impression is that God is an all encompassing, smothering, demanding entity, uncompromising in jealous possession of a follower. Such a God seizes "all in [his] rage / Of Oneness." These impressions combine to highlight the distant voice in "Caught" that regards with ambivalence the value of religious faith and the benevolent character of God.

A related but slightly different emphasis on the distant voice occurs in "The Salamander" where we find a profoundly melancholic view of the value of human life. The poem opens with someone sitting before a fire, staring into "blue waves / Of shuddering heat that r[i]se and f[a]ll, / And blazing ships and blinding caves, / Canyons and streets and hills of hell" (72–73). However, this all too familiar atmosphere is suddenly changed when "amidst it all / I saw a living creature crawl." From this point on the salamander speaks directly to the persona about what he "sees" outside the fire; his melancholic reflections are compared to ones humans make since he looks with "sad eyes . . . as men [look] out upon the skies." Gazing into the dark room, the salamander says "this is the end," the place "where all life dies," the universe of "blank silence, distances untold / Of unimaginable cold." The lights from the room he can see only dimly, since they "Are but reflections cast from here, / There is no other fire but this. / This speck of life, this fading spark / Enisled amid the boundless dark." The creature intimates that the real world, the world of meaning, is found only within the fire; outside there is isolation, barrenness, emptiness. He can only see what is physically in front of him, so the only world he is willing to accept is one that is tangible; that there could be one in the invisible realm beyond his fiery world is unthinkable. And, of course, by implication humankind has a similar mindset; rather than face boldly the prospect of a spiritual world, we, like the salamander, deny anything we cannot perceive as a part of the material world about us. The salamander ends with a nihilistic credo, one suggesting that values are hollow:

> "Blind Nature's measureless rebuke
> To all we value, I received
> Long since (though wishes bait the hook
> With tales our ancestors believed)
> And now can face with fearless eye
> Negation's final sovereignty."

He confronts such nihilism courageously since he faces "with fearless eye, / Negation's final sovereignty." The salamander's affirmation of nihilism implies, if we make the invited comparison between the salamander and the human condition, that human beings need to make a similar discovery and affirmation about their own existence; that is, life may be without meaning, yet our task is to face that reality courageously. The distant voice in this poem contrasts dramatically with the confident, buoyant voice of so much of Lewis's prose.

The melancholic nature of the distant voice continues in "To Charles Williams." This poem records the shock of losing a friend and how it throws one's mistaken view of the human condition into a tailspin: "I can't see the old contours. It's a larger world / Than I once thought it. I wince, caught in the bleak air that blows on the ridge. / Is it the first sting of the great winter, the world-waning? Or the cold of spring?" (105). The old comfortable thought that human life has meaning is challenged by death, and a new, disturbing possibility thrusts itself upon the persona. Indeed, the knowledge that life is fragile causes him to "wince, caught in the bleak air that blows on the ridge," and to question whether or not such a loss is just the tip of the iceberg ("the first sting of the great winter"). Although he allows that he may be overreacting ("Or the cold of spring?"), he never answers the question in the context of the poem, and we are left with the impression that the loss of a friend challenges his wellworn self-assurance about life having ultimate meaning and purpose.

"A Confession," ostensibly about Lewis's dissatisfaction with modern British poetry, also uses the distant voice to underscore man's melancholic situation. For instance, he dislikes T. S. Eliot's imagery in these lines from "The Love Song of J. Alfred Prufrock": "For twenty years I've stared my level best / To see if evening—any evening—would suggest / A patient etherized upon a table; / In vain. I simply wasn't able" (1). In his own description of the evening, Lewis uses a metaphor recalling Greek and Latin allusions: "To me each evening looked far more / Like the departure from a silent, yet crowded, shore / Of a ship whose freight was everything, leaving behind, / Gracefully, finally, without farewells, marooned mankind." Recalling a scene from Dante's *Inferno*, Lewis suggests that humankind is essentially isolated and alone, without a guide, without a Virgil to assist him in his wanderings; we are "marooned mankind." Later he rejects contemporary descriptions of the moon, preferring to call it a "prodigy . . . a riddle glaring from the Cyclops' brow," and a reminder "on what a place / I crawl and cling, a planet with no bulwarks." The phrase "a planet with no bulwarks" speaks of Lewis's melancholic awareness of the human condition as isolated and without moorings and recalls Joseph Conrad's note in a letter: "Most of my life has been spent between sky and water and now I live so alone that often I fancy myself clinging stupidly to a derelict planet abandoned by its precious crew."[7]

The second characteristic of the distant voice is a sense of personal isolation, primarily as a result of terminated friendships. "Scazons" (like "Caught" first published in *The Pilgrim's Regress*) provides early evidence of this aspect of the distant voice, as the poem's persona recalls how an event of the day had triggered his sense of isolation: "Walking today by a cottage I shed tears / When I remembered how once I had walked there / With my friends who are mortal and dead" (118). In "To a Friend" the persona contrasts how his friend's death will serve as "rich soil" for the birth of ideas, while his own life, haunted by fears that "[gnaw] at me for myself," will be as sterile as "the unresponding Moon. / Her gaping valleys have no soil, / Her needle-pointed hills are bare; / Water, poured on those rocks, would boil, / And day lasts long, and long despair" (10405). And in the end of "To Charles Williams" the persona asks: "Of whom now can I ask guidance? With what friend concerning your death / Is it worth while to exchange thoughts unless—oh unless it were you?" (105). The poignant ending of this poem testifies to the depth of Lewis's affection for Williams and, along with the other passages above, communicates a powerful sense of personal isolation.[8]

Several of the undated poems also focus on the loss of *phileo* and the ensuing grief and regret that follow. Perhaps the fullest example of personal isolation as a result of lost friendship occurs in "Lines Written in a Copy of Milton's Works." The poem begins with the persona noting how natural creatures blithely carry on in harmony with one another: "Alas, the happy beasts at pasture play / All, all alike; all of one mind are they" (83). Not only are the animals in harmony, but also they easily change companions and are blessed with disinterested friendship: "None loves a special friend beyond the rest." Indeed, even if a sparrow loses a friend to a bird of prey or to a hunter's arrow, "with a new friend next day, content, he wings his flight." The persona then contrasts this Wordsworthian view of the relationship between the beasts with the more dissonant relationships between human beings. We humans, the persona suggests, cannot unthinkingly and casually find the easy friend since we "in his fellows finds / (Hard fate) discordant souls and alien minds!" Actually, in the effort to find even one close friend, "one heart amidst a thousand like his own," we will encounter a good deal of difficulty. And, ironically, even if we do eventually find such a friend, it will only be temporary:

Or if, at last relenting, fate shall send
In answer to his prayer, the authentic friend,
Him in some unsuspected hour, some day
He never dreaded, Death will snatch away
And leave behind a loss that time can ne'er allay.

Once bereft of that friend, we are left without a companion to "charm to rest each eating care," to share "the secrets of my bosom," or to "while away with delight / Of his discourse the livelong winter night." The last stanza begins with an emphasis upon the persona's sense of isolation: "Alone I walk the fields and plains, alone / The dark vales with dense branches overgrown." In his solitude he feels confined and aimless. Moreover, the imagery of the last two lines of the poem indicates an overwhelming sense of estrangement: "Here, as day fades, I wait, and all around / I hear the rain that falls with sullen sound." The cold dampness of the fading day suggests a pathetic fallacy, especially as the rain falls with "sullen sound."

In addition to the appearance of the distant voice in poems concerning lost friendship or *phileo*, several others deal with lost *eros*. In "As the Ruin Falls" the persona rebukes himself with bitter honesty: "All this is flashy rhetoric about loving you. / I never had a selfless thought since I was born. / I am mercenary and self-seeking through and through: / I want God, you, all friends, merely to serve my turn" (109–10). His confession about his egocentricity continues as he admits that he "cannot crawl one inch outside my proper skin"; he talks of love, he says, but he recognizes that his has not been a giving love: "self-imprisoned, [I] always end where I begin." The other person, the beloved, has taught the persona by example both what loving means (giving) and how miserable his ability to love has been: "Only that now you have taught me (but how late) my lack." But there is an added dimension; the beloved appears to be leaving him, whether because of circumstance or death we cannot be sure: "I see the chasm. And everything you are was making / My heart into a bridge by which I might get back / From exile, and grow man. And now the bridge is breaking." To the beloved he credits his own faltering steps toward a love that is giving; indeed, the beloved has given him the capacity to be less selfish (she has made his heart a bridge) and less isolated (she has helped to end his "exile, and grow man"). His comment that the bridge is now breaking almost certainly refers to his anticipated loss of her. And so he blesses her : "For this

I bless you as the ruin falls. The pains / You give me are more precious than all other gains."

"Joys That Sting" is almost certainly a melancholic reverie about a terminated erotic friendship. Here the persona is saddened "to take the old walks alone, or not at all, / To order one pint where I ordered two, / To think of, and then not to make, the small / Time-honoured joke (senseless all but to you)" (108). That he now only orders "one pint where I ordered two" strongly suggests an erotic or marital connection since two male friends would probably have ordered separately; on the other hand, a husband would normally order for his wife.[9] He goes on to underscore his estrangement and comments that his life is now little more than show:

> To laugh (oh, one'll laugh), to talk upon
> Themes that we talked upon when you were there,
> To make some poor pretence of going on,
> Be kind to one's old friends, and seem to care,
> While no one (O God) through the years will say
> The simplest, common word in just your way.

The grief this poem expresses over the loss of the beloved is both simple and profound: "it is the joys once shared that have the stings." It is possible that "As the Ruin Falls" was written to or for Joy Davidman during her illness and "Joys That Sting" was written after her death as Lewis mourned her; in fact, the tone of the poem is very close to *A Grief Observed* (1961). Regardless, the unwelcomed termination of friendship, be it *phileo* or *eros*, is a central focus in many of his poems that employ personal isolation as a characteristic of the distant voice.

Other than in *A Grief Observed*, the distant voice occurs rarely in Lewis's prose.[10] However, because poetry tends to be a more personal and private medium than prose, this is not surprising. Of course, the appearance of the distant voice in *Poems* argues against those who claim that *A Grief Observed* rings somehow hollow or is proof that his wife's death brought a sudden loss of faith.[11] Undeniably Lewis went through a crisis of faith as a result of Davidman's death, but as the poems noted above suggest, doubt about the nature of God and human meaning were not new to him. He had already wrestled with many of the issues that her death made more concrete, though obviously her death tested him experientially in a way he had not experienced since the death of his mother almost fifty years before. Consequently, the confidence so many of his readers were familiar with deserted him as he agonized over Joy's death.

Lewis's use of the distant voice in these selections from *Poems* is not frequent when viewed in the context of the entire volume; nonetheless, its appearance is noteworthy since it reveals he was not always the confident defender of the faith that his prose apologetics would suggest. That he may have had doubts and questions about God and human meaning does not undermine the value of his apologetics; indeed, to realize that he did struggle with matters of faith makes his apologetics all that more effective and compelling. Were we to think that Lewis was shielded from the doubts that all human beings have would make his prose apologetics too facile, untested by the hard knocks of everyday life. Lewis, as the distant voice in *Poems* illustrates, probably would have agreed with Tennyson: "There lives more faith in honest doubt, / Believe me, than in half the creeds."[12]

Chapter 5 Notes

1. A version of this essay first appeared in *Studies in the Literary Imagination* 22.2 (Fall 1989): 175–184.

2. Thomas Howard, "*Poems*: A Review." *Christianity Today* 9 (June 18, 1965): 30.

3. This manuscript is available in the Bodleian Library, Dep. c. 883–84.

4. *Poems*, ed. Walter Hooper (New York: Harcourt, Brace Jovanovich, 1964), vii (hereafter *P* and subsequent references in the text).

5. At the same time, we must be cautious, as Hooper warns, of "attempting to date [Lewis's] poems on internal evidence "since to do so might lead to "what Lewis himself called the 'Personal Heresy': reading a man's works as autobiography" (viii).

6. George Herbert, "The Collar," in *The Poems of George Herbert* (London: Oxford University Press, 1961), 143.

7. *The Collected Letters of Joseph Conrad: Volume I, 1861–1897*, eds. Frederick Karl and Laurence Davies (Cambridge: Cambridge University Press, 1983), 370.

8. For more see Lewis's tribute to Williams in the "Preface" to *A Preface to Paradise Lost* (London: Oxford University Press, 1942).

9. I am indebted to Dabney Hart for her helpful insight on this point.

10. In *Reflections on the Psalms* (New York: Harcourt Brace and World, 1958) we find an illustrative example: "I have often, on my knees, been shocked to find what sort of thoughts I have, for a moment, been addressing to God; what infantile placations I was really offering, what claims I have really made, even what absurd adjustments or compromises I was, half-consciously, proposing. There is a Pagan, savage heart in me somewhere. For unfortunately the folly and idiot-cunning of Paganism seem to have far more power of surviving than its innocent or even beautiful elements. It is easy, once you have power, to

silence the pipes, still the dances, disfigure the statues, and forget the stories; but not easy to kill the savage, the greedy, frightened creature now cringing, now blustering, in one's soul" (97–98).

11. For example see John Beversluis, "Beyond the Double Bolted Door," *Christian History* 4.3 (1985): 28–31.

12. "In Memoriam (xcvi)," in *Poems of Tennyson* (Boston: Houghton Mifflin, 1958).

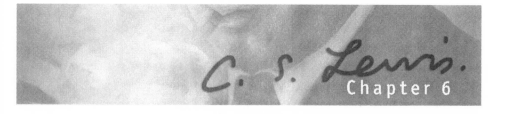

Making the Poor Best of Dull Things: C. S. Lewis as Poet[1]

I am like that odd man Wordsworth knew, to whom
A primrose was a yellow primrose, one whose doom
Retains him always in the class of dunces,
Compelled to offer Stock Responses,
Making the poor best that I can
Of dull things . . . peacocks, honey, the Great Wall, Aldebaran,
Silver streams, cowslip wine, wave on the beach, bright gem,
The shape of trees or women, thunder, Troy, Jerusalem.[2]

Although C. S. Lewis is best known as a prose writer for his clear, lucid literary criticism, Christian apologetics, and imaginative Ransom and Narnia stories, he actually began his publishing career as a poet.[3] Indeed, Lewis consciously considered himself a poet and worked intensely on his poetry for the first two and a half decades of his life. It follows that readers interested in him should become aware of the important role that poetry, particularly older and traditional poetic forms, had in shaping his life as a writer.[4] Accordingly, this essay will illustrate Lewis's early and obsessive desire to be known as a significant poet and suggest ways that a better understanding of his aspirations to become an important poet provides the basis for new critical insights into his work as a prose writer.

Though Lewis alludes to his early love of poetry in *Surprised by Joy*, few have taken the time to trace the implications of this love as he moved from boyhood to young adult. Lewis's letters, particularly to his childhood and lifelong friend Arthur Greeves, as well as his diary entries, provide ample evidence of both his early enthusiasm for the poetry he was reading and his almost frantic desire to achieve acclaim as a poet; furthermore, in them we see his attempt to establish his own theory of poetry, something he pursued throughout his life via a number of different forums. When we examine these sources, we find that he especially enjoyed reading the *Iliad*, Thomas Malory's "Morte D'Arthur," Edmund Spenser's *The Faerie Queen*, *Sir Gawain and the Green Knight*, John Milton's "Comus" and *Paradise Lost*, Percy Shelley's "Prometheus Unbound," William Wordsworth's "The Prelude," and the poetry of Alfred Tennyson, William Morris, Matthew Arnold, and W. B. Yeats (whom he twice met). For instance, about reading the *Iliad* aloud in Greek, Lewis writes to Greeves on September 26, 1914: "Those fine, simple, euphonious lines, as they roll on with a roar like that of the ocean, strike a chord in one's mind that no modern literature approaches."[5] Hearing and reading poetry aloud was always an important principle, as he writes to his brother, Warren, eighteen years later: "By the way I most fully agree with you about 'the lips being invited to share the banquet' in poetry, and always 'mouth' it while I read . . . . I look upon this 'mouthing' as an infallible mark of the man who really likes poetry" (April 8, 1932).[6] Of the "Morte D'Arthur," he notes "it has opened up a new world to me" (January 26, 1915; *CL*, 1, 103).

In reading of Lewis's early delight in poetry, one is struck by the depth of his enthusiasm; his passion for poetry was visceral, and it fed and nourished his aesthetic taste. Letter after letter communicates his love of literature, music, and art, but especially poetry. He consumed it greedily and his appetite was perhaps never sated, although in a telling letter to his brother on August 2, 1928, he does admit that the thrill of discovering a great new poem in English is over:

> There is no longer any chance of discovering a long poem in English which will turn out to be just what I want and which can be added to the *Faerie Queen*, the *Prelude*, *Paradise Lost*, *The Ring and the Book*, the *Earthly Paradise*, and a few others—because there aren't anymore . . . . In that sense I may be said to have come to the end of English

poetry—as you may be said to have come to the end of a wood, not when you have actually walked every inch of it, but when you have walked about in it enough to know where all the boundaries are and to feel the end near even when you can't see it; when there is no longer any hope (as there was for the first few days) that the next turn of the path might bring you to an unsuspected lake or cave or clearing on the edge of a new valley. (776)

There is real sadness in this letter and a longing for the old thrill of discovering a new poem; Lewis's tone here recalls Wordsworth's "Tintern Abbey": "That time is past, / And all its aching joys are now no more, / And all its dizzy raptures."

Lewis's deep affection for the poetry he was reading was a certain stimulus for his own aspirations as a poet. Once again, his letters and diary entries are filled with these longings. To Greeves he frequently writes about the poems he is writing and sending to him for criticism. Such poems include "Loki Bound," "Faeries Must Be in the Woods," "Medea," and others later appearing in his *Spirits in Bondage*. In one long letter of October 6, 1914, Lewis outlines his plan for "Loki Bound" to be patterned after a Greek tragedy, and even offers to collaborate with Greeves to turn it into an opera (75–77). In another letter he talks about his bedtime routine: "I write up my diary for the day, and then turning to the other end of the book devote myself to poetry, either new stuff or polishing the old" (October 12, 1915; 146). Lewis also devoted himself to writing the lyrical poems that are later published in *Spirits in Bondage*. Perhaps he decided to take a break from the narrative poetry he longed to produce, although he did begin work on a prose version of *Dymer* during this same time. Also, because he was involved in officer training for World War I at the time, he may have found it easier to focus on short lyrics than on longer, more sustained pieces. He tells Greeves that "I am in a strangely productive mood at present and spend my few moments of spare time in scribbling verse. When my four months course in the cadet battalion is at an end . . . I propose to get together all the stuff I have perpetrated and see if any kind publisher would like to take it" (June 10, 1917; 321). In spite of the fact that the first publisher he sent it to, Macmillan, rejects it, Lewis does not seem dejected and writes to Greeves that "I am determined not to lose heart until I have tried all the houses I can hear of. I am sending it off to Heinneman next" (August 7, 1918; 392).

Happily, Heinneman accepted his work less than a month later, and his letters begin to show his increasing ambition to achieve acclaim as a poet. For example, he writes to his father, Albert: "This little success gives me a pleasure which is perhaps childish, and yet akin to greater things" (September 9, 1918; 396). To Greeves he says: "You can imagine how pleased I am, and how eagerly I now look at all Heinneman's books and wonder what mine will be like" (September 12, 1918; 397). Several weeks later he gives his father a qualified evaluation of the poems: "I am not claiming that they are good poems—you know the schoolboys' definitions, 'Prose is when the lines go on to the end of the page; poetry is when they don't'" (October 3, 1918; 401). When asked by John Galsworthy for permission to publish one of the poems from *Spirits in Bondage* in a war poetry anthology, Lewis wrote his father that "I naturally consented because it is pleasant 'laudari a laudato viro'" (October 27, 1918; 410).[7] He tells Greeves later when recalling his first meeting with the publisher: "You will understand well how pleasant it was to walk in under a doorway . . . feeling I had some right to be there" (November 2, 1918; 412).

Now a published poet and enjoying the first taste of fame, however modest (most reviews of *Spirits in Bondage* were favorable), Lewis continued his poetic development as additional letters reveal. In a series of letters to Leo Baker, Lewis reflects upon the role and function of poetry. On September 25, 1920, he writes Baker and thanks him for his theory of poetry: "The most valuable part of it, and the part which shd. be insisted on is that 'a poet who is only a poet is not the greatest poet': the assumption that a great poem must have nothing in it but poetry has 'worked like madness in the brain' of too many of us" (508). A poet, Lewis suggests, cannot afford to be only a poet; he must be involved in the lives of men and women. In addition, Lewis intimates how his longing to achieve acclaim as a poet interferes with the actual making of poetry; that is, as he has worked to write great poetry the focus has been on him, not on the poetry, thus marring the very poetry he is striving so heartily to produce. Such critical self-assessment foreshadows an even more penetrating episode several years later; this also may be compared to Lewis's lifelong search for joy, and his repeated realization that when he seeks joy he never finds it. Instead, it must occur spontaneously.

Later in the same letter Lewis attempts to describe the peculiar function of poetry as compared to other arts:

What we want to find is that which is proper to poetry alone: what is the method by which poetry *and no other art* performs the duties shared with all art? Doubtless you would answer that in the same way as I wd. & come to a definition something like this: "Poetry is the art of utilizing the informal or irrational values of words to express that which can only be symbolized by their informal or conventional meanings." These values include chiefly sound & association: also of course their "group" sounds or rhythms which are above and beyond their individual sounds: here is the meaning & justification of metre. Hence the value of the test "could this be said as well in prose?": if the answer is in the affirmative the poem is condemned. (508–09; emphasis Lewis)

Here Lewis reflects too much a workman's view of how poetry happens. That is, he implies that the poet uses language in a particularly structured and precise way to produce a desired emotional effect. While this view links him in a way with the ancient poets he so admired (for example, the shared emphasis on sound and metre), in another important way it suggests a profound difference. For Homer and Virgil poetry was the natural medium of expression; Odysseus and Aeneas live on not because of poetry but because of their characters and the narratives associated with them. Lewis, who wants to imitate them, lacks an Odysseus or Aeneas. Consequently, he focuses too much effort on the practice of poetry rather than on the creation of a story, whether original or borrowed.

This may explain why at about this time Lewis turned his attention to a verse version of *Dymer*. Having finished an earlier prose version in 1917, from 1920 to 1926 Lewis pursued a poetic version with intensity and deliberate single mindedness; his diary, *All My Road Before Me: The Diary of C. S. Lewis 1922–1927*, contains over seventy-five direct references to this effort. In these entries he recounts an almost daily obsession with both his progress on the poem and his ambition to achieve fame as a poet. A study of the diary shows that he completed initial drafts of the first two cantos by the end of June 1922; Canto III by the end of July 1922; Canto IV by the end of August 1922; Cantos V and VI by the end of June 1923; and Cantos VII, VIII, and IX by mid-April 1924. Of course during this process he would go back and forth between one canto and another, revising here and there as he saw the need.

Often he was assisted in this process by the friendly but honest criticism of colleagues, including Baker, Owen Barfield, Alfred Hamilton Jenkin, Cecil Harwood, Rodney Pasley, and Greeves. He completed a final version in the summer of 1925.[8]

At times he writes about his struggles. For instance, early on he notes that "I am very dispirited about my work at present . . . . I have leaned much too much on the idea of being able to write poetry and if this is a frost I shall be rather stranded" (April, 15, 1922).[9] Three months later he is rewriting Canto IV, "with which I am finding great difficulties" (July 30, 1922; 77). Eighteen months later he is at his most dissatisfied: "[I am] discontent with the whole plan of 'Dymer': it seems 'full of sound and fury, signifying nothing'" (January 6, 1924; 281). When revising the proofs just prior to publication, Lewis shares a feeling that many writers have as they look over the product of all their labors: "I never liked it less. I felt no mortal could get any notion of what the devil it was all about. I am afraid this sort of stuff is very much hit or miss, yet I think it is my only line" (July 6, 1926; 422).

But more often than not, he is at least upbeat if not jubilant about his progress. Many entries include comments such as "made some progress," "pleased myself fairly well," "felt fairly satisfied," "pleased myself with it," and "with considerable satisfaction." After several months of work, he writes: "After supper I worked on *Dymer*, bringing it to the end of the storm. I was so transported with what I considered my success that I became insolent and said to myself that it was the voice of a god" (September 30, 1922; 111). A week later he adds: "I read the whole thing through and felt fairly satisfied with the general movement of the story" (October 9, 1922; 115). The following summer, after Harwood praises his most recent efforts, Lewis says Harwood "covered me with enough praise to satisfy the vainest of men" (July 8, 1923; 255).

The greatest insight into Lewis's aspirations as a poet is found in an enclosure to a letter he wrote to Greeves on August 18, 1930, in which he attempts to encourage his friend who has just experienced a critical rejection of a writing project. In the letter, Lewis, who by this time is nearing conversion to Christ, openly admits his belief that because achieving success as a poet had become for him a kind of idol, God had to kill the idol. He writes: "From the age of sixteen onwards I had one single ambition, from which I never wavered, in the prosecution of which I spent every ounce I could, on wh[ich] I really deliberately staked my whole contentment . . . . Suffering of the sort that you are now feeling is my special subject, my profession, my long suit, the thing I claim to be an expert in" (925). Lewis goes on to counsel Greeves that perhaps God is dealing kindly with them now (foreshadowing his own later phrase, a severe mercy) by denying their desires for literary fame because it will save them from the disappointment and despair attendant to those who briefly flame up with literary fame and then flicker quickly and fade quietly into oblivion.

It is the enclosure, however, that is most penetrating. Written as a part of his diary on March 6, 1926, Lewis is brutally honest in analyzing his feelings when *Dymer* is rejected by Heinneman (it was later published by Dent in 1926). As he analyzes his reactions to the rejection, he posits five reasons why he is so disturbed, including the fact that Heinneman had already published *Spirits in Bondage*, he had hoped to make a profit, his desire for personal fame, the desire for the poem itself to achieve a place in literary history, and his desire that his poem though not himself should gain acclaim and thus validate his poetic ability. In a process reminiscent of his logical parry and thrust apologetic technique, he at first discounts each motive. But as he probes deeper, he finally admits that he does desire fame as a poet: "I desire that my value as a poet should be acknowledged by others" (929).

To this he adds that his desire has two aspects: the desire for proof to himself that he is a poet and the desire that his poetic gifts be acknowledged by the world even if he remains anonymous. What follows is one of Lewis's longest passages of self-analysis:

> As far as I can see both these are manifestations of the single desire for what may be called mental or spiritual rank. I have flattered myself with the idea of being among my own people when I was reading the poets and it is unpleasing to have to stand down and take my place in the crowd.... The completion of the poem, [Nevill] Coghill's praise of it, and the sending off to a publisher (after so many years) threw me back into a tumult of self-love that I thought I had escaped .... Worst of all I have used the belief in such secret preeminence as a compensation for things that wearied or humiliated me in real life .... The cure of this disease is not easy to find ... I was free from it at times when writing Dymer. Then I was interested in the object, not in my own privileged position of seer of the object. But whenever I stopped writing or thought of publication or showed the MS. to

friends I contemplated not that of which I had been writing, but my
writing about it: I passed from looking at the macrocosm to looking
at a little historical event inside the "Me." (930)

Lewis goes on to say the only way to cure this disease is to look away from self
to the greater world so that thoughts of self will fade. What is so striking here
is his brutal self-assessment. He confesses baldly that his desire for fame as a
poet is nothing less than spiritual pride. Equally, he notes that poetry per se,
even his poetry, has not been nearly as interesting to him in this process as he
has been. Additionally, we see that his hopes for literary fame as a poet have
been a kind of sop for other disappointments. Indeed, he is clearly embar-
rassed by the recognition that his desire to be a poet has veiled an intense
self-absorption.

Although this diary entry is certainly a watershed in the life of Lewis the
poet, it does not mark the end of his desire for fame as a poet. Instead, it provides Lewis with a moment in time on several occasions later in life (witness
the letter to Greeves where this enclosure is found) when his thirst for fame as
a poet or more broadly as a writer is tempered by the realization that such a
desire is an unhealthy exaltation of self. After 1926 references to his efforts at
writing poetry drop off substantially in his letters and diary entries as a direct
result of his being elected a fellow of Magdalen College; that Lewis feared his
time for poetry would be limited by such a turn of events is prefigured in a
diary entry from February 29, 1924: "I saw that it [a Trinity College fellowship]
would mean pretty full work and that I might become submerged and poetry
crushed out" (*DCSL*, 293).

We know, of course, that he continued to write poetry as his pieces
appeared regularly in newspapers, literary magazines, and scholarly journals.
In letters to other friends he records his continuing impulse to write poetry.
At times he is very confident of his ability as a poet; he writes to Barfield: "I
have written about 100 lines of a long poem in my type of Alexandrine. It is
going to make the Prelude [by Wordsworth] (let alone the *Tower* [by Barfield])
look silly" (March 16, 1932; *CL*, 2, 55). Less than two months later he confesses
about the same poem to Barfield: "I send . . . the opening of the poem. I am
not satisfied with any part I have yet written and the design is ludicrously
ambitious. But I feel it will be several years anyway before I give up" (May 6,
1932; 77). His discouragement about poetry in general appears pronounced

when he writes Barfield seven years later: "I am more and more convinced that there is no future for poetry" (February 8, 1939; 248).

Lewis's debate with E. M. W. Tillyard, published as *The Personal Heresy* (1939), offers another indication of the primacy of poetry in Lewis's life. Although this debate does not explicitly reveal Lewis's passion to be known as a poet, it clearly demonstrates how seriously he considers the necessity for right thinking about the nature of poetry and in particular the role of the poet. In keeping with his view of poetry and the significance of classical models, Lewis rejects modern poetry's emphasis on the poet's personality or character; this he calls the personal heresy. Instead, he argues "that when we read poetry as poetry should be read, we have before us no representation which claims to be the poet, and frequently no representation of a *man*, a *character*, or a *personality* at all."[10] Citing his as an "objective or impersonal theory of poetry," he admits that this notion "finds its easiest application in the drama and epic" (8); given Lewis's consistent early efforts at epic or narrative poetry, this point of view is not surprising. Furthermore, it is not difficult to posit that the personal heresy almost certainly germinates in part from the journal enclosure quoted above; Lewis's powerful indictment of how he had been concerned with his personality when writing poetry provides the basis for his critical distaste for poetry that focuses on the poet.

Yet he does not totally dismiss the significance of the poet's personality; instead, he articulates effectively how it is that a poet's personality may come into a reading of a poem: "[However, when reading a poem], let it be granted that I do approach the poet; at least I do it by sharing his consciousness, not by studying it. I look with his eyes, not at him . . . . The poet is not a man who asks me to look at him; he is a man who says 'look at that' and points; the more I follow the pointing of his finger the less I can possibly see of him" (11). Later he adds that while looking to where the poet points, "I must make of him not a spectacle but a pair of spectacles . . . . I must *enjoy* him and not contemplate him" (12; emphasis Lewis). In his *An Experiment in Criticism* Lewis makes a similar point: "[Literature is valuable] not only nor chiefly in order to see what [the authors] are like but [because we] . . . see what they see [and] occupy, for a while, their seat in the great theatre, [and] use their spectacles and be made free of whatever insights, joys, terrors, wonders or merriment those spectacles reveal."[11] For Lewis poetry is not a private matter, but instead a public one: "[In a poem] it is absolutely essential that each word should suggest not what is private and personal to the poet but what is public, common, impersonal, objective" (*PH*, 19).

Lewis's view of the role of the poet has been under attack since the great Romantic poets, and Wordsworth's claim that poets write about "both what they half create, / And what they perceive." As Lewis sees it, the elevation of the poet's personality has led to "Poetolatry" and "the cult of poetry" displaying "religious characteristics" (65). When Lewis turns to a theory of poetry, he sounds very much like he did in his early letters: "Poetry [is] a skill or trained habit of using all the extralogical elements of language—rhythm, vowel-music, onomatopoeia, associations, and what not—to convey the concrete reality of experiences . . . . [A poem is] a composition which communicates more of the concrete and qualitative than our usual utterances do. A poet is a man who produces such compositions more often and more successfully than the rest of us" (108, 109). Lewis's view suggests that a poet is primarily a workman using the tools of language to reflect on the universal concerns—love, death, meaning—of all men and women. Because the poet is more gifted in the use of language, he can speak poignantly to those common human concerns. However, the poet as a person should be no more worthy of our interest than a plumber; the poet simply articulates more effectively the same basic concerns he shares with the plumber. Toward the end of *The Personal Heresy* Lewis says there are only two questions to ask about a poem: "Firstly, whether it is interesting, enjoyable, attractive, and secondly, whether this enjoyment wears well and helps or hinders you towards all the other things you would like to enjoy, or do, or be" (119–120). It is this pragmatic view of poetry's value that Lewis consistently supports, and, at the same time, may be what keeps him from achieving acclaim as a poet. That is, it may be that Lewis's workman-like efforts to write poetry, to make himself into a poet, inevitably thwarted his poetic sensibilities in verse. Lewis may be the model case illustrating the dictum that poets are born not made.

Even so, Lewis's public discussion with Tillyard complements his continued private correspondence. In a letter to Rhona Bodle he reflects on the way poetry helps make language concrete: "But in reality it is just the clearest, the most concrete, and most indubitable realities which escape language: not because *they* are vague but because language is . . . . Poetry I take to be the continual effort to bring language back to the actual" (June 24, 1949; *CL*, 2, 947; emphasis Lewis). We also have Joy Davidman's evaluation of Lewis's poetry in a letter to Chad Walsh where she takes issue with Walsh's estimate of Lewis as a poor poet:

> By the way, I also read a lot of Jack's poetry and I think you are wrong about it. It's quite new and strange and unfashionable, a complete break with the modern conventions of intellectual and bloodless verse, and for that reason rather difficult to appraise it; but I thought a lot of it was damn good. Technically it's amazing. He's used old forms and given them an entirely new twist. (He liked *my* poetry too—so there!) But you and I will never see eye to eye on verse. (January 25, 1953; emphasis Davidman)[12]

What these letters and diary entries show is the degree to which writing poetry and being a poet were fundamental to the way Lewis saw himself. Though he may have had to suppress his desire to be known as a poet, he certainly longed to be a good one.

Why does Lewis's view of himself as a poet matter? How is it related to his work as a prose writer? What critical insights into his prose can we gain? The answers to these questions require more space than I have here, so let me offer some initial suggestions intended to provoke additional critical study. The fact that Lewis saw himself early in life primarily as a poet begs that we take a new approach in our understanding of his prose, both his nonfiction and fiction, though especially the latter. That is, first I suggest critical exploration of Lewis's prose from the perspective of his being a frustrated poet. Jerry Daniel points the way here when he notes that Lewis has "the soul of a poet . . . [and] all works were 'poetry' to him in the sense that the 'feel' or 'taste' was primary."[13] I believe critical exploration needs to push further into this area. For instance, who can deny the poetic power of Lewis's prose in *Perelandra*? A scholarly examination of Lewis's prose poetry throughout the Ransom trilogy is mandated with a particular emphasis upon how his prose "works" like poetry.[14]

Second, I suggest intense critical inquiry into the rhythm and cadence of his prose as reflecting his deeply-felt poetic sensibility. Although some work has been done on his use of metaphor, I believe we need to focus specifically on how Lewis's use of metaphor is often motivated by poetic rather than rhetorical principles. For example, I would argue that works such as *Mere Christianity* and *The Problem of Pain* are inspired at least partially by poetic sensibilities. In addition, we should examine Lewis's prose imagery as inspired by his deeply felt poetic imagination.

Third, I suggest that Lewis's early (and, as he later judges them to be, unhealthy) aspirations to achieve literary acclaim as a poet inform our understanding of why it is that the danger of spiritual pride surfaces so often in his writings. From Rabadash in *The Horse and His Boy* to Orual in *Till We Have Faces*, from Screwtape to the damned in *The Great Divorce*, from Professor Weston in *Perelandra* to Mark Studdock in *That Hideous Strength*, Lewis examines the subtle yet powerful way in which humans are prone to pride. Can it be that he writes so convincingly of it because he knows so well its pull? These suggestions only touch the surface of where I believe a critical perspective that sees Lewis's prose through the lens of his poetic aspirations may lead. Additional scholarly work in this area should yield a rich harvest and help propel Lewis studies further in the direction of his accomplishments as an artist, as a crafter of words, as a writer per se. Such study will not stand in opposition to his apologetics or polemics but will instead complement and enlarge our understanding and appreciation of them and his prose in general.

In a letter Lewis wrote in 1954 to the Milton Society of America, he thanks them for bestowing upon him an honor:

> [In all my books] there is a guiding thread. The imaginative man in me is older, more continuously operative, and that sense more basic than either the religious writer or the critic. It was he who made me first attempt (with little success) to be a poet. It was he who, in response to the poetry of others, made me a critic, and, in defence of that response, sometimes a critical controversialist. It was he who, after my conversion led me to embody my religious belief in symbolical or mythopoeic forms, ranging from *Screwtape* to a kind of theologised science-fiction. And it was, of course, he who has brought me, in the last few years to write the series of Narnian stories for children.[15]

This imaginative man, whom I believe we may call Lewis's poetic sensibility, bears much critical scrutiny. As his letters and diary entries demonstrate, he longed early in life to walk with Homer, Virgil, and the other ancient poets he so admired. To this end he devoted much of his early literary life and was forever marked by the experience. Though he never achieved the kind of acclaim he desired as a poet, he achieved an even greater acclaim in his prose. Perhaps by "making the poor best of dull things" in his prose, Lewis inadvertently realized his poetic aspirations. The world is undoubtedly richer because this would-be poet found expression for his poetic sensibilities in prose.

Chapter 6 Notes

1. A version of this essay was first published in *SEVEN: An Anglo-American Literary Review* 12 (1995): 79–92.

2. From Lewis's "*Spartan Nactus*," first published in *Punch* 227 (December 1, 1954): 685 (N. W.) Revised and retitled "A Confession" in *P*, 1.

3. His first two published works were volumes of poetry, *Spirits in Bondage* (1919) and *Dymer* (1926). In addition, he wrote many other poems that were later collected by Walter Hooper and published as *Poems* (1964); Hooper also published *Narrative Poems* in 1969, a volume that reprints *Dymer* as well as three other narrative poems.

4. Critical opinion on Lewis as poet has been mixed. Chad Walsh refers to Lewis as "the almost poet" (*The Literary Legacy of C. S. Lewis* [New York: Harcourt Brace Jovanovich, 1979], 35), and Dabney Hart believes that Lewis "will never have a major place in the canon of . . . poets" ("Editor's Comment," *Studies in the Literary Imagination* 22 [Fall 1989]: 128). Charles Huttar agrees and says that Lewis as a poet is a "minor figure" and "barring a revolution in taste, he will never be accorded a higher position" ("A Lifelong Love Affair with Language: C. S. Lewis's Poetry," in *Word and Story in C. S. Lewis*, ed. Peter Schakel and Charles Huttar [Columbia, MO: University of Missouri Press, 1991], 86). With the exception of George Sayer's "C. S. Lewis's Dymer" published in 1980 (*SEVEN: An Anglo-American Literary Review*, Vol. 1), scholars have paid scant regard to Lewis as a poet until recent years. In 1986 Patrick Murphy's "C. S. Lewis's 'Dymer': Once More with Hesitation" appeared in the *Bulletin of the New York C.S. Lewis Society* and was an attempt to rehabilitate *Dymer*. A special issue of *Studies in the Literary Imagination* (Fall 1989) contains two essays on Lewis's poetry: Joe Christopher's "C. S. Lewis, Love Poet" and my "The Distant Voice in C. S. Lewis's *Poems*." In 1991 W. W. Robson, a Lewis colleague and friend, published an article, "The Poetry of C. S. Lewis," in which he reevaluates his own earlier negative view of Lewis's poetry, arguing that in some of Lewis's poems he "touches greatness" ("The Poetry of C. S. Lewis," *The Chesterton Review* 17. 3–4 [Aug.-.Nov. 1991]: 437). In 1992, Luci Shaw celebrated Lewis's poetic "ability to see and probe reality and express it in vivid and illuminating metaphors" ("Looking Back to Eden: The Poetry of C. S. Lewis," *Bulletin of the New York C. S. Lewis Society* 23 [Feb. 1992]: 3). The most comprehensive study of Lewis as a poet is my *C. S. Lewis, Poet: The Legacy of His Poetic Impulse* (Kent, OH: Kent State University Press, 2001).

5. *The Collected Letters of C. S. Lewis, Volume 1: Family Letters 1905–1931*, ed. Walter Hooper (London: Harper Collins, 2000), 71 (hereafter *CL*, 1 and subsequent references in the text).

6. *The Collected Letters of C.S. Lewis, Volume 2: Books, Broadcasts and the War, 1931–1949*, ed. Walter Hooper (London: Harper Collins, 2004), 68 (hereafter *CL*, 2 and subsequent references in the text).

7. "Laudari a laudato viro" may be translated "to be praised by a man who is [himself] praised."

8. In the 1950 reprint of *Dymer*, Lewis provides an even more detailed chronology of the poem's composition. See *Dymer* (London: J. M. Dent, 1950).

9. *All My Road before Me: The Diary of C. S. Lewis, 1922–1927*, ed. Walter Hooper (New York: Harcourt Brace Jovanovich, 1991), 20–21 (hereafter *DCSL* and subsequent references in the text).

10. C. S. Lewis and E. M. W. Tillyard, *The Personal Heresy* (London: Oxford University Press, 1939), 4 (hereafter *PH* and subsequent references in the text.); emphasis Lewis.

11. *An Experiment in Criticism* (Cambridge: Cambridge University Press, 1961), 139.

12. *Out of My Bone: The Letters of Joy Davidman*, ed. Don W. King (Grand Rapids, MI: Eerdmans, 2009), 139 (hereafter *OB* and subsequent references in the text).

13. Jerry Daniel, "The Taste of the Pineapple: A Basis for Literary Criticism," in *The Taste of the Pineapple: Essays on C. S. Lewis as Reader, Critic, and Imaginative Writer*, ed. Bruce L. Edwards (Bowling Green, OH: Bowling Green State University Popular Press, 1988), 9, 11.

14. For examples, see the next two essays, "C. S. Lewis's *The Quest of Bleheris* as Poetic Prose" and "The Poetry of Prose: C. S. Lewis, Ruth Pitter, and *Perelandra*."

15. *The Collected Letters of C.S. Lewis, Volume 3: Narnia, Cambridge, and Joy, 1950–1963*, ed. Walter Hooper (London: Harper Collins, 2006), 516–17 (hereafter *CL*, 3 and subsequent references in the text).

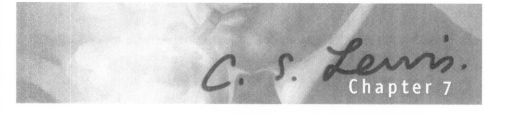

C. S. Lewis's *The Quest of Bleheris* as Poetic Prose[1]

Notwithstanding C. S. Lewis's early desire to achieve acclaim as a poet, a candid survey of his verse reveals he did not. In fact, he wrote his best "poetry" in prose. That is, Lewis's poetic legacy is seen most clearly in his prose where poetic qualities abound—rich lyrical passages, vivid description; striking similes, metaphors, and analogies; careful diction; and concern for the sound of words. While prose works like *Perelandra* and *A Grief Observed* contain the most powerful examples of Lewis's poetic prose, his unpublished prose romance, *The Quest of Bleheris* written between May and October, 1916, is also rich in poetic passages.[2] This essay reviews the genesis of *The Quest of Bleheris*, suggests influences on its composition, offers a summary of the action, and briefly notes the poetic quality of its prose.[3]

The Quest of Bleheris, because unpublished, is known to few.[4] It is an incomplete story of seventeen chapters concerning the adventures of a young knight, Bleheris, as he moves from the relative safety of civilized society to the challenges and dangers of a wilderness experience.[5] Although prose, it is broadly in the poetic narrative tradition of medieval romances such as *Sir Gawain and the Green Knight* and *Sir Orfeo* and medieval dream visions such as *Piers Plowman* and the *Pearl*. Furthermore, we know Lewis wrote *Bleheris* while striving to produce excellent verse, as he wrote Arthur Greeves: "I think Bleheris has killed my muse—always a rather sickly child. At any rate my

verse, both in quality and quantity for the last three weeks is deplorable!"
(June 6, 1916; *CL*, 1, 190). A month later Lewis suggests to Greeves the connection he makes at this time between poetry and prose:

> [What] I meant when I talked about the importance of form was to
> carry a little further what you already feel in prose—that is how some
> phrases such as the Wall of the World, or at the Back of the North
> Wind affect you, partly by sound partly by association, more than
> the same meaning would if otherwise expressed. The only difference
> is that poetry makes use of that sort of feeling much more than prose
> and produces those effects by metre as well as by phrase. In fact, the
> metre and the magic of the words should be like the orchestration
> of a Wagnerian opera—should sort of fill the matter by expressing
> things that can't be directly told—that is, it expresses feeling while
> the matter expresses thought. (July 11, 1916; 209–10)

The greatest influence at this time comes from the prose romances of
William Morris. Lewis's letters to Greeves make frequent reference to Morris
and the delight he has reading *Sigurd the Volsung, The Well at the World's End*,
and *The Wood Beyond the World*. For instance, after re-reading the latter, Lewis
tells Greeves "it has completely ravished me . . . . [It] always brings to mind our
lovely hill-walk in the frost and fog . . . . The very names of the chapters and
places make me happy: 'Another adventure in the Wood Perilous,' 'Ralph rides
the Downs to Higham-on-the-Way,' 'The Dry-Tree,' [and] 'Ralph reads a book
concerning the Well at the World's End'" (November 16, 1915; 153). Lewis
imitates Morris with chapter titles such as "Of my Bleheris and of how he is
betrothed," "Of their journeying to the land of Yesterday," and "Of Bleheris'
first fight." I believe *Bleheris* is Lewis's earliest example of poetic prose and can
be viewed in the tradition of Lewis's efforts at narrative poetry, particularly for
its lyricism, use of traditional figurative language and symbols, and emphasis
upon sound and rhythm.

The first part of *Bleheris* comprises Chapters I-V which introduce the
setting, the characters, and the quest.[6] The story opens with a passage worthy
of medieval romance: "As I sate in the garden in summer time, when the
sun had set and the first stars were trembling into light, and while the
ghostly, little bats were bleating above me, it came to me in mind to write
for you, Galahad, somewhat of the life and dealings of this Bleheris."[7] The

city of Nesses is described next as marked by white stones, five bridges, good wharves, and rich towers, palaces, and halls. In addition there is a powerful stream, Coldriver, plunging into the bay near the city, and in the distance, Cloudy Pass, the only gap between the Great Mountains. In this land lives an old, worthy knight, Sir Lionel, whose prize is his comely daughter, Lady Alice, also known as Alice the Saint because of her great learning and virtue. Alice is the stereotypical object of courtly love: "And every young man of that town, named her alone his good lady and sighed for her, and wrote bransles and ballades upon her" (Fol. 6b). If Alice is the epitome of female beauty, Bleheris represents the pinnacle of male prowess.[8] Moreover, he also is pierced by Alice's beauty, writes verses about her, jousts for her, and sighs that "he was no less sorely smitten in love than Launcelot or Plamides or any of the knights of old song" (Fol. 7a).

Somewhat predictably, Bleheris' mother, Dame Foltete, arranges with Sir Lionel for the two young people to be engaged. Bleheris, however, reacts unexpectedly to this good news; instead of being filled with joy, "in his heart was there no great delight, and he felt dazed as though some evil were come to him" (Fol. 7b). While Bleheris' ambivalent feelings toward this match add psychological interest to his character, Lewis never explains this so we are left wondering why Bleheris feels this way. When he goes to see Alice for the first time after their betrothal, he is "sick at heart, and must needs whisper to himself of his good fortune, as one that would learn a hard lesson" (Fol. 8a). Just as interesting and equally unexplained is her cold response to his first kiss. Later that night Bleheris wanders the streets of Nesses, eventually casting his eyes toward the Great Mountains and trying to analyze his disinterest in Alice. Intrusively, Lewis offers a hint at Bleheris' malady: "For we know well, [Galahad] and I, how easily they that have no sorrow can yet make themselves griefs from the fabrick of their own dreams" (Fol. 9b).

Still, Bleheris tries to force himself to feel passion for Alice, even attempting to write her new love ballads. When this fails, he looks again toward the mountains, recalls wonderful, mysterious stories about them, and then remembers his own desire to journey there for adventure so that he can do mighty deeds and find love as did the heroes of old. This leads him to rationalize that his unease is caused because he is untested and marriage will prevent his questing to discover his manhood. He resolves instead to eschew marriage until after he has journeyed on a quest beyond Cloudy Pass, performed great deeds, and acquired fame for his valor; only then, he believes, will he be worthy of Alice's hand.

After Bleheris awakens the next morning, Lewis's introduces the rose, the central symbol of the tale, though here, too, he never reveals its meaning. Bleheris sees a silk curtain embroidered with roses gently swaying in the breeze with roses that appear to be alive. As he looks at the roses all else seems blocked from his vision and he whispers to himself the word "rose" over and over again, delighting in each repetition and reveling in the thought of such beautiful flowers: "For you must know that from his childhood roses had a strange power upon this Bleheris, and of nothing was he at all so fain: as hereafter you shall hear" (Fol. 11a). Remembering his resolution of the night before, he leaps up and prepares for the day. With his mother he visits Sir Lionel where he reveals his intentions to go on a quest. Although his mother is heart-sick, the old knight is delighted and fully supports the young man's decision. When Alice is asked her thoughts on Bleheris' decision, she replies disinterestedly. This causes Bleheris to be both angry at her coldness and impatient to leave for his quest. However, Sir Lionel manages to convince Bleheris of his need to prepare for his adventures, so the young knight spends three days giving care to practical and spiritual needs. Like Gawain who spends a great deal of time seeing to his armor, both for himself and his horse, Bleheris "looked to all his gear, both armour and steed and weapons." Furthermore, he seeks spiritual counsel from Father Ulfin, devoutly confessing his sins, being absolved, and taking with him a small flask of holy water for protection against evil. Once again the narrator intrudes and signals for the first time a distinctly anti-religious bias underlying the tale by mocking Bleheris' folly in having faith in a holy object.[9]

The first part of the story concludes with Bleheris, about to set off on his journey, realizing that he has no clear quest in mind. Seeking counsel from Sir Lionel, he considers several before somewhat arbitrarily choosing to look for the shadowy figure known only as the Striver, according to some a monster or a fiend while others claim he is a saint or a god. Before he leaves court, he asks for and receives Alice's gloves as a token and remembrance to sustain him during the dark days ahead. This last act, like so much of what Bleheris does in the first five chapters of this tale, reveals that he is playing a part—occasionally he seems cognizant of this, but most often he does not. In effect he is a purposeless, shallow youth, unsure of himself and untested in battle, but determined to go off and have an adventure.

Chapters VI-VII make up the second part of the story and concern Bleheris' first test. Leaving Nesses early the following morning, he rides out into a landscape that Lewis describes in richly evocative poetic prose:

> The world was still fresh and pleasant in the summer dawn: the cool breeze played in the bars of his helmet, there were beads of dew upon every growing thing, & the shadows were still long and faint across the meadows. Before him went a white, well traveled road making ever for the north, and to the right of this, so close that his beast's hoof might almost brush the reeds and bulrushes, Coldriver went gurgling by, deep and green and swift . . . . The pleasant country spread out on the right and the left hand—the golden fields of deep-standing corn, the homely cottages with their long columns of smoke rising in the morning air, the little clumps of woodland where he had wandered full often, and, far to East and West, the blueness of the heathery mountains. (Fols.15a and 15b)

The further he rides, the fewer people he sees and the more isolated he feels. As he approaches Cloudy Pass, he becomes fearful, recognizing in part all he is forsaking by going off on his quest.

However, he encounters a merchant from Nesses on the road and asks which road leads most quickly to the North. He learns it goes through the Sunken Wood, a place the merchant warns him against. Rather than heed the warning, Bleheris foolishly follows the road through the Sunken Wood, deceived by his own excitement and daydream that he is able to play the part of a hero. Summoning all his courage and saying a short prayer, he starts to move down the dark road into the wood, but his fear overpowers him so that he cannot move forward even one pace. He curses his cowardice, sets his teeth, and drives himself forward, but again he fails, this time in the face of a small shadow. The shadow suddenly comes out of the trees, small and hobbling like a child, and so frightens him "that he thought no more of manhood or shame, but set spurs to horse and fled wildly on the other road to his right: nor did he dare to slacken rein nor look behind him until he was well up the mountain side, with the Sunken Wood upon his left hand" (Fol. 18b).[10] Bleheris flees, we surmise, from fear itself. Full of self-loathing, he is at his lowest point as part two ends.

The third part of the story covers Chapters VIII-XI where Bleheris, terribly ashamed of his failure, meets three other knights, eventually joining one of them on a quest that proves disastrous; in the process, however, Bleheris atones in part for his failure at the Sunken Wood. After fleeing the wood, he makes his way to a village hostel where he tries to avoid contact with others, convinced they will be able to see cowardice in his face. In a rare moment of honest self-assessment, he berates himself, realizing that if he is a coward it make little sense to continue his quest. If he is going to run away from a small shadow coming from the trees, how can he believe he will ever be able to fight through the dangers of the north and confront Striver? Yet the thought of returning home so quickly and the embarrassment that would follow spurs him onward. At the hostel he meets three men. The first is tall and thin, though powerfully built; his voice is loud, his eyes piercing, and he often slams his fist on the table to make a point. The second is slimmer and slighter than Bleheris, richly dressed, and, except for a wisp of beard, so beautiful he might have been mistaken for a girl; his voice is muted and sweet, and his half-closed eyes appear to be mulling over some secret, painful memory. The third is middle-aged, strong, tall, and winsome, with a huge golden beard. When he looks at Bleheris, the young man senses his good-natured fellowship and feels his shame ebb away.

This man, Hypertes, inexplicably tells Bleheris he knows of his quest to discover Striver, and then has his two friends introduce themselves. The tall, thin, loud man is Gerce the Desirous because he always seeks tomorrow. The younger, beautiful one is Wan Jadis who is always seeking yesterday. In the conversation that follows, Bleheris learns that Hypertes is a servant of Striver, and that he has come to this hostel in order to point Bleheris in the direction where he will find Striver. However, Wan Jadis invites Bleheris to join him upon his quest for yesterday, telling him the journey lies to the west not far from the mountains. Yesterday, Wan Jadis goes on to say, is a valley of all things passed. Of special interest to Bleheris is Wan Jadis' claim that the queens of old abide there, including Helen, Isolde, and Guenevere, living forever in their beauty and sorrow. Moreover, the valley is a place where all men can hide from hard times of life, surrounded by quiet peace. When Bleheris hears this, he forgets his resolution to seek Striver and joins Wan Jadis.

The next morning the two young men leave the hostel with Hypertes' words in mind that they seek him out when and if they return from their quest. In particular he asks Bleheris to be sure to let him know when he decides to quest for Striver. The two knights set off through a beautiful country with a strong, cool wind behind them. They enjoy good conversation as they ride, and the following day reach the crossroad that will take them to yesterday where Wan Jadis' face flushes with eagerness, and he urges Bleheris onward. For Wan Jadis his long search is nearing a climax, so he can hardly contain himself. As the day wears on well past noon, they enter a narrow valley with a strange beauty; it is a place filled with trees giving off showers of golden leaves even though the autumn has not yet come. As the cool breezes move through the valley, they can peer down the road where the sun almost blinds them with its scarlet blaze. The shower of leaves quickens, and the wind freshens "until it seemed that they were riding a cloud of soft, feathery elves that smote upon them all over: and a golden mist lay about them" (Fol. 24b). As they come out of the narrow valley, Bleheris notices a large rose bush near the shore of a lake.

Wan Jadis, barely able to contain his excitement, urges Bleheris to board a small boat moored near the shore so that together they can sail to yesterday. Bleheris, however, hesitates since a mist shrouds the craft, and he sees it is floating on a muddy marsh; moreover, he sees evil creatures swimming and writhing around it. Nonetheless, Wan Jadis boards the boat, urging Bleheris to join him. Just as Bleheris is about to step into the water to wade out to the boat, however, in the distance he sees something that stops him: a huge, mysterious temple, complete with fluted columns, towering domes, and manicured terraces filled with sad monuments and terrible images. The heavy mist makes it all seem like a dream. Then on the far shore he sees an old woman spinning a thread; when he catches sight of her, he feels sickness sweep over him.[11] Speechless, Bleheris watches in horror as Wan Jadis climbs in the boat, and it slowly drifts away from the shore.

After he recovers his wits, Bleheris springs into the water and tries to grab Wan Jadis' hand, but it is too late. The water turns to slime and thin mud, overflows the sides of the boat, and slimy eels and water spiders twine around Wan Jadis' legs, pulling him under. Even though he is terrified, Bleheris bravely attempts to save Wan Jadis. However, when he makes another step toward the boat, he himself is sucked down by the mud. He would have been lost except for the rose bush growing nearby, since it throws its arms around him and holds him just as if he is its lover. Intent on saving his friend, Bleheris fights against the rose bush, even breaking off its limbs. When he breaks one limb, however, two new ones grab him. His final vision of Wan Jadis is horrible: "Bleheris could see the beautiful, sad face strained and drawn with loathing and the agony of death: it seemed that he strove to speak, but in that moment the slime and mud rose to his white lips, and the evil creeping things crawled over the fair skin, more delicate than porcelain. His eyes cast one more look upon Bleheris: and then the [marsh] closed over his head, and thus Wan Jadis died" (Fol. 26a).

Broken-hearted, Bleheris cries out for his friend, and is answered only by the hollow laugh of the old spinner. He struggles free of the rose bush, collapses upon the ground, and experiences for the first time genuine sorrow. Although he probably does not consciously realize it, he has been tested and proved worthy, and he is no longer acting a part in a play. Looking more closely at the rose bush that saved him, he picks up broken leaves and petals and then buries his face in them, enjoying the sweet fragrance. As he starts to cherish the bush as a friend, he has an unexpected vision: "Then, for a moment, he thought that a madness had come to him: for the tree seemed to be vanished and in its stead he saw a lovely woman kneeling before him, naked but for her hair, half golden and half of a reddish-brown, that streamed over her whole body: her arms were stretched towards him, and he saw that there were manacles of steel upon her wrists—tight and grievous and biting into the soft white flesh. She seemed to be pleading with him" (Fol. 26b). Just as quickly the vision fades away, and Bleheris, fearing what it all means, mounts his horse and rides away from the dead marsh. As the third part of the story ends, Lewis is on the verge of producing a significant literary work. While the first eleven chapters of *Bleheris* are far from perfect, he has managed to write a compelling story filled with prose passages of poetic beauty and populated with characters that, while not terribly complex, are more than cardboard figures. In addition, the allegorical nature of the story has promise and shows the influence of Lewis's reading of *The Romance of the Rose*, especially in his use of the rose bush.[12] Unfortunately, the rest of the tale does not live up to this promise.

Chapters XII-XV concern how Bleheris is reunited with Hypertes and Gerce, and his discovery of an impending great evil. In shock and grief at Wan Jadis' death, Bleheris rides forward intent on some day avenging his friend's death, but still fearful of the old spinner. Along the way he picks a rose from another rose bush and has a second vision where he sees another kneeling woman. As he rides forth, he cannot get the image of the kneeling woman out of his mind, especially her beauty; he is so fascinated with the vision that everything he sees in the land about him appears but to be a reflection of her. Unsure what to make of this, Bleheris, fearing witchery is at work, says his "Pater Noster" and "Ave." He returns to the hostel and receives a note from Father Ulfin telling him that the same day he rode away, Alice left to follow a vision of the cross that came to her in the night. Ulfin charges Bleheris to follow the road north to the city of Ralholt in search of Alice. At the hostel Bleheris is further befriended by a servant, Nut, who offers to be his squire and who warns him against the only other visitor at the hostel, Bethrelladoom. Although we never learn specifically why Bethrelladoom is to be avoided, both Bleheris and Nut sneak away from the hostel late that night and journey north until they reach Wandale where they are given provision by a group of roving dwarves.

Continuing their quest, they travel through desolate wilderness until they meet up with Hypertes and Gerce. While the former greets them warmly, Gerce picks a fight with Bleheris which ends with the two drawing swords and clashing with each other. Hypertes soon intervenes and reconciles the two. When they sit down to eat, Bleheris tells them all that has happened to him since they last met, except he leaves out any reference to his vision of the rose bush. Hypertes is concerned over the appearance of Bethrelladoom and the flight of Alice. Gerce reminds him Bethrelladoom "holds the Rose yet," and at this Bleheris confesses his vision of the rose bush. In a discussion of this between Gerce and Hypertes we learn of two different roses, their possible connection with Bethrelladoom, and whether Alice may also be involved. Sadly, this conversation is muddled and leaves us wondering what to make of it all. The next day they travel north, and the fourth part of the story ends when they reach the outskirts of Ralholt. The narrative failure here reduces the rest of the story to a shadow box, and Lewis fails to capitalize upon the dramatic power of the previous three parts of the story.

Consequently, the last part of the tale, Chapters XVI-XVII, is perfunctory. We journey with them into the city of Ralholt where Lewis expends a great deal of energy describing the houses, temples to Christ and Odin, and the castle of the King. Bleheris is impressed with the rich, lavish surroundings and momentarily forgets his search for Alice: "Bleheris was not over pleased . . . to call to mind that the cause of his coming to Ralholt was to seek out Father Ulfin, and through him the Lady Alice: for now, in such an hour and such a place, they seemed to him very irksome, but more specially that noble and vertuous lady" (Fol. 39). The king of Ralhout eventually invites them all to court where a rich feast is laid out before them. *Bleheris* ends just as the young knight is about to hold a conversation with the king's daughter, and this promising story breaks off, never to be completed. Lewis writes Greeves several times about this. In part, Lewis is befuddled by the allegory he is attempting, and he is unable to conceptualize it effectively. He says, for instance, "the story and not the allegory is the important part" (July 25, 1916; *CL*, 1, 219). By September 27, 1916, he is writing: "I too am wondering whether I should not chuck Bleheris and start something else: partly I have so many ideas and also I think the old fashioned English is a fatal mistake. Any good things that are in it or would be later on, can be worked in elsewhere" (*CL*, 1, 225) By October 1916 he gives up on *Bleheris*.

In spite of the narrative failure of *Bleheris*, Lewis's poetic sensibilities are evident. The story contains many rich lyrical passages. For example, in addition to those already cited, the description of his approach to the Cloudy Pass is indicative: "He [sees] the pleasant country spread out on the right and the left hand—the golden fields of deep-standing corn, the homely cottages with their long columns of smoke rising in the morning air, the little clumps of woodland where he had wandered full often, and, far to East and West, the blueness of the heathery mountains" (Fol. 15b). In fact Lewis is at his best when describing landscapes, perhaps reflecting his own deeply held love for the hills of Down near Belfast and his growing appreciation for Surrey as he studied in the home of his great tutor, W. T. Kirkpatrick. Many of these passages reflect a kind of deliberate verbal pacing creating poetic rhythm:

> It was now past the middle of summer and full hot in the low coun-
> tries, yet here were they gotten to such an height—and moreover the
> freshness of dawn was still upon all things—that a cool, strong, wind
> was blowing across the heather and singing in their ears. On their left
> hand lay the sullen border of the sunken wood, and beneath that the
> height of Cloudy Pass: away to their right the mountain peaks rose
> higher and shut out their prospect: while that part of the mountains
> wherein they rode was a rough land of heath, sprinkled with many
> fair bushes of the prickly gorse, and pierced with masses of grey rock,
> that grew, as it were, through their covering of rank grass where the
> old earth had worn thin. (Fol. 23b)

Also the early similes describing Alice's lips "as cold as might be the lips of the dead," and her beautiful eyes as "calm as the untroubled eyes of an angel painted in the windows of the church" are particularly effective (Fol. 8b).

In addition, he shows a good ear with names like Dame Foltete, Ulfin, and Bethrelladoom.

While it is not justified to see too much poetry in *Bleheris*, it is valid to note the hand of Lewis the poet here. As he himself admits, there is much that does not work, especially the archaic English, the incomplete allegory, and the fragmented narrative. Yet he accomplished much, and this work was so important to him that he never destroyed it. *Bleheris* was a fertile training ground for the narrative poetry Lewis attempted in *Dymer* and "The Queen of Drum" and served as an incubator for the powerful prose poetry we see later in *Perelandra* (1943) and *A Grief Observed* (1961).

Chapter 7 Notes

1. A version of this essay first appeared in *The Lamp-Post of the Southern California C. S. Lewis Society* 23.1 (Spring 1999): 3–15. Quotations from *The Quest of Bleheris* © C. S. Lewis Pte. Ltd.

2. Lewis writes Arthur Greeves about its composition: "I write one chapter every Sunday afternoon, and having started before I came back [Lewis was on holiday at home from April 5 through May 11, 1916], am always two instalments ahead of the one you get: the general course of the story was mapped out from the start, but of course is changed pretty freely whenever I like" (July 25, 1916; *CL*, 1, 219).

3. I defer a full definition of poetic prose until the next essay, "The Poetry of Prose: C. S. Lewis, Ruth Pitter, and *Perelandra*."

4. The original manuscript is housed at the Bodleian Library, MS. Eng. Lett. C. 220/5. Fols. 5–43, dated 1916. The Marion E. Wade Center has a photocopy of the manuscript as well.

5. This parallels the typical medieval romance where the hero accepts a quest that removes him from the safety of the court and takes him to the wilderness where he is tested. After he successfully completes the test, he returns to court a chastened but wiser man. The best known example of this is *Sir Gawain and the Green Knight*. In one of the few essays on Bleheris, "'The Dungeon of his Soul': Lewis's Unfinished 'Quest of Bleheris,'" *SEVEN: An Anglo-American Literary Review* 15 (1998): 37–54, David Downing offers a fine review of this fragment. He argues it is noteworthy "not only because it anticipates so much of Lewis's later imaginative work, but also because it casts new light on the spiritual pilgrimage of a man who became one of the twentieth century's most effective and influential Christian writers—only after spending his teens and twenties as a resolute agnostic" (37).

6. The chapter titles are:
   I: Of the city of Nesses and of certain that dwelt therein
   II: Of my Bleheris and of how he is betrothed"
   III: Wherein Bleheris wastes thy time and mine
   IV: How Bleheris told those folks of what he would do
   V: How Bleheris thinketh on what quest he shall go
   VI: How Bleheris came through the Cloudy Pass

VII: How Bleheris came to the edge of the Sunken Wood
VIII: Of those three that were in the hostel
IX: How Bleheris hearkened to Wan Jadis
X: Of their journeying to the land of Yesterday
XI: How they fared at the Grey Marish
XII: How Bleheris had his first sight of a very evil one
XIII: How Bleheris got him a squire
XIV: Of Bleheris' first fight
XV: How they came a stage further on their way
XVI: How Bleheris is held in great honour & of Gerce the Desirous
XVII: How Bleheris is met with two strangers

7. Fol. 5a (subsequent references in the text). Galahad is Lewis's nickname for Greeves. He writes: "Before you get any further into [Bleheris], let me hasten to warn you that when I said [of] the first chapter, that Bleheris was like you, I hadn't really thought of what I should make him. However I take that back, so that in future when my poor hero does anything mean you won't think I am covertly preaching at you" (June 6, 1916; *CL*, 1, 190). Three years later in Lewis's *Spirits in Bondage: A Cycle of Lyrics* (London: William Heinemann, 1919), one of his poems, "Sonnet," adapts the phrase from this passage "little bats were bleating above me" and we read: "The stars come out; the fragrant shadows fall / About a dreaming garden still and sweet; / I hear the unseen bats above me bleat, / Among the ghostly moths their hunting call" (52).

8. *Bleheris* is not, strictly speaking, a courtly love story although it shares some affinities with such. For Lewis's more mature views on courtly love, see his *The Allegory of Love : A Study in Medieval Tradition* (Oxford: Clarendon Press, 1936).

9. In letters to Greeves, Lewis comments further upon this bias: "I am sorry you disapprove of my remarks in the romance. But you must remember that it is not Christianity itself I am sneering at, but Christianity as taught by a formal old priest like Ulfin, and accepted by a rather priggish young man like Bleheris" (July 18, 1916; *CL*, 1, 216). Later he adds "the meaning of it all is somewhat anti-Christian" (July 25, 1916; 219).

10. Lewis explains the shadow to Greeves: "You ought to know that the 'little, hobbling shadow' doesn't live more in that wood than anywhere else. It follows nervous children upstairs to bed, when they daren't look over their shoulders, and comes and sits on your grandfather's summer seat beside two friends when they talk too much nonsense in the dark" (July 4, 1916; *CL*, 1, 206–07). Later he adds: "I am quite as sorry as you that I can't see my way to working Bleheris back into the Sunken Wood, for I think the idea might be worked a bit more: but don't see how it is to be done without changing the whole plan of the story" (July 11, 1916; 211).

11. In a note on this page of the folio Lewis says: "I meant her to be like the picture of Hela, in the story of Balder." She also shares similarities with the old hag in *Dymer*.

12. Lewis's mature views on allegory appear in *The Allegory of Love*. For instance, he says: "Do not let us be deceived by the allegorical form. That, as we have seen, does not mean that the author is talking about non-entities, but that he is talking about the inner world— talking, in fact, about the realities he knows best" (115).

The Poetry of Prose: C. S. Lewis, Ruth Pitter, and *Perelandra*[1]

An examination of the correspondence from C. S. Lewis to Ruth Pitter (1897–1992) and her journal recollections of the same (with one exception her letters to Lewis have not survived) reveals the two shared a deep love for poetry. Pitter, a poet of no small stature, received copious notes from Lewis about her poetry. In turn, Lewis often asked Pitter's advice about his own verse, admiring her native ability and appreciating her critical insights. In effect, Pitter became Lewis's mentor as a poet. While Pitter was the better poet, she found much to admire in Lewis's verse; ironically, however, it was in the prose of *Perelandra*, the second book of the Ransom trilogy, that she discovered Lewis's most effective poetry. Accordingly, this essay will survey their correspondence and her journals, noting the lively discussions Pitter and Lewis had about poetry, explore the poetic prose of *Perelandra*, and compare Pitter's transcriptions into verse of portions of the end of *Perelandra* to the prose text itself.[2]

Owen Barfield remembers Lewis when he first met him in the early 1920s as one "whose ruling ambition was to become a great poet. At that time if you thought of Lewis you automatically thought of poetry."[3] As earlier essays in this volume have illustrated, Lewis devoted much of his early life to writing poetry;

yet Lewis as a poet remains largely a curiosity to most readers.[4] On the other hand, Ruth Pitter has extensive poetic credentials.[5] In total she produced seventeen volumes of verse.[6] Her *A Trophy of Arms* (1936) won the Hawthornden Prize for Poetry in 1937. In 1955 she became the first woman to receive the William Heinemann Award and the Queen's Gold Medal for Poetry; also during the 1950s she appeared regularly on the BBC program *The Brain Trust*. The Royal Society of Literature elected her to its highest honor in 1974, a Companion of Literature, and she was appointed Commander of the British Empire in 1979. For all this, she remained connected to her country roots. Her poetry offers penetrating observations of the natural world she lovingly celebrates while often moving toward mystical religious themes in the tradition of Thomas Traherne.[7] For instance, "Sudden Heaven" from *A Trophy of Arms* (1936) combines a clipped, terse style with an incisive eye to create a poem of striking power:

> All was as it had ever been—
> The worn familiar book,
> The oak beyond the hawthorn seen,
> The misty woodland's look:
>
> The starling perched upon the tree
> With his long tress of straw—
> When suddenly heaven blazed on me,
> And suddenly I saw:
>
> Saw all as it would ever be,
> In bliss too great to tell;
> For ever safe, for ever free,
> All bright with miracle:
>
> Saw as in heaven the thorn arrayed,
> The tree beside the door;
> And I must die—but O my shade
> Shall dwell there evermore.[8]

"Sudden Heaven" is filled with rich natural images, including "misty woodland's look," "starling perched upon the tree," and "long tress of straw." Yet its real power comes through Pitter's subtle infusion of biblical images, motifs, and allusions such as "suddenly heaven blazed on me," "bliss too great to tell," "bright with miracle," and "the thorn arrayed." Most impressive is her deft use of the tree as an image both of nature, where the starling perches, and the divine, where we envision Christ and his crown of thorns.

While she was brought up in a religious family, her own faith became energized only after listening to Lewis's radio talks (later published as *Mere Christianity*) near the end of WWII. Depressed after a hard work day in a wartime crucible factory, she wondered if she could go on: "I stopped in the middle of Battersea Bridge one dreadful March night, when it was cold and the wind was howling over the bridge, and it was dark as the pit; and I leaned over the parapet and thought: Like this I cannot go on. I must find somebody or something. Like this I cannot go on."[9] She claimed that Lewis's radio talks did much to deliver her from the despair she felt about to consume her as the war was coming to an end.[10] Consequently, out of a sense of gratitude she began to write Lewis shortly after the war was over.

Journal entries show Pitter first wrote Lewis early in July 1946 asking to meet him. In his response to her letter, he expressed surprise that she was hesitant in asking for the meeting: "But what you should be 'trepidant' about in calling on a middle aged don I can't imagine" (July 13, 1946; *CL*, 2, 718). The connection between them was poetry since she recalled that her friend, Herbert Palmer, "at that time was determined to 'bring out' Lewis as a poet" (July, 13 1946).[11] A visit to Lewis followed on July 16, 1946.[12] Afterwards her letter to Lewis recalls the visit:

> I have hunted these out [her *The Spirit Watches* (1939), *A Mad Lady's Garland* (1934), and *The Bridge* (1945)] wishing you to see something more recent than the "Trophy" [*A Trophy of Arms* (1936)], and particularly that you should see "A Mad Lady's Garland," which though only grotesque & satirical . . . I think is my best & most original . . . . My visit to you has discountenanced all the gypsy's warnings of people who say "never meet your favourite authors. They are so disappointing." (July 17, 1946)[13]

Pitter's delight in their meeting is evidenced by her closing remark, but even though they had gotten on so well in their visit,[14] she could not have been prepared for Lewis's high praise in his next letter: "*Trophy of Arms* is enough for one letter for it has most deeply delighted me. I was prepared for the more definitely mystical poems, but not for this cool, classical quality. You do it time after time—create a silence and vacancy and awe all round the poem. If the Lady in [Milton's] *Comus* had written poetry one imagines it wd. have been rather like this." About two poems Lewis is especially ecstatic: "'Cadaverous in Storm' is marvellous and 'then alleluia all my gashes cry' [from 'Solemn Meditations'] just takes one up into regions poetry hasn't visited for nearly a hundred years." Her poetry is so good, Lewis is dissuaded from sharing his with her: "I meant to send you something of mine but I shan't. It all sounds like a brass band after yours. . . . Why wasn't I told you were as good as this?" (July, 19 1946; 720–21).

The high praise of this letter set the tone of Lewis's subsequent correspondence to Pitter. Time and again he was powerfully affected by her poetry, and he lavished praise on her verse. At the same time, however, he could be critical as well. For instance, about one of her longer poems, he says: "As a rule, the bigger a thing is physically the less it works in literature. One ghost is always more disquieting than ten; no good fight in a story can have more than a dozen or so combatants: the death of a million men is less tragic than that of one." Also, he cautions her against coming under the influence of modern poetry: "'Funeral Wreaths' [from *The Bridge*]. No, no, no. The Moderns have got at you. Don't *you* of all people, be taken in by the silly idea that by simply mentioning dull or sordid facts in sub-poetical rhythms you can make a poem. The effect is certain, but it's not worth getting. You know far better than that" (July 24, 1946; 724 and emphasis Lewis). More often than not, however, Lewis only offers compliments, sometimes spiced with characteristic humor. Upon receiving a copy of Pitter's *The Rude Potato* (1941), he writes: "Thanks for the book. I look forward to finding out how rude a potato can be. All the ones I meet are civil enough" (July 21, 1947; 796). And after re-reading *The Bridge* he writes: "A lot of it is stunning good, you know" (August 24, 1949; 973). His greatest praise comes in a letter after he has read *The Ermine: Poems 1942–1952*:

> Dear Miss Pitter, or (to speak more accurately) Bright Angel! I'm in a sea of glory! Of course I haven't had time to read it [*The Ermine*] properly, and there'll be another, more sober, letter presently. This is just a line to be going on with, and to assure you at once that the new volume is an absolute CORKER. I had feared that you might be one of those who, like Wordsworth, leave their talent behind at conversion: and now—oh glory—you come up shining out of the frost

[a writer's block she had endured] far better than you were before. "Man's despair is like the Arabian sun" [a line from "The World is Hollow"]— I seriously doubt if there's any religious lyric between that one and [George] Herbert on the same level. And then my eye strays to the opposite page and gets the "dying-dolphin green" [a phrase from "The Captive Bird of Paradise"]. And "What we merit—A silence like a sword" [a line from "The Other"]. I wonder have you yourself any notion how good some of these are? But, as you see, I'm drunk on them at this present. Glory be! Blessings on you! As sweet as sin and as innocent as milk. Thanks forever, Yours in great excitement, C. S. Lewis. (May 12, 1953; *CL*, 3, 327–28)

Several days later he still is overwhelmed by *The Ermine*: "The brightness does not fade: appealing from Lewis drunk to Lewis sober, I still find this an exquisite collection. When I start picking out my favourites, I find I am picking out nearly all . . . . I do congratulate you again and again. I hope you are as happy about the poems as you ought to be" (May 15, 1953; 328–29).

Given Lewis's deep affection for Pitter's poetry, it is not surprising that he sought her advice about his own poetry. In her he found one who shared similar poetic sensibilities, so he felt comfortable asking her to critique his verse. In fact, he asked her to be straightforward in her criticisms: "Now remember . . . you won't wound a sick man by unfavourable comment . . . . I know (or think) that some of these contain important thoughts and v. great metrical ingenuity. That isn't what I'm worrying about. But are they real poems or do the content and the form remain separable—fitted together only by force?" (July 24, 1946; *CL*, 2, 724). After she offers comments on several of his poems, Lewis writes back: "In most of these poems I am enamoured of metrical subtleties—not as a game: the truth is I often lust after a metre as a man might lust after a woman. The effect I want, even if attained, wd. not be of the elusive kind—more like heraldry or enamel—a blaze" (August 10, 1946; 735). At one point he asks her to judge between two versions of his poem "Two Kinds of Memory":

I want some advice. I have written two different versions of a poem and all my friends disagree, some violently championing A and some B, and some neither. Will you give a vote? Firstly, is either any good? Secondly, if so, which is the good one? Don't be in the least afraid of answering NO to the first question: kindness wd. only be an encouragement to waste more time. . . . I could almost make myself hope for your sake—and lest you spend more time and attention on them than is reasonable for me to exact—that both are bad! (February 2, 1947; 758, 761 and caps Lewis

In her recollection of this letter, Pitter writes:

Both versions are very fine, of course: the skill in form alone is enough to drive a small poet to despair: and then the melody, so strong and so unforced, and the solemn images and the contrasting moods. Strange how memory is here *polarised*, as though he could not have encompassed the paradisal without retaining a hellish pain in recollection, an ever-fresh wound. (NB. These poems should be read aloud, but only by a strong male voice). And see how he deprecates giving trouble, when one was of course only too eager: I have sometimes thought he would devise little jobs because he knew very well what pleasure it would give. (February 2, 1947; Pitter Journal, fol. 38 and emphasis Pitter)

In another instance, she recalls being flattered Lewis would think her view on his poems important: "'Donkey's Delight,' 'Young King Cole,' 'Vitrea Circe,' [are] magnificent poems to my mind, the technique staggering, vocabulary so wide, learned, & choice, discrimination (moral or spiritual) so lofty. As well might a lion request a mouse to criticise his roaring: and yet I can imagine a lion doing so" (July 6, 1947; fol. 52).

On a different occasion, Lewis chides Pitter for waiting so long to send her remarks on poems he has sent her: "On a railway platform this morning (I am just back from Malvern) I made a resolution. I said 'I will no longer be deterred by the fear of seeming to press for an opinion about my poems from writing to find out whether R. P. is dead, ill, in prison, emigrated, or simply never got my letter.' So it was with great pleasure that I found yours awaiting me" (August 31, 1948; *CL*, 2, 874). In her letter she apparently offered criticism about the tone of Lewis's poems, so a month later he writes her still musing on her remarks:

I was silent about yr. criticism because I was still chewing it and have been early taught not to speak with my mouth full. And I'm still chewing and can't really quite eat it. a. Because of a deep suspicion that . . . [your criticism] is really only a rationalisation of a deep and inarticulate (and prob. correct) feeling that mine isn't really poetry after all—a feeling repressed by your kindness and liking for my prose work and coming out in this form. b. By an understanding of the charge (supposing it not to be a rationalisation) wh. is still v. imperfect. But I'll try some more on you anon, and we may hammer it out. (September 29, 1948; 881)

Pitter's journal recollection of this incident provides the most detailed account of her personal evaluation of Lewis as a poet:

Now, I wonder. *Is* his poetry after all not [effective]? About how many poets or poems would readers agree 100% or even 50%? "The peaks of poetry are shiftingly veiled, and different readers catch different glimpses of the transcendental." I should like to know more about the actual process of conception in his case. Did his great learning, a really staggering skill in verse, inhibit the poetry? Did he ever (like most of us) catch some floating bit of emotional thistledown & go on from that, or did he plan on a subject like an architect? (Producing perhaps short epics?) He had a great stock of the makings of a poet: strong visual memory, strong recollections of childhood: desperately strong yearnings for lost Paradise & hoped Heaven ('sweet desire'): not least a strong primitive intuition of the diabolical (not merely the horrific). In fact his whole life was oriented & motivated by an almost uniquely-persisting *child's* sense of glory and of nightmare. The adult events were received into a medium still as pliable as wax, wide open to the glory, and equally vulnerable, with a man's strength to feel it all, and a great scholar's & writer's skills to express and to interpret. It is almost as though the adult disciplines, notably the technique of his verse, had largely inhibited his poetry, which is perhaps, after all, most evident in his prose. I think he wanted to be poet more than anything. Time will show. But if it was *magic* he was after, he achieved this sufficiently elsewhere. (September 29, 1948; fols. 63–64 and emphasis Pitter)

While clearly sympathetic to Lewis's poetry, Pitter believed it was in prose where he made "magic," an assessment shared by many. Specifically, she found his most powerful poetry in the prose ending of *Perelandra*.

Before turning to her poetic transcriptions of the end of Perelandra, a brief examination of the novel confirms that it contains some the most attractive passages of sustained poetic prose that Lewis ever wrote.[15] While the majority of the book is prose narrative, approximately one quarter of the novel may be deemed poetic. Thomas Peters claims "*Perelandra* reads like poetry."[16] In writing about the Ransom trilogy, Kath Filmer argues Lewis's frequent use of metaphor in his poetry is readily transferred to his prose, noting his "fiction has that imaginative, 'magical' quality that he failed to express in his poetry."[17] In explaining what stimulated his writing the story, Lewis characteristically connects it with his poetic impulse of conceiving images: "The starting point for my second novel, *Perelandra*, was my mental pictures of floating islands. The whole of the rest of my labours in a sense consisted in building up a world in which floating islands could exist."[18] Walter Hooper argues the novel may have had its genesis in poetic form, citing the only surviving fragment:

> The floating islands, the flat golden sky
> At noon, the peacock sunset: tepid waves
> With the land sliding over them like a skin:
> The alien Eve, green-bodied, stepping forth
> To meet my hero from her forest home,
> Proud, courteous, unafraid; no thought infirm
> Alters her cheek.[19]

In addition, in recalling all he saw on Perelandra, Elwin Ransom, the novel's central character, corrects Lewis (the character in the novel) for assuming "it's all too vague for you to put in words": "On the contrary, it is words that are vague. The reason why the thing can't be expressed is that it's too definite for language."[20] Indeed, Chapter 3 in its entirety and much of Chapter 4 can be cited as evidence of poetic prose, as in them Lewis creates lavish verbal pictures of the idyllic, paradisal environment Ransom enjoys. What he writes is a lyrical shower of poetic prose unprecedented in his fiction and characterized by a cloudburst of figurative language, including effusive metaphors, similes, and symbols. [21]

For example, after Ransom realizes he is floating and then swimming in the ocean of Perelandra, he tastes the water and is delighted by the first of a series of unanticipated sensuous pleasures: "Though he had not been aware of thirst till now, his drink gave him a quite astonishing pleasure. It was almost like meeting Pleasure itself for the first time. He buried his flushed face in the green translucence, and when he withdrew it, found himself once more on the top of a wave" (30). Naked and awash in the water, Ransom is completely open to experiencing his senses in a unique, primeval fashion. He sees "a rich, varied world in which nothing, for the moment, seemed palpable. . . . [Eventually looking at the sky, he sees] the golden roof of that world quivering with a rapid variation of paler lights as a ceiling quivers at the reflected sunlight from the bath-water when you step into your bath on a summer morning" (29–30). He describes his first sight of the floating islands as "variegated in colours like a patch-work quilt—flame-colour, ultramarine, crimson, orange, gamboge, and violet" (32). Lewis balances his numerous lengthy visual descriptions with ones highlighting smell, as when Ransom first walks through a forest: "The smells in the forest were beyond all that he had ever conceived. To say that they made him feel hungry and thirsty would be misleading; almost, they created a new kind of hunger and thirst, a longing that seemed to flow over from the body into the soul and which was a heaven to feel" (37–38). Ransom also notes the utter silence, yet "the sense of his solitude became intense without becoming at all painful—only adding, as it were, a last touch of wildness to the unearthly pleasures that surrounded him" (38).

However, Ransom's heightened taste buds may be the most memorable episode in this riot of the senses. As he moves through a forest "where great globes of yellow fruit hung from the trees—clustered as toy-balloons are clustered on the back of the balloon-man and about the same size," he picks one. Inadvertently, he punctures a rind and places the opening to his lips:

> He had meant to extract the smallest, experimental sip, but the first taste put his caution to flight. It was, of course, a taste, just as his thirst and hunger had been thirst and hunger. But then it was so different from every other taste that it seemed mere pedantry to call it a taste at all. It was like the discovery of a totally new *genus* of pleasures, something unheard of among men, out of all reckoning, beyond all covenant. For one draught of this on earth wars would be fought and nations betrayed. It could not be classified. He could never tell us, when he came back to the world of men, whether it was sharp or sweet, savoury or voluptuous, creamy or piercing. (38)

As his first day comes to a close, Ransom looks across the ocean to the sunset: "The sea, far calmer now than he had yet seen it, smoked towards heaven in huge dolomites and elephants of blue and purple vapour, and a light wind, full of sweetness, lifted the hair on his forehead. The day was burning to death" (39). All these overwhelming sensuous experiences are linked by feelings of excessive pleasure untainted by guilt, as if old earthly prohibitions against enjoying oneself too much are foreign to this world: "The strange sense of excessive pleasure . . . seemed somehow to be communicated to him through all his senses at once . . . [and] there was an exuberance or prodigality of sweetness about the mere act of living which our race finds it difficult not to associate with forbidden and extravagant actions"(33). The next day Ransom's sensuous feast continues as he encounters wonderfully soothing bubble trees that shower him with a refreshingly cool and intensely aromatic liquid; yellow gourds with a flavor, while not as exotic as the fruit of the previous day, that hints at protein-like heartiness; and a small, friendly dragon who becomes his first companion on Perelandra.

After this Ransom meets the Green Lady, and the poetic prose, while never entirely absent, retires into the background. The rhetorical debates between the scientist Weston, the Green Lady, and Ransom dominate Chapters VII-XIV, culminating in the death of Weston and Ransom's metaphorical descent into Hell and subsequent emergence in Chapter XV. He recovers from his ordeal by being "breast-fed by the planet Venus herself," enjoying sustenance from a grape-like fruit that always seemed to be hanging near his tired, battered body, the "endless sound of rejoicing water," and a reviving song: "Now high in air above him, now welling up as if from glens and valleys far below, it floated through his sleep and was the first sound at every waking. It was formless as the song of a bird, yet it was not a bird's voice. As a bird's voice is to a flute, so this was to a cello: low and ripe and tender, full-bellied, rich and golden brown: passionate too, but not with the passions of men" (197–98). Regaining his strength, he moves down the mountain and enjoys deep blue streamer bushes with "soft, almost impalpable, caresses of the long thin leaves on his flesh," thickets of flowers that shower his head and cover his sides with pollen, and especially the song of a shy, horse-like creature (202–04).

When Ransom eventually meets Malacandra (Mars) and Perelandra (Venus), passages of poetic prose begin to cascade one upon another. In describing their bodies, Lewis writes that, while they are white, "a flush of diverse colours began at about the shoulders and streamed up the necks and flickered over face and head and stood out around the head like plumage or a halo" (212). As the animals gather to witness the enthronement of the King and the Queen (the Green Lady), Ransom sees a wondrous menagerie: "They came mostly in pairs, male and female together, fawning upon one another, climbing over one another, diving under one another's bellies, perching upon one another's backs. Flaming plumage, gilded beaks, glossy flanks, liquid eyes, great red caverns of whinneying or of bleating mouths, and thickets of switching tails, surrounded him on every side" (217). However, the most compelling piece of poetic prose occurs as the King and Queen approach. Ransom notes how the entire atmosphere seems bathed in pure daylight coming from no apparent source, connects this light with holy things, and describes it as reaching perfection on the mountain top "like a lord upon a throne or like wine in a bowl." The light then reveals "Paradise itself in its two Persons, Paradise walking hand in hand, its two bodies shining in the light like emeralds yet not themselves too bright to look at" (218).

Chapter XVII, the final chapter of the novel, provides the richest sustained passages of poetic prose. Pitter's poetic transcriptions of these prose passages actually covers the dialogue in this chapter between several voices regarding the Great Dance—a celebration both of God's loving majesty and the promise of his eventual reconciliation with creation—and consists of twenty-three Spenserian stanzas. As early as April 1947 Pitter told Lewis she was so impressed with the poetic prose ending of *Perelandra*, she wanted to put some of it into Spenserian stanzas.[22] Lewis readily agreed, although he was surprised she wanted to spend her time doing this: "I'm rather shocked your wasting *your* verse on *my* prose. But I hope it'll only be the irritant to start your real activity [she had confided earlier that she was experiencing writer's block]" (April 27, 1947; *CL*, 2, 771 and emphasis Lewis). Two weeks later he asks: "When am I to see the Spenserians? They'll do me good in a way you probably hadn't thought of. In my job one is always ferreting out the 'Sources' of the great poets. Now (serve me right) I shall be a source myself" (May 8, 1947; 776). Pitter reveals in her journal why she felt compelled to turn Lewis's Perelandran prose into verse: "I had been transcribing the paean of praise towards the end of *Perelandra* into irregular Spenserian stanzas simply as a mnemonic: I wished so much to have these enormous transcendental ideas in a form I could memorise & use wherever I happened to be" (July 6, 1947; Pitter Journal, fol. 52).

Pitter's transcriptions, faithful to the source, emphasize the underlying poetic nature of Lewis's prose in *Perelandra*.[23] When Lewis receives her transcriptions, he writes: "I like them—and you manage to be closer to the original in verse than some of my continental translators seem to get in prose. I think that XXI probably wd. be taken in a pantheistic sense by a reader who did not start with the doctrine of the Trinity in mind, but so wd. the original. I think XXIII *has* high eloquence—but of course it is hard for me to judge. IX is specially good" (July 6, 1947; 789 and emphasis Lewis). Somewhat later, apparently in response to her asking if he would object to her publishing her transcriptions, he writes: "I should be delighted if you used your Spenserians for that purpose, and don't really see why you should need my permission" (November 17, 1949; 997).

A comparison of Pitter's transcriptions with the corresponding passages from *Perelandra* offers several insights. First, Pitter's verse often sharpens and clarifies Lewis's prose. For example, the second speech about the Great Dance in *Perelandra* is: "Never did He make two things the same; never did He utter one word twice. After earths, not better earths but beasts; after beasts, not better beasts, but spirits. After a failing, not a recovery but a new creation. Out of the new creation, not a third but the mode of change itself is changed for ever. Blessed is He!" (229). Pitter's "II" closely follows this:

He who has never made two things the same,
He who has never uttered one word twice,
First made the earths, and after them there came
Not better earths but beasts: then there arise
Not nobler beasts but spirits: then He dies
Their death to save the fallen: but these shall be
Not mended, but clothed on in Paradise
With new creation fashioned gloriously:
So change itself is changed for ever. Blest be He!

Her last four lines, assuming they reflect Lewis's meaning—nowhere does he contradict her—clarify the meaning of his original. For instance, Lewis's somewhat vague "after a failing, not a recovery but a new creation" is made more concrete by Pitter's "then He dies / Their death to save the fallen." Similarly, his "out of the new creation, not a third" is considerably sharpened by her expansion: "But these shall be / Not mended, but clothed on in Paradise / With a new creation fashioned gloriously." Moreover, her rhyme scheme, while dependent upon eye rhyme, is an effective enhancement of Lewis's prose.

In a like manner, Pitter's "XVI" is powerful poetry communicating the boundless love, mercy, and compassion of God while at the same time sharpening the meaning of Lewis's original. The passage in *Perelandra* reads: "Each thing was made for Him. He is the centre. Because we are with Him, each of us is at the centre. It is not as in a city of the Darkened World where they say that each must live for all. In His city all things are made for each. When He died in the Wounded World He died not for men, but for each man. If each man had been the only man made, He would have done no less" (232). Pitter's transcription is:

> He is the Centre, and each thing was made
> For Him, and in Him each for ever dwells:
> Not, as in cities of the dark is said,
> Each one for all: but utter love compels
> All to the service of each one. So tells
> The story of the wounded World: He came
> For each man, not for men. His miracles
> Of strongest mercy would have been the same
> If but one living soul had dwelt there in that flame.

While Pitter's version loses the power of Lewis's line "because we are with Him, each of us is at the centre," she considerably clarifies his "He died not for men, but for each man. If each man had been the only man made, He would have done no less" in her expansion: "He came for each man, not for men. His miracles / Of strongest mercy would have been the same / If but one living soul had dwelt there in that flame."

Second, Pitter's verse makes concrete some of Lewis's more abstract imagery albeit with somewhat limited success. Lewis, as noted above, gives Pitter's "IX" special praise:

> The Tree was planted in that world, but here
> The ripened fruit hangs in the heaven high:
> Both blood and life run from the Fountain there,
> Here it runs Life alone. We have passed by
> The first strong rapids: the deep waters ply

On a new course toward the distant sea.
Till now, all has but waited. In the sky
There hangs the promised star, and piercingly
The trumpet sounds: the army marches. Blest be He!

The passage in the original reads: "The Tree was planted in that world but the fruit has ripened in this. The fountain that sprang with mingled blood and life in the Dark World, flows here with life only. We have passed the first cataracts, and from here onward the stream flows deep and turns in the direction of the sea. This is the Morning Star which He promised to those who conquer; this is the centre of worlds. Till now all has waited. But now the trumpet has sounded and the army is on the move. Blessed be He!" (231). Why Lewis thought this stanza merited special praise is not clear, although it may be he thought Pitter's concrete transcription heightened his subtle allusions to both the Garden of Eden (the tree of life) and to Calvary by his use of the Tree.[24] On the other hand, her "till now, all has but waited. In the sky / There hangs the promised star, and piercingly / The trumpet sounds: the army marches" is perhaps too terse an alternative to Lewis's "this is the Morning Star which He promised to those who conquer; this is the centre of worlds. Till now all has waited. But now the trumpet has sounded and the army is on the move." In particular, her "the promised star" forfeits the specificity of "the Morning Star," an obvious reference to Venus; also, by dropping "conquer" Pitter loses Lewis's allusion to Revelation 2:28: "And I will give him the morning star" (NAS). Finally, by omitting "this is the centre of worlds," Pitter obscures an important parallelism that interconnects many of Lewis's paragraphs.[25]

Third, Pitter's transcriptions sometimes blur Lewis's original meaning. For instance, Lewis was concerned her "XXI" "probably wd. be taken in a pantheistic sense by a reader who did not start with the doctrine of the Trinity in mind, but so wd. the original." A comparison of Pitter's transcription with Lewis's original prose supports his concern. The passage in *Perelandra* is: "All things are by Him and for Him. He utters Himself also for His own delight and sees that He is good. He is His own begotten and what proceeds from Him is Himself. Blessed be He!" (233). Pitter's transcription, adding the concrete image of a tree to powerful effect, is:

He made all things, and for Him all was made.
Himself He utters too for His delight,

And sees that it is good. Under the shade
Of His own branches does He sit, and bright
He shines upon Himself: by His own might
Begets Himself from all eternity,
And what proceeds from Him is His by right,
Himself eternally coming to be;
Surely He is His own begotten. Blest be He!

In Pitter's line three ("and sees that it is good") her substitution of "it" for "He" (Lewis's "and sees that He is good") tends to identify the Creator overmuch with the creation.[26] Furthermore, in line eight "Himself eternally coming to be" oddly suggests God continually evolves into what He will become. On the other hand, Pitter's transcription effectively echoes the opening chapter of the book of Colossians where St. Paul emphasizes the "all" sufficiency of Christ: "For by him all things were created: things in heaven and on earth, visible and invisible, whether thrones or powers or rulers or authorities; all things were created by him and for him" (Col. 1: 16).[27]

Finally, Pitter's transcriptions re-configure Lewis's prose into poetic language and cadence, at times making his original more eloquent. For instance, Pitter's transcription of Lewis's third paragraph offers several improvements. His "it is loaded with justice as a tree bows down with fruit" (229) becomes "like a fair tree with bounteous fruit bowed down." Pitter's inclusion of "fair" and "bounteous" heightens the impact of Lewis's line. In like fashion, his "as when stones support and are supported in an arch" (229) is made more eloquent by Pitter's "for not as stones on ground, but bonded tight / Into the living arch." The impact of Lewis's "supported" and "are transformed" is heightened by Pitter's" bonded tight" and "living arch." However, Lewis singled out Pitter's "XXIII" for its "high eloquence":

Yet seeming also is the cause and end
For which Time is so long, and Heaven deep:
Lest if we never met the roads that tend
Nowhere, nor darkness, where the answers sleep
To questions silence must for ever keep:
Nothing could image in our mind that Sea,
That Gulf and that Abyss, the Father. Leap
Into that depth, O thoughts: only to be

Sunk drowned and echoless for ever. Blest be He!

Lewis's original is: "Yet this seeming also is the end and final cause for which He spreads out Time so long and Heaven so deep; lest, if we never met the dark, and the road that leads nowhither, and the question to which no answer is imaginable, we should have in our minds no likeness of the Abyss of the Father, into which if a creature drop down his thoughts for ever he shall hear no echo return to him. Blessed, blessed, blessed be He!" (233–34). At least part of Pitter's success in making this passage more eloquent is her turning Lewis's difficult "the question to which no answer is imaginable" into the memorable "where the answers sleep / To questions silence must for ever keep." Furthermore, Lewis's ambiguous "Abyss of the Father" is helped by the synonyms "Sea" and "Gulf." While, as this brief analysis has shown, Lewis's prose concerning the Great Dance was raw ore that Pitter often transformed into gold, at times her transcriptions actually weakened the poetic prose of *Perelandra*.

Lest we think Pitter's efforts were so much presumptuous self-indulgence, consider the criticism leveled at Lewis when the novel was first published: "Bravely as Mr. Lewis has assaulted the high and mighty symbols of human hope, serious and imaginative as is his purpose, the things he intends . . . cannot be done at the pace and within the structure of narrative prose. It is a subject for verse, and verse at its most immense." The reviewer, Kate O'Brien, adds that "passages in this book which tremble near the absurd because they have to be so much explained, might well have been majestic and beyond question in the simple, inevitable dress of poetry."[28] Accordingly, Pitter's transcriptions, while faithful to the source, suggest both the underlying poetic nature of Lewis's prose in *Perelandra* and offer an imperfect attempt to turn it into verse.[29]

Ruth Pitter was a trusted confidant for Lewis the poet. In other letters to her he expounded at length upon different kinds of poetry, the role of the individual poet, his deep love of Milton, his "experiments" in verse, encouragement that she will overcome her writer's block, the novel experience of having in his "old age" a poem rejected by the *Spectator* ("Very tonic: I'd forgotten the taste of that little printed slip" [January 4, 1947; *CL*, 2, 754]), the "hard" subjects for poetry, and his favorite meters. Undoubtedly Pitter was grateful to be a sounding board, thankful she could in some small way repay Lewis for the radio talks that had helped her avoid the "slough of despond" she felt herself slipping into during the dark days of WWII. Even after his death she paid him compliment by alluding to *Perelandra* in her *Still by Choice* (1966). "Angels" speculates about the real character of an angel ("terrible, tender, or severe?"), and she covertly refers to Lewis's angelic beings, the eldila from the Ransom trilogy: "Or likelier, now we dream of space, Lewis's dread sublime / Pillars of light, no limbs, no face, / Sickening our space and time?"[30] While some might wish to make more of the personal relationship between these two poets than the evidence merits, all we can say with certainty is that they did meet on a number of occasions, but generally in the company of others and always in the context of discussing books, writers, literature, and poetry in particular.[31] Lewis deeply valued the strength and beauty of Pitter's poetry while she found Lewis's greatest poetry in the prose of *Perelandra*. In the end, a shared love of poetry and faith in Christ connect the two writers, links transcending both time and death.

Chapter 8 Notes

1. A version of this essay first appeared in *Christianity and Literature* 49 (Spring 2000): 331–356.

2. The question of whether the focus of this essay is prose poetry or poetic prose should be addressed here. According to *The New Princeton Encyclopedia of Poetry and Poetics*, eds. Alex Preminger and T. V. F. Brogan (Princeton: Princeton University Press, 1993), prose poetry is characterized by "unity even in brevity and poetic quality even without the line breaks of free verse: high patterning, rhythmic and figural repetition, sustained intensity, and compactness" (977). *A Handbook to Literature*, eds. William Thrall and Addison Hibbard (New York: Odyssey Press, 1960), defines prose poetry as "a form of prose with marked (although preferably not too regular) cadence and frequently with extensive use of figurative language and imagery" (383). On the other hand, poetic prose has been defined as "ordinary spoken and written language (prose) that makes use of cadence, rhythm, figurative language, or other devices ordinarily associated with poetry" (*Concise Dictionary of Literary Terms* [New York: McGraw-Hill, 1972], 213). In order to clarify the focus of this essay, I am considering Lewis's poetic prose.

3. From an address given at Wheaton College, Wheaton, IL, October 16, 1964. Transcript available at The Wade Center.

4. For a thorough review of critical works on Lewis's poetry, see my essays "A Bibliographic Review of C. S. Lewis as Poet: 1952–1995, Part One," *The Canadian C. S. Lewis Journal* No. 91 (Spring 1997): 9–23, and "A Bibliographic Review of C. S. Lewis as Poet: 1952–1995, Part Two," *The Canadian C. S. Lewis Journal* No. 91 (Autumn 1997): 34–56.

5. Consider the following critical evaluations. In the preface to Pitter's *First and Second Poems* (London: Sheed & Ward, 1927), Hilaire Belloc praises her poetry as "an exceptional reappearance of the classical spirit amongst us" (7). He likens her verse to a strong stone building and argues really good verse "contrasted with the general run of that in the midst

of which it appears, seems to me to have a certain quality of *hardness* [Belloc's emphasis]; so that, in the long run, it will be discovered, as a gem is discovered in mud" (9). In her poetry he finds "beauty and right order" (10). Belloc also writes in the preface to her *A Mad Lady's Garland* (London: Cresset Press,1934) that Pitter has two peculiar poetic gifts: "A perfect ear and exact epithet. How those two ever get combined is incomprehensible—one would think it was never possible—but when the combination does appear then you have verse of that classic sort which is founded and secure of its own future" (vii). In his *Four Living Poets* (Santa Barbara, CA: Unicorn Press, 1944), Rudolph Gilbert calls Pitter "the poet of purity" and notes "what the poetry reader values most in Pitter's poems is her eloquence . . . . In Pitter one almost looks through the language, as through air, discerning the exact form of the objects which stand there, and every part and shade of meaning is brought out by the sunny light resting upon them" (48–49). Later he adds: "She has a first-rate intuitive gift of observation, a control of poetic language and magical perception that is always to be found in great poetry" (52). In addition, in the *festschrift, Ruth Pitter: Homage to a Poet* (London: Rapp and Whiting, 1969), David Cecil says "she is the most moving of living English poets, and one of the most original" (13). John Arlott refers to her as "a poet's poet" (43), while Thom Gunn notes she "is the most modest of poets, slipping us her riches as if they were everyday currency" (64). Kathleen Raine is more lavish in her praise: "I now see her as one of the poets whose best work will survive as long as the English language, with whose expressiveness in image and idea she has kept faith, remains" (106). In the introduction to Pitter's *Collected Poems* (London: Enitharmon, 1996), Elizabeth Jennings appreciates her "acute sensibility and deep integrity"; her poems "are informed with a sweetness which is also bracing, and a generosity which is blind to nothing, neither the sufferings in this world nor the quirky behavior of human beings" (15). The most complete evaluation of Pitter's poetry is my *Hunting the Unicorn: A Critical Biography of Ruth Pitter* (Kent, OH: Kent State University Press, 2008); hereafter *HU*.

6. Pitter's volumes of poetry are: *First Poems* (London: Cecil Palmer, 1920); *First and Second Poems* (London: Sheed & Ward, 1927); *Persephone in Hades* (Privately printed, 1931); *A Mad Lady's Garland* (London: Cresset Press, 1934); *A Trophy of Arms: Poems 1926–1935* (London: Cresset Press, 1936) and winner of the Hawthornden Prize in 1937; *The Spirit Watches* (London: Cresset Press, 1939); *The Rude Potato* (London: Cresset Press, 1941); *The Bridge: Poems 1939–1944* (London: Cresset Press, 1945); *Pitter on Cats* (London: Cresset Press, 1946); *Urania* (Selections from *A Trophy of Arms, The Spirit Watches*, and *The Bridge* (London: Cresset Press, 1950); *The Ermine: Poems 1942–1952* (London: Cresset Press, 1953) and winner of the Wm. Heinemann Award: Queen's Gold Medal for Poetry, 1955; *Still by Choice* (London: Cresset Press, 1966); *Collected Poems 1926–1966* (London: Barrie & Rockcliff/Cresset Press, 1968); *End of the Drought* (London: Barrie & Jenkins, 1975); *A Heaven to Find* (London: Enitharmon, 1987); *Collected Poems: 1990* (Petersfield: Enitharmon, 1990); and *Collected Poems* (London: Enitharmon, 1996).

7. In her "There Is a Spirit," the preface to *Collected Poems: 1926–1966* (London: Barrie & Rockcliff/Cresset Press, 1968), she writes:

My purpose [as a poet] has never varied. . . . It has been simply to capture and express some of the secret meanings which haunt life and language: the silent music, the dance in stillness, the hints and echoes and messages of which everything is full; the smile on the face of the tiger, or of the Bernini seraph. The silent music is within oneself too, or it would not be detected elsewhere. In the face of mundane joy it says ". . . but all the same"! and in the face of horror ". . . but all the same"! As though the normal targets of consciousness were somehow unreal; life, bursting with its secret, sits hugging itself until we have read the riddle. (xi-xii)

8. This poem has striking affinities with Lewis's "The Day with a White Mark," *Punch* 217 (August 17, 1949): 170; reprinted in *P*, 28. That poem begins with the speaker realizing a surprising turn of events: "All ahead is dark or splashed with hideous light. / My garden's spoiled; my holidays are cancelled; the omens harden; / The plann'd and the unplann'd miseries deepen; the knots draw tight. / Yet I—I could have kissed the very scullery taps. The colour of / My day was like a peacock's chest." Finding unexpected delight in the midst of an otherwise drab day is the thematic focus of the poem. In its conclusion we see Lewis using a phrase that appears as Pitter's title: "Who knows if ever it [unexpected delight] will come again, now the day closes? / No one can give me—or take away—the key. All depends / On the elf, the bird, the angel. I question if the angel himself / Has power to choose when *sudden heaven* for me begins or ends" (my italics).

9. Cited in *Ruth Pitter: Homage to a Poet*, ed. Arthur Russell (London: Rapp and Whiting, 1969), 28 (subsequent references in the text).

10. She noted: "I had to be intellectually satisfied as well as emotionally, because at that time of one's life one doesn't just fall into religion with adolescent emotion. But at last I was satisfied at every point that it was the one way for me. It wasn't the easy road but it was the only possible one" (*Homage*, 28).

11. Because Lewis did not save Pitter's letters, she compiled a journal that reconstructed and summarized the correspondence she had sent to Lewis. The journal is available in MS. Eng. lett. c. 220/3; Bodleian Library. Here folio 18 (hereafter, Pitter Journal; subsequent references in the text).

12. Pitter's diary confirms this date. The entry for July 16, 1947 reads: "Lunch with Lewis? Yes. 1 p.m. Mdln [Magdalen College]." Pitter Pocket diaries and box of 'Treasures' (uncatalogued) Box 31, Diary 1947; Bodleian Library.

13. This is the only surviving letter Pitter wrote Lewis. It is available in the Marion E. Wade Center, CSL /L-Pitter/ 1a.

14. On July 23, 1985, Lyle Dorsett and his wife, Mary, did an oral interview with Ruth Pitter in her home in Long Crendon, Buckinghamshire, England. In the interview, Pitter's recollection of this first meeting is quite different:

> D: How did you come to meet C. S. Lewis?
>
> P: . . . I forced myself on him. I wrote to him and said how his work had delighted, and indeed, more than delighted me. And, would he see me. And he seemed rather grumpy when I got there and said, "I can spare half an hour." Has a deep voice. That was all—
>
> D: Did you go to his—
>
> P: I went to his rooms in—
>
> D: In Magdalen College.
>
> P: In, the college, what was the name of it now?
>
> D: Magdalen.
>
> P: Magdalen, that's right. Yes.
>
> D: About what year was this, Miss Pitter?
>
> P: Oh dear.
>
> D: Was this after the war?
>
> P: No, no it would be while the war was still on. . . . And, well—I think, now I left my book and I don't know whether he wrote to me. But he did say to me at some point, "Why did nobody ever tell me of this?" He was very much struck. He thought the quality of the work was very high.
>
> D: So you went to see him that day and he was a bit grumpy. He said he'd give you about a half an hour.

P: Yes.

D: And while you were there you showed him some of your poetry or you left it with him, did you?

P: Yes, I think it must have been—

D: Did you stay just about a half an hour?

P: Yes. I don't—well, after what he said it was up to me to rise when the end of the half hour. I didn't want to—

D: Did he get any friendlier?

P: What?

D: Did he get any friendlier after you'd been there?

P: Yes, a bit. Not very. I fancy he was always a good deal on the defensive with all sorts of tiresome people.

D: So you left this volume of your verse there. Then did he write to your after that?

P: I think he must have. . .

D: Did you—well, you obviously became a good friend

P: Yes.

D: The two of you became friends.

P: Oh, I may say that, yes, I think so, yes. Yes, we were.

D: What did he think of your poetry?

P: Thought it was very good . . .

This interview is available in the Wade Center; here covers pp. 9–11.

15. Lewis himself thought the novel was one of his two best books, the other being *Till We Have Faces*: "Which do I like best? Now, the answer wd. be *Till We Have Faces* and *Perelandra*" (December 6, 1960; *CL*, 3, 1213–14).

16. Thomas Peters, "The War of the Worldviews: H. G. Wells and Scientism and C. S. Lewis and Christianity," *Mission and Ministry* 11.4 and 12.1 (1998): 47.

17. Kath Filmer, "The Polemic Image: The Role of Metaphor and Symbol in the Fiction of C. S. Lewis," *SEVEN: An Anglo-American Literary Review* 7 (1986): 74.

18. See "Unreal Estates" in *Of Other Worlds: Essays and Stories*, ed. Walter Hooper (London: Bles, 1966), 87. The passages continues: "And then of course the whole story about an averted fall developed. This is because . . . having got your people to this exciting country, something must happen" (87).

19. This fragment first appears in a footnote in Roger Lancelyn Green and Walter Hooper, *C. S. Lewis: A Biography* (London: Collins, 1974), 171.

20. *Perelandra* (New York: Macmillan, 1944), 28 (subsequent references in the text).

21. For more on this, see Filmer, 61–76.

22. Named after Edmund Spenser, Spenserian stanzas contain nine lines rhyming *ababbcbcc*. Pitter employed Spenserians in several poems including, "Resurgam: Or the Glorious and Pitiful History of the Heretical Caterpillar" and "Fowls Celestial and Terrestial or The Angels of the Mind," in *A Mad Lady's Garland* (1934) and "On a Passage from the *Metamorphoses*" from *A Trophy of Arms* (1936).

23. The transcriptions cover *Perelandra*, 229–234, and are available in a holograph notebook beginning: "Transcribed 1970. All unpublished [poems], and of widely varying dates." "Passage from 'Perelandra'" is given first. See Bodleian MS Pitter Verse (uncatalogued), Box 28, 1–11. They were published for the first time in the original version of this essay when it appeared in *Christianity and Literature* 49 (Spring 2000): 331–356, and were reprinted in *C. S. Lewis, Poet: The Legacy of His Poetic Impulse* (Kent, OH: Kent State University Press, 2001), 275–82.

24. Many of the passages relating to the Great Dance have echoes from the book of Revelation. Here, for instance, there is a hint of Revelation 2:7: "'He who has an ear, let him hear what the Spirit says to the Churches. To him who overcomes, I will grant to eat of the tree of life, which is in the Paradise of God'" (NAS).

25. Indeed, of Lewis's twenty-three paragraphs concerning the Great Dance, twelve make similar reference (1, 7, 8, 9, 10, 12, 13, 14, 15, 16, 18, and 22). In Pitter's transcription, however, only eight of her twenty-three stanzas make similar reference (I, X, XII, XIV, XV, XVI, XVIII, and XXII). The lack of interconnection by reference to "centre of the worlds" in Pitter's stanzas as compared to Lewis's paragraphs is especially noteworthy in its appearance in his 7, 8, 9, and 10 while only appearing in Pitter's X.

26. A similar identification of the Creator overmuch with the creation occurs in her interpolation of "His by right" in line seven, leaving "Himself" in line eight as an appositive.

27. The entire passages reads: "For by him all things were created: things in heaven and on earth, visible and invisible, whether thrones or powers of rulers or authorities; all things were created by him and for him. He is before all things, and in him all things hold together. And he is the head of the body, the church; he is the beginning and the firstborn from among the dead, so that in everything he might have the supremacy. For God was pleased to have all his fullness dwell in him, and through him to reconcile to himself all things, whether things on earth of things in heaven, by making peace through his blood, shed on the cross" (Col. 1:16–20).

28. Kate O'Brien, "Review of *Perelandra*," *The Spectator* 170 (May 14, 1943): 458.

29. Before leaving this discussion, it is worth noting the significant role language plays throughout the Ransom trilogy. In addition to the poetry of *Perelandra*, the poetry of the *hyoi*, the acquisition of language by Ransom upon his arrival upon Malacandra, and the advantage this subsequently gives him over Weston and Divine are central foci of *Out of the Silent Planet*. In contrast, poetry is relatively absent in *That Hideous Strength*, in part because a key strategy of N.I.C.E. is to manipulate language and meaning, stripping words of both truth and beauty.

30. *Still by Choice* (London: Cresset Press, 1966), 24. She pays Lewis another tribute in *A Heaven to Find* (London: Enitharmon, 1987) when she writes in "Lewis Appears (Apropos of C. S. Lewis's move to Cambridge [1955], and his possible effect on [F. R.] Leavis and the Logical Positivists)": "Lewis appears, the Trojan Dinosaur, / Eggs of ambivalence distend his Maur. / What meant the Fathers to convey him in? / I wish I knew the Mind of those grave Min." She adds this note to the poem: "'Maur' is 'maw,' misspelt to avoid a false rhyme with 'dinosaur.' 'Min' is the plural of 'man' in Essex dialect" (no pagination).

31. In his 1985 interview Dorsett asked Pitter several questions about the nature of her personal relationship with Lewis; we may take Pitter's own statement as the last word on this subject:

> D: Someone said that if C. S. Lewis was ever going to marry [attributed to Hugo Dyson], that he would marry Miss Ruth Pitter.
>
> P: Oh. Think of that! Did he say that?
>
> D: That is what I've read somewhere that he said to one of his friends.
>
> P: You can't be—
>
> D: No, no, I take that back. I want to correct that. That one of his friends surmised that [what was said was] that if he were to marry, he would marry Miss Ruth Pitter.
>
> P: Well, it's slender, isn't it? All the same it's very gratifying to the feelings. I'm glad to have heard it.

D: Yes, yes, it's a nice thing to have said, isn't it? . . .Well, do you think it would be fair to say that if Miss Ruth Pitter had ever married, maybe she would have married C. S. Lewis?

P: Don't put it to me like that, because honestly I don't know. I think on the whole, I've never been the marrying sort. I think it may be the case, it was just as well I were not called upon to make that decision. Well, I—I'm left with the hope that we shall meet again in heaven (p. 11 of the interview).

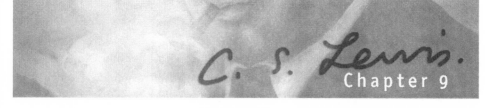

Chapter 9

Quorum Porum: The Literary Cats of T. S. Eliot, Ruth Pitter, and Dorothy L. Sayers[1]

The fascination people have with cats escapes me. While I don't hate cats, my interest in them rarely exceeds benign indifference. For instance, while my wife and children love to pick up our current feline, Molly, I endure her presence as long as she stays outside on our porch or in the garage. When she meows for lap time, I give her a friendly but firm brush off.[2] So I find it amusing that a number of writers wax poetically and philosophically on cats. In a letter to a friend C. S. Lewis writes: "We were talking about cats and dogs the other day and decided that both have consciences but the dog, being an honest, humble person, always has a bad one, but the cat is a Pharisee and always has a good one.[3] When he sits and stares you out of countenance he is thanking God that he is not as these dogs, or these humans, or even as these other cats!" (March 21, 1955; *CL*, 3, 587).[4] Lewis's anthropomorphic analysis of cats links him with three other writers who have written slim collections of verse dedicated to cats: T. S. Eliot's *Old Possum's Book of Practical Cats* (1939),[5] Ruth Pitter's *Pitter on Cats* (1947),[6] and

Dorothy L. Sayers' "War Cat," (1943), *A Cat's Christmas Carol* (Christmas 1947) and "From the *Catalects of Pussius Catus II*" (1948).[7] The rhyming couplets favored by Eliot, Pitter, and Sayers contribute to the serio-comic tone of all the poems, and while a discussion of the stylistic similarities these poems share would be interesting, I limit my focus here to how each writer finds in the life of cats fascinating insights into the human experience. Specifically, Eliot personifies human pride, Pitter explores human melancholy, and Sayers parodies human selfishness.

Old Possum's focuses upon the pride of specific cats as almost every poem highlights a particular named cat. There is Growltiger, a river cat; Mungojerrie and Rumpleteazer, cat burglars; Old Deuteronomy, an old, wise cat; Rumpuscat, a dog intimidator; Mistofflees, a magician; Macavity, a mysterious cat; Asparagus (aka Gus), a theatre cat; Skimbleshanks, a railroad cat; and Morgan, a pirate cat. Eliot's attention to a cat's pride is stated in the first poem of the volume, "The Naming of Cats." Here he offers that every cat must have three different names. The first is a "family name" such as Peter, James, Plato, or Electra: "All of them sensible, everyday names." The second is a "particular name": "But I tell you, a cat needs a name that's particular, / A name that's peculiar, and more dignified, / Else how can he keep up his tail perpendicular, / Or spread out his whiskers, or cherish his pride?" (11). Eliot offers a quorum of such names: Munkustrap, Quaxo, Coricopat, Bombalurina, or Jellylorum. The third name, however, is the most important since, unlike the first two names that might be shared by any number of cats, it is absolutely unique to each cat: "But above and beyond there's still one name left over, / And that is the name that you never will guess; / The name that no human research can discover— / But THE CAT HIMSELF KNOWS, and will never confess" (11; caps Eliot). Eliot ends the poem with a snapshot of a cat's pride in his secret name:

> When you notice a cat in profound meditation,
>> The reason, I tell you, is always the same:
> His mind is engaged in a rapt contemplation
>> Of the thought, of the thought, of the thought of his name:
>>> His ineffable effable
>>> Effanineffable
> Deep and inscrutable singular Name.[8] (11–12)

Each poem in the volume goes on to illustrate some attribute of pride linked to the cat celebrated in the poem.

For instance, the old gumbie cat, Jennyandots, is proud of her household management; she insists that the mice under her care behave so as to lend dignity to the home she so meticulously manages: "She is deeply concerned with the ways of the mice— / Their behaviour's not good and their manners not nice; / So when she has got them lined up on the matting, / She teaches them music, crocheting and tatting" (15). In addition, she is an excellent cook, using food as another means of keeping her mice in line:

> As she finds that the mice will not ever keep quiet,
> She is sure it is their irregular diet
> And believing that nothing is done without trying,
> She sets right to work with her baking and frying.
> She makes them a mouse-cake of bread and dried peas,
> And a *beautiful* fry of lean bacon and cheese.
> (15–16; emphasis Eliot)

Even the cockroaches under her command are kept from loitering: "She thinks that the cockroaches just need employment / To prevent them from idle and wanton destroyment. / So she's formed, from that lot of disorderly louts, / A troop of well-disciplined helpful boy-scouts" (16). Jennyanydots' efficacy managing the house is indisputable: "So for Old Gumbie Cats let us now give three cheers— / On whom well-ordered households depend, it appears" (16).

Rum Tum Tugger is proud of his particularities, since he wants what you don't want him to want, or, conversely, he doesn't want what you want him to want. He is unusually picky and finicky, always wanting things his way:

> If you offer him pheasant he would rather have grouse.
> If you put him in a house he would much prefer a flat,
> If you put him in a flat then he'd rather have a house.
> If you set him on a mouse then he only wants a rat,
> If you set him on a rat then he'd rather chase a mouse. (21)

No matter what you do, Rum Tum Tugger isn't satisfied. If he is in, he wants out; if he is out he wants in. Whether it is lodging or food, "he only likes what he finds for himself" (22). More maddening, even his offers of affection are only on his terms: "The Rum Tum Tugger doesn't care for a cuddle; / But he'll leap on your lap in the middle of your sewing, / For there's nothing he enjoys like a horrible muddle" (22). Yet, all we can do is accept that Rum Tum Tugger "is a Curious Cat— / And there isn't any need for me to spout it: / For he will do / As he do do / And there's no doing anything about it!" (22). This cat's pride is that he always causes trouble.

Macavity, the mystery cat, is a master criminal. Indeed, his reputation is so great, Scotland Yard calls him the Hidden Paw:

> Macavity, Macavity, there's no one like Macavity,
> He's broken every human law, he breaks the law of gravity.
> His powers of levitation would make a fakir stare,
> And when you reach the scene of crime—*Macavity's not there*!
> You may seek him in the basement, you may look up in the air—
> But I tell you once and once again, *Macavity's not there*!
> (40; emphasis Eliot)

He is described as tall and thin, the feline equivalent of shady and shifty. His eyes are sunken in, his face creased in thought, his coat disheveled, his whiskers unkempt, his walk snake-like; when he appears to be dozing, he is really wide awake, casing the joint. In spite of his record, outwardly he's respectable, and he has never been solidly linked to a crime; not even his footprints are in the file of Scotland Yard. More than a common criminal, Macavity has been implicated in both international and commercial espionage for he is a "fiend in feline shape, a monster of depravity" (41). He is so clever and proud, "he always has an alibi, and one or two to spare" (41). Indeed, all other notorious cats "are nothing more than agents for the Cat who all the time / Just controls their operations: the Napoleon of Crime!" (42).

The high society cat, Bustopher Jones, is proud of his appearance. He is the best dressed cat in town. Wearing "his coat of fastidious black," he is a veritable Beau "Brummell of Cats; / And we're all of us proud to be nodded or bowed to / By Bustopher Jones in white spats!" (49). He frequents all the upscale clubs and is easily recognized by his well-groomed look. Food is a special delight: "When he's seen in a hurry there's probably curry / At the *Siamese*—or at the *Glutton*; / If he looks full of gloom then he's lunched at the *Tomb* / On cabbage, rice pudding and mutton" (50). Indeed, Bustopher's diet has been too rich: "It can be no surprise that under our eyes / He has grown unmistakably round. / He's a twenty-five pounder, or I am a bounder,

/ And he's putting on weight every day: / But he's so well preserved because he's observed / All his life a routine, so he'll say" (50). This stoutest of cats is a legend as he proudly parades down the Pall Mall. Eliot ends the volume by linking the pride of cats with that of people:

> You now have learned enough to see
> That Cats are much like you and me
> And other people whom we find
> Possessed of various types of mind.
> For some are sane and some are mad
> And some are good and some are bad
> And some are better, some are worse—
> But all may be described in verse. (55)

Whether it is pride of place or pride of race, pride of skill or pride of thrill, pride of dress or pride of crest, Eliot's cats are gentle satires on human pride, giving *Old Possum's* a practical yet light-hearted tone.

Pitter on Cats also offers a practical view of cats; however, rather than focusing upon the pride of individual cats, Pitter surveys the melancholy life of cats. In a sense her cat poems explore the hard daily challenges cats face; accordingly, there is a dark, gritty undercurrent throughout *On Cats*. For example, there are poems on cat "covens" where caterwauling is given a Latin dignity; on orphaned but street savvy cats; on the dangers new kitten litters face; on a neutered tomcat's final "glorification"; on the excessive human petting of cats; and on cats having to endure the ways of humans. While *On Cats* maintains vestiges of a serio-comic tone like *Old Possum's*, the recurring melancholic theme of the former volume gives it a darker edge than the latter. This darker, more realistic tone is set in the opening lines of the volume. "Quorum Porum" opens ominously: "In a dark garden, by a dreadful tree, / The Druid Toms were met. They numbered three, / Tab Tiger, Demon Black, and Ginger Hate. / Their forms were tense, their eyes full of fate" (7). In a scene reminiscent of the opening of *Macbeth* and the three witches chanting "Fair is foul, and foul is fair. / Hover through the fog and filthy air," Pitter has her three druids engage in a caterwaul challenge[9]:

> An hour of ritual silence passed: then low
> And marrow-freezing, Ginger moaned "OROW,"

Two horrid syllables of hellish lore,
Followed by deeper silence than before.
Another hour, the tabby's turn is come;
Rigid, he rapidly howls "MUM MUM MUM";
Then reassumes his silence like a pall,
Clothed in negation, a dumb oracle.
At the third hour, the black gasps out "AH BLURK!"
Like a lost soul that founders in the murk;
And the grim, ghastly, damned and direful crew
Resumes its voiceless vigilance anew. (7; caps Pitter)

The poem ends when the three "stiffly rise, and melt into the shade, / Their Sabbath over, and their demons laid" (7). Although there is something of the mock epic about this poem, in the tradition of Chaucer's "The Nun's Priest's Tale," at the same time Pitter deftly captures the ominous ethos of an evening showdown between her brooding druids.[10]

In a letter of May 8, 1947, Lewis makes playful compliments to Pitter about *On Cats*, particularly wondering about "Quorum Porum" and the Latin declension of porum: "Thank you for the *De Porum Moribus* (How does the whole declension go? Puss, Puss, Purrem, Purris, Purri, Purre, Purres, Purres, Porum, Pibus, Pibus?). A very cheerful and companionable work. I think the first piece is the best" (*CL*, 2, 776). Pitter comments:

> "I had sent Lewis a copy of my 'Pitter on Cats': he is referring to the first (and yes, much the best piece in it), 'Quorum Porum,' i.e. a meeting of cats: 'quorum' a competent number, 'porum,' genitive plural of 'puss.' Now, if declined as a boy would, in the commonest way for nouns in '-us,' this has decidedly (childishly) rude results. Those concerned for the elegance of their Latinity will be grateful to Lewis for his ingenious & graceful declension, so skillfully avoiding the pitfalls (which of course were the object of the exercise)." (Pitter Journal, fol. 48)[11]

That a cat's life is always tenuous and dangerous is the focus of "Mister The Blitzkit (For K.)."[12] In its portrayal of an orphaned kitten looking for a home, Pitter captures the youthful, but worldly wise savvy of Blitzkit: "Little Mister, six weeks old, / Hungry, frightened, dirty, cold, / Has no mother, home, nor dinner, / But he's sharp for a beginner" (9). Street-wise, Blitzkit, in hiding, surveys the humans that pass him on the street, since "from their faces he can tell / Who would treat a kitten well." He rejects a policeman ("good but gruff . . . [who] pop him in a certain van"); a nice looking matron (whose "four fat kids" would eat all the stew and "give him hell"); and then, in order, a warden, a soldier, and a sailor. At this point poor Blitzkit is at his nadir: "Cripes, he could down a bit of food. / And O hell, here comes the rain" (9).

However, before he gives in to despair, he sees the mark, a kindly looking young woman:

> In her countenance he reads
> That she will satisfy his needs.
> Food, fire, bed—he ticks them off—
> Worm-dose, mixture for his cough,
> Velvet mouse for when he plays,
> Brush and comb, and holidays
> In the countryside afar,
> Or boarded out with loving char. (10)

Certain she will "pick him up correctly / And always touch him circum-spectly," he darts out in front of her and looks up "with piteous grace." His street-smart savvy serves him well:

> Six weeks old—but what a grip
> On the art of salesmanship!
> Youth, dirt, fear, all play their part
> In the lady's feeling heart.
> A word of love, a mutual kiss,
> And he is hers, and she is his. (10)

Blitzkit's melancholic present is redeemed for a bucolic future; she takes him home, gives him warm milk, and "a nice old woolen vest." As he drifts off in peaceful sleep, he knows she will brush his fur: "And in the evening she will seal / Their love with a substantial meal, / And let him lay his clever head / Close to her own warm heart, in bed" (11).[13]

If Pitter's druid cats represent dark melancholy and Blitzkit street-wise savvy, Plainey of "The Neuter-Cat's Apotheosis" illustrates that there is still life left in old bones. Certainly he has seen better days:

Aged, thin-legged, tabby-and-white, and wise,
Poor Plainey held his tongue, and used his eyes.
Full seventeen years a hunter's life he led,
With seldom better food than broth and bread,
The heartless mess that rural England pours
On dirty plates for faithful carnivores.
And what with this, and his declining years,
He showed thin fur, stiff joints, and cankered ears. (15)

Much of his reputation rests upon the day early in his life when he "KILLED THE STOAT," yet now "as a mere yard-cat, he had his share / Of want, and cold, and wretchedness to bear" (caps Pitter). A special torment to him is the Demotic Venus, the female of the yard: "She, / Never had any sort of use for he: / Insultingly aware he was no suitor, / She cuffed his chops because he was a neuter." In addition, food, really his only comfort now, is not very good. Although he sometimes finds some "eave-scooped nestlings" in the spring, such pickings are meager and "not a bellyful." Furthermore, he distained "to eat rats and such" since "rodentophagy's a feline vice" (15). And sleep, which ought to have been another comfort, is thwarted by summer cold and "winter meant the cart-shed and its drip" (16).

However, Plainey's life is invigorated when a mean-spirited neighbor sells out:

And Kick-cat Hall, where Plainey dared not show
His clay-hued nose for fear of sudden blow,
And where conditions gave his nerves the jitters,
Became (O happy day) a nest of Pitters.
These kindly people served a charming god
Whose creed associated Cats with Cod;
Who put into their heads, when fowls they had,
That Giblets make the feline bosom glad. (16)

Plainey finds himself welcomed into this new kitchen and condescends to permit the new owners to pet and groom him from time to time. More blessings follow one Christmas when his new hostess, who is wrestling to remove dry meat from a turkey "that she does not deem a treat, / But half despises," hears his plaintive purring: "'Hard times . . . have taught me discipline; / I ask no more than some odd piece of skin" (17). So moved is his hostess that she rips off an entire leg and holds it down to Plainey. He knows what to do:

> For sudden Plainey leapt,
> And seized the trophy like a true adept;
> And who shall say whether his clutching claws
> First touched it, or his well-instructed jaws?
> One moment, with the hunter's cunning old,
> He stayed to jerk it to a better hold:
> The next, like skimming Monoplane was seen
> (With turkey-leg for wings) to scour the green. (16–17)

Retreating into his lair under the woodpile, he realizes "a neuter lifetime's frustrate love: / To have enough" (18). Even though Plainey experienced many hard-knocks in life, his encounter with grace via the Christmas turkey leg is his apotheosis; he transcends his heretofore melancholic existence by feasting on this gift of the incarnation.

If Plainey finds grace, the mother cat in "The Matron-Cat's Song" personifies one who knows how to bear trouble with a loving, yet detached resignation. The poem opens immediately after she has given birth to her latest litter:

> So once again the trouble's o'er,
>   And here I sit and sing;
> Forgetful of my paramour
>   And the pickle I was in:
> Lord, lord, it is a trying time
>   We bear when we're expecting,
> When folk reproach us for the crime
>   And frown with glance correcting. (34)

Admitting that she feared someone would kill her kittens soon after they were born, she has found an ironic sanctuary: "The surly cook, who hates all cats, / Hath here a little closet, / And here we nest among her hats— / Lord save me when she knows it!" (34). Reflecting on her litter, she smiles to herself as she thinks about the future of her "girls": "Lord, lord, to think upon the sport / Which doth await the hussies; / They'll be no better than they ought, / Nor worse than other pussies" (34–35). However, her real pride is in her boys, with one minor hesitation: "How harsh their manly pelts will be, / How stern and fixed each feature— / If they escape that cruelty / Which man doth work on nature!"[14] (35). Considering her immediate future, she resigns herself to caring for her kits. Though their voices are small, they will still demand her whole attention; more problematic, however, is that their noisy caterwaul will attract "dishonourable mention," possibly leading to their discovery and unhappy end. She ends her melancholic musings by noting: "But then, alas, I shall not care / How flighty they may be, / For ere they're grown I'll have to bear / Another four, or three" (35). The matron cat's practical wisdom and seasoned experience speak to all who find a loving but detached resignation the best way to plow through life's stony fields; that is, she resolves to do what she can for her kittens because she loves them, but she will not get bogged down trying to manage things beyond her control.

If Eliot's cats are light-hearted and Pitter's melancholic, Dorothy L. Sayers' are selfish: they seek comfort and soul's ease. "War Cat," her first published cat poem, is an imaginary dialogue between a tender-hearted mistress and her little cat who has been doing his part during the war-time difficulties of London.[15] The mistress begins with an apology to her underfed cat; given the scarcity caused by the war, table scraps don't exist: "I am sorry, my little cat, I am sorry— / If I had it, you should have it; / but there's a war on" (lines 1–3). She goes on to note that even humans are eating poorly these days; all that's left "is nothing for you / but cat's biscuit/ and those remnants of yesterday's ham" (11–13). Her cat mews back reproachfully:

> "Mistress it is not nice;
> the ham is very salt
> and the cat-biscuit very dull,
> I sniffed at it, and the smell was not enticing.
> Do you not love me any more?
> Mistress, I do my best for the war-effort;
> I killed four mice last week,
> Yesterday I caught a young stoat,
> you stroked and praised me,
> you called me a clever cat.
> What have I done to offend you?
> I am industrious, I earn my keep;
> I am not like the parrot, who sits there

using bad language and devouring
parrot-seed at eight-and-sixpence a pound
without working for it."[16] (24–34)

Next the cat complains of his mistress's sense of justice and charity, recalling similar arguments legions of humans have had through the ages with their resident deity. When the cat realizes that reason will not alter his mistress's will, he tries to evoke her emotion and pity, rubbing himself against her legs and noting that his ribs "are rubbing together / for lack of food" (43–44). Again he explains his inability to eat the meal she has proffered him: "I cannot eat this— / my soul revolts at the sight of it. / I have tried, believe me, / but it was like ashes in my mouth" (46–49). In the end, the cat accuses his mistress of having removed her favor from him, of shutting up her "bowels of compassion," and of condemning him to die "of starvation / and a broken heart" (54–55).

The mistress defends herself, pointing out that everyone is suffering the same kinds of deprivations. She even says he should count himself lucky compared to other cats in Europe: "If you were a little Greek cat, / or a little Polish cat, / there would be nothing for you at all, not even cat-food: / indeed you would be lucky / if you were not eaten yourself" (59–64). Then she adds that fishermen have gone to great lengths to help manufacture the cat-biscuit he so thoroughly rejects, and that there is simply no remedy. Indeed, she becomes irked by his ingratitude and decides to give away his meal: "If you will not be comforted / we will put the contents of your saucer / into the chicken-bowl— there! / all gone! nasty old cat-food— / The hens, I dare say, / will be grateful for it" (74–79). Yet, even she relents a bit and promises her crying cat she will try to drop by the butcher's shop to see if there are any scraps.

However, by the time she puts on her shoes and hat and takes up her shopping bag, she finds her cat on the table and the chicken-bowl licked clean. When she realizes this, she explodes:

Hell-cat, Hitler cat, human,
all-too-human cat,
cat corrupt, infected,
instinct with original sin,
cat of a fallen and perverse creation,
hypocrite with the innocent and limpid eyes—
is nothing desirable

till somebody else desires it?
is anything and everything attractive
so long as it is got by stealing?
Furtive and squalid cat,
green glance, squinted over a cringing shoulder,
streaking hurriedly out of the back door
in expectation of judgment,
your manners and morals are perfectly abhorrent to me,
you dirty little thief and liar. (95–110)

Still, the tender-hearted mistress cannot resist his "pretty, wheedling ways, / (not to mention the four mice and the immature stoat)" (113–14). In the end, finding she already has her hat on, she decides to go the butcher, holding out the hope some little tasty morsel may be found for her deceitful yet charming cat. The theme of comfort, particularly tasty food, runs through all Sayers' cat poems, so the feline of "War Cat" becomes an archetypal figure. The world may be falling apart, but just get him good grub; perhaps the collapse of civilization as we know it may not be so bad if tempered by a full stomach.

"From the *Catalects of Pussius Catus II*" is an amusing parody on the wisdom of the philosopher cat, Pussius Catus, given on the occasion of his Christmas blessing.[17] Pussius' poem is actually a homily offering instruction on why the life of a cat is superior to that of a pig: "This is our yard, and in it stands Our Mistress (on hind legs with hands) / The other one (the quadruped) was Fatima, but now she's dead."[18] Pussius, so sure of himself that he views his mistress as just another kind of cat, moralizes that when Fatima first arrived "she was not large / But Lord, how she did feed and feed, a very prodigy of greed. / She was, in short, a perfect Pig, and so when she got very big / A lorry came and she was taken to where pigs vanish into bacon." The self-assurance of Pussius concludes the poem:

Hear Pussius Catus moralise: to be a pig is most unwise.
Better by far to be a cat who if he likes can put on fat
And grow majestic and immense regardless of the consequence,
Since tho' he bulge with fish and meat he never will be fit to eat.
So because Pussies and Mankind are so enlightened as to find
Each other quite uneatable, Puss can afford to wish you well,
Hoping your Christmas may be good and beautiful with glorious food!

Sayers' humor via Pussius is delightful as she intimates the conspiratorial relationship assumed but almost never spoken (can it ever be?) between humans and cats. It is within this comfortable conspiracy that Pussius so self-confidently luxuriates. Of course, he is blind to his own moralism, because, while it is unwise, perhaps even a sin, for a pig to overeat, Pussius pontificates that it is just fine to become a "fat cat." "From the *Catalects of Pussius Catus II*" is a didactic sermon in the best tradition of self-serving cats everywhere.

A Cat's Christmas Carol has nothing to do with Dickens' story of Scrooge and Tiny Tim.[19] Instead, it is a cat's eye view on the night of Christ's birth, and, like most of Sayers' cat poems, food is an important topic:

> The Twelve days of Christmas are here,
> The best in the whole of the year,
> With turkey and meat
> For my masters to eat,
> And with joy and with giblets for me,
>   For me,
> With joy and with giblets for me!

As we move through the poem it becomes clear this Palestinian cat connects the mysterious events she sings about with some larger universal meaning she cannot quite fathom. However, of one thing she is certain: all these mysterious events combine to insure she will receive the promise of the poem's refrain: "And with joy and with giblets for me, / For me, / With joy and with giblets for me!" Whether it is arrival of "an angel exceedingly bright," or "The Shepherds who heard him . . . / And ran at the top of their speed / With pipe and with horn / To salute the New-Born," or "The Magi . . . / Very grand in their robes and their crowns, / With a gift of great worth / For the King of the Earth," the Palestinian cat is certain of this comfortable thought: "And with joy and with giblets for me, / For me, / With joy and with giblets for me!"

Sayers' retelling of the Christmas story focuses in the end on the birth of Christ as the cat sings: "The Baby who lay in the stall / Was delighted to welcome them all; / He received them with grace / And a smile on His face." Yet this incredible act of God's love—God becoming man, the Incarnation of the infinite to save the finite—is imperceptible to the Palestinian cat:

All praise to His bountiful name!
I do not quite know why He came;
But I'm sure this is true—
It had something to do
With joy and with giblets for me,

For me,

With joy and with giblets for me!

Like Pussius Catus, the Palestinian cat can never quite get out of herself. Even her praise to "His bountiful name" resonates with allusions to a fully stocked dish of her favorite dainties, especially, it would seem, giblets. Perhaps Sayers is gently parodying the human tendency to miss the import of great events, particularly God's improbable entry in human history, because of our devotion to personal agendas and self-fulfillment. Regardless, Sayers' selfish cats are interesting counterpoints to Eliot's proud ones and Pitter's brooding ones.

Before closing this look at these literary cats, it is worth noting that all three authors received various notes from friends, and in some cases from each other, regarding their poems on cats. For instance, Sayers sent Pitter a copy of her cat poem, *Aeneas at the Court of Dido* (1945),[20] with the enclosed note: "Dear Miss Pitter, I hope the enclosed may give you a few moments of entertainment in exchange for the vast pleasure I have had from your book of verses *On Cats*" (June 9, 1947; *HU*, 158). Later that same year Sayers sent Pitter a copy of her *A Cat's Christmas Carol* as a private 1947 Christmas card and enclosed the following note: "I meant to send this in time for your cats to sing at Christmas, but had momentarily mislaid your address. But it may be suitably sung till Twelfth Day! With all good wishes for 1948" (158). Lord David Cecil writes Pitter on June 23, 1947, about *On Cats*: "I have never thanked you for your book of cat poems. It was very bad of me, because I simply loved them. Your cats are much more genial and full-blooded and comfortable than [T. S.] Eliot's which always seem to me to suffer from a touch of New England primness. Yours have a nice Dickensian vitality. I am so pleased to be acquainted with them" (158–59).[21] Lewis, probably offering a comment on Eliot's *Old Possum's*, writes Pitter: "I think just as you do about the Anglo-Cats. Their prevailing quality is the very non-catholic one of disobedience. They will obey neither our own book nor Rome" (Feb. 8, 1947; *CL*, 2, 762).[22]

In spite of my genuine respect for Eliot, Pitter, and Sayers, as well as Lewis and Lord David Cecil, I remain nonplussed when it comes to cats. Even their literary cats don't cause me to warm up to felines in general. Sadly, the fascination people have with cats is a puzzle to me. What is so special about cats? It escapes me![23]

Chapter 10 Notes

1. A version of this essay first appeared in *SEVEN: An Anglo-American Literary Review* 18 (2001): 25–45.

2. I must not begrudge Molly some praise. She survived more than five years the busy road that fronts our house; her predecessors never managed a year.

3. T. S. Eliot says something similar in "The Ad-dressing of Cats" from *Old Possum's Book of Practical Cats* (London: Faber and Faber, 1939): "Now Dogs pretend they like to fight; / They often bark, more seldom bite; / But yet a Dog is, on the whole, / What you would call a simple soul" (55); subsequent references in the text.

4. Also, in other letters Joy Davidman and Lewis include other references to cats. On June 6, 1958, Joy writes: "Is your pet a cat or dog? I've found that cats stand these changes and separations pretty well—one of mine, when I was ill, took possession of a new home and mistress and had them completely under his thumb in a week. (If one can speak of a cat's thumb?)" (*CL*, 3, 952). On February 24, 1961, Lewis writes: "I hope your vet is not a charlatan? Psychological diagnoses even about human patients seem to me pretty phoney. They must be even phonier when applied to animals. You can't put a cat on a couch and make it tell you its dreams or produce words by 'free association.' Also, I have a great respect for cats—they are very shrewd people and would probably see through the analyst a good deal better than he'd see through them" (1243). Still later on July 3, 1962, he adds: "We are both ruled by cats. Joy's Siamese—my 'stepcat' as I call her—is the most terribly conversational animal I ever knew. She talks all the time and wants doors and windows to be opened for her 1000 times an hour" (1355–56).

5. Eliot's *Old Possum's Book of Practical Cats* is certainly the best known of these volumes as a result of the long running stage production, *Cats*. Seven of the fifteen poems in *Old Possum's* are written in rhyming couplets (one of these is in triplets): "The Old Gumbie Cat," "Growltiger's Last Stand," "Mungojerrie and Rumpelteazer," "The Pekes and the Pollicles" (in triplets), "Macavity: The Mystery Cat," "Gus: The Theatre Cat," and "The Ad-dressing of Cats." Four are in *ababcdcd*: "The Naming of Cats," "The Song of the Jellicles," "Old Deuteronomy," and "Cat Morgan Introduces Himself." Two are in *waxa ybzb* (actually these can be read as two longer lines of rhyming couplets): "Bustopher Jones: The Cat about Town" and "Skimblehanks: The Railway Cat." Two follow an irregular pattern of rhyme: "The Rum Tum Tugger" and "Mr. Mistoffelees." The "sing-song" nature of the poems is constant regardless of his use of tetrameter, hexameter, heptameter, and octameter. Interestingly, Eliot shuns pentameter.

6. *Pitter on Cats* (London: Cresset Press, 1946) relies primarily on tetrameter and pentameter; occasionally she alternates lines of trimeter and tetrameter (or these can be read as lines of heptameter with internal rhyme) or tetrameter and pentameter. The major exception is "Musa Translated" written in unrhymed hexameters and heptameters. Just as in *Old Possum's*, most of the poems (eight of thirteen) in *On Cats* are written in rhyming couplets (three are in heroic couplets): "Quorum Porum," "Mister the Blitzkit," "The Neuter-Cat's Apotheosis" (heroic couplets), Three Cheers for the Black, White and Blue," "The

Safety-Valve" (heroic couplets), "Granny-Winks," "The Celebrated "Cat Purser O'Hara," and "The Kitten's Ecologue" (heroic couplets). Two are in *ababcc*: "The Talking Family" and "The Spartan Boy." Two are in *abab cdcd*: "The Commensals" and "The Matron-Cat's Song." One is unrhymed: "Musa Translated"; subsequent references in the text.

7. Sayers' "War Cat" is of irregular meter and does not rhyme. *A Cat's Christmas Carol* employs stanzas rhyming *aabbccc*. The characteristic pattern of the stanzas is as follows: two lines of tetrameter followed by two lines of trimeter (one could force a reading of these lines as a single line of pentameter with internal rhyme); the last three lines are the refrain "And with joy and with giblets for me, / For me, / With joy and with giblets for me!" "From the *Catalects of Pussius Catus II*" is thirteen octameter lines employing internal rhyme; in effect, then, it reads like rhyming tetrameter couplets. Additional Sayers' "cat poems" include: *Aeneas at the Court of Dido* (1945), "Cousin Parker's Cat's Christmas Card" and "From the *Catalects of Pussius Catus I*"(1948), "Torquato Tasso to the Cats of St. Anne's (a translation; 1952), and "For Timothy, in the Coinherence" (1973). For more information on her poetry, see *The Poetry of Dorothy L. Sayers*, ed. Ralph E. Hone (Trowbridge, Wiltshire: The Dorothy L. Sayers Society, 1996).

8. The secret name could be an indirect allusion to a similar concept in Revelation. For instance, Revelation 2:17 says: "He who has an ear, let him hear what the Spirit says to the churches. To him who overcomes, to him I will give some of the hidden manna, and I will give him a white stone, and a new name written on the stone which no one knows but he who receives it" (NAS). Also, Revelation 19:12 says: "And His eyes are a flame of fire, and upon His head are many diadems; and He has a name written upon Him which no one knows except Himself" (NAS).

9. A later poem in the volume, "Mister The Blitzkit (For K.)" also shares allusions to *Macbeth* since it begins: "Double, double, toil and trouble, / Crumps and bumps and lumps of rubble." This poem is discussed below.

10. This poem has also elicited a number of other favorable reactions from her readers. For example, J. A. Elliot sent Pitter the following letter:

Dear Miss Pitter,

I write to tell you that my family and I have enjoyed "Quorum Porum" very much. We read it first in *Lilliput*, and it is a fact, incredible as you may think it, that my son, who is fifteen, has a copy in his pocketbook. Or, to be correct, he *had* a copy. I got your Cresset Press volume recently and was deeply aggrieved to find "Quorum Porum" a bit different. My boy's school just had a Founder's Day, and I visited him there. Among other things I told him about this. I think you would have enjoyed the resulting discussion. It was decidedly like the intemperate fury of two Shakespeareans on discovering some crime in a new edition, or, at any rate, some departure from tradition. *Someone* had been tampering with the Original Text. So my son produced the First Edition from his pocketbook and we studied it. We prefer "save *for* the involuntary caudal thrill" to the same line without the word "for." We prefer this line to come *after* "the horror was that they should sit so still," not before it. And lastly, we prefer "wearing negation like an oracle" to the Cresset volume line.

I should say that I have enjoyed the Cresset volume enormously. I think the rest of it is just as good as "Quorum Porum." Especially "Musa Translated." Therefore, I thank you on behalf of this family for the fun we have had from learning Q. P. and for the fun we are going to have with your last volume. (July 2, 1947; *HU*, 298 and emphasis Elliot)

11. Pitter's nephew, Mark Pitter, a classics teacher at Oakham School and her literary executor, offered a critique of Lewis's declension in a letter to his aunt of Feb. 29(?), 1982:

My dear Aunt Ruth,

    If you are going to start with a noun whose nominative singular ends in 'us(s)', you have a choice of three: a) 2nd decl. masc. noun in us, as you state . . . , b) 3rd decl. neuter in us, -eris . . . and this won't suit Quorum Porum, because I wager that none of the feline hierophants at that assembly were neuters, 3) 4th decl. masc. or fem. nouns in ?s, ūs . . . . Pace C. S. Lewis, the 5th decl. won't work for puss, because its nominative singular ends invariably in es, which banjaxes the whole shooting match, for it gives us pes, which means 'foot,' and which anyway is 3rd declension, which is quite enough to confuse allcomers . . . . I reckon to vote with the indolent schoolboy and adopt the 2nd declension, ruderies included. Ruderies of this sort are innocent enough, anyway. I think you're right in saying that C. S. Lewis thus avoided the object of the exercise: he should have read more Aristophanes, the perfect example of the Rude being transcendentally innocent. (*HU*, 298–99)

12. K. was shorthand for Pitter's business partner and housemate, Kathleen O'Hara.

13. In a letter of September 22, 1949, Lewis recalls a visit to Pitter that may suggest the "true" character of the cat who inspired this poem: "You gave us a lovely day. A fine hazy air of cornucopia ('beyond all rule or arte, enormous bliss') hangs over it . . . . My only regret is that my acquaintance with the *Blitzekatze* didn't prosper as I shd. have wished. My duty to your colleague [Kathleen O'Hara]; it was a great pleasure to meet her" (*CL*, 2, 982). Pitter said about this cat: "The Blitzekatze was our cat, which we had found in the ruins after an air-raid" (Sept. 22, 1949; Pitter Journal, fol. 81).

14. An obvious reference to neutering.

15. First published in *Time and Tide* 24 (Dec. 4, 1943): 994. Reprinted in *The Poetry of Dorothy L. Sayers*, 43.

16. Another Sayers' cat poem, "Pussydise Lost," portrays a miffed cat; this time the cat is bewildered by an unfathomable theological conundrum:

> I bought my gods a sacrifice—
> A little creeping mouse:
> They said: "A cat that catches mice
> Does credit to the house."
>
> Next day I sacrificed a bird—
> A noble singing thrush:
> The gods let fly an angry word,
> Likewise a scrubbing brush.
>
> Why are the trees of paradise
> Set round with prohibitions?
> The gods, mysterious and all-wise
> Impose these strange conditions. (*Everybody's Weekly*, June 7, 1952)

While Sayers' tone here is whimsical, there is no mistaking the connection she suggests between how this cat's struggle to understand the dark ways of her masters is akin to human efforts to plumb the divine will. In addition, the poem makes obvious allusion to the theme of Milton's *Paradise Lost*: "To justify the ways of God to men."

17. Her "From the *Catalects of Pussius Catus I*" offers a similar comic effect:

> I often think that men would be
> More restful if they were like me;
> If all the food they ever ate
> Were handed to them on a plate,

If clothing sprouted from their skins,
And if they did not shave their chins,
But just could take things as they find them,
And need not shut the door behind them. (copy available in the Marion E.
Wade Center)

18. As this poem was privately printed, copies of it may only be viewed at the Bodleian Library or at the Marion E. Wade Center.

19. Privately printed; copies of it may only be viewed at the Bodleian Library or at the Marion E. Wade Center.

20. For the complete text of the poem, see *The Poetry of Dorothy L. Sayers*, 145–48. Written in iambic tetrameter quatrains of alternate rhyme, this has been called "one of [Sayers'] most beautifully crafted poems." With its obvious allusions to Virgil's *Aeneid* (Books III and IV), Dante's *Inferno* (Canto II, 32; IV, 122; and XXVI, 93), and the ravages of World War II Europe, the poem is a *tour de force*, as it relates the story of a "lean, hard-bitten Tom"/Aeneas who is newly landed on English soil, his equivalent of Carthage. Utilizing a tone muted but reminiscent of that of "War Cat" and "Pussydise Lost," Tom/Aeneas chronicles his struggles, wondering "what fierce wrath could urge / Heaven, or for what obscure offence, / Five years to vex us with the scourge / Of famine, fear, and pestilence." Allusions to how falling bombs devastated the cat population of his former land so that "huge starving hordes of mice and rats" over-ran his country are followed by the tale of his sojourn by sail to the shores of England. True to Virgil's account, the cat Queen/Dido (though motivated less by lust than by admiration), invites Tom/Aeneas to stay with her: "We too have seen the vengeful brand / Strike from the sky; but yet we live / Favoured of Heaven, and what our land / Can offer you, we freely give." The poem ends with Tom/Aeneas musing on a theological puzzle worthy of "Pussydise Lost":

Cat's eyes may not avail
 To pierce the awful pantry-door
Where Justice in her iron scale
 Weighs out the meed of less and more.

Enough that some dark deed of shame
 By cats has set all Heaven at odds;
For these prodigious woes proclaim
 That there is war among the gods.

Paralleling the human propensity to associate pain and suffering with God's wrath aroused because of human sin, Tom/Aeneas attributes the existential dilemma of suffering cats to feline deeds of darkness that have inflamed the human gods against them.

21. Pitter and Eliot used to attend Chelsea Old Church in London, often taking communion at the same time. After her *A Trophy of Arms* (London: Cresset Press,1936) won the Hawthornden Prize for Poetry in 1937, Pitter gives Eliot the news while they stand together in a bus queue; he graciously replies "And you much deserve it." Cited in Peter Dickinson, "Ruth Pitter," *The Canadian C. S. Lewis Journal* 79 (Summer 1992): 1–3.

22. Still another Sayers' cat poem is "For Timothy, in the Coinherence" (1973). Written in memory of a cat belonging to Sayers' long-time friend, Muriel St. Clare Byrne, it is a prayer hoping for the resurrection of Timothy and makes allusions to Charles Williams (particularly the last word in the title), Dante (the epigraph is from *Paradiso*, Canto XXVIII, 129), and Genesis 1–3 and 6–9 (the Garden of Eden and the Ark). The poem is available in *The Poetry of Dorothy L. Sayers*, 157–158.

23. After I finished this essay, I left it unattended on my desk. Several days later I noticed the pages shuffled and pawed about. As I examined them more closely, I discovered the following epitaph scratched across the bottom of the last page. While the name of the author cannot be confirmed, the note itself has given me pause: "Sigh. I often wonder if he has any brain at all. He just doesn't get it! . . . . Yet, he insures that each day my plate is filled 'with joy and with giblets for me, / For me, / With joy and with giblets for me!'"

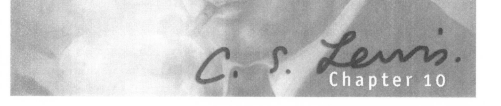

Devil to Devil: John Milton, C. S. Lewis, and Screwtape[1]

Before C. S. Lewis was ten years old, he wrote in his diary: "I read *Paradise Lost,* reflections there-on" (March 5, 1908).[2] While it is unclear how much of John Milton's masterpiece he actually read and understood at this young age, this entry marks Lewis's early affection and admiration for Milton's verse. Furthermore, this entry foreshadows the pervasive presence of poetry in Lewis's literary maturation. For instance, Lewis's correspondence with Arthur Greeves is an amazing record of his all-consuming love of poetry, particularly Milton. Lewis tells Greeves that "Comus" is "an absolute dream of delight" (September 27, 1916; *CL*, 1, 225), and that "it is agreed to be one of the most perfect things in English poetry" (August 4, 1917; 332). His praise of *Paradise Lost* is more frequent and sustained. For instance, he writes Greeves after reading the first two books of *Paradise Lost* that "[I] really love Milton every time I come back to him" (February 7, 1917; 274). A month later he adds: "I have finished 'Paradise Lost' again, enjoying it even more than before . . . . In Milton is everything you get everywhere else, only better. He is as voluptuous as Keats, as romantic as Morris, as grand as Wagner, as weird as Poe, and a better lover of nature than even the Brontes" (March 6, 1917; 290). To another friend he says: "To see Milton's real greatness one need but notice the fresh joy and reality of his Eden . . . [as compared to] the over-ripe stanzas which describe [Spenser's] garden of Acasia" (August 14,

1920; 504). Furthermore, dozens of his letters to various correspondents contain lines from *Paradise Lost* that Lewis uses to illustrate points or ideas he is discussing. In short, it is no exaggeration to say that the greatest influence on Lewis's poetic maturation and development was Milton; further, while Lewis came to fall under the sway of many other great writers, I believe Milton is the greatest single literary influence on the work of Lewis.[3] Accordingly, it is no surprise to find that Lewis's *The Screwtape Letters* owes a debt to Milton, especially *Paradise Lost* (hereafter *PL*). In what follows I will briefly note Milton's influence on selected early works of Lewis and use this as a springboard to explore a number of specific Miltonic influences on *The Screwtape Letters*.

The first indications of Milton's pervasive influence appear in *Spirits in Bondage* (hereafter *SB*). Lewis's initial title for this book was *Spirits in Prison*, but when his father pointed out that a book by this title had already been published by Richard Hitchens, Lewis took the title from a passage in Book I of *PL*. Toward the end of Book I Satan prefaces his call for a council of the fallen angels to discuss their strategy against God by saying: "For this Infernal Pit shall never hold / Celestial Spirits in Bondage, nor th' Abyss / Long under darkness cover."[4] Furthermore, when he explains the sub-title of *SB*, "A cycle of lyrical poems," Lewis writes his father:

> The sub-title "A cycle of lyrical poems" was not given without a reason: the reason is that the book is not a collection of really independent pieces, but the working out, loosely of course and with digressions, of a general idea . . . . To call it a cycle is to prepare the reader for this plan and to induce him to follow the order of the poems as I have put them . . . . Of course one could dispense with a sub-title altogether, but I rather approve of the old practice by which a book gives some account of itself—as *Paradise Lost*—*a heroic poem in twelve books*—*The Pilgrim's Progress*—*being an account of his journey from this world to the next,* (September 18, 1918; *CL*, 1, 399–400 and emphasis Lewis)

Thus in his conception of *SB*, Lewis uses *PL* as an artistic point of departure.

Another indication of Milton's influence upon Lewis is the poem "Milton Read Again (in Surrey)" which appears in *SB*. Written as a panegyric in the style of John Keats' "On First Looking into Chapman's Homer" and William Wordsworth's "London, 1802" (another poem praising Milton), "Milton Read

Again" is a tribute to Milton. Though it is impossible to date this poem precisely, it was likely written between 1914–1917 while Lewis was studying with his great teacher, W. T. Kirkpatrick, in Surrey, south of London. Lewis's delight at being sent to study with the "Great Knock" (as Kirkpatrick was affectionately called by Lewis and his father) and his withdrawal from Malvern College and all he detested there creates the context for this poem. In particular, Lewis appears to be celebrating his recent re-reading of *PL*: "Three golden months while summer on us stole / I have read your joyful tale another time, / Breathing more freely in that larger clime / And learning wiselier to deserve the whole" (*SB*, 32). He calls Milton his Master, and thanks him for guiding him and showing him "treasures rare"; before he read Milton he was unable to see the natural beauties of the Surrey countryside. Now, however, he compares his reading of Milton to one who returns to walk a familiar wood, suddenly overcome with "the weird spirit of unexplained delight, / New mystery in every shady place, / In every whispering tree a nameless grace, / New rapture on the windy seaward height." Here, Lewis credits Milton with guiding him to the treasures of poetry, opening his eyes to a rich imagination where before his has been barren.[5]

Skipping ahead more than twenty years, we learn that when Lewis writes his brother Warren a letter on July 20, 1940 about his initial conception of *The Screwtape Letters* (hereafter *SL*), he refers to Milton. He begins by saying that he and a friend had recently heard Hitler speaking on the radio:

> I don't know if I'm weaker than other people: but it is a positive revelation to me how *while the speech lasts* it is impossible not to waver just a little. I should be useless as a schoolmaster or a policeman. Statements which I *know* to be untrue all but convince me, at any rate for the moment, if only the man says them unflinchingly. The same weakness is why I am a slow examiner: if a candidate with a bold, mature handwriting attributed *Paradise Lost* to Wordsworth, I shd. feel a tendency to go and look it up for fear he might be right after all. (*CL*, 2, 425; emphasis Lewis)

When the letter continues, Lewis explains the genesis of *SL*; in addition, he offers an example of how one might fall under the sway of a powerful speaker:

> I have been to Church for the first time for many weeks owing to the illness . . . . Before the service was over—one cd. wish these

things came more seasonably—I was struck by an idea for a book wh. I think might be both useful and entertaining. It wd. be called *As one Devil to Another* and would consist of letters from an elderly retired devil to a young devil who has just started work on his first "patient." The idea wd. be to give all the psychology of temptation from the *other* point of view. e.g. "About undermining his faith in prayer, I don't think you need have any difficulty with his intellect, provided you never say the wrong thing at the wrong moment. After all, the Enemy will either answer his prayers or not. If he does *not*, then that's simple—it shows prayers are not good. If he *does*—I've always found that, oddly enough, this can be just as easily utilized. It needs only a word from you to make him believe that the very fact of feeling more patient after he's prayed for patience will be taken as a proof that prayer is a kind of self hypnosis." (426–27; emphasis Lewis)

This powerful voice eventually becomes Screwtape, and a reading of *SL* reveals that, if nothing else, Screwtape evolved into an unflinching, compelling speaker, capable of swaying toward evil even the sturdiest saint.

Moreover, it is worth noting that Screwtape is a direct literary descendant of Milton's Satan, not to mention the real-life Hitler. Accordingly, I believe the influence of Milton's *PL* is transparent in *SL*. For instance, both works were written or conceived during times of war: for Milton it was the turmoil of 1640–1660 when the Parliament led a rebellion culminating in the execution of Charles I in 1649 and the establishment of Oliver Cromwell's government, while for Lewis it was 1930–1939 and the early years of World War II. War, by the way, is a key characteristic of the literary epic, the literary genre of *PL*, and all of Screwtape's letters are written under the shadow of the "European" war. In *PL* Milton explores imaginatively how a war in heaven might have occurred; indeed, he devotes three books, almost one quarter of *PL*, to Satan's rebellion and the subsequent war in heaven. In *SL* Lewis portrays Screwtape and his colleagues in a perpetual dogfight with the Enemy (God) and the forces of heaven. In *PL* Milton shows that the war in heaven was one between Michael and Satan, not God and Satan. In fact, in Book VI Milton underscores this point by showing that God is no more threatened by Satan's rebellion than an elephant is threatened by a gnat; he leaves it to Michael to lead the legions of angels against Satan and the rebel angels. This same point is reinforced in the preface to *SL* when Lewis writes: "Satan, the leader or dictator of devils, is the opposite, not of God, but of Michael."[6]

While the pervading war metaphor is one transparent link between *PL* and *SL*, a second one concerns the nature of the devils in each work. For example, in *PL* Satan argues that he is self-created. In Book V Satan is rebuked for his rebellion by the angel Abdiel; in part Abdiel chastises Satan for his lack of gratitude toward the God who condescended to create him and all things: "As by his Word the mighty Father made / All things, ev'n thee, and all the Spirits of Heav'n / By him created in thir bright degrees" (lines 836–38). Satan scorns Abdiel's argument and offers one worthy of an offended child:

> That we were form'd then say'st thou? And the work
> Of secondary hands, by task transferr'd
> From Father to his Son? strange point and new!
> Doctrine which we would know whence learnt: who saw
> When this creation was? remember'st thou
> Thy making, while the Maker gave thee being?
> We know no time when we were not as now;
> Know none before us, self-begot, self-rais'd
> By our own quick'ning power. (853–61)

In effect, Milton's Satan makes the nonsense argument that since he cannot remember when God formed him, that is proof he is self-created.

Lewis considers this point in the preface to *SL*: "The commonest question is whether I really 'believe' in the Devil. Now, if by 'the Devil' you mean a power opposite to God and, like God, self-existent from all eternity, the answer is certainly No. There is no uncreated being except God. God has no opposite" (vii). Furthermore, in Lewis's *A Preface to Paradise Lost*, written in 1942 only a year or so after *SL*, Lewis analyzes Satan's argument this way:

> Now, of course, the property of a self-existent being is that it can understand its own existence; it is *causa sui*. The quality of a created being is that it just finds itself existing, it knows not how nor why. Yet at the same time, if a creature is silly enough to try to prove that it was not created, what is more natural than for it to say, "Well, I wasn't there to see it being done"? Yet what more futile, since in thus admitting ignorance of its own beginnings it proves that those beginnings

lay outside itself? Satan falls instantly into this trap . . . as indeed he cannot help doing—and produces as proof of his self-existence what is really its disproof.[7]

Milton's Satan is as self-deceived on the matter of his origin as he is on a host of others issues, including that he is as wise, intelligent, resourceful, just, and fair-minded as God.

Another influence of *PL* upon *SL* with regard to the nature of the devils concerns the idea that the fallen angels fell through an abuse of their free wills and that, accordingly, their natures are depraved. While there are multiple examples of this in *PL*, perhaps the best place to see this is at the beginning of Book II where the fallen angels, banished to hell, hold a council at their newly created palace, *Pandemonium*. Called by Satan, the council debates the issue of what they should do to oppose God now that they have been expelled from heaven. Four fallen angels speak. Moloch argues for open war. Belial argues for inactivity, suggesting if they stay quiet then perhaps God's wrath against them will lessen. Mammon claims they can take the substance of hell and create an imitation of heaven—they can make a heaven of hell. Beelzebub, Satan's mouthpiece, scorns all these plans and directs their focus on the newly created world inhabited by "some new Race call'd Man"; he argues they should

> Seduce them to our Party, that thir God
> May prove thir foe, and with repenting hand
> Abolish his own works. This would surpass
> Common revenge, and interrupt his joy
> In our Confusion, and our Joy upraise
> In his disturbance; when his darling Sons
> Hurl'd headlong to partake with us, shall curse
> Thir frail Original, and faded bliss,
> Faded so soon. Advise if this be worth
> Attempting, or to sit in darkness here
> Hatching vain Empires. (368–78)

Satan, via Beelzebub, manipulates the council in such a way as to insure that his will is followed; in effect, he abuses their already abused wills in pursuit of his political agenda. Later, Milton's God in Book III comments on the different way in which he will treat the fallen angels vs. fallen man: "[The fallen angels] by their own suggestion fell, / Self-tempted, self-depraved: Man falls deceiv'd / By th' other first: Man therefore shall find grace, / The other none" (129–32). That is, Milton's God reserves a harsher punishment for the fallen angels because they abused their own wills, while he promises grace to human beings since their wills are to be deceived by the fallen angels.

In the preface to *SL* Lewis considers the same point: "The proper question is whether I believe in devils. I do. That is to say, I believe in angels, and I believe that some of these, by the abuse of their free will, have become enemies to God and, as a corollary, to us. These we may call devils. They do not differ in nature from good angels, but their nature is depraved. *Devil* is the opposite of *angel* only as Bad Man is the opposite of Good Man" (vii; emphasis Lewis). Throughout *SL* Lewis offers us numerous opportunities to see the results of the abuse of free will in Screwtape, and by allusion, in his colleagues Glubose, Scabtree, Triptweese, and Toadpipe. Perhaps the most obvious example of this is the repeated difficulty of Screwtape and the forces of hell to understand what motivates God to "love" (a word Screwtape can hardly get out of his mouth) humans. At one point Screwtape even has to backtrack and apologize for using the word:

> The truth is, I slipped by mere carelessness into saying that the Enemy really loves the humans. That, of course, is an impossibility. He is one being; they are distinct from Him. Their good cannot be His. All His talk about Love must be a disguise for something else—He must have some *real* motive for creating them and taking so much trouble about them. The reason one comes to talk as if He really had this impossible Love is our utter failure to find out that real motive . . . . Members of His faction have frequently admitted that if ever we came to understand what He means by Love, the war would be over and we should reenter Heaven. And there lies the great task. We know that He cannot really love: nobody can; it doesn't make sense. If we could only find out what He is *really* up to! (96–98; emphasis Lewis)

Screwtape's refusal to comprehend God's love is an abuse of his free will. That is, there actually is no intellectual barrier to Screwtape's understanding the idea of God's love; indeed, as this passage shows, he has already "slipped into" using such language. The real reason Screwtape and the other devils flatly reject the idea of God's love is that to do otherwise would violate their independence from God. To accept God's love would mean bringing their wills in accordance with his. This they willfully choose not to do. As Luther put it, the opposite of belief is not unbelief; it is self-sufficiency. Screwtape and the other devils choose by an act of their wills to live independently from God; they want nothing to do with him, relying instead upon their own wits and stratagems. Although they would never admit this, they are cosmic orphans, intentionally separating themselves from God. Indeed, they are allergic to God. They willfully choose to live outside his grace, mercy, and love. They cannot understand what motivates God's love because they choose by an act of their wills not to come under the covering of his loving concern.[8]

Before leaving the matter of the devils in *PL* and *SL*, we should note Lewis's argument in the preface to *SL* when he says that literature's best devils are Dante's, not Milton's: "[Dante's] devils . . . in their rage, spite, and obscenity, are far more like what the reality must be than anything in Milton. Milton's devils, by their grandeur and high poetry, have done great harm" (ix). What Lewis means here is that Milton's creative genius caused him to create in his fallen angels creatures so seemingly noble that, in spite of their rebellion against God, some readers actually end up admiring them. William Blake, the early English Romantic poet, put it this way: "The reason Milton wrote in fetters when he wrote of Angels & God, and at liberty when of Devils & Hell, is because he was a true Poet and of the Devil's party without knowing it."[9]

Regardless, and Lewis's claim notwithstanding, I suggest Screwtape and his colleagues have more affinities with Milton's fallen angels than Dante's devils. While Lewis's devils lack the majesty and grandeur of Milton's fallen angels, they are more than Dante's cardboard characters. Dante's devils are bogeymen; scary enough it is true, but flat and one-dimensional. On the other hand, Milton's fallen angels muster the power of poetry and rhetoric; they are advertising kingpins, television and newspaper reporters, university professors, or master politicians. They steal past our defenses and slide quietly into ours wills; they blind us to what they are doing, all the while moving us toward the outer darkness. Screwtape is certainly the heir of Milton's Satan and the fallen angels, not Dante's chaotic, gibbering, inarticulate, pitchfork-wielding monsters.

The best example of this is revealed in the way that both Satan and Screwtape use poetry as rhetoric; that is, both appropriate poetic language to advance their political agendas. There can be little debate that Milton's

Satan is a great poet; he has the gift. To illustrate, consider his reaction to finding himself in hell; though he clearly sees hell is a far cry from heaven, his language is worthy of a Homeric hero:

> Farewell happy Fields
> Where Joy for ever dwells: Hail horrors, hail
> Infernal world, and thou profoundest Hell
> Receive thy new Possessor: One who brings
> A mind not to be chang'd by Place or Time.
> The mind is its own place, and in itself
> Can make a Heav'n of Hell, a Hell of Heav'n.
> What matter where, if I be still the same,
> And what I should be, all but less than hee
> Whom Thunder hath made greater? Here at least
> We shall be free; th' Almighty hath not built
> Here for his envy, will not drive us hence:
> Here we may reign secure, and in my choice
> To reign is worth ambition though in Hell:
> Better to reign in Hell, than serve in Heav'n. (I, 249–263)

Here Satan manages to convince himself that his fall from heaven into the noxious pit of hell is actually a good thing; he believes his own rhetoric. He is the political candidate who, after being soundly thrashed at the ballot box, still clings tenaciously to his platform—down but not out.[10] While Satan's poetic rhetoric is unwittingly directed at himself here, there are countless examples throughout *PL* wherein we see him exercise verse arguments to bring about his will.

On a smaller scale, Screwtape also has the gift. While it is true his letters are not in verse, the rhetorical quality of his poetic prose appears in a number of passages. For instance, notice how the rhythmic cadence of the thesis/antithesis pattern in the following passage functions much like the blank verse of *PL*: "We want cattle who can finally become food; He wants servants who can finally become sons. We want to suck in, he wants to give out. We are empty and would be filled; He is full and flows over" (46). In another passage where Screwtape tells Wormwood—the demon Screwtape is advising as he tempts his first human "patient"—that time works on hell's side for two reasons, his prose approaches free verse (as I indicate by the printing below):

The routine of adversity,
the gradual decay of youthful loves and youthful hopes,
the quiet despair (hardly felt as pain) of ever overcoming the
chronic temptations with which we have again and again defeated
them,
the drabness which we create in their lives,
and the inarticulate resentment with which we teach them to
respond to it—
all this provides admirable opportunities of wearing out a soul by
attrition

. . . .

Prosperity knits a man to the World.
He feels that he is "finding his place in it,"
while actually it is finding its place in him.
His increasing reputation,
his widening circle of acquaintances,
his sense of importance,
the growing pressure of absorbing and agreeable work,
build up in him a sense of being really at home on Earth,
which is just what we want. (143)

Screwtape's rhetorical poetic prose, like Satan's, is used on some occasions to convince himself of the legitimacy of his cause, but more often than not it is used to direct Wormwood toward an efficacious temptation of his patient. Given the grand scale of *PL*, Milton's Satan is the greater poet; however, Screwtape knows how to use poetic prose to accomplish much the same purpose: separate humans from the love of God. To paraphrase Blake, in Screwtape we see Lewis was a true Poet and of Milton's party without knowing it.

Another parallel I want to draw between Milton's Satan and Screwtape is that both are master politicians. That is, whatever his other considerable skills (and they are many), Screwtape is a master politician cut from the same cloth as Milton's Satan. Throughout *PL* Satan controls and manipulates those under his dominion, and Lewis's Screwtape does the same. For example, I have already noted how Satan uses Beelzebub during the council in hell to put forth his platform; like a smart politician who lets his lieutenant be the front man, thus letting the lackey bear the weight of a failed policy while ready to grab for himself the glory of a successful policy, so Satan manipulates Beelzebub and the fallen angels. Later Satan manages to convince Sin and Death, two monstrous figures guarding the gates of hell, to let him out of hell by promising them he will bring them food: the souls of human beings.[11] Still later he slips past the angel Uriel who guards earth, utilizing lies and flattery. His effectiveness as a political maneuverer culminates in Book IX when he uses lies and half-truths to seduce Eve to his party; in effect, he manipulates her into believing that God does not have her best in mind.

Similarly, Lewis's senior tempter is manipulative; he advises Wormwood on how to use prayer, the church, the "right" kind of friends, the world, pride, gluttony, habits, spiritual dryness, humility, war, fear, cowardice, party affiliation, boredom, humor, sex, time, and jargon to tempt the patient. Screwtape is clever, imaginative, witty, and perceptive. In addition, he has a keen intellect and can analyze with uncanny insight (for the most part) what kinds of things hell can use to attack humans spiritually:

> You will say that these are very small sins [flippancy, boredom, sloth]; and doubtless, like all young tempters, you are anxious to be able to report spectacular wickedness. But do remember, the only thing that matters is the extent to which you separate the man from the Enemy. It does not matter how small the sins are, provided that their cumulative effect is to edge the man away from the Light and out into the Nothing. Murder is no better than cards if cards can do the trick. Indeed, the safest road to Hell is the gradual one—the gentle slope, soft underfoot, without sudden turnings, without milestones, without signposts. (64–65)

Screwtape's mastery as a manipulator becomes frightfully clear to Wormwood too late; his last letter begins "My dear, my very dear, Wormwood, my poppet, my pigsnie . . . I have always desired you, as you (pitiful fool) desired me. The difference is that I am the stronger. I think they will give you to me now; or a bit of you. Love you? Why, yes. As dainty a morsel as ever I grew fat on" (156), and ends "Most truly do I sign myself Your increasingly and ravenously affectionate uncle Screwtape" (160). The grimly humorous truth is that Screwtape has been manipulating Wormwood all the time into a pie, casserole, or fricassee—the central entrée serving for a hellish banquet.

The final parallel I make between Milton's Satan and Screwtape is the humiliating ignominy each experiences. In Book X Satan returns to hell anxious to announce his success against Adam and Eve. However, at the moment when he finishes boasting of his success, instead of hearing applause from the fallen angels: "Contrary he hears / On all sides, from innumerable tongues / A dismal universal hiss, the sound / Of public scorn" (506–09). Before he realizes what is happening, he and the fallen angels are transformed into monstrous serpents, thus explaining the hissing he hears. Further, they are compelled to climb a grove of trees and bite into the same kind of fruit Eve had been tempted to eat; however, instead of tasting sweetness, they "Chew'd bitter Ashes, which th' offended taste / With spattering noise rejected: oft they assay'd, / Hunger and thirst constraining, drugg'd as oft, / With hatefullest disrelish writh'd thir jaws / With soot and cinders fill'd" (566–70). Milton adds that this monstrous transfiguration occurs yearly, "this annual humbling certain number'd days, / To dash thir pride, and joy for Man seduc't" (576–77). The fallen angels, as Milton conceives it, are put through this humiliating transformation and forced feeding by God once a year as a punishment for what they have done to Adam and Eve and as a reminder of his authority over them.

It is this scene of highest irony in *PL* that Lewis echoes in letter twenty-two of *SL*. In the letter Screwtape is sharply critical of Wormwood's failure to keep the patient from falling in love with a Christian girl: "I have looked up this girl's dossier and am horrified at what I find. Not only a Christian but such a Christian—a vile, sneaking, simpering, demure, monosyllabic, mouselike, watery, insignificant, virginal, bread-and-butter miss! The little brute! She makes me vomit" (111). As he rages on, the letter breaks off and we are told it is finished by another hand:

> In the heat of composition I find that I have inadvertently allowed myself to assume the form of a large centipede. I am accordingly dictating the rest to my secretary. Now that the transformation is complete, I recognize it as a periodical phenomenon. Some rumour of it has reached the humans, and a distorted account of it appears in the poet Milton, with the ridiculous addition that such changes of shape are a "punishment" imposed on us by the Enemy. (114–15)

I think Lewis enjoys this joke he pulls on Screwtape, his debt to Milton transparent.[12]

Having made the argument that Screwtape is the literary descendant of Milton's Satan, I should point out the notable differences between *PL* and *SL*. *PL* is a literary epic in verse comprising twelve books and following the rather strict literary format of that genre; *SL* is an epistolary novel of thirty-one letters and has a loose narrative structure, appropriate to letter writing. *PL* has a hell much in the image of those found in Virgil and Dante; *SL* has a hell organized along the lines of a gigantic corporate or totalitarian bureaucracy. In *PL* the fallen angels work together against the Enemy ("devil with devil damned / Firm concord holds"); in *SL* Screwtape and the other devils are literally in a dog-eat-dog competition. *PL* has a cosmic focus since it is Milton's attempt "to justify the ways of God to men"; *SL* has a more limited concern since it is Lewis's contention that "my heart—I need no other's—showeth me the wickedness of the ungodly." *PL* has a tone of high seriousness; *SL* has a comic tone, although our laughter at times is uncomfortably close to home. *PL* has a large cast of characters and we are given multiple points of view; *SL* is the peculiarly unique perspective of one creature. If *PL* is a macro vision of spiritual warfare, *SL* is a micro vision.

In conclusion, while we laugh at Screwtape, we also fear him, and rightly so. He is no Underwood Deviled Ham devil. Instead, Screwtape writes with a stiletto; via his lucid, diabolical epistles he offers disturbing insights into the nature of temptation. As a result, instead of glib, pre-packaged, spiritual truisms, *SL* offers us a spiritual backhand, and the slaps are painful and a bit unnerving. At the same time, Lewis's fascinating insights into the psychology of temptation are more nourishing than the devotional pabulum mass-produced by some market-driven writers. *SL* is an "anti-devotional" demanding we take serious stock of our spiritual lives. Whether Milton's influence is wholly responsible for the sharp, penetrating insights of *SL* is debatable; however, as I have argued in this essay, *SL*'s most important literary antecedent is *PL* and Milton's Satan is the father of Screwtape.

Chapter 10 Notes

1. A version of this first appeared in *Lamp-Post of the Southern California C. S. Lewis Society* 26, nos. 3–4 (Fall-Winter 2002): 6–18.

2. Cited in Walter Hooper's *C. S. Lewis: A Companion and Guide* (London: HarperCollins, 1996), 459.

3. Anecdotally, while I was compiling the index to my book, *C. S. Lewis, Poet: The Legacy of His Poetic Impulse*, I was not surprised to note that the largest number of references to writers who specifically influenced particular poems of Lewis was Milton.

4. John Milton. *Paradise Lost*, in *Complete Poems and Major Prose*, ed. Merritt Y. Hughes (New York: Odyssey Press, 1957), lines 657–59 (subsequent references in the text).

5. Lewis's debt to Milton at this time is primarily poetic, not theological, though given Lewis's later conversion and his *A Preface to Paradise Lost*, we may see in "Milton Read Again" the seeds of his interest in Christianity lying dormant.

6. This preface appears in the paperback version published by Macmillan in 1961; here vii. Unless otherwise noted, subsequent references will be in the text and come from *The Screwtape Letters* (New York: Macmillan, 1943).

7. *A Preface to Paradise Lost* (London: Oxford University Press, 1942), 97–98.

8. Note as well this passage:

> Think of your man as a series of concentric circles, his will being the innermost, his intellect coming next, and finally his fantasy. You can hardly hope, at once, to exclude from all the circles everything that smells of the Enemy: but you must keep on shoving all the virtues outward till they are finally located in the circle of fantasy, and all the desirable qualities inward into the Will. It is only in so far as they reach the will and are there embodied in habits that the virtues are really fatal to us. (I don't, of course, mean what the patient mistakes for his will, the conscious fume and fret of resolutions and clenched teeth, but the real center, what the Enemy calls the Heart). All sorts of virtues painted in the fantasy or approved by the intellect or even, in some measure, loved and admired, will not keep a man from Our Father's house: indeed they may make him more amusing when he gets there. (SL, 37)

9. William Blake, "The Marriage of Heaven and Hell," in *Blake's Poetry and Designs*, eds. Mary Lynn Johnson and John E. Grant, 2nd edition (New York: Norton, 2008), 71.

10. While it is beyond the scope of this essay, it should be noted that Milton understood intimately the politics of his own day since he served as the Secretary of Foreign Tongues under the government of Oliver Cromwell. Having sat through any number of political meetings, he undoubtedly used his knowledge in the portrayal of Satan and the other fallen angels.

11. In *PL* Sin is Satan's daughter and Death is his son.

12. Screwtape's rage here is one of the few times we see Dante's influence upon Lewis's conception of the devils.

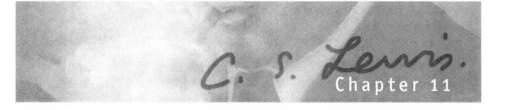

The Nature Poetry of Ruth Pitter[1]

It is unfortunate that Ruth Pitter (1897–1992), an important twentieth-century British poet, is little known in America. When her name is recognized, it is usually in the context of "the woman who should have married C. S. Lewis." While it is too much to call this essay an attempt to "rehabilitate" Pitter, it is accurate to describe it as an effort to expose how Pitter's poetic impulse, the desire "to express something of the secret meanings which haunt life and language," places her in the mainstream of twentieth-century British poetry. Because she was never associated with a literary group or movement, Pitter has not attracted widespread critical notice, in spite of the many writers who admired her work.[2] For instance, Owen Barfield was a great admirer of Pitter. Barfield, like Pitter and Lewis, shared a love for traditional English poetry and distaste for modernist verse. After a luncheon with Pitter, on August 1, 1949, Barfield writes Pitter and offers high praise for her poetry, particularly "Fowls Celestial and Terrestrial" from *A Mad Lady's Garland* (1934)[3]: "It is, in its own right, a very noble poem with a life to it that occasionally makes one catch one's breath. And if a poem doesn't make me catch my breath, I may feel very politely towards [it] & be quite glad to read it, but—well! You know the difference. That is the battle from 1930 onwards." His compliments continue when he adds:

I can well understand that you enjoyed writing the Garland most. You *are* the Trophy [a reference to Pitter's 1936 volume, *A Trophy of Arms*], but you only wear the Garland, and therefore can keep on taking it off and looking at it . . . . I wish I could get hold of the *Trophy* somehow. And have you a lending copy of *Persephone in Hades* [a reference to Pitter's 1931 volume], which the [local] library does not possess? I have a special weakness for Persephone and hope it is really about her and not about a giant grain elevator of that name in Wisconsin or a pylon in Beverly Hills.

Pitter must certainly have felt pleased by the way he ends this letter: "May I keep the [*Mad Lady's Garland*] a little longer, please? Why don't we all live in your 'Heroic Couplets' mansion and spend our time reading our own poetry to each other, and the great poems of antiquity together, except of course when we were dancing . . . on the sunken lawns and playing the viol de gamboys?"[4]

Barfield's delight with Pitter's poetry is well documented in other letters to her.[5] Among other attractive qualities of her verse, Barfield enjoyed her intense, passionate, yet controlled insights about the human condition and her musings on the spiritual life. However, this essay will focus on her nature poems; many are mystical reflections on the natural world and illustrate her deeply felt sense of place. In particular, the Hainault Forest in Essex, an ancient grove of oak, chestnut, beech, and elder on the outskirts of greater London, was a beloved spot for the young Pitter.[6] Within five miles of the London suburb of Ilford where Pitter grew up, Hainault Forest was a favorite place for family walks and day trips. In 1914 Pitter's parents, poor elementary school teachers, managed to rent a small cottage there and Pitter's delight was unbounded. Weekends and summer holidays were now consumed with visits to the cottage, and it became the family's second home. Free to wander in the forest, Pitter developed an acute eye for the natural objects she encountered. The symbolic power of the cottage and the forest find outlet in her mature poems written from 1935 to 1953; repeatedly she returns imaginatively to the cottage and the forest in dozens of poems. In short, Hainault Forest is the most dynamic and pervasive force powering her fertile imagination, and it becomes a "spot in time" that sustains and nurtures her poetic sensibilities for the rest of her life.

For instance, in the autobiographical poem, "The Cottage," written in 1926 shortly after the death of her father, George, Pitter vividly remembers him in Hainault Forest:

> . . . My father of that utter loneliness
> Was part; he was a man of great desires
> Confused, frustrated: the imperfect he
> Rejected, and so had nothing in this life.
> He talked with spirits of the tenuous air,
> And far in the black wood I often saw
> His homeward lantern, and would hear him make
> Cheerful discourse to one that answered not.
> A bodiless music in the frosty dark
> One night we heard: one night the snowy owl
> Swooped down, and sitting on the gate did cry
> As boding woe: he told me one was dead,
> A dwarf that lived at hand, and it was so.
> He had a friend, a rat, most hoar and old
> And blind: he fed and cheered it, caring not
> For any ravage that such creatures do;
> And fox and squirrel held his store as theirs,
> And the sad hound and hard-used lurcher came
> To warm them, and when sick they searched for him.
> And one that found him not lay down and died
> On the deserted threshold in the dark.
>
> And he was harvested last harvest time:
> I gathered in his thin, neglected crops
> Untended since the sowing, and rooted out
> Self-seeded hundreds of forget-me-nots;
> And I shall gather in his crops no more;
> Saving the lifelong crop of bitter weeds
> He sowed in me, that make me hate my kind
> But not hate him; such offspring was his fate,
> And such a father mine; a majesty
> Of darkness orders man's unhappy ways,
> And to that empire do I bow, and keep

A steadfast silence. Ours not tragedy,
Nor the perfection of catastrophe,
But the slow victory of the rotten void,
Where nothing triumphs over piety,
Even as in this soil the fungous slime
Rots the proud body of the English oak.

There his old garment hangs upon the door:
There lean his spade and mattock, hedging-hook,
With all their kind: most strange, he does not come,
And I am told he will not come again.
Yet far in the dark wood I hear him make
Cheerful discourse to one that answers not:
And still the hound comes and seeks the fire,
The ghostly place hath but one ghost the more.[7]

This passage evokes Pitter's abiding love both for the cottage and for her father. As the rich imagery of the cottage and forest suggest, she regularly returns to them in her mind. More importantly, however, these lines reveal her recognition of her father's hard life and nostalgia for their shared times of simple companionship at the cottage. She acknowledges his affect on her personality—sowing in her "bitter weeds . . . that make me hate my kind"—yet, she sees in this a strength since it has toughened her and made her accept that for humankind "darkness orders man's unhappy ways." Her description of his clothes and tools are so apt we almost smell his scent and as we run our eyes over the handles worn to smoothness. And the final lines verge on the mystical. That this poem was not published during her lifetime offers commentary on Pitter's reluctance to expose her heart; yet this poem is one of her most compelling, and it illustrates how intensely her memories of Hainault Forest stayed with her.

Pitter's mother, Louisa, grieved the death of her husband but found solace by purchasing a little country house at the North End, near Dunmow, Essex. This place soon succeeded the deteriorating cottage in Hainault Forest as Pitter's favorite spot when she wanted to escape London, and for many years she cherished the dream of one day retiring to this Essex retreat. Pitter, who never married, earned a living as an artisan in Chelsea, eventually opening in June 1930 an ornamental painting business with her friend Kathleen O'Hara. Then a near catastrophic event occurred. Only two months after beginning their business, while Pitter was opening a small can of cellulose paint, it exploded and the lid flew up, severely injuring her left eye—not only lacerating it but also coating it with amyl acetate and pieces of hard pigment.[8] The terrible injury to her eye actually became a catalyst for the maturation of her imaginative life. Reduced to an invalid and unable to keep up her frenetic work schedule, Pitter took advantage of her physical inactivity by exploring in profoundly deep ways, ways she had never attempted before, the full exercise of her poetic imagination. Indeed, one of her most powerful poems, "Stormcock in Elder," had its genesis during this period. As the poem opens, we see that Pitter has imaginatively retreated to the cottage in Hainault Forest:

> In my dark hermitage, aloof
> From the world's sight and the world's sound,
> By the small door where the old roof
> Hangs but five feet above the ground,
> I groped along the shelf for bread
> But found celestial food instead.

Expecting only to find physical nourishment, surprisingly, she finds something more sustaining:

> For suddenly close at my ear,
> Loud, loud and wild, with wintry glee,
> The old unfamiliar chorister
> Burst out in pride of poetry;
> And through the broken roof I spied
> Him by his singing glorified.

What then follows is a concrete, detailed description of the stormcock, the English missal thrush, made all the more remarkable because this vivid physical description is based on Pitter's memory from her days in Hainault Forest:

> Scarcely an arm's length from the eye,
> Myself unseen, I saw him there;
> The throbbing throat that made the cry,
> The breast dewed from the misty air,
> The polished bill that opened wide
> And showed the pointed tongue inside:

The large eye, ringed with many a ray
Of minion feathers, finely laid,
The feet that grasped the elder-spray:
How strongly used, how subtly made
The scale, the sinew, and the claw,
Plain through the broken roof I saw;

The flight-feathers in tail and wing,
The shorter coverts, and the white
Merged into russet, marrying
The bright breast to the pinions bright,
Gold sequins, spots of chestnut, shower
Of silver, like a brindled flower.

Soldier of fortune, northwest Jack,
Old hard-times' braggart, there you blow!
But tell me ere your bagpipes crack
How you can make so brave a show,
Full-fed in February, and dressed
Like a rich merchant at a feast.

One-half the world, or so they say,
Knows not how half the world may live;
So sing your song and go your way,
And still in February contrive
As bright as Gabriel to smile
On elder-spray by broken tile.[9]

In effect, then, the eye injury led to the emergence of a genuine poetic voice as she began to write poems less crafted "while the eye was in action" and more by the insights of her unconscious mind. Her enforced blindness caused her to turn within to "see." As a result, she explored her inner poetic voice in new and dramatically transforming ways. Where she once embraced nature visually like the young Wordsworth, her blindness forced her to explore her memories of nature and natural objects in a more deliberate, reflective, and intuitive manner. This pause, this inner exploration, gave her the time to penetrate the mysteries of life whereas before she wrote about the surface of human existence in a flat, unconvincing, ethereal tone. The retreat within, perhaps combined with the fear of never seeing again, drove her to a closer examination of her own poetic vision. Where she once maintained a detached, impersonal relationship with her poetry, now she made personal connections with the subjects of her verse, often with startling insights about the human condition—its joys, doubts, loves, fears, commitments, uncertainties, convictions, and longings.

Driven into the fertile mine of her imagination, Pitter learned how to draw on past memories, much in the manner of Wordsworth's "spots of time," in order to find the substance of great poetry with the cottage and its surroundings in Hainault Forest as the controlling foci of a vast poetic reservoir. Indeed, over the next twenty-five years, the period of her most memorable and powerful work, she draws frequently and deeply from this well of memory. In poem after poem the "blind" poet retreats back to her forest of memories, delighting in the sights, sounds, smells, and touch of the paths, trees, birds, flowers, meadows, brooks, and inhabitants of Hainault Forest. Those early years near the cottage had inadvertently developed into a well head of stored memories; the poetic energy that had only trickled out in her poetry up until her thirtieth year began to gush out into a flowing stream through the mid-1950s. Had she not suffered the eye injury and the forced idleness it precipitated, she may have never had the chance to make the imaginative descent into this poetic well-spring. In effect, Pitter's eye injury (from which she later recovered) was a key event that unlocked her voice as a poet. Out of a potential disaster, she reaped a benefit she could never have anticipated.

A Trophy of Arms is a collection of poems rich with the influence of Hainault Forest. While "Stormcock in Elder" discussed above harkens back to the forest cottage, her beloved "dark hermitage," her deep affection for this place is more vividly portrayed in "The Lost Hermitage" as, during a return trip to the hut, she insists that

My heart dwells here
In rotten hut on weeping clay,
Tends here her useful herbs, her bloom;
Will not away,
May not be startled to one tear,
Is tenant of her little room
Forever. (41)

Even though she cannot live at the hut, imaginatively she will always inhabit it. She lists the many birds there (stockdove, stormcock, finch, blackbird, jay, starling, titmouse, nightingale, and "song-thrush hatched in a cup of mud") as well as particular images such as "frost on the grass, / The lonely morning, the still kine, / Grief for the quick, love for the dead." Pitter claims "all these are laid / Safe up in me, and I will keep / My dwelling thus though it be gone." Her memory will lovingly stay upon the ramshackle cottage whether she is back in Chelsea or the cottage tumbles in upon itself: "My store is not in gold, but made / Of toil and sleep / And wonder walking all alone." By her affirmation of the permanence of the cottage in her imaginative life and its power to renew her, Pitter's "The Lost Hermitage" has links to Yeats' "The Lake Isle of Innisfree."[10]

Pitter's nostalgic affection for the cottage is also apparent in "O Where Is the Dwelling":

O where is the dwelling I love the most,
And what but the one poor place can please,
Where the penny I lost and the faith I lost
Lie buried beneath enchanted trees?

O there is the dwelling I love the most,
And thither for ever my feet are bound,
Where the youth I lost and the love I lost
Lie buried, lie buried in holy ground. (46)

Of note here is how she connects her longing for this place with a series of profound losses, including faith, youth, and love; that is, while there is pain associated with the forest cottage, it is more than assuaged by the "enchanted" and "holy" ground this place has in her imagination. Pitter's ability to communicate simply in her verse is one mark of her growing poetic maturation. She continues this theme in "The Return" although in this case she longs to escape imaginatively the toil of everyday life in London: "So, since the battle goes so ill, / Let me lie down and dream of home: / Tonight I'll lie upon the hill / Between the bough and the grass" (85). She sees in her mind the tree where the nightingale sings, the mists drifting over the brooks, and the heavily scented lilies, woodbines, and hyacinths. Yet in this instance her memories are not enough to sustain her:

To no end but to be old and poor,
To lose the good, and to get the bane:
To find no door like the rotting door
Which I find not again:
To weep in my bed at night
And forget the tear of delight.

Drawing strength from these images momentarily refreshes her although the imaginative return to the cottage cannot trump the gritty reality of her every-day circumstance.

Other poems are also inspired by experiences in Hainault Forest. "The Viper" is a lovely piece reminiscent of Emily Dickinson's "A Narrow Fellow in the Grass." Yet while Dickinson objectively focuses upon the visual as the snake "wrinkled and was gone" leaving the viewer with "a tighter feeling / And Zero at the Bone," Pitter emphasizes instead a connection of "the lovely serpent" with the spiritual: "Fair was the brave embroidered dress, / Fairer the gold eyes shone: / Loving her not, yet did I bless / The fallen angel's come-liness; / And gazed when she had gone" (26). In "The Strawberry Plant" Pitter writes perhaps her best descriptive poem as she details the particular "rocky niche" where she spies a perfect strawberry plant:

She sat enthroned and perfect; for her crown
One bud like pearl, and then two fairy roses
Blanched and yet ardent in their glowing hearts;
One greenish berry spangling into yellow
Where the light touched the seed: one fruit achieved
And ripe, an odorous vermilion ball
Tight with completion, lovingly enclasped
By the close cup whose green chimed with the red
And showered with drops of gold like Danaë:
Three lovely sister leaves as like as peas,
Young but full-fledged, dark, with a little down:
Two leaves that to a matron hue inclined;
And one the matriarch, that dressed in gold
And flushed with wine, thought her last days her best.
And here and there a diamond of dew
Beamed coolly from the white, smiled from the gold,

Silvered the down, struck lightning from the red.
The overhanging rock forbade the sun,
Yet she was all alight with water-gleams
Reflected, like the footlights at a play:
Perfection's self, and (rightly) out of reach. (65)

That this humble yet beautiful plant cannot be plucked thoughtlessly by a passer by gives the poem a wonderfully lasting impression; we can envision in our minds this delicate natural beauty sitting forever undisturbed in her rocky throne.

Reviews of *A Trophy of Arms* were overwhelmingly positive.[11] Accordingly, it was not entirely surprising that *A Trophy of Arms* won the Hawthornden Prize in 1937.[12] Unfortunately for Pitter and the rest of Europe, World War II effectively began with the Nazi blitzkrieg of Poland on September 1, 1939. Pitter, like the vast majority of her countrymen, supported the war and was willing to sacrifice in order to insure that might did not triumph over right. Of course, no one could have known how severely such resolve would be tested, including, in her case, the eventual failure of her thriving business as an artisan.

Her next volume of poetry, *The Spirit Watches* (1939), written under the growing shadow of the war, contains several poems illustrating Pitter's imaginative retreat to Hainault Forest. "Time's Fool" is a careful visual reconstruction of her memories of the cottage. The poem begins ironically as Pitter admits she is time's fool, although not heaven's, because in spite of her longing to rekindle her memories of the cottage, "yet hope not for any return." Her tender affection for the cottage comes through as she recalls its contents: "The rabbit-eaten dry branch and the halfpenny candle / Are lost with the other treasure: the sooty kettle / Thrown away, become redbreast's home in the hedge, where the nettle / Shoots up, and bad bindweed wreathes rust-fretted-handle. / Under that broken thing no more shall the dry branch burn."[13] To refer to these worn out, tattered objects as "treasure" heightens the poignancy of her memories and serves to re-inforce her almost childlike determination to hold on to this spot in time. She goes on and claims that all these objects, while poor and of little comfort, were to her at one time "all comfort" because there "the heart was at home." Again, her memories are powerfully evocative: "The hard cankered apple holed by the wasp and the bird, / The damp bed, with the beetle's tap in the headboard heard, / The dim bit of mirror, three inches of comb." No amount of logical knowledge about the apparent meanness of the cottage can negate its powerful hold upon her imagination:

> I knew that the roots were creeping under the floor,
> That the toad was safe in his hole, the poor cat by the fire,
> The starling snug in the roof, each slept in his place:
> The lily in splendour, the vine in her grace,
> The fox in the forest, all had their desire,
> As then I had mine, in the place that was happy and poor.

Pitter's strong sense of nature's pull, the desire to merge with and be a part of this place, her longing for a return to her adolescent happiness is rarely seen more effectively than in this poem.

"The Hut" continues this theme, picturing the cottage as gradually being overcome by nature. "Stuck, like a snail upon a wall, / On what we called a hill," the hut leans against an apple tree "whose laden branches lay / On the hot roof voluptuously, / And murmured all the day" (28). Imagining that a dryad is warming the hut for her own mysterious purposes, Pitter's notes how "the sapling ash had mined the floor, / The chimney flew the bine" and "the doorway was without a door, / But flaunted eglantine." Not only have trees, vines, and flowers invaded the hut, but animals have as well: "The swallow built upon the beam, / The rat was much at home." Yet this woodsy home is the imaginative center of Pitter's world since "there one foolish child would dream, / Where sorrow could not come." The cottage is also the focus of "Bloweth Where It Listeth" which takes its title from John 3:8: "The wind bloweth where it listeth, and thou hearest the sound thereof, but canst not tell whence it cometh, and whither it goeth: so is every one that is born of the Spirit." In the poem Pitter suggests that while her body is bound to an earthly spot, her spirit "like any wandering moth . . . flits abroad in air; / Seeking the unsought, and loving what is lone" (58). Not surprisingly, her spirit ranges over the earth until it comes "to a cottage in a solitary lane, / Where the sparrow, nested in the neighbouring tree, / Brooded the shabby eggs which no one loved but she." Seeing a "poor soul" within, her spirit peers "in anxiously, to mark the look of care, / But for once in this sorry life sorrow was not there." Indeed, while sorrow has once been there, it has now fled away, leaving her spirit joyful and content, taking comfort and solace with her: "For it took her tenderness with it as it went: / For it goes about blessing, and will not be gainsaid, / The wild weed in the waste land, the ruined wall, and the dead; / And the hearts of poor women in the cold country-side / It goes about blessing, and will not be denied." In effect, her spirit's retreat to the cottage nourishes Pitter as it returns to her conscious mind.

"Lament for the Landless" broadens to consider the nurturing power of nature and the harm caused to those who have no direct access to the countryside: "Love of the earth leaps up, and falls in a sigh for my fellows / . . . Alas, for the man who has never smelled the thick-flowering / [Grape] vine in its bursting glory / . . . Alas for the disinherited, the earthless, the uprooted— / No crocus, no primrose, no blessing of natural increment" (48). Other natural objects lamented include the flower of the plum, the hedge-sparrow's brood "with buttercup-yellow gullets," strawberry and violet plants, and "the azure crescent / Of the [robin's] half-eggshell." The lament peaks when Pitter posits: "Who is forlorn of these is the godforsaken." Accordingly, she opts for immediate sensuous experience: "I eat of the fruit of the tree where the good dog lies / Meshed in the quiet root, and my hand busy / On wrinkled stems that were planted by the forgotten." Additionally, she wants to merge with nature: "And I must be numbered with them and neglect the seasons, / Though somehow I know that a flower is remembered for ever, / And eyes, and the shape of a bird for ever remembered." All those cut off from the natural environment are pitiable and worth lamenting. These four poems harkening back to the cottage and the forest communicate not only Pitter's visceral love of nature but also indicate her secret desire to withdraw from the coming conflict, the distant but coming chaos and destruction of war.

Several poems in *The Spirit Watches* concern nature's pattern of life and death, joy and pain, and how this pattern speaks to the human condition. For instance, in "The Vine in Bloom," a poem inspired by the lush grape vines kept by her mother at the Essex cottage, Pitter explores the beauty of the cycle of life by contrasting her personal aging with nature's pattern of rebirth:

It matters not to grow old, when the vine is breaking:
The years have no weight when the holy vine is in bloom:
Soon I must be sleeping, but this shall still be waking,
The promise of birth is breathed in the word of doom;

She gives me the flower now, then the cluster that comes in its room,
But soon I must be giving and the vine taking. (9)

That is, as she sees the vine so heavy with blossoms that it sags to the point of breaking, rather than feeling sorry for herself as she consider her own "fullness" of years, Pitter does not fear death. There is "no grudge, . . . no quarrel" between her and the vine; instead, the comforting, eternal verity of nature's ongoing activity brightens her day and is heightened by the last image in the poem: "And the speckled bird, / Murmuring her care and her busy kindness, is heard / Nourishing next year's songs in the bonny laurel." In the end, Pitter emphasizes her sense of joy rather than pain in this musing upon death and rebirth.

"Burning the Bee-Tree" similarly reflects upon nature's ongoing, revitalizing power. She describes the final fiery destruction of a tree that once housed an active bee hive: "We threw their tower down on the mould, / And split it open wide, / But they had taken away their gold, / And there was none inside" (12). As others gaze on what's left—"the embalming stain," "a few shards of comb," and "a breath as of the clover-plain"—Pitter watches the "spiced funeral vapours" curl upwards and wonders: "What do you see above, what fair / Visions salute your eyes, / What reverend memories repair / The breach of centuries?" This final destruction of the hive's empire, however, does not evoke sadness; rather, as in "The Vine in Bloom," Pitter finds solace in the unending cycle of nature this event suggests. The burning bee-tree becomes an archetype for all that nature renews and re-combines: "The labour, and the bitter stings, / The cells' meticulous range, / Honey, which makes a perishing thing / Immortal, do not change." Far from leading her to bitterness, the burning bee-tree encourages Pitter to recommit herself not only to life, but, more importantly, to writing poetry: "Life, make one couplet that I sing / As deathless, and as strange!" While death is an implicit certainty, Pitter finds in nature's cycles and rhythms continuity rather than finality; we die but our lives are only a part of a larger, on-going reality.

Finally, "The Bush-Baby" is a wistful desire for connection to the animal world. Standing outside a lemur enclosure in the local zoo, Pitter intuitively longs for a closer relationship with the furtive, delicate creature: "I would rather hold this creature in my hand / Than be kissed by a great king. / The love for what I do not understand / Goes from me to this slight thing" (46). In the velvet coat and round, nocturnal eyes she sees "an image out of Paradise," and she blesses the bush-baby. Pitter ends by focusing upon humankind: "To see a glory in another kind, / To love, and not to know. / O if I could forsake this weary mind / And love my fellows so!" The character of the natural world—forests, gardens, or animals—to offer beauty, rest, and peace is almost always preferred by Pitter over interaction with other human beings. And the deeply impressed memories of the cottage and Hainault Forest are at the heart of such longings for retreat to the natural world.[14]

Like most Londoners, Pitter suffered great mental and physical anguish throughout WWII. In addition to short rations and short tempers, the nightly bombing raids were horribly frightening.[15] Not surprisingly, then, her next volume of poetry, *The Bridge: Poems 1939–1944*, is an introspective volume of poetry influenced by her wartime experiences. Several poems coalesce around nature and her memories of the cottage in Hainault Forest. Because of the dangers of living in Chelsea at this time, Pitter writes poems that are dreamy returns to the cottage. In "Retrospect" she envisions her spirit returning to the cottage, "a sylvan place, a distant time, / An owlish and an elvish air."[16] Her spirit "looks upon the ragged tree, / It broods along the darkening glade; / It sees what I no longer see." Yet she cannot make the kind of connection she desires with her spirit: "It hears what is to me unheard: / If it could only speak to me, / Shaping the wonder to a word, / If it could speak the ancient spell." In "Rainey Summer" she tries to "remember, though we cannot write it, the delicate dream." Notwithstanding this claim, she does a wonderful job remembering: "We repose in our secret place, in the rainy air, / By the small fire, the dim window, in the ancient house; / Kind to the past, and thoughtful of our hosts, / Shadows of those now beyond thought and care, / Phantoms that the silence engenders, the flames arouse" (45). The exactness of her memories recall "Stormcock in Elder": "The secret bird is there, . . . betrayed / By the leaf that moved when she slipped from her twig by the door, / As the mouse unseen is perceived by her gliding shade, / As the silent owl is known by the wind of her flight." The sustaining power of the cottage is again underscored in the poem's final lines: "We remember the delicate dream, the voice of the clay; / Recalling the body before the life was begun, / Stealing through blood and bone with bodiless grace / In the elfish night and the green cool gloom of the day."

Still another poem that harkens back to the cottage is "The Hill of the Kindred" which opens: "Would you remember if I asked you / The ruin in the hanging wood?" (51). She recalls the close grove, the hill side, the broken stones, and the "cold black gaping chimney-place, / . . . Like a skull's face." Perhaps by contrast with the ruins Pitter sees all about her in London after the nightly bombings, the memory of the ruined cottage is sustaining: "A ruin is to me / A place of peace, where restless care, / Parting, and toil, and usury, / And all our sorrows buried are." But beyond remembering the literal ruin, she recalls the people who once were there: "I think how she who baked the bread / On this poor hearth when it was warm / Sleeps like a queen among the dead." This almost certainly alludes to her mother, Louisa, as Pitter recalls the delightful days that she and her family spent in the Hainault Forest before World War I. The solace she imaginatively experiences as she lays her "head / Down on the green neglected stone, / Loving the cold hearth of the dead" gives her the strength to carry on in the midst of hardship: "Not timid, like an untried child, / Nor bitter, like an angry lover; / For life and I are reconciled, / The grief is done, the care is over."

Several poems relate to specific experiences in nature. "The Tall Fruit-Trees" is an exuberant celebration of autumn harvest as Pitter glories in the joys of climbing heavily loaded plum, pear, and apple trees: "But while I am able O let me ascend the plum-tree / And poke my head out at the top, where the lovely view / Has a foreground of scarlet plums with a wash of blue, / And I am away from earth in the starlings' country" (30). The pleasure she receives from this high vantage point suggests a deep desire to ascend life's everyday toil and pain, lost instead in the swaying fecundity of the great trees. While Pitter's poem lacks the existential subtleties of Robert Frost's "After Apple Picking" ("For I have had too much / Of apple-picking: I am overtired / Of the great harvest I myself desired"), it nonetheless reflects Pitter's strong affection for the natural environment: "But the great old trees are the real loves of my heart, / Mountains of blossom and fruit on the stalwart timber." "The Bat" recounts Pitter's unexpected pleasure in handling an injured bat brought into the house by her marauding cat. Initially she is horrified to see the bat since she thinks it "unholy" and has always thought its "murky and erratic wing" was "made of stuff / Like tattered, sooty waterproof, / Looking dirty, clammy, cold, / Wicked, poisonous, and old" (32). Yet because "even fear must yield to love / And pity makes the depths to move," she picks up the creature in order to save it from the cat. As she lifts the night flyer, she is curiously moved: "Strange revelation! Warm as milk, / Clean as a flower, smooth as silk!" In contrast to what she had believed, she finds the bat's body to be delicately charming: "O what a piteous face appears, / What great fine thin translucent ears! / What chestnut down and crapy wings, / Finer than any lady's things." As the tiny, fragile creature clings to her, Pitter is not repelled; instead she sympathizes with it, and blesses it as she releases it: "Warm, clean, and lovely, though not fair, / And burdened with a mother's care; / Go hunt the hurtful fly, and bear / My blessing to your kind in air." This sense of connectedness between all living creatures is one that finds expression in many of Pitter's nature poems, and the unexpected pleasure this heretofore frightening creature brings is reminiscent of her reaction to the snake in "The Viper" from *A Trophy of Arms*.

"Wild Honey" is a measured harangue at the stupidity of a man who is consumed with the surface and the trivial: "You, the man going along the road alone, / Careless or wretched, rarely thoughtful, never serene, / Possessing nothing worth having; man of the sickly pleasure, / Man of the mawkish, wrong-headed sorrows, typical man" (52). This superficiality causes such a man to pass by and miss a rich, sweet, and sustaining vein of goodness:

> There in the riddled tree, hanging in darkness,
> There in the roof of the house and the wall-hollow,
> The new like pearl, the old like magical amber,
> Hidden with cunning, guarded by fiery thousands
> (See where they stream like smoke from the hole in the gable),
> There in the bank of the brook the immortal secret,
> In the ground under your feet the treasure of nations,
> Under the weary foot of the fool, the wild honey.

This parable on humankind's tendency to live on the surface and its inability to see the nurturing truth of nature beneath the crust of everyday activity is neatly done, and Pitter's descriptions of where the wild honey may be found are masterful. She suggests we waste our time with the facile, the obvious, the mundane, while missing richer sources of meaning and purpose, a notion she also explores in "Burning the Bee-Tree" from *The Spirit Watches*.

Several nature poems in *The Bridge* concern birds. "Freemasons of the Air" is a careful observation of sandmartins flitting and darting about a sandy bluff as they scrape out their nests: "With turning wing and forky tail, / And highest in the diamond light / The swifts like boomerangs in flight, / The spirits who can sleep on high / And hold their marriage in the sky" (17). Pitter finds simple delight in watching these birds joining together to build their homes: "They sport, they sing in unison, / Their noble spirits make them one." If the implication is that humans should learn something about unity from the sandmartins, Pitter offers a patent moral in "The Crow," a poem about how an injured crow is cared for by a group of children. In spite of their kindness to him, the crow never warms to his captors; instead, "friendship [he] damned with all he knew" (21). Pitter uses this bitter crow as a jumping off point for comparison to someone from her past: "I knew a man, I knew a man / As thin as any grudging crow. / He also had his bitter *damn* / For all his jailers here below. / And also for the one above. / His hatred was a kind of faith" (emphasis Pitter). She wishes this man could be born again so that he would "think less of getting, more of giving; / In short, to learn the art of living." Although there is no way to establish who she has in mind, it is not hard to speculate this is a poem about her father, George; his socialist principles were sickened by the poverty and misery he saw in the lives of the elementary aged children he taught, and Pitter's memories of him discussed earlier in "The Cottage" support this possibility.[17]

The Ermine, which appeared eight years later in the spring of 1953, is a volume filled with poems inspired by stories or memories from her childhood or with poems exploring death and the spiritual life. While no poems can be linked directly to Hainault Forrest, several poems reflect natural scenes or settings, including "The Cedar," written to memorialize a favorite cedar of Lebanon that Pitter loved looking at when she stayed at the Penns, the home of her friend, the poet Dorothy Wellesley. Peering out of the upper floor windows and into the garden below, Pitter sees more in the cedar than just trunk, branches, and nettles. Instead, it becomes a conceit for the landscape of the world—its microcosm becomes a macrocosm:

> Plant or world? Are those lights and shadows
> Branches, or great air-suspended meadows?
> Boles and branches, haunted by the flitting linnet,
> Or great hillsides rolling up to cliffs of granite?
> Those domed shapes, thick-clustered on the ledges,
> Upright fruit, or dwellings thatched with sedges? (21)

Her imagination sees much more than the majestic tree; in fact, it "is a country hanging in the morning. / Scented alps, where nothing but the daylight changes, / Climbing to black walls of mountain ranges." In this vivid description, Pitter offers a vision of pleasure and comfort, a "dwelling of the blessed in the green savannahs."

"Hill and Valley" (To D. C.), a poem dedicated to her friend, Lord David Cecil, is almost certainly set in the countryside near Oxford. In this poem Pitter tries to capture the peace of an idyllic scene, moving imaginatively from a lush hillside down "by deep drinking-places where the cattle go" (22). She hears mowing "falling with whispers" and the shrill cry of a lark, and she watches in silence as "grape-coloured shadows" lengthen down the hill. For a moment she wants to stay there where she "could mind the sheep on the hill for ever," but then she believes she was "made to live by a great river, / Watching the cattle drinking in dimpled gleams, / Winding the wands of willow that spring by the streams." Although she and O'Hara would soon move out to the Oxford countryside and settle in the village of Long Crendon, when she writes this poem she is still living in Chelsea near the Thames, the "great river." Longing on the one hand to live closer to the natural environment, on the other hand she senses that her present calling keeps her in the city. Consequently, she delights in the quiet, natural setting of this hill and valley, using them as memories that she can later draw upon for refreshment.

"The Tree at Dawn" takes us on an early morning mowing expedition where Pitter contrasts the overwhelming beauty of the scene—probably set near the Essex cottage—and the felicity of the animals nearby with human discontent and unhappiness. Up before the rising of the sun, "in the cold grey, and all alone," she takes up her scythe ("the hook"), "and while the dew would serve my turn / I cut the nettles strong, / The mowing grass and parsley-fern / The garden hedge along" (3). Reflecting on the quiet isolation of this experience, she muses: "How lonely seem the creatures then; / How lonely, even trees; / But the conceiving minds of men / Are lonelier than these." Echoing ideas she explored earlier in "Lament for the Landless" from *The Spirit Watches*, Pitter says nature's great advantage over man is that its objects are not aware of their loneliness: "They do not know themselves alone, / And knowing would not care; / But holiness invests each one / In the grey morning air." Struck by this thought, Pitter drops her scythe—ceasing her "sacrilege"—and peers intently as light begins to infuse the scene: "Still as a plant I stand, and look, / And now no longer break / The breathing silence with my hook, / But watch the colours wake." Her attention focuses upon a gigantic tree with its great bole of "glittering green ore," its boughs "dark green as the deepest sea," its sap that contains "the spirit of the dreadful night," and its fruit that "burn in the light of their last dawn, and bleed."

Then she turns this vision of the tree upon herself, noting that while the fruit of the tree "bleeds," the tree is not in pain; she contrasts this with her own experience: "For all the pain / Is in me who behold, / And mine, not his, the crimson stain." Pitter's "bleeding" is her awareness of her disconnect from other humans; this is a pain that nature can never know. As the light continues to grow, it mystically illumines the tree and other objects beyond it:

> But his that life mysterious,
> > And sacred, as I well see,
> And well companioned; glorious
> > Beyond the great old tree
> The pale-blue velvet cabbages
> > Stand lovely as a dream,
> And violet and pink sweet-peas
> > Clearer begin to gleam,
> With white that glimmered long ago,
> > When from my bed I came.

The intensity of this mystical experience is fleeting, ironically washed out by the rising sun: "The clouds begin to glow, / The east begins to flame; / The god leaps up, the day is here, / The heat pours from the sky: / The tree is commonplace and dear, / And I am only I." In this poem we move along with Pitter as she rises before dawn, intent on getting some practical work done—to fulfill the agenda she set that day for herself—and experience instead her unexpected sense of isolation and loneliness in the face of nature's mysteries. For a moment we behold her "dappled-dawn" epiphany and find supernal value in the familiar objects of nature that she also explores in "The Bird in the Tree" from *The Spirit Watches*, but then the common light of day turns all into the ordinary, the mundane. Perhaps in no other poem does Pitter capture as effectively her intuitive understanding of the mystical power of nature than in "The Tree at Dawn."

In "The Captive Bird of Paradise" Pitter reflects upon a beautiful bird of paradise she loves to watch in a nearby zoo. Although the bird's beauty is confined by the bars of the cage, Pitter has a mystical connection with the bird. Indeed, for Pitter this bird is a miraculous creature. She longs to understand, to connect, to know intuitively all the bird stands for: "Give me the bird of Paradise, though dying, / Exiled and doomed, ravished from the Elysian / Forest where I shall never see it flying" (18). Her descriptions of the bird's colors are memorable, including "the rose-death purple mantled on with fire" and "the dying-dolphin green." The poem ends with Pitter, although regretting that she will never see an even more mysterious bird, the phoenix—"Though I shall never see the sudden turning / Into a sphery monstrance, globe of splendour, / The ecstasy that is beyond our learning, / The action and the attitude that render / Love back to whence it came, the phoenix burning"—she will be more than compensated by experiencing a mystical communion with the bird of paradise: "Give me the bird of paradise, the wonder." The bird as an object of natural beauty powerfully drew Pitter; in the bird Pitter longed to make a mystical connection to transcendent beauty.

"Hen Under Bay-Tree" is less about the natural setting and more an allegorical comment upon Pitter's life. Self-effacingly, she pictures herself as "a squalid, empty-headed Hen, / Resolved to rear a private brood" (43). As a result, she flies up from "the social pen" and perches in "noblest solitude" on the branches of a baytree. We should not miss the irony here, since Pitter, who never married or had children, portrays herself as brooding hen; on the other hand, of course, her "offspring" are her poems, and her flight to the baytree connotes the laurel wreath, the classical token of honor given to poets. Noting the sense of being cut off from those who would understand her, Pitter says the hen waits: "Alert she sits, and all alone; / She breathes a time-defying air." While above her songbirds shake the tree with their carols, the hen is content to occupy the lower branches: "Unworthy and unwitting, yet / She keeps love's vigil glorious; / Immovably her faith is set, / The plant of honour is her house." While some might object to ending the poem with such an obvious moral, Pitter affirms through the hen several things. First, as a poet she is a loner, and given her penchant for following traditional forms and rejecting the modernism of T. S. Eliot and his imitators, this is no surprise. Second, as a poet, she will be true to her muse, and never get involved in self-promotion. Third, as a poet she will affirm the redemptive power of love in all its manifestations.

Finally, as a poet, the only validation she needs is having written the kind of poetry she believes in—the kind of poetry that speaks directly to the heart, to the soul, to the spirit of others.[18]

Pitter could little have known that after *The Ermine* she would live almost forty years. During these years she was very active, winning the William E. Heinemann Award for *The Ermine* and the Queen's Gold Medal for Poetry in 1955, writing dozens of essays, appearing regularly on BBC radio and television, and publishing three more volumes of poetry—*Still by Choice* (1966), *End of Drought* (1975), and *A Heaven to Find* (1987).[19] And while she continues to publish occasional nature poems in these volumes, she no longer retreats to Hainault Forest; instead, her thematic focus shifts primarily to reflections on aging and the spiritual life. When Pitter died on February 29, 1992, her passing was widely hailed as a great literary loss. One writer called her "one of the truest and most dedicated poets of her time; and it is a standing rebuke to English letters that her voice—clear, precise and unflustered amidst unfathomable depths—should have only lately sounded in the wilderness . . . . Pitter's beautifully contrived utterance calls her readers to attention; her seamless simplicity holds them transfixed. In her ordered scheme neither obscurity nor banality had any place."[20] He also added perceptively: "Her poetry combines grit and tenderness, hardness and fragility, sensual experience and intellectual vision. Yet somewhere behind these multiple antitheses, she would hint, there lies the single unattainable truth." Another writer said "she came to enjoy perhaps the highest reputation of any living English woman poet of her century."[21] He also noted her isolation from the mainstream poetry of her day: "Few who took the trouble to read her came away unimpressed by her Traherne-like dedication to Christianity or by her refusal to write except in her own voice. Her poetry behaves as if all the literary movements of the past century, from Georgianism to Concrete Poetry, had simply never happened . . . . In this, as in her wholly genuine modesty and disregard for fame, she was unique among her contemporaries. She was concerned only with verse." Ann Margaret Ridler affirmed that Pitter's "whole life was devoted to her craft, her writing grounded in the natural world, in common things and people portrayed with love and a painterly clarity."[22] Ridler went on to say that Pitter "celebrated a triumphant faith in an all-pervading divinity. Though at times she conveys a profound desolation, again and again she affirms the miracle of rebirth . . . . Her finest work reveals a strong certitude of visionary splendours within, through and beyond the natural world, and in this respect she was a true modern metaphysical." Perhaps the key to understanding Pitter's poetry is found in her essay, "We Cannot Take Less," that aired as a BBC radio address under the title "Hunting the Unicorn." Once again she recalls an early experience from Hainault Forest:

> I was sitting in front of a cottage door, one day in spring, long ago; a few bushes and flowers round me, a bird gathering nesting-material, the trees of the forest at a little distance. A poor place—nothing glamorous about it . . . [when] suddenly everything assumed a different aspect—no, its *true* aspect. For a moment, it seemed to me, the truth appeared in its overwhelming splendour. The secret was out, the explanation given. Something that had seemed like total freedom, total power, total bliss—a good with no bad as its opposite—an absolute that *had* no opposite—this thing, so unlike our feeble nature, had suddenly cut across one's life—and vanished . . . . What *is* this thing? . . . Is it—could it be, after all—a hint of something *more real* than this life—a message from reality—perhaps a particle of reality itself? If so, no wonder we hunt it so unceasingly, and never stop desiring and pining for it. (Feb. 17, 1961; *HU*, xvii and emphasis Pitter)

Ruth Pitter's nature poetry, fueled by her vivid memories of Hainault Forest, often takes us to hidden places—to the secret things of life, to the things just beyond the material, to the very meaning of life. Many times we catch glimpses of the hidden treasure. If human life is lived behind a veil faintly obscuring reality, Pitter's nature poems often lift the edge of the veil. In her hunt for the unicorn, many of us join the pursuit, because, like Pitter, we cannot take less.

In the introduction to Pitter's *Collected Poems* (1990), Elizabeth Jennings praises Pitter's "acute sensibility and deep integrity"; Jennings claims that her poems "are informed with a sweetness which is also bracing, and a generosity which is blind to nothing, neither the sufferings in this world nor the quirky behavior of human beings."[23] Philip Larkin, who edited the *Oxford Book of Modern Verse*, included four of her poems, writing to a friend that her poetry was "rather good," high praise coming from one of the most respected twentieth-century English poets.[24] As I have tried to illustrate in this study of her nature poetry, Ruth Pitter deserves a wider reading and a more judicious critical appraisal. If she "enjoyed the highest reputation of any living English woman poet of her century," it is time that both her life and her art be given the exposure and recognition they so richly deserve.

Chapter 11 Notes

1. A version of this essay first appeared in *CSL: Bulletin of the New York C. S. Lewis Society* 38 (July-August 2007): 1–10, 12–17.

2. See the *festschrift*, *Ruth Pitter: Homage to a Poet*, ed. Arthur Russell (London: Rapp and Whiting, 1969). Pitter, in contrast to T. S. Eliot, Ezra Pound, and W. H. Auden, is a traditional poet in the line of George Herbert, Thomas Traherne, William Wordsworth, John Keats, Thomas Hardy, A. E. Housman, W. B. Yeats, and Philip Larkin. Unlike the modernists, she rarely experiments with meter or verse form, nor does she explore modernist themes or offer critiques of modern English society. Instead she works with familiar meters and verse forms, and her reluctance to alter her voice to follow in the modernist line explains in part why critics have overlooked her poetry.

3. *A Mad Lady's Garland* (London: Cresset Press, 1934).

4. Barfield's correspondence to Pitter is available in her uncatalogued papers in Bodleian Library; emphasis Barfield.

5. I cite this correspondence in full in *HU*, 150–53.

6. Though reduced somewhat in size in the hundred plus years since Pitter's birth, this tract of forest is still largely intact, preserved by the Woodland Trust.

7. *HU*, 32–33. .

8. For more on this injury, see *HU*, 37–38.

9. *A Trophy of Arms: Poems 1926–1935* (London: Cresset Press, 1936), 39 (subsequent references in the text). Pitter's own gloss on the poem's origin connects it to her eye injury: "This poem is very singular to me because it was composed when I had temporarily quite lost my sight as the result of an accident. I'd seen the bird many years before, but it was only then, when I was blind, that its image came back to me in the most minute detail . . . . The small details . . . would not have been seen consciously while the eye was in action. But the image from the unconscious mind came back more complete than anything directly seen" (*HU*, 40).

10. After describing how he will go to Innisfree and build a small cabin "of clay and wattles," Yeats ends his poem: "I will arise and go now, for always night and day / I hear lake water lapping with low sounds by the shore; / While I stand on the roadway, or on the pavements grey, / I hear it in the deep heart's core."

11. See James Stephens, "Preface" to *A Trophy of Arms*; John Gawsworth, "Review of *A Trophy of Arms*," *New English Weekly*, September 24, 1936; Hilaire Belloc, "Two Poets" (review of *A Trophy of Arms* and A. E. Housman's *More Poems*), *G. K.'s Weekly*, October 26, 1936, p. 146; Eda Walton, "Miss Ruth Pitter's Poems" (review of *A Trophy of Arms*), *Times Literary Supplement*, October 3, 1936, p. 784; Dilys Powell, "Ruth Pitter's New Poems," *London Mercury*, October, 1936; Michael Roberts, "The Eternal Fog," *Spectator* 157 (October 16, 1936): 652; Siegfried Sassoon, *The New Statesman & Nation* 12 (December 19, 1936): 1034. In earlier letters to Pitter, Sassoon is highly complimentary. In a letter of October

22, 1936, he writes: "Please allow me to congratulate you on your beautiful book of poems. Until I bought 'A Trophy of Arms' I was entirely unaware of the existence of your exquisite work; but when I read 'Sudden Heaven' I felt so grateful to you that I harken to thank you . . . . Hoping that this letter will give you a little pleasure" (*HU*, 289). Two months later after his review of *A Trophy of Arms* appeared, he writes: "It was a great privilege to be able to praise your poems in print—a proud & pleasant privilege, in fact, to continue the alliteration! Your poems have qualities which I admire so deeply & gratefully. What I wrote about them was like a well-meaning elephant in a garden . . . . I only hope that my review has helped to make you more widely appreciated . . . . I very much hope to meet you one of these days" (December 22, 1936; *HU*, 289); and Dallas Kenmare, "The Triumph of 'Pure Poetry,'" *Poetry Review* (1937): 373–380. In addition, Pitter received many letters offering thanks and praise for her work. Perhaps the greatest praise came from Lord David Cecil, winner of the Hawthornden Prize in 1929 for *The Stricken Deer*, and later a great friend and supporter:

> Dear Miss Pitter, I hope you will forgive a total stranger writing to you. But I feel
> I must tell you how very beautiful I think your poems [*A Trophy of Arms*]. I read
> them last week in a fit of drab depression brought on by the condition of the world:
> and I cannot tell you what a ray of light spread out on my horizon to discover that
> some one cared still to write such firm spontaneous glowing poetry—could feel the
> essential normal beauties of soul & body, so freshly, so strongly, so unsentimentally.
> I read your mad Lady's Garland too & had liked that very much especially the Fowls
> Terrestrial & Celestial: but in your new book you have soared still higher. Thank you
> very, very much. (September ? 1936; cited in *HU*, 82)

12. The Hawthornden Prize, oldest of the major British literary prizes, was established in 1919 by Alice Warrender to recognize annually the best work of imaginative literature by a writer under forty-one years old. Edward Shanks won the initial award in 1919 for *The Queen of China*. Later winners included Edmund Blunden for *The Shepherd* (1922), Sean O'Casey for *Juno and the Paycock* (1925), Virginia Sackville-West for *The Land* (1926), Siegfried Sassoon for *Memoirs of a Fox-Hunting Man* (1928), Lord David Cecil for *The Stricken Deer* (1929), James Hilton for *Lost Horizon* (1934), Evelyn Waugh for *Edmund Campion* (1936), David Jones for *In Parenthesis* (1938), Graham Greene for *The Power and the Glory* (1941), and Ted Hughes for *Lupercal* (1961). When Pitter won the prize the monetary value was about $500; as of 2002 the award was worth $10,000.

13. *The Spirit Watches* (London: Cresset Press, 1939), 10 (subsequent references in the text).

14. The critical reception of *The Spirit Watches* was mixed. See Stephen Spender, "Review of *The Spirit Watches*," *The New Statesman & Nation* 18 (December 9, 1939): 834; Desmond Hawkins, "Recent Verse" (review of *The Spirit Watches*), *Spectator* 163 (December 15, 1939): 876; "The Watching Spirit" (review of *The Spirit Watches*), *Times Literary Supplement*, December 23, 1939; Eric Forbes-Boyd, "Two English Poets" (review of *The Spirit Watches*), *Christian Science Monitor*, February 24, 1940, p. 11; Louise Bogan, "Review of *The Spirit Watches*," *The New Yorker* 16 (April 20, 1940): 92; Louis Untermeyer, "Review of *The Spirit Watches*," *The Christian Century* 57 (April 24, 1940): 547; May Sarton, "Two Poets: W. B. Yeats and Ruth Pitter," *The University Review* [Kansas City] October 1940, pp. 63–65.

15. For more on this see *HU*, 84–140.

16. *The Bridge: Poems 1939–1944* (London: Cresset Press, 1945), 38 (subsequent references in the text).

17. Initial reaction to *The Bridge* was favorable. See "From Death to Life" (review of *The Bridge*), *Times Literary Supplement*, April 7, 1945, p. 164. In his *Four Living Poets* (1944), Rudolph Gilbert had anticipated this reviewer, calling Pitter "the poet of purity" and noting "what the poetry reader values most in Pitter's poems is her eloquence . . . . In Pitter one almost looks through the language, as through air, discerning the exact form of the objects which stand there, and every part and shade of meaning is brought out by the sunny light resting upon them" (48–49). Later he added: "She has a first-rate intuitive gift of observation, a control of poetic language and magical perception that is always to be found in great poetry" (52); Wilfrid Gibson, "Review of *The Bridge*," *The Manchester Guardian*, May 23, 1945, p. 3; "Two Contemporary British Poets Who Build Bridges" (review of *The Bridge*), *Christian Science Monitor Weekly Magazine Section* July 7, 1945, p. 15; "Review of *The Bridge*," *Kirkus* 13 (December 15, 1945): 552; G. W. Stonier, "Review of *The Bridge*," *New Statesman & Nation* 29 (April 28, 1945): 276; "Review of *The Bridge*," *New Yorker* 22 (February 23, 1946): 91; Randall Jarrell, "Review of *The Bridge*," *Nation* 162 (May 25, 1946): 633; Christopher Morley, "Testament against Terror" (review of *The Bridge*), *The Saturday Review of Literature*, 29 (March 23, 1946): 12; Fredrick Brantley, "Sparrow's Skull" (review of *The Bridge*), *New York Times*, May 5, 1946, p. 8; Babette Deutsch, "Delight and Dismay" (review of *The Bridge*), *Poetry: A Magazine of Verse* 68 (May 1946): 103; Theodore Maynard, "Review of *The Bridge*," *The Catholic World* 163 (July 1946): 373.

18. Certainly critics found *The Ermine* to be her most mature work of poetry. See "The Mortal Lot" (review of *The Ermine*), *The Times Literary Supplement*, August 21, 1953.

19. Her growing fame also provided her with opportunities to write regularly for magazines. For instance, Mary Grieve, the editor of *Woman: World's Greatest Weekly for Women*, contacted Pitter in August 1958, and asked: "I wonder if you would ever think about writing particularly for women? They say seven million women read *Woman* every week" (Aug. 5, 1958; *HU*, 228). After meeting, they agreed Pitter would write six articles on gardening, and her first essay appeared on October 25, 1958, under the running head "The Flower of Peace: A Countrywoman's Diary." Grieve was so pleased with Pitter's work that she commissioned six more and then another six; eventually the essays appeared weekly until December 5, 1959. For more, see *HU*, 228–30. Underlying all of Pitter's gardening thoughts is the sense of divine blessing and Edenic bliss, perhaps best illustrated in her November 1, 1958 article:

> A little Scotswoman with a heartbreakingly pretty voice once said to me, while we were talking about flowers, "Don't you miss the Garden of Eden?" Yes, that's just what I *do* miss. I miss it desperately. Think of it! To live in a paradise; in a perfect garden, in a perfect climate, where there is no sorrow, no sin, no suffering, no death. To live on glorious fruits and to see nothing but heavenly flowers and beautiful creatures, and to have divine Love itself dwelling with you! We all miss it, and we miss it all the time. But we are promised *heaven*, and that is more wonderful still. So I plant and tend my garden, and struggle on in spite of disappointments and failures; and every time I see some rich plant in bloom, or some beautiful, wholesome fruit ready to pick, I remember the beauty of that lost garden in the old, wonderful story with its deep meanings. And I look forward; forward to the promised place of bliss, with beauties and delights that no one can ever begin to imagine. (*HU*, 229; emphasis Pitter)

Pitter's search for lost Eden perhaps compelled her gardening instinct. In spite of nature's fallen status, in the garden she could best glimpse the kindness, goodness, and benevolence of God. While human relationships would always be complicated by sin, the promise of the garden and its paradisal vestiges drew Pitter to the beauties of the natural world.

20. *The Daily Telegraph*, March 2, 1992.

21. *The [London] Times*, March 3, 1992.

22. "Capturing the Dance in Stillness," *The Guardian*, March 3, 1992.

23. *Collected Poems: 1990* (Petersfield: Enitharmon, 1990), 15.

24. *Selected Letters of Philip Larkin*, ed. Anthony Thwaite (London: Faber & Faber, 1992), 412–13. The poems he includes are: "The Eternal Image," "Time's Fool," "But for Lust," and "Hen Under Bay-Tree."

Joy Davidman and the *New Masses*: Communist Poet and Reviewer[1]

Although best known as C. S. Lewis's wife, Joy Davidman was a gifted writer, publishing a volume of poetry, *Letter to a Comrade* (1938), two novels, *Anya* (1940) and *Weeping Bay* (1950), and the non-fiction book, *Smoke on the Mountain* (1953), her interpretation of the Ten Commandments.[2] However, these works are not the sum total of Davidman's literary output; from April 1938 through July 1945 Davidman's poetry, book reviews, and movie reviews appeared regularly in the *New Masses*, the semi-official weekly magazine of the Communist Party of the United States of America (CPUSA). These works of Davidman merit careful critical consideration. Accordingly, in what follows I offer a brief review of the history and literary/political agenda of *New Masses*, how Davidman came to be connected with it, and a critical evaluation of her work published there.

New Masses was the literary descendant of two radical periodicals.[3] *Masses* (1911–1918) was, according to Daniel Aaron, a "spectacular organ of socialism, anarchism, paganism, and rebellion."[4] Such a critical judgment is not surprising, given the masthead statement that appeared in every issue during the early editorship of Max Eastman:

THIS MAGAZINE IS OWNED AND PUBLISHED COOPERATIVELY BY ITS EDITORS. IT HAS NO DIVIDENDS TO PAY, AND NOBODY IS TRYING TO MAKE MONEY OUT OF IT. A REVOLUTIONARY AND NOT A REFORM MAGAZINE; A MAGAZINE WITH A SENSE OF HUMOR AND NO RESPECT FOR THE RESPECTABLE: FRANK, ARROGANT, IMPERTINENT, SEARCHING FOR THE TRUE CAUSES; A MAGAZINE DIRECTED AGAINST RIGIDITY AND DOGMA WHEREVER IT IS FOUND; PRINTING WHAT IS TOO NAKED OR TRUE FOR A MONEY-MAKING PRESS; A MAGAZINE WHOSE FINAL POLICY IS TO DO AS IT PLEASES AND CONCILIATE NOBODY, NOT EVEN ITS READERS—THERE IS A FIELD FOR THIS PUBLICATION IN AMERICA. (Cited in Aaron, 22; caps in original).

Politically *Masses* advanced a socialist agenda and for that caught the eye of the United States government; matters came to a head just prior to America's entry into World War I when *Masses* loudly opposed conscription. By April 1917 it was banned from the U. S. postal service and Eastman and his colleagues were indicted for conspiring to obstruct the draft (36). Although the trial ended with a hung jury, *Masses* never recovered.

After the suppression of *Masses*, *The Liberator* (1918–1924) appeared, largely subsuming and intensifying the socialist agenda of *Masses*. With Eastman as editor and others on his editorial staff, including Floyd Dell and Joseph Freeman, *The Liberator* marched steadily toward enthusiastic support for the Bolsheviks in Russia. Mike Gold, who joined the editorial staff of *The Liberator* in 1921, soon began to urge an even more revolutionary agenda for the periodical than Eastman; in particular, Gold vigorously pushed what he called proletarian literature—poems and stories by and about workers and their plight. In 1922 *The Liberator*, with its philosophical base squarely set in Bolshevism, was turned over to the Worker's Party, a transparent organ of the CPUSA. Since it was no longer primarily a periodical directed by artists and writers, *The Liberator*, now with an entirely political agenda, lost the interest of most of its former writers and readers; it folded in 1924.

With the demise of *The Liberator*, Gold and others established *New Masses* (1926–1948), largely in an effort to re-capture the spirit of *Masses*; that is, they wanted to combine literature and politics as had the earlier periodical. *New Masses* (hereafter *NM*) was published initially as a monthly beginning May 1926, and, as a result of financial difficulties and political in-fighting, Gold became the sole editor from 1928–1930. In a bellweather article published in January 1929, "Go Left, Young Writers," Gold pressed for the emergence of a proletarian writer, a "wild youth of about twenty-two, the son of working class parents, who himself works in the lumber camps, coal mines, and steel mills, harvest fields and mountain camps of America . . . . He is a Red but has few theories. It is all instinct with him. His writing is no conscious straining after proletarian art, but the natural flower of his environment."[5] Such writers could only be effective if they based their work upon personal experience: "Write. Your life in mine, mill, and farm is of deathless significance in the history of the world. Tell us about it in the same language you use in writing a letter. It may be literature—it often is. Write. Persist. Struggle" (189). In that same issue of *NM*, Martin Russak added: "A real proletarian writer must not only write about the working class, he must be read by the working class . . . [and he must embody] bitter hatred, absolute class solidarity, and revolutionary passion."[6] In September 1930 Gold offered more detail about the nature of what he called "proletarian realism" in his "Notes of the Month": such literature dealt "with *real conflicts* of men and women who work for a living. It has nothing to do with . . . sickly mental states nor mental anguish"; it "does not believe in literature for its own sake, but in literature that is useful, has a social function"; it would be written in "as few words as possible"; it would contain "swift action, clear form, the direct line, cinema in words"; and it would do "away with lies about human nature. We are scientists; we know what a man thinks and feels" (*A Literary Anthology*, 206–08; emphasis Gold).[7]

Such a view of literature threatened to reduce it to thinly veiled propaganda; at the same time, such literature supported the revolutionary aims of the CPUSA in the 1930s. Given the tremendous social upheaval resulting from the stock market crash in 1929 and the subsequent Great Depression, the CPUSA found fertile ground in the thousands of unemployed, homeless, and displaced. Yet, ironically, readership of *NM* lagged so badly that it ceased publication in September 1933 with a circulation of only 6,000 copies a month. When it reappeared as a weekly in January 1934 with Granville Hicks as editor, it had, by necessity, broadened its revolutionary agenda; by December

1934 its circulation had increased to 25,000 weekly, and Gold stepped back from editorial involvement.[8]

By advocating and publishing proletarian literature, the re-invented *NM* carried forward the banner of the CPUSA in a highly public fashion. The short story, "Quiet and Safe," by Len Zinberg is representative of one stream of proletarian realism that appeared in *NM*. Offered from the perspective of a strike breaker, the story purports to give us an inside view of his cowardly psychology. In recounting his tentative journey toward the picket lines, the strike breaker worries that there are no policemen around to protect him; he imagines being attacked by those on the picket line: "Those dirty bastards waiting to slug him, and there was no cops! Those saps, just hoping to smack him one, and they would hit him. He could feel the dull smacking sound of a fist on a jaw, on a soft eye, on a nose, on a soft stomach; a lot of fists landing on his face." Whatever authorial distance Zinberg began writing the story with disappears in the next paragraph when we read: "As he wiped the sweat from his thin oval face, he saw the door of the building open and a cop come out. The scab thought, the sonofabitch must have been smoking in the hallway, not even looking out for me."[9]

Now that readers know for certain they are reading about a scab, they can be sure he will be paid in full by the end of the story. The little forced tension created in the story concerns how the scab manages to get past the picket line by attaching himself to a mailman; smirking to himself about how he has fooled the strikers, the scab takes an elevator up to his work place only to find he is early and locked out. When he hears the elevator coming up again, he is in a panic, certain the strikers are coming to beat him up. However, when he sees it is the mailman, the denouement occurs and the story ends: "The mailman was passing him and the scab grinned and said 'Hello, *pal*. Kind of . . .' The postman swung from his knees as he turned, a heavy roundhouse blow that sent the scab crashing against the wall; then he slipped to the floor . . . . The scab lay there quietly, a slim trickle of blood running out of the side of his mouth and down over his broken jaw" (153). In spite of Zinberg's intention that we find irony in how the story ends, given its title, cartoon characters, facile understanding of human nature, and transparent hatred for the "scab," the story is more laughable than convincing.

The poetry appearing in *NM* was sometimes not much better. For instance, in the introduction to "Eight New Poets" we read the following:

"[These poems are] indicative of the extent to which the social crisis and the agitation for a literature with social emphasis and proletarian bias has permeated the general literary scene and influenced a new group of writers. A number of them have no connections with working-class organizations, but their sympathies are definitely with the proletariat. This symposium is presented with the hope it will stimulate a new interest in and encourage a social poetry."[10] "Winter Haven" describes the plight of "cold boys, loading gunnysacks with coke"; "Monday Morning" offers a snapshot view of a hobo jungle and sardonically notes that "strong coffee is almost as good as lysol is, to wash / the ache from the bones"; "Dirge for the Fearsome" mocks those who lack the courage to fight for labor; "Poem in the Pressroom," "'Fired!'" and "Phyllis and Corydon" lament the helplessness of workers against their bosses; "Meaning" considers a worker and his wife in their struggle to survive and find meaning in life; "Death of Barbusse" attempts to evoke the revolutionary spirit of W. B. Yeats; "Intellectual to Worker" is an ironic dramatic monologue in which a writer tries to convince a laborer that the work each does supports the revolution. Perhaps the key example in this collection of eight poems of proletarian realism is "Sonnet":

> The living soul is nailed upon a graph
> and money bends the index toward despair
> but, cushioned soft, our half-hog humans laugh
> the child's way, ego's—their private joy sole care.
> And still they throw as gypsies do a card,
> staking the world come fortune lapse or thrive;
> still pitch coins to a ghetto-ghost in the yard;
> still yap "Stay yoked!" and still, "Be glad alive!"
> here's paradox, puffed to your size: reject your class,
> parcel your pity off for a fool's iota,
> fatten yourself like a pet bug under glass,
> live for yourself and lo! death's sure your quota!
> But death damned more, to end as fascist meat,
> hung like a butchered rabbit by your feet. (13)

Whatever the merits this has in advancing proletarian realism—and I am not convinced there are many—has there ever been an uglier poem?[11]

Not everything appearing in *NM* was as crude as these examples; indeed another stream appeared containing writings by many luminaries of contemporary American literature, including William Carlos Williams, Robinson Jeffers, Theodore Dreiser, Sherwood Anderson, John Dos Passos, Edmund Wilson, Erskine Caldwell, Langston Hughes, Richard Wright, and Ernest Hemingway. Lesser lights included Granville Hicks, Horace Gregory, James Farrell, Margaret Walker, Muriel Rukeyser, and, of course, Joy Davidman. These writers, largely uncomfortable with the propagandist stream, subtly helped transformed the meaning of proletarian literature from Gold's early definition to a literature written by those "who have clearly indicated their sympathy to the revolutionary cause" (Aaron, 283). Writing in the *Partisan Review*, Arvin Newton argued that "all proletarian writers . . . are under a solemn obligation to fight tooth and nail against philistinism in all its nauseating forms; to rise above parochialism both of time and place; and to save from the black night of fascism all of the past that is really humane and of good report."[12] A case in point was the active support of *NM* to the loyalists during the Spanish Civil War. In the June 22, 1937, essay, "Fascism Is a Lie," Hemingway writes: "Really good writers are always rewarded under almost any existing system of government that they can tolerate. There is only one form of government that cannot produce good writers, and that system is fascism. For fascism is a lie told by bullies. A writer who will not lie cannot live or work under fascism."[13] Had Hemingway known of the similar bullying of communism in the Soviet Union, he might have changed the title of his essay to "Totalitarianism Is a Lie"; be that as it may, his essay suggests how interest in proletarian literature flourished in the pages of *NM* throughout the 1930s.

Joy Davidman's connection to communism and *NM* was a gradual process that began sometime in the mid-1930s. In her autobiographical essay, "The Longest Way Round," she describes in part how she became attracted to communism. Although she came from a financially secure, middle-class family, she witnessed the terrible social conditions brought about by the Great Depression:

> To live entirely for my own pleasures, with hungry men selling apples
> on every street corner, demanded a callousness of which I seemed
> incapable. Maybe no rational person would worry about the rest of

the world; I found myself worrying, all the same. And I wanted to *do* something, so I joined the Communist Party . . . . I entered the Party in a burst of emotion, without making the slightest effort to study Marxist theory. All I knew was that capitalism wasn't working very well, war was imminent—and socialism promised to change all that. And for the first time in my life I was willing to be my brother's keeper. So I rushed round to a Party acquaintance and said I wanted to join.[14]

Joining was not as easy as she thought; after two failed attempts in which Party officials bungled the records, she finally received her membership card in 1938.[15] In addition to the social and economic crises she saw, her own situation at the time as a "permanent substitute teacher" in the New York City high school system, a designation that effectively blocked her path to a permanent teaching license, also contributed to her movement toward the CPUSA; in effect, she was chattel in the excess teacher labor pool. With the literary success of *Letter to a Comrade* in 1938, Davidman found herself as a potentially useful tool of the Party.

Within a short time of joining the CPUSA, Davidman, eager to use her talents as a writer, sought out a way to help the Party. Since she had been reading *NM* for some time, particularly the poetry, she eventually made her way to the offices of *NM* and offered her services. Almost immediately she was brought on board as a poetry editor. No lover of proletarian literature herself—she believed many of the poems previously published in *NM* were bad poems in spite of their proletarian rhetoric—she set about to raise the quality of verse appearing in *NM*. At the same time, she learned that she must support the agenda of the Party through her *NM* work. In "The Longest Way Round" she writes: "I was accepted almost at once as a journalist and critic on the Party's semiofficial magazine, *New Masses*. And I began to learn . . . that my judgment of a book or movie must depend, not on its artistic merit, but on its Marxist orthodoxy, or even on whether its author was a liberal contributor to the Party's needy treasury" (*OB*, 91).[16] In addition she found "that, at the sight of a hero, a martyr, or a genius, I must say, not, 'How wonderful!' but, 'How can we *use* him? . . . . [To the Party] I willingly gave my spare time, my spare cash, my love of truth, and my artistic conscience" (91–92; emphasis Davidman). Nonetheless, she maintained some independence: "There were, however, some signs of health in me. I made jokes at the Party's expense; I continued, in the teeth of the Party's contempt, to read fantasy; and I utterly failed to read the dreamy books we called 'proletarian novels'" (92).

Initially it appeared that she would make her primary contribution to *NM* as a poet. Though she was only twenty-three years old, her first poem in *NM*, "Strength through Joy," appeared in the April 5, 1938, issue. A satiric attack on fascism, the poem illustrates the essential poetic voice of Davidman: focused, concentrated, hard, insisting on being heard, earnest, serious, determined, confrontational, zealot-like, insightful, and penetrating. For instance, she neatly parodies the Satanic pride of Hitler:

> For I am he
> the maker of honor, the hand bestowing judgment
> seen in a cloud, the jaws of desolation,
> begetter of dead men, eater of my sons,
> and when any man is gnawed by the mouth of a cannon
> I grow new teeth. I am filled with iron,
> with fire and exhalations; I am magnificent,
> honor the nails of my feet and the parings thereof
> each being capable of killing. I am precious
> and a treasure to women; honor then my knees
> and the clasp of my thighs. And I will give you,
> you, my dear children, my loving children, you
> wearing my symbol on the fat of your arm
> the beautiful moment, the moment of beautiful pain
> with which you burst into flames; the high, the radiant
> and honorable death.[17]

In "Prayer Against Indifference" appearing four months later she uses a similarly hard-edged voice, asking that she be castigated if she ever fails to be outraged at injustices such as wars, ruined men, and "bloody children lying dead." Instead, she prays for "eyes that will not shut; / Let me have truth at my tongue's root; / Let courage and the brain command / The honest fingers of my hand." If ever she fails these—of particular note is the allusion to her craft as a writer and its demand she write and publish the truth—she begs that she be destroyed: "And when I wait to save my skin / Break roof and let my death come in."[18]

Other *NM* poems by Davidman are less confrontational; at the same time, however, they reflect issues held dearly by the CPUSA or those holding a revolutionary ideology. For instance, several poems illustrate sympathy for the loyalists' efforts against the fascist forces in Spain. "Near Catalonia" is a measured lament for the woefully undersupplied loyalist forces:

> We have the sweet noise of the sea at our back
> And before us the bitter shouting of the gun
> And the brass wing of aeroplanes and the sun
> That walks above us burning. Here we wound
> Our feet on metal fragments of the bomb,
> The sword unburied and the poisoned ground.
> Here we stand; here we lie; here we must see
> What we can find potent and good to set
> Between the fascist and the deep blue sea.

The poem then notes the things the loyalist soldiers lack: adequate defense against the bombs, airplanes, and poison gas of the fascist forces. All they have to offer in defense against the enemy is captured in the poignant conclusion:

> We have only the bodies of men to put together,
> The wincing flesh, the peeled white forking stick,
> Easily broken, easily made sick,
> Frightened of pain and spoiled by evil weather;
> We have only the most fragile of all things the man,
> And the heart the most iron admirable thing of all;
> And putting these together we make a wall.[19]

"Pacific Shore," a poem almost certainly written in 1939 during Davidman's brief sojourn to Hollywood as a movie screen writer, shifts away from Spain and tenderly explores a family's quiet despair at having been evicted from their farm apparently for failure to meet their mortgage: "What do we do now? / Plant our bodies in the ebb and flow? / Harvestless man, wife and son and daughter, / bury ourselves in the nice cheap water?" What should they do? Simply accept the way capitalism has driven them off their land? Davidman concludes the poem with a veiled call to revolution: "Turn around and take it back again, / turn again and take the country back / that the bank nibbled in the honest man's track / . . . Turn back, turn back our faces to the sun."[20]

Perhaps Davidman's most unusual poem appearing in *NM* is "Peter the Plowman." It begins with apocalyptic images and dire warnings that people should face the truth about the evils of capitalism rather than hurrying "to get back to the shady nook in hell / where they lie down with arms around their worry / in decent privacy." But then the poem focuses upon the prophetic role of the poet:

> I the songmaker, the sun's conscious lover,
> had my vision, not in dreamy weather,
> nor in lightning nor the burning bush,
> but soberly in winter while the sun
> lit up the loneliness of everyone;
> saw myself and all the songmakers
> as hollow bugles to the people's mouth
> speaking the Judgment word. I heard
> the tombs explode; I saw the dead arise.

Divorcing the poet's prophetic insight from any religious origin ("nor the burning bush"), Davidman suggests instead it comes from the cold light of day. Poets find that through them, seemingly inexplicably, "rolled the everlasting sound / dragging sleepers up from underground." The poem then ends with perhaps Davidman's most explicit statement of how she sees herself as a poet:

> Poet, poet, you are the people's trumpet;
> golden and clean put yourself to their lips,
> tear yourself apart to shout their word
> so that no gun is louder, no fear is louder,
> no frightening bell is louder in its steeple;
> till all the sunlight shines on all the people.[21]

If this ending is Davidman's *NM* poetic manifest in brief, and I believe it is, it explains why all her *NM* poetry is outward looking—that is, it is poetry concerned with showing the moral and economic bankruptcy of the two worldviews she most despised at the time: fascism and capitalism.

In general Davidman's *NM* poems, while written in the tradition of proletarian literature, are nonetheless well done; although she had a political agenda driving her selection of subject matter, her poems are not simply set pieces. She uses irony effectively and her imagery is evocative if well-worn. The central problem with her *NM* poems is their outward focus on social issues; that is, these are all public poems revealing little about her personal experience.[22] We are never given an inside view of Davidman's understanding of the human condition; instead, she paints on a very broad canvas her perceived understanding of the plight of her proletarian subjects. While poetry does not, of necessity, have to give readers an inside view of the human condition, perhaps the most compelling, penetrating, and moving poetry does precisely that. Whatever the merits of public poetry, most readers find private poems—ones that expose what it means to be human, ones that reveal artfully and truthfully the heart, the soul, the mind, and the spirit—to be more interesting. And certainly Davidman was capable of such poetry as roughly half of the poems in *Letter to a Comrade* illustrate.

However, poetry was not the primary literary contribution Davidman made to *NM*; instead it was her facility as a book, theater, and movie reviewer—especially the latter—that best portrays her contribution to the cause.[23] During her most active period as a writer and editor for *NM*, March 1941 through July 1943, she was publishing a book, theater, or movie review in almost every issue.[24] Her initial reviews, published from December 1938 through May 1939, were book reviews. An early review, that of Kenneth Porter's volume of poetry, *The High Plains*, on February 7, 1939, illustrates an important element found in almost all her reviews: a biting pen. Davidman begins kindly enough: "In an age when so much verse is verbally profuse and emotionally costive, technically dazzling and stale with the pedantry of an Ezra Pound, it is sometimes refreshing to come upon a book wherein purpose and passion somewhat outrun technique."[25] However, her pen turns sharp later on when she dismisses some of the religious poems; in particular, she says Porter's "The Lord's Supper" rises "to singular heights of silliness . . . with its comparison of a mountain to a sliced cake." In correspondence with Porter later she tries to ameliorate her criticism:

> I was rather hasty in calling "The Lord's Supper" silly, I'm afraid. Looking at it now, I see it was the whole sacramental idea which annoyed me; I'm inclined by nature to call anything sacramental sentimental, being an iron materialist. As for the imagery, I've seen the mountains you speak of and I know the symbolism, but the whole

philosophy of the poem is so unlike mine, and so unlike, indeed, that of your own later work, that I could wish you had followed your first impulse in not printing it.

In the letter Davidman goes on to admit her tendency toward sharp criticism: "I must tell you something about that review; it's probably the most favorable I've ever written, for the cat in me comes out in reviewing; and it was originally half of a longer review, the other part of which was devoted to a book which I boiled in oil by way of contrast. But I cut that out, attacked by an uneasy conscience because I knew the book's author" (February 19, 1939; *OB*, 16–17).

Davidman's candid admission of her aggressive tendency to unsheathe her pen is borne out in many later reviews. She did not suffer fools lightly. For example, she begins one review: "When all the hack ideas in Hollywood are laid end to end, you get something like the package labeled *Come Live with Me*."[26] Then she adds: "The laughs are spaced as widely as a seven-year-old's teeth . . . and Jimmy Stewart's attempt to get into his wife's arms is nothing you ought to see after a heavy meal" (30). About Barbara Stanwick's acting in one film, Davidman writes: "[Her] girl reporter is a soggy stain on the film. She does her emotional scenes as a series of impassioned squawks."[27] In one of her most blistering reviews she savages the World War II movie *I Wanted Wings*:

> This reviewer has always considered herself fairly articulate, yet, face to face with *I Wanted Wings*, she feels the poverty of her vocabulary. All the words that describe it adequately are unprintable . . . . [The film] makes no bones about its intentions. It is a recruiting poster in style, sentiment, and static quality. If you imagine yourself compelled to stare at such a poster for two solid hours, you will have some idea of the entertainment value of this juicy offering . . . . Using the crudest of appeals, *I Wanted Wings* alternates uplifting pep talks with uplifted blondes. A more flaccid script would be hard to imagine . . . . It is astonishing, indeed, how many women there are in the Air Corps (Hollywood version). They attend court-martials, they stroll across the field cheerfully snapping pictures of bombers, they stow away in airplanes. And they never wear any underwear, or much overwear for that matter . . . . [It] is a limping affair; you find yourself looking closely at the screen to make sure the projector

hasn't stopped. There are, of course, some extremely beautiful and intelligent airplanes, that contrast favorably with the human performers . . . . If Miss Veronica Lake ever puts on a brassiere, her acting ability will disappear.[28]

She is equally severe with *That Uncertain Feeling*, a film that "is a soufflé that has been left standing too long . . . . Its final consistency is such that you could sell it as an old rubber tire, and not even a goat would notice the difference in taste."[29] About *Penny Serenade* she remarks: "All that you can get from [this film] can be obtained more economically by slicing an onion. Besides, an onion doesn't smell that bad" (30–31). About "a repulsive young [actor] named Victor Mature, who is being served up as a skinful of sex appeal," she opines: "Having appeared in several bad movies, Mr. Mature is within the province of this reviewer, who would trade her rights in him for enough fertilizer to nourish the snapdragons in her windowbox."[30] Perhaps her most terse dismissal of a film is the following: "There is only one thing wrong with *Young Mr. Pitt*; it is a lie."[31]

A good deal of Davidman's venom against Hollywood is undoubtedly connected with her unsuccessful sojourn there to write screenplays. Yet she could also appreciate good work coming from Hollywood. In her review of *Rage in Heaven* she reveals her own earlier involvement with the film and candidly admits that it is now a much better picture than she left it: "*Rage in Heaven* has passed through many hands since James Hilton let it fall with a dull thud. This reviewer had a crack at writing it, too, in her Metro-Goldwyn-Mayer days, and it is with great magnanimity that she admits the film is much better than she or James Hilton left it. Purged of its original drooling sentiment, *Rage in Heaven* is a swift and exciting study of yet one more psychopathic murderer" ("Huey Hooey," 31). In another reference to her time in Hollywood, she writes: "Writing a film script is much like writing anything else; you get a bright idea, you put it on paper quickly in the first flush of inspiration, and then the hard work starts."[32] Another insight into Davidman's Hollywood experience comes in her book review of Leo C. Rosten's *Hollywood: The Movie Colony—The Movie Makers* (New York: Harcourt Brace, 1942). She opens by saying the book "is extensive but not intensive, like a very little manure spread over a very big field." Rather than objective research, Rosten, argues Davidman, has relied upon gossip, generality, and prejudice. She says the book is "a deliberate whitewashing of the producer caste," and that it "is not a survey of Hollywood; it is an appeasement of Hollywood—the Hollywood of reaction, labor-baiting and Red-baiting, and cheap escapism."[33]

Her most damning indictment of Hollywood comes in an essay in which she considers its screen portrayals of women, an implicit critique perhaps suggesting reasons for her own lack of success there. "Women, Hollywood Version" is essentially a charge that the men running Hollywood are male chauvinists. She begins by citing a line from the movie *Tom, Dick, and Harry* where the female lead, Ginger Rogers, says: "It's as natural for a girl to want to make a good marriage as for a man to want to get ahead in business." Davidman then argues that the male producers of the movie would be surprised that such a line might open them to a charge of misogyny. Long before feminism was a cultural given, Davidman argued several of its principal tenets:

> In the United States, the emancipation of women is part and parcel of the democracy we are fighting for. Increasingly, women succeed along lines once reserved for men; as in the Soviet Union and Britain, women replace men whenever possible in the war effort. Nor are their homes worse run, their children worse cared for. On the contrary; as any psychologist knows, women who have realized their potentialities as creative human beings make better mothers than frustrated women who must take all their ambitions out on their children. Thus the films are lagging behind the country. Their half-unconscious war against the emancipation of women certainly gives unintended support to one of the tenets of fascism—the deliberate debasement of womanhood.[34]

She next points out that most Hollywood movies promote a vision of women intimating that their lives are "entirely what [men choose] to make [them]." Wives are shown to be happy not when they exercise their own desires and aspirations, but rather when they "know their place" and settle for being good wives, mothers, and home-makers. "The cardinal point of woman's emancipation—the admission that she can have a successful career and a successful marriage—is almost never made" in popular Hollywood films (29). Instead, films are filled with caricatures of women: the crotchety schoolteacher, the frustrated and unglamorous professional woman, or the office sourpuss.

Soviet films, by way of contrast, are praised by Davidman for their portrayal of women who have successful careers and marriages. Hollywood, on the other hand, glorifies female beauty and accordingly objectifies women into sex objects:

> In forcing women into the harem, the important thing is to make the women like it; they must be induced to accept their unhealthy fate as highly moral and emotionally desirable. Consequently we have [a whole school] of films, glorifying a morbidly passive and self-effacing female type; the great range of movies, superficially quite inoffensive, which never say a word derogatory to women yet present them in a dependent and inferior position as a matter of course . . . . The routine film heroine has no integrity, no sense, no reliability. She is always breaking off her engagement when a more enticing prospect comes along; yielding spinelessly to the blandishment of the brash youth whom she began by resenting; falling among thieves and Nazi spies; dancing helplessly in the background while the villain conks the hero; slapping faces at insults to her imbecile "dignity"; making an idiot of herself at baseball games. But ah, she has beauty! She has S[ex] A[ppeal], and has It. (29–30)

Davidman claims the reason for this sexual exploitation is simple: money. In addition, "this nakedly financial motive" shows "the plain fact that film-makers write as they think. If they regard woman as a commercial article, that is because pretty girls come to Hollywood from all over the country to trade in their beauty. Beauty is a drug on the market in southern California" (30). Although she does not argue movies are the sole cause of a woman's lack of genuine self-esteem, she does see a vicious cycle: "The movies, out of carelessness or miseducation or corruption, imitate and prettify some of the worst features of daily life; and life promptly imitates the movies" (31). In her conclusion, she offers a possible solution: "The true corrective is in the education of the American people. When the people at last repudiate completely all expressions of male chauvinism, the movies will hastily follow suit" (31).

The importance of "Women, Hollywood Version" is three-fold. First, it illustrates Davidman's willingness to take on an entire industry—one that had essentially chewed her up and spat her out—with energy, insight, and candor. Many of her arguments against the way in which movies trivialize women and glorify sex are still valid, albeit much has changed in Hollywood's portrayal of women during the last seventy-five years. Second, it shows her expressing radical positions that she never bothers to document—for instance, the claim that "any psychologist" knows working women make better mothers "than frustrated women who must take all their ambitions out on their children." This is the zeal of the revolutionary, the argument of one who knows she is right, the righteous word of one whose authority is her own sense of moral superiority. Finally, it reveals a passionate personality intent on righting the wrongs perpetuated by a system she finds repellant, exploitive, and manipulative.

Although Davidman has much criticism for Hollywood, she consistently praised one genre of films it produced: "This reviewer has said nasty things about Hollywood. Yet today she wishes to make partial amends. There is at least one branch of the film art in which Hollywood remains supreme. I refer, of course, to the screwball comedy. When they want to fill a picture with lunatics, boy, do they fill it with lunatics."[35] For instance, her first movie review in *NM*, "Marxist Mania," had nothing to do with the father of communism. Instead, she lavishes praise on *Go West*: "For slapstick as it ought to be, thank God, there are still the Marx brothers.[36]" Davidman also gave high marks to many Disney films: "*Dumbo* is the most delightful Disney so far . . . [with] a circus full of animals, all with personality, all of remarkable and interesting shape." She compliments the color and draftsmanship of the illustrators, the lively music, and "the general atmosphere of affectionate gaiety." Davidman especially praises the parade of pink elephants: "So you think *you've* seen pink elephants? Hah. Precision requires me to add that they are not all strictly pink; how about the neat little number in a rather surprising plaid?"[37] She also enjoyed well-done musicals; regarding *Louisiana Purchase* she uncharacteristically coos: "[It] is enchantingly carried out all through; its wit is gay and natural, its plotting extraordinarily cogent, and its bright and light and fantastic technicolor is admirably suited to the unreal world of the musical film . . . . *Louisiana Purchase* is a darling picture. As this reviewer is beginning to melt slightly at the edges, we had better stop here."[38]

Another genre of films she consistently reviewed was, not surprisingly, the war movie. Although she could be savage, as her evaluation of *I Wanted Wings* has already shown, Davidman actually wanted there to be better movies about the realities of the war—in part because she was an American and in part because she was a communist intent on exposing fascism at every turn. In time there were better produced war movies. Among many she singled out for commendation were *Target for Tonight, Mrs. Miniver, Ring of Steel, One of Our Aircraft Is Missing, Wake Island, Commandos Strike at Dawn, Air Force, Hangmen also Die, Action in the North Atlantic,* and *Bataan.* She commends *Mrs. Miniver* as "an American war film to be proud of . . . [for] its adult dignity, the restrained power of its tragedy, and its foursquare approach to the fact of the people's war."[39] In *One of Our Aircraft Is Missing* Davidman is thrilled to find "that the [story of] trapped airmen can make a first-rate, sober, and genuinely heroic film." Of the film's portrayal of Nazis, she says: "They are always there, a lurking terror: never quite seen, hence all the more horrible. They snarl orders outside a church full of praying people; they growl at each other round the corner where the Englishmen are hiding . . . . The movie as effectively portrays our enemy as it presents the heroism of our allies."[40] *Commandos Strike at Dawn* draws high praise because "this film of the fighting Norwegian people says, at last, exactly the right things about an occupied nation, about quislings, and about Nazis."[41] She singles out *Hangmen also Die* as so great a film "that the critic's task becomes humble study of [its] methods . . . . [It] may well be America's finest artistic comment on the war."[42]

Davidman also had the good fortune to be writing movie reviews for *NM* during a period in which appeared some of the finest movies ever made, including *Citizen Kane, The Maltese Falcon, How Green Was My Valley, Casablanca, Keeper of the Flame,* and *The Ox-Bow Incident.* She says *The Maltese Falcon* makes "the movie detective story completely adult . . . . Sam Spade, the amorous but grim detective, is more effective than Sherlock Holmes ever was, proving in Humphrey Bogart's adroit hands that a detective can be human and doesn't have to wear a funny hat." Characterization, she argues, is the particular strength of the film: "The detective, the villains, the sweet little liar of a heroine, are all memorable people. Even the widow in the background, weeping, is an incisive study of one kind of fraud."[43] *Keeper of the Flame,* which ignited a firestorm of critical controversy for implying there existed a secret conspiracy to promote American fascism, is a critically important film according to Davidman because "now as never before American fascism must be stamped out, before it loses the war for us; and *Keeper of the Flame* is a bright weapon to kill it with." She also heaps praise on an unlikely place: Hollywood. "The producers of MGM who backed the picture are to be congratulated." And while she also has compliments for the director, George Cukor, and the key actors, Spencer Tracy and Katherine

Hepburn, it is the anti-fascism message she most endorses: "The driving force of the film . . . transcends individual contributions, uniting them into a single clear statement: the enemies of the people are moving among us under cover of darkness. They must be exposed."[44]

However, the most important group of films that Davidman reviewed for *NM* were the dozens coming out of the Soviet Union. Predictably, Davidman only found praise for these films; while it is certainly true that some of them deserved her commendation, it is also true that she did not exercise the same critical eye with them than she did with the American, British, and French films she reviewed. In other words, she followed the Party line in reviewing the Soviet films; thus, they were essentially all good films—no matter the weaknesses and flaws—because they came out of the Soviet Union and implicitly illustrated how communism was a superior form of government than either capitalism or fascism. For instance, in her first review of a Soviet film, *The New Teacher*, she inadvertently reveals her bias: "*The New Teacher* . . . is rather a lovely thing . . . . It is hard to put into words just why . . . . All one can say is that the picture dances and leaps with the joy of life."[45] Regarding the Soviet documentary, *Soviet Frontiers on the Danube*, she says: "You can see what happy people really look like. When the Red Army marched into Bessarabia, years of misery and persecution were wiped out . . . . The Soviets need no guards between themselves and the people; throughout the villages, the entire population swarms out, clambers over the tanks, brings little bunches of wild flowers and presses them into soldiers' hands." While an impartial reviewer would at least suggest the possibility that such scenes are obviously part of a propaganda campaign, Davidman never entertains the thought. Instead, she sings its praises: "One could go on forever without conveying a tenth of the emotional power of *Soviet Frontiers*. This reviewer does not, ordinarily, label films 'must'; but *Soviet Frontiers* is a 'must' picture. You have to go and see it; you can't afford not to."[46] The editors at *NM* and their CPUSA comrades must have been delighted.

Other glowing reviews include *Wings of Victory* ("It has remained for the Soviets to produce the first great film on flying, because only the Soviet, only a socialist state, could understand that the man is more important than the plane"), *The Girl from Leningrad* (its fighting scenes "are perhaps the best of all shots of modern war"), *Guerrilla Brigade* ("Never was a Soviet film a more magnificent tribute to the common man—his suffering, his heroism, his triumphs. Indeed, it is hard to think of *Guerrilla Brigade* as a film at all, or of its men and women as actors; the thing is a piece of living history"), *This is the Enemy* (". . . has brilliantly solved the problem besetting all our novelists, playwrights, and screen writers; the problem of integrating a struggle of individuals against Nazis with the great struggle of humanity"), and *In the Rear of the Enemy* ("It happens to be a rather tremendous film; but it is still more tremendous as a statement of the brotherhood of peoples").[47] About the musical *Volga-Volga*, she positively gushes: "Do the Soviets *have* to come out on top in everything? They already have the best diplomats, the best kindergartens, the best economic system, the best life—but is that enough for them? No; they go and get the best musical comedies too. I turn green. I gnash my teeth with envy."[48]

It remains to offer an overall critique of Davidman talents as a reviewer. First, she was conscientious and regular in her reviews; even if she disliked a film, she would explain why, although sometimes it must be admitted with a poisoned pen. Second, she was not always caustic and could be quite generous; for example, about *Out of the Fog* she says: "[It] is so good as to leave this reviewer without a chance to exercise her poison pen. A tale of decent, ordinary human beings threatened by a gangster, the film has obvious symbolism, and its final rallying of the gentle people to destroy the gangster is the rallying of the oppressed the world over."[49] Third, although my essay has not shown this, she often wrote about the technical excellences or failures of a film, including lighting, camera angles, editing, musical scores, and direction; another way to put this is that she took her craft as a movie reviewer seriously. Fourth, although she often sold-out her critical soul when it came to reviewing movies from the Soviet Union, in other regards she was an honest reviewer who explained her reasons for liking or disliking a film. Fifth, she used language effectively; she never wasted words, opined thoughtlessly, prattled for effect, or pandered to the lowest common denominator. Fifth, she treated film as art; accordingly, she tried to write movie reviews that respected film for its potential to move viewers toward a great understanding of the human condition.

In total Davidman published in *NM* more than a dozen poems, over ninety movie or play reviews (covering more than one hundred and ninety works), fifteen book reviews, and a dozen or so opinion pieces.[50] After her CPUSA and *NM* days were over, Davidman freely admitted that she sold out her personal and literary soul to the Party, linking her with many other lapsed American communists of the 1930s. She explains part of her disillusionment with communism in a letter to William Rose Benét, thanking him for a recent poem, "To a Communist," in which he offered an even-handed evaluation of the failures of communism while avoiding personal attacks[51]:

> It's quite true, I'm afraid, that Marxism is just another of man's hope-less attempts to foresee and control the future, and a crystal ball would have done nearly as well . . . . As for me, I had to have a direct and shattering experience of God, and then to plow my way through Lenin's *Materialism*, surely the world's most unreadable book . . . in order to find out that Marxism was philosophically nonsensical, logically unsound, historically arbitrary, and scientifically half false from the start and the other half overthrown by Einstein's first work[52] . . . . Thank you . . . for giving us credit for our good intentions, no matter what road they paved. For almost all of us had them. I've met a few definitely paranoid communists, and few embittered failures, but Lord knows the majority of us were just well-meaning half-edu-cated schlemihls, and none a bigger schlemihl than I.[53] (October 31, 1948; *OB*, 79–80)

Such candor was characteristic of her life, at times alienating her from some but attracting her to others. We know C. S. Lewis was attracted to Davidman's quick mind and sharp wit; he says as much in *A Grief Observed*: "Her mind was lithe and quick and muscular as a leopard . . . . It scented the first whiff of cant or slush; then sprang, and knocked you over before you knew what was happening. How many bubbles of mine she pricked! I soon learned not to talk rot to her unless I did it for the sheer pleasure."[54] Lewis's words of praise for Joy Davidman are hard to document outside her *NM* writings, but for those who take the time to review her *NM* poems, book and movie reviews, and opinion pieces, a clearer picture of who she was and perhaps why Lewis loved her begins to emerge. Lewis loved her wit, her logic, her repartee, her brilliance, her penetrating mind, and her good humor; all these are evident in her *NM* work. He puts it best: "She was my daughter and my mother, my pupil and my teacher, my subject and my sovereign; and always, holding all these in solution, my trusty comrade, friend, shipmate, fellow-soldier. My mistress; but at the same time all that any man friend (and I have good ones) has ever been to me" (39). It is a delightful irony that one who had been a communist poet and reviewer—quite publicly making her case in the pages of *NM*—later won the heart of the greatest Christian author of the twentieth century.

Chapter 12 Notes

1. A version of this essay first appeared in *The Chronicle of the Oxford C. S. Lewis Society* 4, no. 1 (February 2007): 18–44.

2. *Letter to a Comrade*, winner of the Yale Younger Poet competition for 1938, appeared to signal the beginning of a significant writing career as Davidman also won in the same year the Loines Memorial award ($1000) for poetry given by the National Institute of Arts and Letters. *Anya* and *Weeping Bay* received modest but generally favorable critical scrutiny while *Smoke on the Mountain* continues to be read and quoted by those doing intensive study of the Decalogue.

3. For more on the history of the CPUSA and the *New Masses*, see Daniel Aaron, *Writers on the Left* (New York: Harcourt, 1961); Michal R. Belknap, *Cold War Political Justice: The Smith Act, the Communist Party, and American Civil Liberties* (Westport, CT: Greenwood Press, 1977); Arthur C. Ferrari, "Proletarian Literature: A Case of Convergence of Political and Literary Radicalism," in *Cultural Politics: Radical Movements in Modern History* ed. Jerold M Starr (New York: Praeger, 1985); Barbara Foley, "Women and the Left in the 1930s," *American Literary History* 2 (Spring 1990): 150–169; Michael Folsom, ed., *Mike Gold: A Literary Anthology* (New York: International, 1972); Granville Hicks, *Granville Hicks in the* New Masses (Port Washington, NY: Kennikat Press, 1974); Irving Howe and Lewis Coser, *The American Communist Party: A Critical History* (New York: Praeger, 1957); Maurice Isserman, *Which Side Were You On? The American Communist Party during the Second World War* (Middletown, CT: Wesleyan University Press, 1982); Harvey Klehr, *The Heyday of American Communism: The Depression Decade* (New York: Basic Books, 1984); David Madden, ed., *Proletarian Writers of the Thirties* (Carbondale, IL: Southern Illinois University Press, 1968); James E. Murphy, *The Proletarian Moment: The Controversy over Leftism in Literature* (Chicago: University of Illinois Press, 1991); Alfred North, ed., *New Masses: An Anthology of the Rebel Thirties* (New York: International Publishers, 1969); Fraser M . Ottanelli, *The Communist Party of the United States: From the Depression to World War II* (New Brunswick, NJ: Rutgers University Press, 1991); Walter Rideout, *The Radical Novel in the United States 1900–1954* (Cambridge: Harvard University Press, 1956); Alan M. Wald, *Exiles from a Future Time: The Forging of the Mid-Twentieth-Century Literary Left* (Chapel Hill, NC: University of North Carolina Press, 2002).

4. *Writers on the Left* (New York: Harcourt, 1961), 18 (subsequent references in the text).

5. "Go Left, Young Writer," *New Masses* 4 (January 1929): 3–4. Reprinted in *Mike Gold: A Literary Anthology*, ed. Michael Folsom (New York: International, 1972), 188 (subsequent references in the text).

6. Cited in Arthur C. Ferrari, "Proletarian Literature: A Case of Convergence of Political and Literary Radicalism," in *Cultural Politics: Radical Movements in Modern History*, ed. Jerold M. Starr (New York: Praeger, 1985), 175.

7. In fairness, Gold's view on the nature of proletarian literature softened and broadened over time. For more on this see James E. Murphy, *The Proletarian Moment: The Controversy over Leftism in Literature* (Chicago: University of Illinois Press, 1991) and Walter

Rideout, *The Radical Novel in the United States, 1900–1954* (Cambridge: Harvard University Press, 1956).

8. See Ferrari, 179, and Rideout, 149–50.

9. "Quiet and Safe," *New Masses* 28 (July 12, 1938): 152 (subsequent references in the text).

10. *New Masses* 22 (February 16, 1937): 11.

11. For an example of the kind of non-fiction "proletarian realism" appearing in *NM*, see Milton Blau's "I Never Found a Job," *New Masses* 35 (April 16, 1940): 17–18.

12. Arvin Newton, "A Letter on Proletarian Literature," *Partisan Review* (February 1936): 14.

13. "Fascism Is a Lie," *New Masses* 23 (June 22, 1937): 4. See also Alan Calmer, "The Proletarian Short Story," *New Masses* (July 2, 1935): 17–19; "Portrait of the Artist as a Proletarian," *Saturday Review of Literature* (July 1937: 3–4, 17); and Philip Rahv, "Proletarian Literature: A Political Autopsy," *Southern Review* (Spring 1939): 616–28.

14. "The Longest Way Round," in *These Found the Way: Thirteen Converts to Protestant Christianity*, ed. David Wesley Soper (Philadelphia: Westminster Press, 1951). Reprinted in *OB*, 90; emphasis Davidman.

15. Oliver Pilat, "Girl Communist [Joy Davidman]: An Intimate Story of Eight Years in the Party," *The New York Post*, November 2, 1949.

16. In a letter to Aaron Kramer of January 26, 1948, just as she was about to abandon communism, she explained this as well: "In the old days, on *New Masses* . . . I was yielding to the prevailing expediency of our criticism, to the opportunism which has been a serious disease among us for years—the sad notion that you gotta give a comrade an extra break. How many bad films I was ordered to praise because their authors had contributed money to the cause, out in Hollywood! Now the trouble with this attitude in criticism is that it is suicidal . . . . [We end up fooling] our own people. We have, by our dishonest criticism, and I use the word advisedly, led a whole generation of young left-wingers to believe that technique does not matter, characterization and psychology and the sense of beauty and even the ability to write good clear English do not matter; as long as [one's] book is politically sound it's a book. We have destroyed not only Marxist criticism but Marxist creative writing for the time being. What has happened to the upsurge of the early thirties? Many competent writers have been forcibly *driven* away by insistence of dishonest and half-literate critics on censoring their work" (*OB*, 56; emphasis Davidman).

17. "Strength through Joy," *New Masses* 27 (April 5, 1938): 5.

18. "Prayer Against Indifference," *New Masses* 28 (August 9, 1938): 17. Poems with a similarly strident tone against fascism or injustice include "Apology for Liberals," *New Masses* 28 (August 16, 1938): 4; Rpt. in *Letter to a Comrade*, 90; "The Devil Will Come," *New Masses* 32 (June 27, 1939): 6; "For the Gentlemen," *New Masses* 38 (December 31, 1940): 23; "Sonnet to Various Republicans," *New Masses* 53 (December 19, 1944): 10; "Quisling at Twilight," *New Masses* 56 (July 31, 1945): 4.

19. "Near Catalonia," *New Masses* 29 (October 18, 1938): 18. See also "Poem for Liberation," *New Masses* 52 (September 12, 1944): 8.

20. "Pacific Shore," *New Masses* 39 (March 25, 1941): 24. See also "For the Happy Man," *New Masses* 38 (February 18, 1941): 36; and "Here in the City," *New Masses* 40 (July 8, 1941): 20.

21. "Peter the Plowman," *New Masses* 44 (September 15, 1942): 15.

22. I realize that in criticizing her *NM* poems in this way I am open to the charge of having a bourgeois poetical sensibility—exactly the kind of sensibility Mike Gold and other proletarian critics of the 1930s would have both abhorred and vigorously attacked.

23. It is worth noting in brief here two other activities Davidman participated in during the period of her Communist fervor. First, she joined the Communist writer's guild, League of American Writers, and actively promoted their events. For instance, she invited Stephen Vincent Benet to attend a meeting: "The League wants me to ask you if you'd care to appear at an anti-war poetry meeting . . . . We're going on record, while we can, against America's entering the war; and we should be grateful if you would consent to read some appropriate poems of your own" (June 3, 1940; *OB*, 30). Second, she was on the faculty of the School for Democracy, an anti-fascist and pro-Communist institution in New York City. Records show that for the fall 1943 term she taught "Poetry Workshop."

24. There are two notable gaps in Davidman's publications in *NM* that should be explained here. The first one occurred from June 1939 through December 1940; the cause of this gap was her six month move to Hollywood in spring 1939 in an abortive attempt to write movie screenplays. Since she had been unpaid at *NM*, the $50 a week salary offered by MGM as a part of its Junior Writer Project was very attractive. For more on this, see Pilat, November 5, 1949, and Lyle Dorsett, *And God Came In: The Extraordinary Life of Joy Davidman, Her Life, and Marriage to C. S. Lewis* (New York: Macmillan, 1983).The second gap occurred from November of 1943 through August 1944; the cause for this gap was her pregnancy and the eventual birth of her first son, David Lindsay Gresham on March 27, 1944. Douglas Howard Gresham was born November 10, 1945.

Marriage to William Lindsay Gresham on August 2, 1940, and the birth of her sons combined with a general disillusionment with the CPUSA eventually led Davidman to sever her connections with the party and *NM*. She says in "The Longest Way Round": "My husband had lost his enthusiasm for Communist speeches in Spain. What war did for him childbirth did for me. My little son was a real thing and so was my obligation to him; by comparison, my duty to that imaginary entity the working class seemed the most doubtful of abstractions. I began to notice what neglected, neurotic waifs the children of so many Communists were . . . . By 1946 . . . I had no time for Party activity, and was glad of it" (*OB*, 92–93).

25. "Kansas Poet" (book review of *The High Plains* by Kenneth Porter), *New Masses* 30 (February 7, 1939): 26.

26. "Humdrum Cinema" (movie reviews of *Come Live with Me* and *So Ends Our Night*), *New Masses* 38 (March 18, 1941): 29 (subsequent references in the text).

27. "Huey Hooey" (movie reviews of *Meet John Doe* and *Rage in Heaven*), *New Masses* 39 (April 1, 1941): 31 (subsequent references in the text).

28. "Rover Boys on Wings" (movie reviews of *I Wanted Wings* and *Topper Returns*), *New Masses* 39 (April 8, 1941): 28–29.

29. "Three Films" (movie reviews of *That Uncertain Feeling, The Flame of New Orleans,* and *Penny Serenade*). *New Masses* 39 (May 20, 1941): 30 (subsequent references in the text).

30. "Neptune's Pets" (movie reviews of *Washington Murderdrama, Power Dive,* and *Border Vigilantes*), *New Masses* 39 (June 10, 1941): 28–29.

31. "False History" (movie review of *Young Mr. Pitt*), *New Masses* 46 (March 23, 1943): 30.

32. "Fantasy and Fun" (movie reviews of *Million Dollar Baby* and *Singapore Woman*), *New Masses* 40 (August 19, 1941): 30.

33. "Quack, Quack" (book review of *Hollywood: The Movie Colony—The Movie Makers* by Leo Rosten), *New Masses* 42 (February 10, 1942): 24.

34. "Women: Hollywood Style," *New Masses* 44 (July 14, 1942): 28 (subsequent references in the text).

35. "Shining Screwballs" (movie reviews of *Love Crazy* and *Shining Victory*), *New Masses* 39 (June 17, 1941): 28.

36. "Marxist Mania" (movie review of *Go West*), *New Masses* 38 (March 4, 1941): 27.

37. "Other Movies" (movie reviews of *Dumbo*, *All That Money Can Buy*, and *Target for Tonight*), *New Masses* 41 (November 4, 1941): 27; emphasis Davidman.

38. "Dinner Knives" (movie reviews of *The Man Who Came to Dinner* and *Louisiana Purchase*), *New Masses* 42 (January 20, 1942): 29–30.

39. "Under the Bombs" (movie reviews of *Mrs. Miniver*, *Nazi Agent*, and *Ring of Steel*), *New Masses* 43 (June 30, 1942): 29.

40. "Dutch Underground" (movie reviews of *One of Our Aircraft Is Missing*, *George Washington Slept Here*, *A Yank at Eton*, and *Iceland*), *New Masses* 45 (November 17, 1942): 29–30.

41. "Commandos Strike at Dawn" (movie reviews of *Commandos Strike at Dawn* and *China Girl*), *New Masses* 46 (February 9, 1943): 27.

42. "But the People Live" (movie review of *Hangmen also Die*), *New Masses* 47 (May 4, 1943): 28.

43. "The Maltese Falcon" (movie reviews of *The Maltese Falcon*, *It Started With Eve*, and *The Man Who Seeks the Truth*), *New Masses* 41 (October 21, 1941): 28.

44. "Keeper of the Flame" (movie reviews of *Keeper of the Flame*, *Chetniks*, and *Hitler's Children*), *New Masses* 46 (March 30, 1943): 28–29.

45. "Soviet Love Story" (movie reviews of *The New Teacher* and *That Hamilton Woman*), *New Masses* 39 (April 22, 1941): 28.

46. "Soviet Frontiers" (movie reviews of *Soviet Frontiers on the Danube* and *Underground*), *New Masses* 40 (July 15, 1941): 27.

47. "Perfect Landing" (movie reviews of *Wings of Victory* and *The Land is Bright*), *New Masses* 41 (November 25, 1941): 26; "The Girl from Leningrad" (movie review of *The Girl From Leningrad*), *New Masses* 42 (January 6, 1942): 26; "Guerilla Brigade" (movie reviews of *Guerilla Brigade* and *The Ghost of Frankenstein*), *New Masses* 43 (April 21, 1942): 28; "This Is the Enemy" (movie reviews of *This Is the Enemy* and *Laugh, Town, Laugh*), *New Masses* 44 (July 7, 1942): 30; and "Heroes are Human Beings" (movie reviews of *In the Rear of the Enemy*, *Desperate Journey*, *Manilla Calling*, and *Tales of Manhattan*), *New Masses* 45 (October 13, 1942): 30.

48. "Volga-Volga" (movie review of *Volga-Volga*), *New Masses* 39 (May 27, 1941): 25; emphasis Davidman.

49. "The Face of China" (movie reviews of *Ku Kan* and *Out of the Fog*), *New Masses* 40 (July 8, 1941): 29.

50. Davidman's last publication in *NM* was "Quisling at Twilight," 56 (July 31, 1945): 4. The last time her name appeared on the *NM* masthead as a contributing editor was 59 (April 16, 1946): 1.

51. See "To a Communist," *Saturday Review of Literature* (October 23, 1948): 39.

52. In an earlier letter to V. J. Jerome she is even more caustic about Lenin's *Materialism*: "I got an awful shock when I read *Materialism* . . . . What possesses us to offer *this* as a statement of our philosophy? No wonder we can never get anywhere with educated bourgeois thinkers! The book is pathetic; merely from the standpoint of construction it is rambling, repetitious to idiocy, irrelevant; its language, probably further corrupted by the translator, is of an almost hysterical violence and bad manners. Even the jokes ain't funny; they're just insults. As for its logic, it is unbelievable; the premises are wrong, the conclusions are wrong, and they're non sequiturs anyway" (January 21, 1948; *OB*, 52–53

and emphasis Davidman). Later in this letter Davidman favorably contrasts C. S. Lewis with Lenin, noting in particular strengths she has found in *That Hideous Strength*.

53. In a later letter to Benét, Davidman gave her opinion as to the demise of *NM*: "What killed [*NM*] was simply the entire incompetence of its editors; they didn't know there was such a thing as a technique of editing, and refused to consider the possibility of learning it. They didn't know anything about their readers and did nothing to find out; their position was that reading *New Masses* was a moral duty, so it didn't have to be interesting" (February 1, 1949; *OB*, 99–100).

54. *A Grief Observed* (London: Faber and Faber, 1961), 8 (subsequent references in the text).

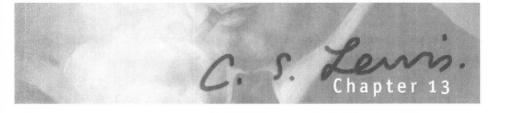

Fire and Ice: C. S. Lewis and the Love Poetry of Joy Davidman and Ruth Pitter[1]

Despite widespread interest in the life and work of C. S. Lewis, little critical work has been done exploring the nature of Lewis's relationship with women other than Lyle Dorsett's 1983 biography of Joy Davidman, *And God Came In*.[2] While this is not the place for an exhaustive study, I do want to bring to light a heretofore untapped source of information regarding Lewis's relationship with not only Davidman, but also the British poet Ruth Pitter: the love poetry of each woman. Readers of Lewis have long wondered how it was that Lewis fell in love with Davidman, while those who have also known of his prior relationship with Pitter are frankly puzzled that he chose to marry Davidman rather than Pitter. Reduced to its essence, my contention is that Davidman "won" Lewis because of her passionate, aggressive, "winner-take-all" attitude toward romantic love as revealed in her love poetry, while Pitter "lost" Lewis because of her dispassionate, reserved, "you-must-win-me" attitude toward romantic love as revealed in her love poetry. Reading biography into or out of an author's literary work is risky business, opening one to Lewis's charge of committing the "personal heresy."[3] Nonetheless, and even though I was schooled in New Criticism and the maxim that a poem should be valued as a work of aesthetic beauty and artistic integrity in and of itself and not as a biographical artifact, I find the insights of such a biographical reading of Davidman's and Pitter's love poetry compelling. At a minimum I believe these insights inform a deeper understanding of Lewis's decision to marry Davidman rather than Pitter.

First some background on Lewis's relationship with Ruth Pitter. Pitter had developed a warm, friendly relationship with Lewis long before Joy Davidman came on the scene. Due to the efforts of two mutual friends, Herbert Palmer and Lord David Cecil, she began corresponding with him in July 1946, and soon they were writing each other regularly. Pitter, who was an established poet and winner of the Hawthornden Prize for poetry in 1937 for her volume *A Trophy of Arms: Poems 1926–1935* (1936), impressed Lewis because she wrote the kind of verse he admired and wished to emulate. In many letters he lavishes praise on Pitter's poetry. Pitter, of course, was pleased by Lewis's praise and friendship.[4] She had long admired him, and was even in spiritual debt to him since she directly connected her move out of depression and her eventual conversion to Christianity to having heard Lewis's BBC radio broadcasts during World War II.[5] In many letters she writes about her excitement over her friendship with Lewis. She writes her friend Nettie Palmer: "My most exciting adventure of late has been making the acquaintance of C. S. Lewis. I think more of his work than anybody else's now . . . what a privilege to know anyone so learned and so humane. He is a poet too—has sent me some pieces in MSS. Almost appallingly clever in form, and fits the profoundest thoughts into it entirely without distortion . . . . I do glory in knowing this man, and to think that he admires my work" (August 5, 1946; *HU*, 145).[6] Soon Lewis is inviting Pitter to luncheons at Magdalen College. About one invitation Pitter writes: "The thing that looms largest on my present horizon is the prospect of a luncheon at Magdalen College on the 9th [October 1946]. C. S. Lewis has very friendly & unexpectedly invited me . . . . I've always had a curious hankering after University society, due no doubt to ignorance: and the idea of entering those venerable courts as a guest instead of a mere sightseer seems to cure a certain ache" (October 2, 1946; *HU*, 146).[7] And about yet another luncheon Pitter writes: "I'm going to Oxford on Friday, to assist at a 2-day debate on whether women ought to be parsons. I think not, though it's not easy to say why. It's going to be held in C. S. Lewis's rooms at Magdalen [College], & some of us are going to lunch with him afterwards. This interests me a good deal more than the debate" (December 28, 1949; *HU*, 153). Pitter's delight in getting to know Lewis better through meetings like these was keen, perhaps leading her to harbor hopes for an even closer relationship. While Lewis, at least in his letters, never encourages a relationship beyond friendship, he clearly was comfortable with Pitter and enjoyed spending time with her.

Over the next several years Pitter continued to receive copious notes from Lewis about her poetry, and, in turn, he often asked Pitter's advice about his own verse, admiring her native ability and appreciating her critical insights. She became a sounding board for Lewis's verse. In effect, then, Pitter became Lewis's mentor as a poet.[8] It is not hard to imagine the satisfaction Pitter received being called upon for her opinion, particularly since she admired him as writer, scholar, and sage, ever mindful of how his radio broadcasts had helped to bring her out of her wartime depression. While it is impossible to document how often Lewis and Pitter met before Davidman came on the scene, the historical record suggests such meetings ranged in the neighborhood of several dozen. Indeed, in part because of these frequent meetings, many of Lewis's friends believed he was attracted to Pitter. For example, in his biography of Lewis George Sayer recalls:

> Ruth Pitter was one of the very few modern poets whose work [Lewis] admired. His writing to her of his appreciation developed into a witty and profound correspondence and occasional meetings between them . . . . I [drove him to see Pitter] three times between 1953 and 1955 . . . . It was obvious that he liked her very much. He felt at ease in her presence—and he did not feel relaxed with many people—and, in fact, seemed to be on intimate terms with her. The conversation was a mixture of the literary and the domestic . . . . Each suggested amusing and improbable books for the other to write. Herbs were pinched and tasted in the cottage garden. Homemade drinks were sampled. She asked for the recipe of my moselle-like elder-flower wine. Jack did not contribute much to this domestic conversation, but it was clear that he enjoyed it . . . . It was clear that he enjoyed both the idea and the reality of domesticity . . . . After one visit in 1955,

he remarked that, if he were not a confirmed bachelor, Ruth Pitter would be the woman he would like to marry . . . . [When I said it was not too late, he said] "Oh yes it is . . . I've burnt my boats."[9]

Lewis's friend Colin Hardie was insistent that Pitter would have been a better match for Lewis than Davidman. According to Walter Hooper in a letter he wrote to Pitter on February 14, 1975, during a visit to Colin and Christian Hardie the subject of Davidman came up. Hooper writes:

> Rather interestingly, I had never heard them speak of Joy Davidman before. During this visit Christian told me about a luncheon party at which Lewis introduced her to Joy, hoping, Christian thinks, that she would take [Joy] under her wing and become friends. I asked what came of it, and Christian confessed that she felt such a strong dislike of Joy that she couldn't bring herself to be nice to her. Colin, who had sat listening to this conversation, suddenly burst out with "Jack should have married Ruth Pitter"—and nothing more was said about Joy. (*HU*, 197)

And of course other friends of Lewis found his marriage to Davidman odd. For instance, J. R. R. Tolkien, allegedly consistently referred to Davidman as "that woman," and Owen Barfield, who had his own lively correspondence with Pitter, may also have been puzzled at Lewis's decision to marry Davidman.

Whatever Lewis's feelings for Pitter, they were not powerful enough to cause him to pursue her. Instead, once Davidman came on the scene, Lewis was drawn to Joy. Perhaps naively, Lewis hoped the two women might become friends, and so he arranged for the three of them to dine together at the Eastgate Hotel in Oxford on February 1, 1954. In her most terse journal entry recalling her correspondence with Lewis, Pitter writes: "It was at this luncheon that I met Mrs. Gresham for the first and last time" (Pitter Journal, fol. 123). In spite of Lewis's best intentions, there is no evidence that the two women he most cared about at that time in his life ever warmed to the other. The icy relationship between Davidman and Pitter is not surprising. Moreover, in the Bodleian Library there remains sealed correspondence between Pitter and Hooper which may reveal further evidence of Pitter's disaffection for Davidman; however, this correspondence may not be opened until the death of Joy's sons, David and Douglas Gresham.[10]

His friendship with Pitter notwithstanding, Lewis later fell in love with Davidman and married her . . . twice. Why? I believe part of the answer is revealed in the love poetry written by each woman. Pitter, born in 1897, came to sexual maturity during the height of World War I. The devastating effect of the war on an entire generation of young men, decimating the pool of marriageable men, caused Pitter, like many British women of this era, to give up thoughts of marriage. In the early 1920s, Pitter, who earned a living as an artisan painting decorative furniture, became fast friends with another artisan, Kathleen O'Hara, and the two women agreed to become business partners, opting for independence, establishing a career, and looking for a little home to retire to when their working days were over. Pitter herself recalls this period as rather normal, noting that she and O'Hara belonged to a generation of surplus women. Thereafter they shared household expenses and living quarters until O'Hara's death in 1973.

It would be misleading, therefore, to suggest that love poetry dominates Pitter's work; in fact, it does not. More often than not Pitter's poetry concerns her deep, almost mystical love of the natural world, her musings upon the human condition, and her search for transcendent truth. Yet at times she did write about romantic love, albeit with some skepticism. Pitter, while neither frigid nor a prude, grew to have a circumspect view of the possibility of passionate love. To Herbert Palmer she writes: "Have kept out of love as much as possible, as my psychology is such a muck-heap that it takes all my skill to carry on, without jarring impacts, which would ruin all my careful improvements. I lurk, intensely observant, in the undergrowth" (November 14, 1936; *HU*, 41). In a later essay she wrote:

> Although my private myths [about romantic love] flourished obstinately over the years and against odds too, as one after another of the inadequate opposite numbers faded away, I began to have glimmerings about the dishonesty of the whole thing. I was growing up; terribly slowly, but inexorably. The ideas of Freud and Jung began to pervade human society, and I couldn't help becoming aware of them. But the biggest eye-opener was when somebody fell romantically in love with *me* . . . This was a horrible experience, because it was quite obvious that he wasn't in love with me, myself. He didn't know me, didn't want to. All he asked was that I should *pretend* to be the woman

of his vision. He was looking past me—looking over my shoulder at a ghost. There is hardly a word in the language rude enough to reply to this attitude, I felt, choking with indignation, and throwing his flowers out of the window. And all the time I had been trying to do this very thing to other people. (41–42; emphasis Pitter)

Pitter's recognition that this man had been in love with love and not with her, helped her see this as similar to her own failure. While this angered her for the moment, she noted: "Most of us don't get the chance to be silly-romantic for more than a very short period of our lives. Romantic love is a flowering. Surely there's a time of life when these bright dreams and alluring myths are all right. You can't live on flowers, of course, but, oh Lord, how sweet they are!"[11]

Consequently, while Pitter did have friendly relationships with several men throughout her life (including Eric Blair, a.k.a. George Orwell), and was probably sexually involved with several, she also had a powerful sense of self-protection—both against a broken heart and for her fiercely held Muse. No poem better expresses this sentiment than "If You Came" from *The Spirit Watches*:

If you came to my secret glade,
Weary with heat,
I would set you down in the shade,
I would wash your feet.

If you came in the winter sad,
Wanting for bread,
I would give you the last that I had,
I would give you my bed.

But the place is hidden apart
Like a nest by a brook,
And I will not show you my heart
By a word, by a look.

The place is hidden apart
Like a nest of a bird:
And I will not show you my heart
By a look, by a word. [12]

While the speaker promises the visitor physical comfort, including shelter and nourishment, and while there is sensual detail in her promise to wash his feet and give him her bed, she will not give her secret self, her heart's true being, because it "is hidden apart." Indeed, the penetrating core of the poem is the speaker's affirmation that she "will not show you my heart, / By a look, by a word." At the same time, her initial invitation to the visitor is genuine and winsome, suggesting she is open to romantic pursuit, but it has to be initiated by the man. The discovery of her heart is possible, yet the poem ends abruptly, leaving the sense that no pursuit, no discovery was attempted. In commenting on this poem later, Pitter says:

> There is a deep instinct, a biologically sound one, I think, in women's heart—that in love they must be sought out. They have a right of veto, but they mustn't make advances, even if they are deeply in love. In fact, the proof of a true lover is that he knows this and will discover their feelings however well they hide them. If he isn't interested enough to find out their secrets, he cannot be accepted. In . . . "If You Came," the woman is saying that she will surrender completely, but only if the lover can find out her hidden heart, which she conceals as jealously as a bird hides its nest in the woods. (*HU*, 280–81.)

At another point she says: "This poem enshrines . . . the biological fact that a woman expects to be found out about. She expects to be discovered, however secret she makes herself" (43). If this is what a man needed to do win and woo Pitter, Lewis was neither by nature nor inclination given to such pursuit. As he had told Sayer, he had "burnt his boats." He would never be the pursuer.

Of course, "If You Came" is not the only poem Pitter writes about love, but it does indicate the overall tone of her attitude: romantic love, while beautiful, intense, and desirable, is a threat and an ultimately unfulfilling alternative to her devotion to poetry. Several earlier poems in *A Trophy of Arms* coalesce around the idea of romantic love. "Early Rising" focuses upon the sense of lost or unspoken love. Pitter begins "I arose early, O my true love," and then describes the quiet, pre-dawn beauty of the forest: "It was an hour of Eden."[13] Happy musings follow, but they are negated by the poem's ending:

> And I was sad, O my true love,
> For the love left unsaid:

> I will sing it to the turtle-dove
> That hugs her high-built bed:
> I will say it to the solemn grove
> And to the innocent dead. (32)

A more bitter tone is evoked in "Weeping Water, Leaping Fire" as Pitter angrily rejects the idea of love, given the hardships of life she faces:

> Weeping water, leaping fire
> God and my grave are my desire.
> With swarming strife and scanty joy,
> Little ease and long annoy,
> I am damned and drowned in rue—
> With love then what have I to do? (48)

In spite of the poem's second stanza's less violent tone, she still ends it asking "then what have I to do with love?" The final two lines appear to address Cupid (or perhaps the boy in question): "Lovely boy, I know you lie: / Frown as you will, but pass me by." If "Weeping Water, Leaping Fire" insists love should be avoided, "True Love's not Told" argues that it is impossible to communicate about love. Actually Pitter links this idea to a series of other incommunicable things ("righteousness hath no witness"), and then appeals to Dame Truth who effectively remains mum. The impossibility of human communication about love on earth is reinforced by the poem's conclusion: "What said I even now? True love's not told; / I'll tell my love when we shall meet in heaven, / My love: till then my love I shall not know" (55). Despite a kind of leap of faith here at the end, the fact remains there is no possibility of connecting to her beloved on earth.

Contrasting to these jaundiced views of romantic love, "Fair is the Water" is a more hopeful expression regarding romantic love. Set in a favorite forest, the poem denotes the life-giving effect of water on the land, "on the braided tresses of the barley," and on the rose. However, the emotional peak of the poem comes in its conclusion: "Fairest is water when the heart at evening / leads the fond feet to the familiar places: / fairest is water when it falls in silent / dew where thou liest" (58). The ending is admittedly ambiguous since we wonder about where the person is lying. Is he asleep in a nearby bed? Is he beneath the earth? Or is he only in her memory? Another poem, "As When the Faithful Return," is a poignant statement about unrequited yet patient, hopeful, faithful love: "As when the faithful return to valleys beloved, / little lamenting the winter, alone with the pensive / genius, the soul of the place, and when the profane ones / fly with the summer, and lewdness and folly are vanished: / so I with thine image at last shall abide in silence" (45). The persona insists that when others deride, forget, or reject the beloved, "mine shalt thou be in dateless eternal affection." More than that, the persona senses the beloved will eventually return to her: "Quiet and clean is the house, and here I await thee: / thou by familiar groves, by the river of water, / under the snow-laden yew, the sun-gilded rose, / reverend with years, with youth immortality blooming, / silent advancest, and sittest down in my dwelling." The simplicity of the diction and the crisp, evocative phrases ("quiet and clean," "snow-laden," and "sun-gilded") contribute to the beauty of the lyric's suppressed passion. As these five poems from *A Trophy of Arms* suggest, and in contrast to statements by Pitter about avoiding romantic entanglements, her heart's affection could not simply be silenced.[14]

"The Swan Bathing" from *The Bridge* is about her favorite bird (she published almost a dozen poems featuring the swan). However, the overtly sexual context of this poem is unique in her work. Even the title of the poem connotes a sensuous, if not sensual, experience, and this is made explicit in the opening lines: "Now to be clean he must abandon himself / To that fair yielding element whose lord he is" (18).[15] Throughout the swan is the image of masculine activity and the river of feminine passivity, and the picture Pitter paints as the swan washes himself is clearly one of sexual encounter and climax:

> There in the mid-current, where she is strongest,
> Facing the stream, he half sinks, who knows how?
> His armed head, his prow wave-worthy, he dips under:
> The meeting streams glide rearward, fill the hollow
> Of the proud wings: then as if fainting he falls sidelong,
> Prone, without shame, reveals the shiplike belly
> Tumbling reversed, with limp black paddles waving,
> And down, gliding abandoned, helplessly wallows,
> The head and neck, wrecked mast and pennon, trailing.

His passion spent—as the "wrecked mast and pennon, trailing" metaphor and its obvious verbal echo of penis makes explicit—he continues his dominance:

"It is enough: satisfied he rears himself, / Sorts with swift movement his disordered tackle, / Rises, again the master; and so seated / Riding, with spreading wings he flogs the water / Lest she should triumph."

The violence of his mastery is further reflected by the river: "In a storm of weeping / And a great rainbow of her tears transfigured, / With spreading circles of his force he smites her / Till remote tremblings heave her rushy verges / And all her lesser lives are rocked with rumour." Once his dominance is assured, the swan and the river "are reconciled." Having expended himself, he moves on: "With half-raised pinion / And backward-leaning head pensively sailing, / With silver furrow the reflected evening / Parting, he softly goes." While the primary attention of the poem up until this point has been the swan, the end focuses tenderly upon the river. As the swan sails away, "one cold feather / Drifts, and is taken gently by the rushes; / By him forgotten, and by her remembered." The all too common stereotypical end of sexual consummation—the male's conquest, satisfaction, and then moving on versus the female's submission, partial satisfaction, and longing for intimacy more lasting than mere copulation—is beautifully and poignantly portrayed with this ending. Although Pitter often insisted she avoided romantic entanglements and was extremely guarded about affairs of the heart, only someone who had experienced a physically intense, if ultimately short-lived, sexual relationship could have written a poem as passionate as "The Swan Bathing."

Other poems in *The Bridge* about romantic love lament how it is thwarted by lust. This is nowhere clearer than in "But for Lust": "But for lust we could be friends, / On each other's neck could weep: / In each other's arms could sleep, / In the calm the cradle lends" (50). But even the possibility of genuine friendship is trumped by unbridled *eros*: "But for passion we could rest, / But for passion we could feast / On compassion everywhere." Despite lust's destructive certainty, Pitter insists tender, compassionate love is possible: "Even in this night I know / By the awful living dead, / By this craving tear I shed, / Somewhere, somewhere it is so." "Lament for One's Self" also deals with how lust bedevils love. Presented as a dialogue between an impartial narrator and an unhappy respondent, the difficulty of finding love that sustains and fulfills is highlighted: "Did you find the true heart / For whom you were born? / Never, for cold lust did part / Us in this place forlorn" (54). Moreover, even friendship is hard to find: "It is either that we all are mad, / Or my heart was born blind, / For every kind of love went bad / Between me and my kind."

However, as with the hopeful ending of "But for Lust," "Lament for One's Self" resists despair:

No matter what the body felt,
No matter what it saw,
My inmost spirit ever knelt
In a blind love and awe:

And dead or living knows full well,
Sick or whole it knows,
The secret it may never tell
Of joy and repose. (55)

Even though human experience and past encounters argue the contrary, Pitter never gives up on the hope that selfless love will win out.

This is true in a slightly different way in the "Vision of the Cuckoo," a poem portraying Pitter as bitterly outraged over thwarted love. As she watches and listens to a cuckoo in the roses outside her window, Pitter reflects upon its "sweet voice, sour reputation" (20). Even more significant, "I with the eye possess you and your meaning." The cuckoo's reputation as one who lays her eggs in another bird's nest, leaving her chicks to be raised by the foster mother gives Pitter the means of laying aside her own fierce anger: "I by the world and by myself offended, / Bleeding with outraged love, burning with hate, / Embattled against time my conqueror / In mindbegotten, misbegotten space, / Drink with fierce thirst your drop of absolution." In the cuckoo Pitter sees "no love, no hate, no self; only a life, / Blooming in timelessness, in unconceived / Space walking innocent and beautiful." That the cuckoo can move on and resign the past to the past, stimulates Pitter to make a similar resolution: "Guiltless, though myriad-life-devouring; / Guiltless, though tyrant to your fellow-fowls, / You live; and so in me one wound is healed, / Filled with a bright scar, coloured like the roses." As in "But for Lust" and "Lament for One's Self," in "Vision of the Cuckoo" Pitter veers away from despair and finds a way to cope with her disappointments in love.

After *The Bridge* Pitter does not publish any more love poems. This is important because *The Ermine* (1953), her next and finest volume (it won both the William Heinemann Award and the Queen's Gold Medal for Poetry—the first time a woman won the latter award), contains poems written between

1942–1952, the very years when her friendship with Lewis began and matured. Why no love poems? I suggest several possibilities. First, given her desire to be the pursued and not the pursuer, she would never tip her hand through her verse; accordingly, in her poems she would not indicate in any way whether she was excited or frightened by the possibility of romantic love—not with Lewis or any other man. Second, given that *The Ermine* is something of a poetic journal of her spiritual pilgrimage toward Christianity, its concern is with *agape* rather than *eros*. Third, given that Pitter was fifty-six when *The Ermine* was published, she may have tired of investing her muse in poems about romantic love; a sore heart can as easily dampen the desire to write about love as it can ignite it. Fourth, if she believed Lewis might have feelings for her, why risk putting something in print that might frighten him away? Finally, if Lewis was not interested in her, why embarrass herself and him by writing about it like a school girl? In all this, however, I think we need to keep in mind as well the stereotypical view that the English, particularly of the era of Lewis and Pitter, did not wear their hearts on their sleeves; matters of the heart were best kept private.

If, therefore, Pitter was both personally and culturally prone to holding back with regard to matters of romantic love—waiting, indeed, to be pursued—Davidman was both personally and culturally prone to reaching out with regard to matters of romantic love. Even before her marriage to William Gresham, she had been sexually active, and no doubt she had been pursued herself on many occasions.[16] However, she was also very used to being the pursuer; after her marriage fell apart and once she fell in love with Lewis, she pursued him with single-minded devotion. In saying this I am in no way criticizing Davidman. As Chaucer says, "Love is a mighty Lord," and a strong-willed person such as Davidman would have been even more given than other women to winning the love of the man she most admired. Accordingly, after her rejection of communism and after her conversion to Christianity, in which the writings of Lewis played no small part, she decided to seek out a relationship with him.[17]

Because the American literary critic, Chad Walsh, had published the first critical study of Lewis in 1949, *C. S. Lewis: Apostle to the Skeptics*, Davidman sought him out; a friendship resulted and through Walsh Davidman began corresponding with Lewis in January 1950. A lively correspondence developed, one enjoyed as much by Warren Lewis as by his brother.[18] By the fall of 1952 Davidman had sailed to England and invited Lewis to meet her at a luncheon in the Eastgate Hotel in Oxford. Lewis, who obviously enjoyed being with Joy, reciprocated and invited her to luncheon at his rooms in Magdalen College, much as he had done previously with Pitter, and then followed this up with the very unusual invitation that she spend Christmas at his home, the Kilns.[19] Dorsett observes: "It is likely that Joy was already falling in love with C. S. Lewis. [Her cousin, Renee] believed that [Joy] had fallen in love with Lewis's mind during their extended period of correspondence, and since Joy's marriage was in a shambles, it does not require an overly active imagination to believe this. Lewis perhaps was growing infatuated with Joy; at least he delighted in her company, or he never would have continued the round of luncheons" (*And God Came In*, 86).

Although unlike Pitter who published multiple volumes of poetry, Davidman's only volume of verse, *Letter to a Comrade* (1938), which won the Loines Memorial award ($1000) for poetry given by the National Institute of Arts and Letters, appeared twelve years before she began corresponding with Lewis.[20] What can this volume possibly tell us about Davidman's romantic conquest of Lewis? Quite a lot, I would argue. First, there is a definite, clear voice in these poems: focused, concentrated, hard, insisting to be heard, earnest, serious, determined, not suffering fools lightly, confrontational, zealot-like, insightful, and penetrating, yet at times needy, open, vulnerable, tender, and desperately longing for romantic love. This voice suggests someone who, once knowing what she wants, will move heaven and earth to obtain it. Second, while many of the poems reflect Davidman's communist agenda of the time, particularly her biting critique of American political, social, and economic policies, many others comment upon the nature of beauty, the certainty of death, and, ironically, the person of Jesus Christ. For instance, her haunting "Snow in Madrid" (partially quoted by Debra Winger in the 1993 film version of *Shadowlands*) is a delicate poem of "terrible beauty":

> Softly, so casual,
> Lovely, so light, so light,
> The cruel sky lets fall
> Something one does not fight.
>
> How tenderly to crown
> The brutal year

The clouds send something down
That one need not fear.

Men before perishing
See with unwounded eye
For once a gentle thing
Fall from the sky.[21]

And in "Againrising" Davidman offers a poem from the perspective of Christ on the cross. She takes us through the critical hours on the day of his crucifixion, beginning with "The stroke of six / my soul betrayed; / as the clock ticks / I am unmade" and ending with "The dawn great wide; / the clock struck five, / and all inside / I was alive" (81). This is a curious affirmation of Christ's resurrection since Davidman's ethnicity as a Jew might have militated against such a view.[22] What all this suggests is someone who loves beauty and has an innate longing for spiritual fulfillment—qualities shared by Lewis.

However, the third and most interesting thing about the poems in *Letter to a Comrade* concerns the ones that explore romantic love. As a whole, these poems reveal a woman intent upon experiencing *eros* as comprehensibly as possible—its joys, its ecstasies, its sensual delights, its soaring passions. Moreover, these poems reveal a woman pursuing with single-minded intensity a lover who will completely satisfy her—and if once she finds this lover, she will never let him go. In some of the love poems Davidman offers a hard-edged view of what it takes to survive as a woman. For example, her "To the Virgins" is nothing like Robert Herrick's "To the Virgins, to Make Much of Time." While the latter is a breezy entreaty for virgins to enjoy sexual activity as soon as possible in order to thwart time's effect on the body, the former is a steely eyed warning to virgins to put themselves first and to be wary of love: "Whatever arrow pierce the side / Or what confusion wring the mind, / Cherish the silver grin of pride / To stiffen your mouth in a whistling wind. / . . . Love yourself / And show the pleasant world your teeth" (20). To Herrick's *carpe diem* Davidman counters with self-preservation. Similarly, her "This Woman" rejects traditional ideas of femininity: "Now do not put a ribbon in your hair; / Abjure the spangled insult of design, / The filigree sterility, nor twine / A flower with your strength; go bare, go bare" (54). Instead, Davidman says a woman should take on the hardness of a tree: "Branching from the broad column of your flesh / Into the obdurate and fibrous mesh / Stubborn to break apart and stiff to hew; / Lost at your core a living skeleton / Like sharp roots pointing downward from the sun."

Notwithstanding this hardness, however, many poems celebrate passion and the ecstasy of physical love. Sometimes she is an enchantress weaving spells to bind her lover to her as in "Sorceress Eclogue": "I for my lover / cook magic over woodfires to call him home. / . . . This is magic made with a leaf and a leaf; / by this incantation his body drawn home" (58). Through her incantations she will pull him toward her so that "I shall kiss you with your mouth sticky with honey / your eyelids stuck together with sleep; / the summer shall enclose us in the heavy heat" (59). Highlighting both sensuous and sensual details, in the end she will have him: "I shall put my hands over your hands / and feel the blood beginning in your arm / and run my hands over the hair on your arm" (60). At other times she is helplessly driven to her lover as in "Little Verse":

Do not speak of him
Lest I leave you
To flow like water
About his doorstep

Or like a moth
Touch his eyelids
With sleepy dust;
Or like a lover

Trouble his hearing
With sweet lust;
Or leave my body
Upon his doorstep. (77)

And still at other times she is lonely, looking for her lover to quell her melancholy, always it seems through physical contact as she suggests in "*Il pleure dans mon Coeur*": "Only turn your lips to my lips and let your hair / lie in my hand or tangle in my hand, / and fall asleep, and let your body stand / between my sorrow and the weeping air" (50).

But most often she is a possessive, aggressive lover. For instance, in "Night-Piece" Davidman claims she will build protective rings around her lover:

I shall make rings around you. Fortresses
In a close architecture of wall upon wall,
Rib, jointed rock, and hard surrounding steel
Compel you into the narrow compass of my blood
Where you may beat forever and be perfect,
Keep warm. The blood will keep you warm, the body
Will curl upon you not to let the air
Sting you with ice. And you shall never be wounded
By your bright hostile business of living, while
I and my charitable flesh survive . . .
. . . Nor shall you
Suffer one touch of pain or recollection of evil
While you are in my bed. (42)

Her zeal to protect, shelter, nurture, and cull out her lover is akin to that of John Donne in poems such as "The Good-Morrow," "The Sun Rising," and "Break of Day." However, Davidman is perhaps even more determined to possess her lover than Donne was; consider what she says about the multiple rings she shall build around her lover:

Now the first ring
Is the devious course of my blood going all around you
And you with a blind mouth growing in my flesh
In the likeness of a child. You cannot break free,
For I have locked a little of your life
Into my life; and the second ring to enclose you
My breast and arms; then a smooth round light
And a wall winking with sleek and brittle windows
With darkness cowering at them; the cold starry endless enemy
Crowding you in, crushing my arms around you
To keep off black terrors.

Her blood, her breasts, her arms encircle and protect her lover, and her obsession for him culminates in the poem's final lines: "Keep warm, / My lover. Lie down lover. If there is peace / Arrested in any memorable fragment of time / I have shut you in with it and drawn a circle" (43). Pitter could no more have written a poem like this than ice can form in a volcano. The energy, the passion, the aggressive desire to possess communicated by this poem certainly suggests something about Davidman's approach to romantic love. If she wanted a man, she would go for him; unlike Pitter who would wait for her heart to be found out, Davidman would not only seek her lover, she would build fortresses around him, not so much to protect him from the outer world as to assure that only she could have him.

A similar poem is "The Empress Changes Lovers," brilliantly written from the perspective of an empress's discarded lover.[23] Stung by her decision to throw him over, he warns her that she will not find it so easy to forget their passion:

> . . . You shall recall
> Forever the tingle and flash of my body embracing you,
> The way my strength came forth, the angles of my elbows,
> The placing of my ribs, long clasps of thighs
> And a flat back; you'll not obliterate
> Any of my tricks of touching you to give you pleasure,
> And worse for you you'll not forget your pleasure,
> As thus and thus you prickled up your skin
> And licked out with your rough dry catlike tongue
> To which I tasted salt. Kill what you like;
> You will not kill the antic of your own body
> That remembers me, nor the words, the physical attitudes
> And warm rooms, qualities of light, and secretive fabrics
> That mean my name; the very smell of my flesh in passion.
> But you'll remember, and you will regret
> As long as flesh likes pleasant things, and the tenderness
> By me created in you will absently come to haunt you
> Without a name, and faceless, dumb, and eyeless
> Ask for my body. (73)

Davidman's explicit description of and details about sexual love here suggest a frankness akin to D. H. Lawrence. While we never learn why the empress has decided to put him off, her former lover has the last word, mocking her future lovemaking sessions: "Never your special lust for me and its answers, / And the peculiar and lovely delight you had in me; never / The pleasure your senses got from me merely by wanting. / I'm saying you will not have me ever again" (74). In this poem love is reduced to animal passion—flesh, sweat, heat, climax, and a longing for more and more. There is no holding back in this kind of love; it wants what it wants when it wants it, and no amount of self-denial can thwart the driving passion of this kind of erotic love. Once again, Pitter was simply incapable of writing a sexually charged love poem like this.

Yet in spite of poems expressing the full pleasure and excitement of passion, Davidman also suggests in other romantic poems that the core of the beloved—the essence of the person—cannot be touched by the lover. There is a separateness, a distance that even passion cannot overcome. For example, "Division" begins by celebrating a rich passion that knows sweet climax:

> Behold how sweetly we have come together;
> Rich night and air, the dark embracing air
> And union of the ceiling and the floor
> Enclosing passion; love, cool formal sheets,
> And secret wool of blankets. And so sweetly
> We come together; so the clasp, the spasm
> Answer each other, suitably invent
> Exhaustion sweeter than content. (78)

Recalling something of Maria's phrase "the earth moved" from Hemingway's *For Whom the Bell Tolls* to describe the ecstasy of lovemaking, Davidman suggests the soaring nature of the lovers' passion with the phrase the "union of the ceiling and the floor." Still, passion alone is not enough: "Is there no more / To say? the body answering a body / In its own fashion perfect as a flower; / Is there no more to say?" As she explores these questions and others she wonders why the consummation of physical passion is not enough to satisfy her deepest longings: "Shall I have of you / The lovely mud, unreasoning, the flesh / Beautifully and unimportantly nourished, / While the irrelevant brain stares off into space / At a blank wall; is there no more to say?"

As close as physical passion brings them, it never satisfies the longing of her soul to meet another soul "face to face":

> I will not eat you; I desire of you
> Not to devour your separate nature; never
> Shall I suck out your soul. Let us keep lonely;
> But I would see the eyes of loneliness

In your eyes meeting me; I would perceive
In this queer universe, life and the spirit,
And from the locked and isolated self
Salute the world outside.

And here is the poem's greatest irony: passionate lovers are nonetheless lonely, unable to make deep soul connections:

I clamorous, I the imperative,
I the fond conqueror of your love, the lover,
The lion crying in the wilderness,
I conscious of your life, your thought, your soul
(Call it) now hold your body quite as closely
As one can meet another, and the body
Asks and is satisfied, complete, made perfect,
While the brain stares at nothing. (79)

Indeed, the poem's opening ecstasy celebrating passion is undercut by Davidman's suggestion that her lover is just another object, another thing that has physical substance but no reality beyond that:

You are not real.
You are like wood and rock, like earth, like satin;
You are a touch, a taste. You are the animal
Gold rippling thighs of horses; or disturbing
And twisting cats; you are the muscles of tigers,
The objective eyes of owls. You are not life;
I am life. I find your accidental body,
I take you for my pleasure, and all's done;
And I am sweetly fed. No more, no more?

While passion clearly brings her some solace, her lover remains separate, distant, and apart. Accordingly, only her interior life has meaning for her; it is only there she will find fulfillment. Yes, she will continue to enjoy her lover's body, but as the final question hints, there is "no more" she can expect from him. In addition, she will never turn away from physical passion since she could "no more" bear isolation than he. Finally, "no more" may be a plaintive query to the universe, asking in effect: "Is there no more to life than sexual pleasure? Is there nothing beyond the physical, no transcendent reality that lovers can experience?"

The last romantic poem to consider is "Yet One More Spring." Ostensibly about the spring time, the poem actually focuses upon death: "What will come of me / After the fern has feathered from my brain / And the rosetree out of my blood; what will come of me / In the end, under the rainy locustblossom / Shaking its honey out on springtime air / Under the wind, under the stooping sky?" (65). Davidman wonders rhetorically if she will be "voiceless" and "unremembered." In answer she provides one of her most powerful poetic passages:

> Out of my heart the bloodroot,
> Out of my tongue the rose,
> Out of my bone the jointed corn,
> Out of my fiber trees.
> Out of my mouth a sunflower,
> And from my fingers vines,
> And the rank dandelion shall laugh from my loins
> Over million-seeded earth; but out of my heart,
> Core of my heart, blood of my heart, the bloodroot
> Coming to lift a petal in peril of snow,
> Coming to dribble from a broken stem
> Bitterly the bright color of blood forever.

She will be no "shrinking violet" in death. The rich, concrete imagery of these lines suggest a vigor, a fierce sensibility, an intensity that indelibly marks Davidman's verse as uniquely hers. Every part of her will rise again through the natural objects she will infuse.

If the poem were to stop here, it would be a great success. Yet Davidman does not limit her legacy to mere re-incarnation in nature. Where she will be best remembered is in the heart of her lover:

> But I would be more than a cold voice of flowers
> And more than water, more than sprouting earth
> Under the quiet passion of the spring;
> I would leave you the trouble of my heart
> To trouble you at evening; I would perplex you
> With lightning coming and going about my head,

Outrageous signs, and wonders; I would leave you
The shape of my body filled with images,
The shape of my mind filled with imaginations,
The shape of myself. I would create myself
In a little fume of words and leave my words
After my death to kiss you forever and ever. (65–66)

Her promise to live on in the mind of her lover is striking, and anyone who has read Lewis's *A Grief Observed* will be struck by how these lines presage much of what he says about Davidman there. Indeed, if it was somehow possible, which I admit it is not, the final lines from this poem are Davidman's prothalamion (a song celebrating a marriage to be) and epithalamium (song celebrating a marriage just completed) to Lewis.[24] If ever a poet foresaw how her memory would affect her lover, it was Davidman in this poem. She could not have known, of course, that this lover would be Lewis, nor could he have had any inclination that he was being "pre-loved" by Davidman with such intensity, but later events suggest the inevitability of their coming together as friends, companions, and ultimately lovers.

In the final analysis, what can we learn from the love poetry of Pitter and Davidman that might explain why Lewis was drawn to Joy? First, while Davidman was an active participant in matters concerning romantic love, Pitter was an observer, prone more to "lurking" in the undergrowth, as she put it, than pursuing romantic love. Moreover, Davidman had numerous sexual relationships with men before Lewis; she was vastly more experienced in matters of how to please a man sexually than Pitter. Pitter, while living in the "Bohemian" ethos of London's Chelsea, and thus probably sexually active at times, was almost certainly less sexually active than Joy; she surely was more circumspect since only in "The Swan Bathing" is she explicit about the sexual nature of romantic love. Second, Davidman, as an American, was culturally more prone to reach out for what she wanted; Pitter was culturally more prone to hoping for what she wanted. Put another way, Davidman was bold, aggressive, and determined while Pitter was shy, passive, and reticent. Third and related to the previous, Davidman had the American penchant for wanting to know and get close to a celebrity; Pitter, while also thrilled at getting to know Lewis, exercised the reserve often associated with her countrymen. Fourth, Davidman, though she had to earn a living as a writer, probably had more time on her hands than did Pitter; Pitter, as an artisan, worked hard to earn a living, often twelve to sixteen hour days, six days a week. Davidman had the time to pursue Lewis; Pitter did not. Finally, Davidman was looking to escape from a terrible marriage; Pitter was living a happy if hard life independent from reliance on a man. Davidman needed a man; Pitter did not.[25]

In the end only Lewis knows what drew him to Davidman rather than Pitter. He certainly was not naïve. If Joy "swept him off his feet," he was a willing participant. While he may have enjoyed Ruth's company, poetry, and cooking (she was by all accounts a marvelous cook), her own reticence to push herself forward militated against Lewis being the pursuer. Nothing in Lewis's life before Joy demonstrated that he was capable of pursuing a woman; it would have to come from the other side. He had to be made to fall in love; otherwise, he would have remained a bachelor. Of the two women, only Davidman knew how to do this as her love poetry so convincingly illustrates. Pitter, on the other hand, wanted to be pursued. Fire and ice, Joy Davidman and Ruth Pitter. Lewis chose heat and light.

Chapter 13 Notes

1. A draft version of this essay was read to the Oxford C. S. Lewis Society, November 2, 2004, and a version of this essay first appeared in *SEVEN: An Anglo-American Literary Review* 22 (2005): 60–88.

2. Lyle Dorsett, *And God Came In: The Extraordinary Life of Joy Davidman, Her Life, and Marriage to C. S. Lewis* (New York: Macmillan, 1983). More recently, Candice Fredrick and Sam McBride have published *Women Among the Inklings: Gender, C. S. Lewis, J. R. R. Tolkien, and Charles Williams* (Westport, Conn.: Greenwood Press, 2001), a helpful though not entirely satisfying feminist perspective. Also, Lewis's collected letters offer wonderful evidence of his lively correspondence with a number of other women, including Mary Neylan, Sister Penelope Lawson, C.S.M.V., and Dorothy L. Sayers.

3. Lewis addressed this topic as early as March 30, 1930, in a paper he read to the literary group, the Marlets. Entitled "The Personal Heresy in Poetics," the paper introduces themes Lewis expands upon later in *A Personal Heresy* (London: Oxford University Press, 1939). In *C. S. Lewis: A Biography* (New York: Harcourt Brace Jovanovich, 1974), Roger L. Green and Walter Hooper note the paper "attacked the notion that poetry is the 'expression of personality' and is useful for putting us into contact with the 'poet's soul': in short, that a poet's 'Life' and 'Works' are two diverse expressions of a single quiddity" (125). The fullest expression of Lewis's ideas on this follows in *The Personal Heresy*, originally a series of scholarly essays between Lewis and E. M. W. Tillyard. Lewis rejects modern poetry's emphasis on the poet's personality or character; he comes to call this emphasis the "personal heresy." Instead, he argues "that when we read poetry as poetry should be read, we have before us no representation which claims to be the poet, and frequently

no representation of a *man*, a *character*, or a *personality* at all" (4; emphasis Lewis). Yet he does not totally dismiss the significance of the poet's personality. Instead, he articulates effectively how a poet's personality may affect the reading of a poem: "[However, when reading a poet], let it be granted that I do approach the poet; at least I do it by sharing his consciousness, not by studying it. I look with his eyes, not at him . . . . The poet is not a man who asks me to look at him; he is a man who says 'look at that' and points; the more I follow the pointing of his finger the less I can possibly see of him" (11). Later he adds that while looking to where the poet points, "I must make of him not a spectacle but a pair of spectacles . . . I must *enjoy* him and not contemplate him" (12); emphasis Lewis. Later in *An Experiment in Criticism* (Cambridge: Cambridge University Press, 1961) Lewis makes a similar point: "[Literature is valuable] not only nor chiefly in order to see what [the authors] are like but [because] . . . we see what they see [and] occupy, for a while, their seat in the great theatre, [and] use their spectacles and be made free of whatever insights, joys, terrors, wonders or merriment those spectacles reveal" (139). However, as David Downing notes in his *Planets in Peril: A Critical Study of C. S. Lewis's Ransom Trilogy* (Amherst: University of Massachusetts Press, 1992), "Lewis's point in *The Personal Heresy* is not that biographical materials about an author are of no use in helping interpret his or her works. What he objects to, rather, is the relegation of the text to a secondary, or mediary, role in favor of one's primary interest: the 'mind' or the 'genius' of the author" (9). In the discussions that follow, I do give the texts of Pitter's and Davidman's love poems primacy, for I believe both to be very good poets. At the same time, I use the texts in order to perform biographical criticism, making every effort to offer sound, reasoned commentary on the relationship between the texts and each woman's personal relationship with Lewis.

4. In addition, because she lacked a university education, the favor of an academic like Lewis validated her work in a way that few can imagine. For more on Lewis and Pitter see "The Poetry of Prose: C. S. Lewis, Ruth Pitter, and *Perelandra*" (earlier in this volume); "The Anatomy of a Friendship: The Correspondence of Ruth Pitter and C. S. Lewis, 1946–1962." *Mythlore* 24 (Summer 2003): 2–24; "Silent Music: The Letters of Ruth Pitter." *Bulletin of the New York C. S. Lewis Society* 35 (Spring 2004): 1–15; and *HU*, 141–222.

5. In an interview on BBC Radio Pitter recalled:

There were air raids at night. The factory was dark and dirty. And I remember thinking—well—I must find somebody or something because like this I cannot go on. I stopped in the middle of Battersea Bridge one dreadful March [1943?] night when it was cold, and the wind was howling over the bridge, and it was as dark as the pit, and I stood and leaned against the parapet and thought—like this I *cannot* go on. And it didn't come to me at once but some time afterwards I heard the broadcast talks of C.S. Lewis, and I at once grappled them to my soul, as Shakespeare says. And I used to assemble the family to hear because I thought that they were so good that even from the point of view of enjoyment people shouldn't miss them, and I got every word of his that I could, and I could see by hard argument there was only the one way for it. I had to be intellectually satisfied as well as emotionally because at that time of life one doesn't just fall into it in adolescent emotion, and I was satisfied at every point that it was the one way and the hard way to do things. (June 24, 1955; *HU*, 118 and emphasis Pitter.)

6. Also, on August 6, 1946, Pitter writes Theodore Maynard about this meeting:

I had an adventure recently. I have been struck all of a heap by the writings of C. S. Lewis, but should never have thought of trying to make his acquaintance: but it came about through a friend, quite without my own volition, and I went down to

Oxford and sought him out in his study at Magdalen. It was a great success from my point of view. He only knew about my work vaguely, but I sent him the "Trophy," and he was quite enthusiastic. He has sent me some MS poems of his own—he calls himself a "failed poet"—but such metrical skill without the slightest distortion of profound thought I never did see—didn't think English (or any tongue) capable of it. He doubts, however, whether it's true poetry. It would be glorious to find out where he's sticking, either in the work or in his estimate of it, and I mean to try—sadly hampered as I am by want of the analytical faculty. (*HU*, 294)

7. Warren Lewis confirms Pitter's attendance in his *Brother and Friends: The Diaries of Major Warren Hamilton Lewis*, eds. Clyde S. Kilby and Marjorie Lamp Mead (San Francisco: Harper & Row, 1982): "Thursday 10ᵗʰ October: 'Yesterday J gave a mixed lunch party in the New Room, at which I found myself sitting next Ruth Pitter, the poetess; inter alia she told me of how in her youth she known AE in Galway'" (195–96). Earlier on Sept. 4, 1946, Pitter had written Maynard: "I'm so glad you know C. S. Lewis's works. All denominations seem to agree on this—the Abbot of Buckfast told me he thought Lewis particularly good at devils!" (*HU*, 294).

8. For instance, on February 2, 1947, Lewis asks her to judge between two versions of his poem "Two Kinds of Memory":

I want some advice. I have written two different versions of a poem and all my friends disagree, some violently championing A and some B, and some neither. Will you give a vote? Firstly, is either any good? Secondly, if so, which is the good one? Don't be in the least afraid of answering No to the first question: kindness wd. only be encouragement to waste more time. . . I could almost make myself hope for your sake—and lest you spend more time and attention on them than is reasonable for me to exact—that both are bad! Otherwise, I have set you a troublesome exercise: the botheration being that you have to read one *first* and can therefore never bring a quite open mind to the second (by the way, B was conceived first but A completed first). All good wishes and don't let this be a nuisance. (*CL*, 2, 758–61; emphasis Lewis)

9. George Sayer, *Jack: C. S. Lewis and His Times* (San Francisco: Harper & Row, 1988), 211–12.

10. While the exact nature of this correspondence will fall to future scholars to publish, Pitter, motivated by an understandable but uncharitable bitterness, convinced herself that Joy used her illness (bone cancer) to manipulate Lewis into marrying her and caring for her two sons. Pitter writes about this in "The Alabaster Box, or This Awful Power," a document that I date to the mid-1970s.

11. In a later interview with Hilary Smith, Pitter said:

If one had a miserable love affair, and, of course, a little bohemian life and one had many, then this was not this stuff . . . I wanted at all. I think instinctively I was anticipating *Monsieur de Rougemont* . . . *L'amour dans l'accident [or l'occident]* and . . . C. S. Lewis's *Allegory of Love*, because I always had an instinct about mixing love up with things; [it] never seemed right when you'd done it. It wasn't I minded showing my feelings, but the result seemed impure. One hadn't enough control to present the solution one wished. ("The Poet Speaks," March 24, 1964; *HU*, 41)

In another later interview with John Wain, she said: "I would look at the boy next door and I would look at young men one met in the course of one's work, and one would say to one's self that they are simply not relevant. One might be very fond of them, but one would realize that, as I always say it would be cruelty to animals to marry them, because there was always this ruling passion [writing poetry], this major preoccupation, in which the poor dears had no share" (BBC radio, October 31, 1968; cited in *IIU*, 42). Still later in an interview with Hallam Tennyson, she added: "I always said to myself: my true love or none. I will not marry unless I feel I cannot exist without that person. And though it were quite often painful, one realized that this extremely nice person, one would be glad to know better—well to him my work was only marginal. But to me it was absolutely primal, and if the work was only marginal to him, then he was only marginal to me" (BBC radio. November 7, 1977; *IIU*, 42).

12. *The Spirit Watches* (London: Cresset Press, 1939), 23 (subsequent references in the text).

13. *A Trophy of Arms: Poems 1926–1935* (London: Cresset Press, 1936), 31–32 (subsequent references in the text).

14. Related poems include "Simile" (3), "On a Passage from the *Metamorphoses*" (8), and "The Flower-Piece" (34).

15. *The Bridge: Poems 1939–1944* (London: Cresset Press, 1945), 18 (subsequent references in the text).

16. It is worth noting at this point that the heroine of Davidman's first novel, *Anya* (New York: Macmillan, 1940), is sexually active in and outside of marriage.

17. For more on her conversion, see her autobiographical essay, "The Longest Way Round," in *These Found the Way: Thirteen Protestant Christianity*, ed. David W. Soper (Philadelphia: Westminster Press, 1951); reprinted in *OB*, 83–98.

18. See *Brothers and Friends: The Diaries of Major Warren Hamilton Lewis*.

19. Lewis was clearly overwhelmed by this visit. On December 19, 1952, Lewis writes his godson, Laurence Harwood, about Joy's visit: "Here's something for usual expenses. I am completely 'circumvented' by a guest, asked for one week but staying for three, who talks from morning till night. I hope you'll all have a nicer Christmas than I. I can't write (write? I can hardly think or breathe. I can't believe it's all real)" (*CL*, 3, 268).

20. In addition to *Letters to a Comrade* and *Anya*, Davidman also published a second novel, *Weeping Bay* (New York: Macmillan, 1950), and she edited and contributed some poems to *War Poems of the United Nations* (New York: Dial Press, 1943). She also published the nonfiction book, *Smoke on the Mountain: An Interpretation of the Ten Commandments* (London: Hodder & Stoughton, 1953), with a foreword by C. S. Lewis.

21. *Letter to a Comrade* (New Haven, CT.: Yale University Press, 1938), 40 (subsequent references in the text).

22. She also explores the crucifixion in "I the Philosopher," 32.

23. The point of view in this poem could be that of the empress, but the verbal cues in the poem argue for a male perspective. For instance, at one point the persona says: "Let no recollection / Of any time when you were a woman come / Grinning at you with mortality written on bare teeth."

24. Immediately proceeding "Yet One More Spring" is a poem entitled "Prothalamion" (64). It, too, bears witness to Davidman's intimation that there may be a lover for her in the future that will fulfill her.

25. Moreover, it will not have escaped some readers that when Lewis first met Joy she was 37 and he was 54; on the other hand, Pitter was 55. We can hardly accuse Lewis of having clay feet if he was more attracted to the younger woman.

Reviews and Review Essays

Other Worlds[1]

The fantasy worlds of C. S. Lewis, J. R. R. Tolkien, Charles Williams, and George MacDonald offer Christian readers an escape from the harsh realities of this world. Tolkien suggests that we should liken our thoughts of escape to those of a prisoner rather than a deserter. A prisoner wishes to escape the dirt, filth, and stuffiness of his cell; a deserter runs away because he lacks the courage to face reality. So when Christians enjoy the world of a fantasy novel for its justice or mystery or beauty, they are not deserters; instead, they are prisoners dreaming of another world where the air is fresh, life is new, and hope is real.

To understand why fantasy literature holds such allure, five general characteristics distinguish it from other literary genres. The first is setting, since most fantasies are concerned with "other" worlds. The physical setting and composition of these worlds are not unlike our own: they contain rivers, seas, oceans, mountains, trees, flowers, suns, moons, stars, animals, and peoples. But there are marked differences: the rivers and seas contain magic water; the mountains are more mysterious; the trees and flowers are more alive; and the animals are humanlike—they can talk.

The second is the unique way writers transition their characters from our world to the other world. For example, in MacDonald's *Lilith*, Mr. Vane enters Lilith's world by following a huge talking raven through a mirror that has been precisely adjusted in relationship to the sun. In Lewis's *The Lion, the Witch and the Wardrobe*, a group of children accidentally enter Narnia through the back wall of a closet. Those of us who delight in such transitions long to enter magic worlds. Kathryn Lindskoog tells of hearing this story: "A few years

233

ago I learned of a family here in Oxford who, one Sunday afternoon, finished reading their little boy *The Lion, the Witch and the Wardrobe* . . . . While the parents were having tea downstairs, such a terrible racket began upstairs they thought the house was falling in. They rushed up to find their son with a hatchet. He had smashed through the back of his parent's wardrobe and was hacking away at the wall behind it. I'm told the only way to save the house was to read him another story of Narnia."[2]

Fantasy literature is further identified thirdly by its inhabitants. These inhabitants are typically the many creatures of our childhood (and adult) imaginations: witches, ogres, dragons, trolls, werewolves, goblins, giants, wizards, elves, and dwarves. Talking lions, mice, beavers, badgers, horses, bears, wolves, dogs, and squirrels abound, as well as mythical creatures such as fauns, satyrs, wood nymphs, water sprites, unicorns, minotaurs, and centaurs. Tolkien goes so far as to create an entirely new creature to inhabit Middle Earth: the hobbit, whose outstanding characteristics are stealth, hairy feet, and love of food, drink, and tobacco. But another creature lives in these fantasy worlds—human beings, and our presence helps draw our imagination into other worlds. Unless we can actually visualize ourselves living, breathing, and moving through such places, there is little hope that we will seriously pursue the other worlds of fantasy literature.

The fourth distinguishing mark of fantasy literature turns around two thematic commonplaces: the conflict between good and evil and the quest. In MacDonald's *The Princess and the Goblin*, both themes are apparent. Princess Irene is captured by the comically grotesque king of the goblins to be a bride for his simpleton son. Curdie, a young miner and the personification of goodness, is called upon to regain the little princess, and his quest leads him through various battles and conflicts. Tolkien's *Lord of the Rings* trilogy also employs both themes. The quest concerns the journey to the Cracks of Doom where an ancient and powerful ring (carried by hobbit Frodo Baggins) must be destroyed. Along the way, Frodo and company are assisted by the forces of good while the forces of evil attempt to capture the ring.

In *The Charwoman's Shadow* by Lord Dunsany, the conflict between good and evil involves a deceptive wizard and his naïve assistant, Ramon Alonzo. In order to pay back the wizard for having learned magic, Ramon must give the wizard his shadow. Unfortunately, Ramon discovers that spiritual salvation can only be complete when one is accompanied by his shadow, and thus his quest becomes the recovery of his shadow. Lewis also integrates Christian symbolism into his themes. In *The Lion, the Witch and the Wardrobe* we find the clearest example of this integration. Aslan the lion and Jadis the witch become embroiled in a struggle for the life of the human child Edmund. According to ancient Narnian law (Deep Magic), all traitors were to become the property of Jadis. Slightly bewitched by Jadis, Edmund had betrayed his brother and sisters and stood under condemnation of death. Aslan, however, recalling an even older Narnian law (Deeper Magic—if a willing victim is killed in a traitor's stead, Death will start to work backwards) offered himself for Edmund. Here the parallel to the atonement is obvious. The importance of these two themes cannot be overemphasized. They give fantasies a vision of life centered upon morality; when we enter another world, we do not lose sight of the necessity for moral responsibility. Evil actions in Narnia are no less evil because they occur in a fantasy world. Evil is evil no matter where it occurs, and good is good regardless of the environment.

Finally, most fantasies have a happy ending. Many people view happy endings as unrealistic. They argue that life usually ends unhappily. As A. E. Housman says in a poem from *A Shropshire Lad,* "Therefore, since the world has still / Much good, but less good than ill, / And, while the sun and moon endure / Luck's a chance, but trouble's sure / I'd face it as a wise man would / And train for ill and not for good." These critics are right, of course; happy endings are infrequent in everyday human experience. However, since fantasies occur in other worlds, we should not expect realistic endings. Happy endings are real for fantasies. And they are valid because they momentarily lift us from the bleakness of our own world.

But are works of fantasy literature really valuable? Shouldn't we be hesitant about giving over our minds and imaginations to stories that take us out of the real world? Lovers of fantasy literature will point out that such stories give us a feeling of mystery and wonder about life. Places where trees and animals talk, where mice and men fight together, and where life appears more attractive awaken our minds to wonder and longing. Fantasies can become the means by which our imaginations are baptized so that we can more fully experience the beauty of our own world. Literary critic Robert Crossley has ably expressed this: "What keeps successful fantasy from self-indulgence or that decadence of mere novelty is that . . . [the eye is directed] back to the richness of ordinary things. With access of knowledge and power the reader may return to his own world, his consciousness of self, others, and environment refreshed and cleansed."[3] Lewis puts it another way when he says that little boys read of enchanted woods and "the reading makes all real woods a little enchanted."[4]

Fantasy is also valuable because it hints at our final union with God. Various passages of Scripture emphasize the reawakening of nature when Christ returns: "Let the field exult, and everything in it! Then shall all the trees of the wood sing for joy before the Lord, for he comes" (Ps. 96:12–13), and "Let the floods clap their hands; let the hills sing for joy together before the Lord, for he comes to judge the earth" (Ps. 98:8–9). In many fantasies the reawakening of nature has already occurred, and the longing such an awakening creates within readers helps them anticipate God's final reconciliation with nature and with humankind.

And, yes, fantasy is also a means of escape. I am not suggesting that Christians should avoid the realities of this world by losing themselves in other worlds. Christ did not pray that we be taken out of the world (Jn. 17:15). We are to accept our responsibilities in this world and do them well. However, we must not be burdened by the pressures of this world. Fantasies offer us an escape from the ugliness of this world, and such escapism is not negative, but courageous. As Christian prisoners in a world that is often dirty, disgusting, and demeaning, our escape is not desertion, but deliverance.

The importance of fantasy literature should not be glorified, but neither should it be belittled. According to Tolkien, the greatest fantasy of all time is the life, death, and resurrection of Christ. This happy ending, which he terms the Great Eucatastrophe, "is supreme; and it is true. . . . God is the Lord, of angels, and of men—and of elves. Legend and history have met and fused."[5] The greatest fantasy of all is the very one that came true.

Demythologizing C. S. Lewis: A Review of A. N. Wilson's *C. S. Lewis: A Biography*

(New York: Norton, 1990)[6]

C. S. Lewis once wrote that "we learn from Freud and others about those distortions in character and errors in thought which result from a man's early conflicts with his father."[7] This curious statement, since elsewhere Lewis expresses disapproval for Freud, could serve as the thesis for A. N. Wilson's *C. S. Lewis: A Biography*. Indeed, Wilson goes out of his way to give us a Freudian reading of Lewis's life and attempts to demythologize a man he says has been made into "a saint in the minds of conservative-minded believers" (x).

Wilson's Freudian analysis of Lewis's life is evident when he comments on Lewis's adolescent sexual pre-occupations: "Like many sexually naive people, Lewis supposed that if he eliminated the consciously erotic elements of his sexuality from the surface of life, he would be able to dispel the habits and characteristics of which these [sado-masochistic] tastes were a mere symptom." In addition, he makes much of how the death of Lewis's mother when he was nine upset his emotional balance and caused him to bottle "up within himself" (47) feelings throughout his adult life. Furthermore, Wilson argues that Lewis's relationships with Mrs. Janie Moore and his late marriage with Joy Davidman indicate that "the quest for his lost mother dominated his relations with women." Lewis's love-hate relationship with his father is also given a very close Freudian analysis. Wilson notes this when he writes: "Presumably there is no pediatrician or child psychologist in the world who would recommend that a nine-year-old boy, within a fortnight of his mother's death, should be sent away from home . . . to a school run on harshly unfeeling lines. But this is what happened to C. S. Lewis" (11). That his father would send him away from the security of his home in Little Lea into the brutal world of the English public schools was enough to create a long-time disgust within the boy for his father, according to Wilson.

Especially damaging was Albert Lewis's failure to come to the emotional aid of his son during times of crisis. For example, Albert neglected to see his son off to the trenches in France in 1917, and, perhaps more disturbing, he did not visit his wounded son during his recovery in an English hospital. At one point Lewis wrote his father: "It is four months now since I returned from France and my friends suggest laughingly that 'my father in Ireland' of whom they hear, is a mythical creation" (58). Wilson culminates this part of his biography in a chapter entitled "Redemption by Parricide," where he argues that Lewis's inability to support himself financially without his father's help and his father's death in 1929 haunted him. Twenty-five years later he wrote: "I treated my own father abominably and no sin in my whole life now seems so serious" (114).

Readers will accept Wilson's Freudian reading of Lewis's life according to their own pre-suppositions; at times his claims are laughable while at others he may be close to the truth. What is certain is that he makes a pointed attempt to portray Lewis as a believable man, "warts and all." Wilson does not hesitate to note Lewis's brusque manner during tutorials, his enjoyment of bawdy stories, his love of verbal combat with colleagues with whom he disagreed, and his almost certain sexually illicit relationship with Mrs. Moore. Of the latter, Wilson writes: "While nothing will ever be proved on either side, the burden of proof is on those who believe that Lewis and Mrs. Moore were *not* lovers" (58; emphasis Wilson). Indeed, according to Wilson, Lewis's relationship with Mrs. Moore dominated his life after the death of his father. About Lewis's relationship with Joy Davidman, Wilson has little new to add, although he does an effective job of revealing the depth and extent of Lewis's grief when she died.

From a literary point of view the book is strongest when Wilson analyzes Lewis's writings. He is a perceptive literary critic and does an excellent job of showing how Lewis's books are an accurate reflection of his beliefs. A case in point is Wilson's analysis of *The Discarded Image*, a book he calls "perhaps the most completely satisfying and impressive" (151) one Lewis ever published. Wilson shows how Lewis re-educates a modern audience so that it can appreciate the thought, imagery, and metaphor of an ancient book. However, Wilson is less credible when he claims that the scene when the children pass through the wardrobe in *The Lion, the Witch and the Wardrobe* can be viewed psychologically as an "unconscious image of the passage through which Lewis first entered the world from his mother's body" (228).

Near the end of the book Wilson takes pains to argue that two separate groups of Lewis devotees have perhaps gone too far in their reverence for Lewis as "lay defender of the faith." The first is represented by the Marion E. Wade Center at Wheaton College which he says attempts to keep "alive the image of an evangelical Lewis" (304) while the second is represented by Walter Hooper's C. S. Lewis Society in Oxford "where a High Church, celibate C. S. Lewis is reverenced" (304). Wilson is unfair to both groups, and his mocking them does him no credit. At the same time, he is right to argue that "we do Lewis no honour to make him into a plaster saint. And he deserves our honour" (xviii).

This is the fourth important Lewis biography since his death. Roger Lancelyn Green and Walter Hooper's *C. S. Lewis: A Biography* (1975) is a scholarly though bland study. William Griffin's *Clive Staples Lewis: A Dramatic Life* (1986) is interesting but is limited since it attempts to tell Lewis's life in a month-by-month, year-by-year format through the use of Lewis's already published writings. George Sayer's *Jack: C. S. Lewis and His Times* (1988) is competently written and throws some new light on Lewis's life, especially his Oxford experience (Sayer was both a pupil and later close friend of Lewis). Wilson's biography goes beyond all these; it is not definitive, but because Wilson uses newer sources (for example, the unpublished Lewis Papers) with greater frequency than the other biographers, his book offers a more comprehensive and forthright picture of one of this century's greatest Christian writers. Although his Freudian reading of Lewis is sometimes over the top, the book is still worth a fair reading.

C. S. Lewis as Artist:
A Review of *Word and Story in C. S. Lewis*

Eds. Peter Schakel and Charles Huttar
(Columbia, MO: University of Missouri Press)[8]

Since the death of C. S. Lewis there have been hundreds of books and articles published about his life and work. The vast majority have focused on Lewis as Christian apologist; only a handful have treated Lewis as artist. Happily, *Word and Story in C. S. Lewis* is a notable exception to this pattern. Peter Schakel and Charles Huttar, professors at Hope College, have done a fine job of gathering a collection of cogent, articulate essays concentrating on Lewis's ideas about language and narrative. The thesis of the book is "that an awareness of Lewis's ideas about language and narrative is essential to a full understanding and appreciation of his thought and works, and that this awareness is essential for all readers of Lewis" (1), regardless of whether they read him for his apologetics, his literary criticism, his children's stories, his essays, his science fiction, or his poetry.

Word and Story is conveniently divided into two parts. The first half is devoted to how Lewis effectively and consciously uses language as an artist, and takes as its point of reference the final paragraph of Lewis's essay "Bluspels and Flalansferes," a passage the editors claim to be "near the heart of Lewis's theories regarding language" (2). The essence of the paragraph is that poets use "old words" and "new metaphors" to create meaning "which is the antecedent condition both of truth and falsehood." Lewis goes on to say that "reason is the natural organ of truth; but imagination is the organ of meaning" (2). Essays on Lewis's ideas about metaphor, semantics, the relationship between language and faith, philology, imagery, the relationship between language and consciousness, and poetry follow and provide the thematic focus of this part of the book.

Of special interest to many readers will be the essay on Lewis's poetry, a neglected part of Lewis's corpus. Although Huttar notes that "barring a major revolution in taste (86)" Lewis will never be regarded highly as a poet, he points out that the poetry is an important source for Lewis's ideas about language, especially "its illusive and elusive nature" (87). He also shares examples of Lewis's "sheer love of the sounds of words" as in the rhyme found in one poem, *popinjays/stopping praise* and the frequent appearance of alliteration in Lewis's poetry (87). Huttar briefly discusses as well Lewis's antipathy toward modern poetry, especially as practiced by T. S. Eliot and propounded by I. A. Richards. The essay on poetry ends by examining poems that reveal Lewis's belief that language is "a fundamental human attribute, one that reveals both our greatness and our limitations" (103). The limitation of language is most evident when it is directed to God: "To 'attempt the ineffable Name,' he wrote in the poem 'Footnote to All Prayers'. . . is to risk worshiping an 'idol' shaped by one's 'own unquiet thoughts'; the language of prayer references only 'frail images' in the speaker's mind, 'which cannot be the thing Thou art'" (106).

Like the first half of the book, the second half responds to a short passage from Lewis, this time one found in "On Stories" where he suggests his theory of narrative:

> To be stories at all they must be series of events: but it must be understood that this series—the plot, as we call it—is only really a net whereby to catch something else. The real theme may be, and perhaps usually is, something that has no sequence in it, something other than a process and much more like a state or quality. . . . In life and art both, as it seems to me, we are always trying to catch in our net of successive moments something that is not successive. (5)

Actually there are two groups of essays in this half of the book. The first group concentrates on how Lewis uses story to make abstract or theological notions concrete. Because "a gap always exists between experiencing a thing and thinking about that thing," Gilbert Meilander says that Lewis uses myth "to bring experience not of some isolated tidbit of life which passes away but of what has timeless, universal significance" (149). Other essays in this section distinguish between Lewis's ideas about "story as Logos (something said) and story as Poiema (something made)" and what I call the "rhetoric" of stories; that is, the persuasive power of stories to communicate spiritual and moral truth. The second group of essays turn to the narrative models Lewis relied upon (medieval prose romance, medieval allegory, eighteenth century "novel of ideas") as well as the structural devices he employs, particularly "juxtaposition of story against story" (as in *Perelandra*), the "dialectic of multiple worlds" (as in the *Narnia* stories), and the "linear and circular patterns of movement" (as in *Till We Have Faces*).

Although half of the book focuses on Lewis's ideas about language and the other half on his ideas about narrative, the two halves are not disjointed. Part of the reason for this is that the essayists in each section often refer to how Lewis's ideas about language and narrative were influenced by Owen Barfield, Lewis's great friend and critic (Barfield dedicated his own *Poetic Diction* to Lewis by writing "Opposition is true friendship"). Indeed, the editors wisely invited Barfield to write the afterword in which he comments on the achievements of the book.

Word and Story is a valuable contribution to Lewis studies. Its thoughtful investigation of Lewis's ideas on language and narrative is long overdue and should help to open further explorations of Lewis as an artist and conscious craftsman. Although these essays may appear to focus on material too esoteric for the non-specialist reader of Lewis, most are very well-written and appealing. Schakel and Huttar deserve the thanks of both academic and general readers of Lewis for bringing together a volume of essays that avoids the pedantic and yet moves us beyond the limits of the well-ploughed field of Lewis's apologetics.

Surprised by Love:
A Review of *Shadowlands* (1993)
Directed by Richard Attenborough, Savoy Pictures[9]

Richard Attenborough's *Shadowlands* is a stunning film about C. S. Lewis's relationship with Joy Davidman. Anthony Hopkins as Lewis gives an academy award winning performance, particularly capturing Lewis's awkwardness with women and reticence in showing emotion. Indeed, a motif returned to time and again is Lewis's suppressed feelings. When Joy chides him for his bookishness, touting instead the importance of experience, he quietly asserts that "personal experience is not everything." The rest of the film challenges this belief.

Debra Winger, an unexpected choice to play Joy, is equally effective. From the first, her faint New York accent shocks and serves to remind how totally foreign she was to the closed academic milieu of Lewis's Oxford. As an American Jew, former member of the Communist party, and divorcee, Joy was the last woman Lewis might have fallen for. Yet, as Winger so aptly plays her, Joy's wit, sharp mind, verbal swordplay, openness, and frank invasion of Lewis's world overwhelms him. He is surprised by love.

Counterpoised to their relationship is the theme of pain. On several occasions Lewis is shown speaking to large groups of admirers about the way in which God uses pain as a tool to "chisel human character." Utilizing passages almost verbatim from *The Problem of Pain*, he confidently asserts that pain is "God's megaphone to arouse a deaf world." However, once Lewis begins to feel for Joy and to witness her terrible suffering with bone cancer, his bookish self-confidence is shattered; her pain forces him to face both his awakened emotions and his heretofore unchallenged faith. In a poem almost certainly written during this time, Lewis writes: "Thus, what old poets told me about love / (Tristram's obedience, Isoud's sovereignty. . .) / Turns true in a dread mode I dreamed not of, / —What I once studied, now I learn to be" (*P*, 109). As Lewis helplessly observes Joy's suffering, the film poignantly plumbs the depth of human pain and the capacity of Christian faith to endure.

The film's greatest weakness is its failure to demonstrate the vitality of Lewis's faith. While not completely slighted, Lewis's faith is given only token recognition. For instance, the film fails to show that immediately after marrying Joy in the hospital, the Anglican priest, at Lewis's specific request, performed a service of healing; subsequent to that, Joy's cancer went into remission. In addition, although prayer is mentioned several times, only once do we see Lewis in prayer, and even this is relegated to Joy's death bed scene. Equally disturbing is the way Joy's faith is muted. This is especially ironic since Lewis's books on Christian apologetics had been so instrumental in her faith development; moreover, their common faith in Jesus Christ had been the original source of their friendship.

In spite of this, the film is very much worth viewing. The cinematography is beautiful, the supporting cast is excellent (especially Edward Hardwicke as Warren Lewis and Joseph Mazzello as Douglas Gresham), and the screenplay by William Nicholson is powerful. The film illustrates the essence of Lewis's love; in a letter he says his feelings for Joy "began in Agape, proceeded to Philia, then pity, and only after that became Eros" (*CL*, 3, 884). Joy's suffering was the catalyst that broke the floodgate of Lewis's passion. When Lewis and Douglas huddle together in the attic to weep bitterly over their loss, we see Lewis the man no longer hiding in the shadow of his books. This experience purges him, focusing for all of us that this world is only shadowlands. Real life, as he and Joy knew so well, comes after, in the golden valley of heaven. As Lewis puts it at the end of the last Narnia story, "the term is over: the holidays have begun. The dream is ended: this is the morning" (*LB*, 173). *Shadowlands* affirms both the value of human love, and to a lesser extent, the sustaining power of faith.

A Review of *C. S. Lewis: A Companion and Guide*
Ed. Walter Hooper (London: HarperCollins, 1996)[10]

While there is little new in Walter Hooper's *C. S. Lewis: A Companion and Guide*, it does contribute to furthering our appreciation of the work and life of Lewis. On the one hand, Hooper offers summaries of Lewis's most popular works including the Chronicles of Narnia, the Ransom Space trilogy, *The Screwtape Letters*, *The Great Divorce*, autobiographical works like *Surprised by Joy*, his books on Christian apologetics and literary criticism, and, unexpectedly, but deservedly, his poetry; to general readers of Lewis, these summaries will be helpful. On the other hand, why Hooper only provides summaries of some of Lewis's works is never adequately explained. Still, Hooper offers as complete a bibliography on Lewis's writing as may ever exist and new supplementary material on Lewis's life, particularly the important people who influenced and helped shape him; both scholars and general readers will find nuggets here.

For instance, Hooper includes detailed accounts of Lewis's friends and colleagues as well as fascinating insights into the quality of Lewis's character. We learn that when Pauline Baynes, Lewis's illustrator for the Narnia stories, wrote to congratulate him for *The Last Battle* winning the Carnegie Medal for the best children's book of 1956, he replied: "Is it not rather 'our' Medal?" (625). Peter Bide, Lewis's former pupil whom he asked to perform both a church sanctioned marriage between Lewis and Joy Davidman and a service of healing for Joy, says Lewis was "baffled" by the position the Anglican Church held regarding his wanting to marry Joy; in the end he acquiesced to both requests: "Jack was a special case. Not only did I owe [him] a considerable intellectual debt but the ordinary demands of friendship would have made it churlish to say no" (634). Warren Lewis says Hugo Dyson, long-time Lewis confidant, Inkling, and Shakespearean, best captured the nature of his brother's relationship with Mrs. Janie Moore: "'O cursed spite that gave thee to the Moor': poor [Jack's] whole catastrophe epitomized in nine words!'" (652). Another pupil, Dom Bede Griffiths, wanting to convince Lewis of the merits of Roman Catholicism, found Lewis resistant because he only wanted "to speak of those [matters] which *unified* Christians" (671; emphasis Griffiths). Dorothy L. Sayers, whom Lewis said was the first important person to write him a fan letter, was never a member of the Inklings, though Lewis liked her for "her extraordinary zest and edge of her conversation—as I like a high wind" (725).

Hooper also reveals Lewis had once been the object of marital fraud. Apparently early in 1951 a Mrs. Hooker represented herself as Mrs. C. S. Lewis and stayed at the Court Stairs Hotel for over a year, all the while assuring the proprietors her husband would pay her bill as soon as he arrived. When confronted in Oxford by the hotel managers, Lewis explained that he was not married. In the legal action that Lewis reluctantly initiated upon the advice of his solicitor, Owen Barfield, Mrs. Hooker was arrested and subsequently convicted; during the process it was discovered this was a fraud Mrs. Hooker had practiced previously. Still, Lewis found the legal action horrible: "The actual scene in court was horrid. I never saw Justice at work before, and it is not a pretty sight. Any creature, even an animal, at bay, surrounded by its enemies, is a dreadful thing to see: one felt one was committing a sort of indecency by being present" (58–59). This bizarre incident ended with Mrs. Hooker showering Lewis with letters from prison insisting that if they were not married they were certainly engaged. Lewis learned she was dying and was begging to see him one last time; however, when he visited her in prison, he learned that she lied even about this. He wrote: "Poor creature . . . there's not much left of her when one takes away the fantasies" (63).

The book's great weakness is its lack of analysis. There is no section devoted specifically to analyzing Lewis's achievements as a writer, artist, or apologist; even in the summaries of Lewis's books we rarely find Hooper going beyond the obvious. He does often provide helpful background information regarding when and how books came to be, but his analysis and synthesis lack focus and sustained emphasis. When he discusses, for example, allegory in the Chronicles of Narnia, Hooper does little more than pull together other passages where Lewis refers to allegory; he neglects a thorough, critical investigation of the place of allegory in Lewis's corpus. Admittedly, scholarly analysis may have been beyond the scope of Hooper's efforts in this volume, but in a book that runs to almost one thousand pages one expects significant critical insight. A related weakness is the absence of a critical bibliography.

Though Hooper has been often maligned in recent years, especially over the authorship of *The Dark Tower* and related matters, he deserves thanks for this volume. While not a definitive piece of scholarship, it is a solid contribution to the growing collection of information on the twentieth century's most popular Christian writer; it deserves a place on the bookshelf of both acolyte and critic. Hooper avoids excessive panegyric and hagiography, yet this is, nonetheless, a tale tenderly told. *C. S. Lewis: A Companion and Guide* is a loving testimony to a writer the author unashamedly loves.

A Review of Wesley A. Kort's
C. S. Lewis: Then and Now

(Oxford: Oxford University Press, 2001)[11]

If Doris T. Myers fine book *C. S. Lewis in Context* (Kent, Ohio: Kent State University Press, 1994) offers readers an understanding of the public context of language when Lewis wrote his best fiction in the 1940s and 1950s, Wesley A. Kort's *C. S. Lewis: Then and Now* attempts to place Lewis's work in the context of twenty-first century America. Kort, of the Department of Religion at Duke University, has written a thoughtful, penetrating book. While he could have narrowly focused on the sociology of religious ideas in Lewis's work, Kort avoids this pitfall; instead he takes readers "into what I think of as the most useful aspects of Lewis's work for people [particularly university students] attempting to articulate 'world and life views' that are both relevant to our current location and informed by religious beliefs" (9). Although Kort believes Lewis is "dated," he nonetheless argues that "in his work there are strategies, critical moves and insights, and large bits of construction worth imitating and using" (5). In particular, Kort finds much to admire in Lewis's avoidance of the two errors characteristic of contemporary American Christianity: viewing modern culture as "inevitable and irremediable" and believing that "religion can be self-enclosed" (5). Accordingly, Kort's goal is to take the insights of Lewis "then"—roughly his writings of the 1940s and 1950s—and try to apply them to contemporary American culture "now."

In his first chapter, "Retrieval," Kort notes that literary studies have moved away from formalism and disciplinary orthodoxy and toward interdisciplinary studies as well as matters of theory and practice that engaged Lewis, including education and curricula, value theory, the continuities between high and popular culture, the relation of power and ideology to beliefs and ideas, and the moral consequences of intellectual and technological imperialism. As a result, "the combination of literary with historical, theoretical, cultural, critical, and moral/religious ingredients normalizes Lewis's work in current literary studies" (13). Much of the rest of the chapter considers how Lewis's work goes a long way toward retrieving and reconstructing a relation between religious belief and English culture.

The next chapter, "Reenchantment," explores how "Lewis believes that religion can be rightly understood only by people who live in a world that is at least to some degree *enchanted*" (33; emphasis Kort). In addition to providing an historical review of how the world came to be disenchanted for most people, Kort refers to Lewis's *The Abolition of Man* as the primary text where Lewis analyzes and critiques this disenchantment. In large measure, Kort argues that Lewis sees human relationships as all-important; however, since the current cultural movement has been toward more and more isolation and individuation, disenchantment has been the inevitable result. He summarizes what we can learn from Lewis: "For the world once again to be enchanted . . . we must recognize (1) that we have a cultural location, (2) that our characteristic methods of analysis are partial and strategic, (3) that the larger world has a real or potential value and meaning which must be recognized, and (4) that as individuals and groups we have value not primarily in isolation from or opposition to others but in relationships with them" (49). The third chapter, "Houses," considers "the place of spatial language in Lewis's work" (53). Citing examples from works as varied as *Surprised by Joy, The Lion, the Witch and the Wardrobe, That Hideous Strength, Till We Have Faces, Mere Christianity,* and *The Screwtape Letters,* Kort shows how Lewis uses "housing as a metaphor for an adequate sense of the world and of one's relations to and within it" (65).

The core of the book is "Culture," both the literal middle chapter of seven and the longest one in the book. Lewis believes, according to Kort, that religion, particularly Christianity, permits people to give an account of the world that makes more sense than the ones posited by secular attitudes. Further, Kort says Lewis "gives culture a critical role in the formation of such an account, and we should ask why he does that" (73). While Christian accounts of the world will not look the same from one cultural context to another, Lewis suggests there are three components of a Christian account: "the 'pattern' at one end, the 'changing conditions of history' at the other, and, between them, the adaptation—culture, that is—playing its mediating role" (74). In other words, Lewis views culture as a mediator between reality and belief; all three should direct a person outward, not inward, and the surest sign of "sick" culture is when the majority no longer "recognize[s] that there are things outside the self that are more important" (77). Modern culture for Lewis must be critiqued because it encourages self-centeredness and materialism, which "aggravate and reinforce one another and conspire to destroy culture" (78). Referring again to *The Abolition of Man*, Kort shows how Lewis attacks English educational theories of the 1940s and 1950s that advanced (albeit perhaps unintentionally) self-centeredness and materialism. A real strength of the chapter is when Kort explains how Lewis sees culture as related to Christianity. Kort notes that Lewis's ideas "puts him outside the circle of Christians for whom faith and human cultures are unrelated or even opposed to one another" (87). At the same time, Kort acknowledges Lewis believes that while "Christianity potentially has positive internal relations with human cultures, it has contrary relations with dominant characteristics of modern Western culture" (87). Kort summarizes this discussion deftly:

> Despite the negative characteristics of modern culture, human culture can have a positive relation to religion, and such a positive relation is needed by both. Christianity is not necessarily distorted or compromised by being related to human culture. On the contrary, it is by means of culture that Christianity is related to the particulars of people's everyday lives. Cultures are needed for their enabling and preparatory effects for a Christian account of the world, and cultures grant Christian accounts of the world their specificity, their variety, and their relevance to actuality. It is a sign of the disease of modern culture that attempts to relate Christian beliefs and practices to it [that results] in compromise and distortion. (89)

The rest of the chapter considers whether or not there are matters of continuity between cultures (for example, shared or "universal" values or beliefs), the relations of cultures to one another (Kort notes this is precisely Ransom's dilemma when he first engages the *hrossa* on Malacandra in *Out of the Silent Planet*), and the role of language and literature in cultural engagements.

As important as culture is for Lewis, Kort says that character (also the title of the fifth chapter) is more significant. He quotes from Lewis's famous sermon, "The Weight of Glory" ("Nations, cultures, arts, civilizations—these are mortal, and their life is to ours as the life of a gnat. But it is immortals whom we joke with, work with, marry, snub, and exploit—immortal horrors or everlasting splendours"), and then remarks: "Culture is a part of all that someday will pass away; but the person is part of what will not. Lewis is primarily concerned with character . . . because he believes that is what Christian faith requires" (100). A central argument in this chapter is Kort's assertion that for Lewis character is largely shaped by personal morality; that is, while moral rules are helpful guidelines, the complexity of human behavior cannot be reduced to simply following a set of rules: "Right relations can only arise for a person who is morally constituted, who has character, and character is a matter of the right relation not only between a person and other people but also between aspects of a person's life and between a person and his or her goals" (104).

The next chapter, "Pleasure," explores the recurring theme of pleasure in Lewis's work. One perceptive insight Kort offers is that often in Lewis's work (for instance in *That Hideous Strength*), modern society, which stresses exuberance and pleasure-seeking, is typically portrayed as nothing like a garden of delight. Kort also examines why real pleasures are so edifying, the relationship between pleasure and joy, and how modern society successfully reduces and distorts human desire and pleasure. "Celebration," the last chapter, considers how frequently communal delight in pleasure leads to celebration in Lewis's work. Kort believes that celebration in Lewis "refers to and is based on the relations anchored in Creation. These relations are inclusive. Celebrations are therefore not limited to people; animals and plant life are also included" (142). Readers will be challenged by Kort's assertion that for Lewis Creation is a more important theological catalyst for celebration than is the Atonement.

If the book has a weakness, it is the conclusion where Kort asks: "What would it be like to attempt a project similar to Lewis's here on American soil?" (161). While admitting the numerous difficulties that such a project entails, Kort nonetheless sees it as valuable: "While there is much to reject, oppose, and correct in the culture, there also are traits that need to be surfaced and reinforced. What is called for is neither wholesale rejection of the culture nor uncritical endorsement of it. Needed instead is a sagacious discrimination of those aspects of American culture that can be related to traditional beliefs, beliefs that may yet provide some support for more adequate accounts of the world and of our relations within and to it" (163–64). He then posits a collective focus upon the "surprisingly rich and complex moral and spiritual content [of] . . . American culture that can be retrieved and shared" (164). He suggests the important principles that shaped the founding history of America, including the Wisdom books of the Bible, might be drawn upon toward the development of a sapiential religious system. Such a religious view that might inform American culture would include the need for human beings to maintain a relation with the natural context of their lives, the affirmation of human diversity, and the assertion that people "should imagine a better, more morally and spiritually resonant common life for the future" (168). Although I wish Kort well realizing this project, I doubt it will ever get off the ground, not only because of inertia but also because of human selfishness as well as the American propensity toward individualism and self-isolation.

I admire much of what Kort does in this book. Blessedly, he avoids the irritating tendency of many writers on Lewis to re-state what Lewis says. Instead, he offers a fresh, articulate, and theologically informed reading of Lewis. I found myself several times noting new insights about Lewis's work I had not seen before. While I do not believe (as Kort does) that "Lewis, were he with us, would throw his weight behind this project," I do believe Lewis would have been sympathetic to such an effort. Lewis held firmly to belief in the core values of the civilized life, the so-called "stock responses," including honor, courage, bravery, honesty, charity, respect, and so on. Throughout his writings he never wavers from anchoring himself to such stock responses; for him they are the common denominator, most fully describing what it means to be human. In whatever ways Kort's project might undergird the promotion of stock responses, Lewis would have applauded him, both then and now.

A Review Essay on *The Collected Letters of C. S. Lewis,* Ed. Walter Hooper[12]

In what promises to be his last major effort at advancing studies on C. S. Lewis, Walter Hooper offers in *C. S. Lewis, Collected Letters: Volume I, Family Letters, 1903–1931,* the first of a planned three-volume set of the Oxford don's and Cambridge professor's collected correspondence. That the entire set will not be the complete letters is regrettable, but given the reticence of publishers to invest in such an effort, we should be grateful to Hooper for what he has been able to publish. Knowledgeable readers will quickly see that *Volume I* is comprised primarily of letters previously published in *Letters of C. S. Lewis,* edited by Warren Lewis (London: Fount, 1988 [1966]) and *They Stand Together: The Letters of C. S. Lewis to Arthur Greeves (1914–1963),* edited by Walter Hooper (New York: Macmillan, 1979). What makes *Volume I* a valuable addition to Lewis studies is two-fold. First, the letters previously published in *Letters of C. S. Lewis* are actually only fragments; in *Volume I* they are printed in their entirety. In addition, the first fifty-eight pages contain letters never before published, covering the time of Lewis's formative years from ages seven to fourteen. Second, *They Stand Together* has been out of print for almost twenty years. For readers interested in Lewis's literary, spiritual, intellectual, cultural, and social maturation, the letters to Greeves are absolutely essential. In one volume, therefore, we have concentrated a cache of critically important biographical information on Lewis.

While the earliest letters are predictably filled with grammatical conundrums and misspellings, more importantly they overflow with discussions regarding the imaginary world, Boxen, that Lewis and his brother, Warren, were excitedly yet consciously creating. For instance, Lewis writes Warren in 1916: "I am sorrey [sic] that I did not write before. At present Boxen is *slightly* convulsed. The news has just reached her that King Bunny is a prisoner. The colonists (who are of course the war party) are in a bad way: they dare scarcely leave their houses because of the mobs. . . . But the able general Quicksteppe is taking steps for the rescue of King Bunny (the news somewhat pacified the rioters)" (3; emphasis Lewis).

Lewis's closeness to his brother, a deep affection he maintained throughout his life, is also evident in these early letters. Their reliance on each other is often revealed in conspiratorial passages where the two work to keep their father, Albert, oblivious to their schemes. In November, 1913, while at Malvern College, Lewis responds to a letter from Warren in which he suggests they collude to travel home together to Belfast at the next holiday (Warren was in Surrey at this time being tutored by W. T. Kirkpatrick, later Lewis's most important teacher): "Although always quite ready to fall in with your wishes whenever they are within the bounds of possibility, I always like to point out some of the more glaring absurdities in the same. It has not occurred to you that this simultaneous attack on the paternal purse will savour somewhat too much of preparation" (36). Lewis then reproduces for Warren a paragraph he has composed and plans to send their father in which he cleverly suggests all the advantages there would be for the two boys to travel together; Lewis adds that this paragraph will come at "the end of a long and cheerful letter, when he [Albert] will be bucked up" (36).

The sense of conspiracy the two boys had regarding their father lasted until his death on September 25, 1929, and had its genesis, according to Lewis, after the death of his mother in 1908. In his autobiography, *Surprised by Joy*, Lewis notes that his father's grief over the death of his wife had the unfortunate effect of driving a wedge between him and his sons:

> Under the pressure of anxiety his temper became incalculable; he spoke wildly and acted unjustly. Thus by a peculiar cruelty of fate, during those months the unfortunate man, had he but known it, was really losing his sons as well as his wife. We were coming, my brother and I, to rely more and more exclusively on each other for all that made life bearable; to have confidence only in each other. I expect that we (or at any rate I) were already learning to lie to him. (*SJ*, 19)

Lewis's letters about Albert consistently illustrate condescension at best or contempt at worst. Indeed, Lewis's poor opinion of his father becomes tiresome, particularly since at that time Lewis himself was living as a hypocrite; that is, until at least 1925 when he finally secured a position as tutor at Magdalen College, Oxford, he was accepting money from his father, at least in part to support Mrs. Janie Moore and her daughter, Maureen, a detail Lewis connived to keep from his father. After his father's death, however, Lewis's tone changes radically. Left alone to handle Albert's estate since Warren was in the Far East serving in the army, Lewis writes his brother:

> As time goes on the thing that emerges is that, whatever else he was, he was a terrific *personality*. . . . How he filled a room! How hard it was to realize that physically he was not a very big man. Our whole world, the whole Pigiebotian [a euphemism the boys developed to refer to oddities they connected to Albert's behavior] world, is either direct or indirect testimony to the same effect. Take away from our conversation all that is imitation or parody (sincerest witness in the world) of his, and how little is left. The way we enjoyed going to Leeborough [their home in Belfast] and the way we hated it, and the way we enjoyed hating it: as you say, one can't grasp that *that* is over. And now you could do anything on earth you cared to in the study at midday or on Sunday, and it is beastly. (827; emphasis Lewis)

Lewis's later shame over his behavior toward his father also comes out in a letter to Greeves when he "remembered how abominably I had treated *my* father" (June 7, 1930; 903 and emphasis Lewis).

Lewis's correspondence with Greeves is fascinating as we see him exploring a multitude of topics, engaging in lively debates, and reflecting on what he is learning. In particular, the letters provide insight into his aesthetic, sexual, and spiritual development. For instance, in letter after letter he writes about his love of books, both as examples of great literature and as objects themselves; other letters reveal his deep affection for nature, especially landscapes; still others focus upon his growing love of great music, with Wagner being a special favorite. Most notable, perhaps, is how these early letters reveal his deep affection for poetry and his conscious efforts to write great poetry. In a letter dated July 11, 1916, Lewis writes: "I thought a person like you would sooner or later come to like poetry . . . . Poetry makes use of . . . feeling much more than prose and produces those effects by metre as well as by phrase. In fact, the metre and the magic of words should be like the orchestration of a Wagnerian opera—should sort of fill the matter by expressing things that can't be directly told" (209–10). Later that year he confides to Greeves: "I am at present engaged in making huge plans both for prose and verse none of which I shall try. I begin to see that short, slight stories & poems are all I am fit for at present & that it would be better to write & finish one of such than to begin & leave twenty ambitious epic-poems or romances" (October 4, 1916; 228).

Lewis and Greeves also wrote to each other about their sexual fantasies. While this will make some readers uncomfortable, as a young man Lewis had at least a brief fixation on sadism. He writes Greeves on June 3, 1917: "I hope you are right as to the possibilities of my finding my particular kind of love. [Another student] tells me that the person to read on my subject is a Frenchman of the 17th century called the Visconte de sade: his books, however, are very hard to come by" (313). Even more unsavory is a line from a letter he writes one week later: "I am afraid I must have given myself away rather as I went round imploring everyone to let me whip them for the sum of 1*s.* a lash!" (319). Although Lewis's interest in sadism is disturbing, it is clear from later letters this was a passing fancy and not a lifelong addiction.

Lewis's letters about God illustrate his movement from being a pompous, sophisticated, religious know-it-all to a broken, humbled, spiritual seeker. For example, in an early letter to Greeves the eighteen-year-old Lewis writes:

You ask me my religious views: you know, I think, that I believe in no religion. There's absolutely no proof for any of them, and from a philosophical standpoint Christianity is not even the best. All religions, that is all mythologies to give them their proper name are merely man's own invention—Christ as much as Loki. . . . Often, too, great men were regarded as gods after their death—such as Heracles or Odin: thus after the death of a Hebrew philosopher Yeshua (whose name we have corrupted into Jesus) he became regarded as a god, a cult sprang up, which was afterwards connected with the ancient Hebrew Jahweh-worship, and so Christianity came into being—one mythology among many, but the one that we happen to have been brought up in. . . . Now all this you must have heard before: it is the recognised scientific account of the growth of religions. Superstition of course in every age has held the common people, but in every age the educated and thinking ones have stood outside it, though usually outwardly conceding to it for convenience. . . . I must only add that one's views on religious subjects don't make any difference in morals, of course. A good member of society must of course try to be honest, chaste, truthful, kindly etc.: these are things we owe to our own manhood & dignity and not to any imagined god or gods. (October 12, 1916; 230–31)

Twelve years later, however, with World War I battlefield service, intensive study as an Oxford undergraduate, and several years teaching experience as a tutor at Magdalen College all behind him, Lewis moves from atheism to the threshold of theism. Although he is capable of writing to his father slighting comments about someone who "gets a number of young men together (some reports say women too, but I believe not) and they confess their sins to one another. Jolly, ain't it? But what can one do? If you try to suppress it . . . you only make martyrs" (March 31, 1928; 751), two years later in a letter to Greeves of January 30, 1930 he is himself engaging in analysis of his own sins:

Things are going very, very well with me (spiritually). On the other hand, one knows from bitter experience that he who standeth should take heed lest he fall, and that anything remotely like pride is certain to bring an awful crash. The old doctrine is quite true you know— that one must attribute everything to the grace of God, and nothing to oneself. Yet as long as one *is* a conceited ass, there is no good pretending not to be. My self satisfaction cannot be hidden from God

. . . [but] *Pride* [is] my besetting sin . . . . During my afternoon med-itations . . . I have found out ludicrous and terrible things about my own character. Sitting by, watching the rising thoughts to break their necks as they pop up, one learns to know the sort of thoughts that do come. And, will you believe it, one out of every three is a thought of self-admiration: when everything else fails, having had its neck broken, up comes the thought "What an admirable fellow I am to have broken their necks!" I catch myself posturing before the mirror, so to speak, all day long. I pretend I am carefully thinking out what to say to the next pupil (for *his* good, of course) and then suddenly realise I am really thinking how frightfully clever I'm going to be and how he will admire me. I pretend I am remembering an evening of good fellowship in a really friendly and charitable spirit—and all the time I'm really remembering how good a fellow I am and how well I talked. And then when you force yourself to stop it, you admire yourself for doing *that*. It's like fighting the hydra (you remember, when you cut off one head another grew). There seems to be no end to it. Depth under depth of self-love and self admiration. (877, 878; emphasis Lewis)

In February 1930 he feels the Hound of Heaven drawing nearer when he writes Owen Barfield: "Terrible things are happening to me. The 'Spirit' or 'Real I' is showing an alarming tendency to become much more personal and is taking the offensive, and behaving just like God. You'd better come on Monday at the latest or I may have entered a monastery" (882–83).

Lewis movement to faith in Christ is amplified in three particular letters he writes to Greeves. On December 24, 1930 Lewis writes: "I think the trouble with me is *lack of faith*. I have no *rational* ground for going back on the argu-ments that convinced me of God's existence: but the irrational deadweight of my old sceptical habits, and the spirit of this age, and the cares of the day, steal away all my lively feeling of the truth, and often when I pray I wonder if I am not posting letters to a non-existent address" (944–45; emphasis Lewis). On October 1, 1931 he adds: "I have just passed on from believing in God to def-initely believing in Christ—in Christianity. I will try to explain this another time. My long night talk with [Hugo] Dyson and [J. R. R.] Tolkien had a good deal to do with it" (974). All this culminates in his letter of October 18, 1931:

What has been holding me back . . . has not been so much a difficulty in believing as a difficulty in knowing what the doctrine *meant*:
you can't believe a thing while you are ignorant *what* the thing is.
My puzzle was the whole doctrine of Redemption: in what sense the
life and death of Christ "saved" or "opened salvation to" the whole
world. . . . What I couldn't see was how the life and death of Someone
Else (whoever he was) 2000 years ago could help us here and now . . . .
Now what Dyson and Tolkien showed me was this: that if I met the
idea of sacrifice in a Pagan story I didn't mind it at all: again, that if
I met the idea of a god sacrificing himself to himself . . . I like it very
much and was mysteriously moved by it: again, that the idea of the
dying and reviving god (Balder, Adonis, Bacchus) similarly moved
me provided I met it anywhere *except* in the Gospels. The reason was
that in the Pagan stories I was prepared to feel the myth as profound
and suggestive of meanings beyond my grasp even tho' I could not
say in cold prose "what it meant." Now the story of Christ is simply a
true myth: a myth working on us in the same way as the others, but
with this tremendous difference that *it really happened*: one must be
content to accept it in the same way, remembering that it is God's
myth where the others are men's myths: i.e. the Pagan stories are God
expressing Himself through the minds of poets, using such images
as He found there, while Christianity is God expressing Himself
through what we call "real things" . . . . Does this amount to a belief
in Christianity? At any rate I am now certain (a) That this Christian
story is to be approached, in a sense, as I approach the other myths.
(b) That it is the most important and full of meaning. I am also *nearly*
certain that it really happened. (976–77; emphasis Lewis)

Simply put, without these letters we would have no way of tracing Lewis's
movement from atheist to agnostic to theist to Christian since *Surprised by Joy*
only quickly sketches his conversion. If for no other reason, these letters make
Volume I required reading. In addition to the letters, Hooper provides extensive footnotes in which he thoroughly explains passing references to people,
places, books, and ideas. Also invaluable are a "Biographical Appendix" of
forty-seven pages and an exceptionally detailed index. *Volume I* is a book that
rewards both the Lewis scholar and general reader.

The second volume, *C. S. Lewis, Collected Letters: Volume II, Books, Broadcasts, and War 1931–1949*, also does not disappoint. The most notable feature of *Volume II* is how it begins to fill in details of Lewis's life that have heretofore remained incomplete. For instance, many Lewis biographies and even his own autobiography, *Surprised by Joy*, concentrated attention either upon his early life and conversion (1898–1931), or his late marriage to Joy Davidman and the final years of his life (1950–1963). Now we are able to see how Lewis's faith in Christ energized and changed him, as well as how his fears, hopes, biases, convictions, and commitments governed his thoughts, writings, and actions during the bulk of his years as an Oxford don. Moreover, often we read passages in his letters that are early drafts of ideas later appearing in his books and essays, all illustrating Lewis's conscious efforts to float important ideas before committing them to print.

I was particularly struck by Lewis's honest admission of his fears. This is true whether he is writing about his brother, Warren, who served in Shanghai during the Japanese war on China (1931–33), or about physical pain, or especially about the impact of World War II. Lewis's genuine affection for Warren is well-documented, so it is not surprising that he writes his brother lengthy letters offering minute descriptions of everyday events at their shared home, the Kilns, in Headington, or in his rooms at Magdalen College. Readers used to thinking of Lewis as merely cerebral will chuckle to hear Lewis tell Warren about his "public works," their euphemism for landscaping the grounds at the Kilns. But the letters are often a subterfuge for his fears for Warren's safety. For instance, he writes Warren on February 15, 1932: "It is impossible from here to form any idea of the only aspect of the thing that concerns me: *viz*: the actual and probable distance between [you] and the firing . . . . The result is that my fancy plays me every kind of trick. At one time I feel as if the danger was very slight . . . [but] at another I am—exceedingly depressed. All the news is of the sort that one interprets over and over again with new results in each new mood. A beastly state of affairs" (46). A year later after Warren's safe return and retirement from the army, Lewis confides to Arthur Greeves: "We both have a feeling that 'the wheel has come full circle,' that the period of wanderings is over, and that everything which has happened between 1914 and 1932 was an interruption: tho' not without a consciousness that it is dangerous for mere mortals to expect anything of the future with confidence. We make a very contented family together" (February 4, 1933; 95).

When Lewis writes his friend Leo Baker about pain on June 24, 1936, he previews ideas later reworked in *The Problem of Pain* (1940):

I must confess I have not myself yet got beyond the stage of feeling physical pain as the worst of evils. I am the worst person in the world to help anyone else to support it. I don't mean that it presents quite the intellectual difficulties it used to, but that my nerves even in imagination refuse to move with my philosophy. In my limited experience the sufferer himself nearly always towers above those around him: in fact, nothing confirms the Christian view of this world so much as the treasures of patience and unselfishness one sees elicited from quite commonplace people when the trial really comes. (196)

Two years later he links his fears to the growing threat of WWII in a letter to Dom Bede Griffiths:

I have been in considerable trouble over the present danger of war. Twice in one life—and then to find how little I have grown in fortitude despite my conversion. It has done me a lot of good by making me realize how much of my happiness secretly depended on the tacit assumption of at least tolerable conditions for the body: and I see more clearly, I think, the necessity (if one may so put it) which God is under of allowing us to be afflicted—so few of us will *really* rest all on Him if He leaves us any other support. (April 29, 1938; 225–26 and emphasis Lewis)

Another dozen letters offer additional insight into Lewis's fears about WWII, culminating in his June 2, 1940 letter to Owen Barfield: "The real difficulty is, isn't it, to adapt ones steady beliefs about tribulation to this *particular* tribulation; for the particular, when it arrives, always *seems* so peculiarly intolerable" (419; emphasis Lewis). Ironically, Lewis's fears would be severely tested three weeks later with the fall of France on June 22,1940. Lewis's honest admissions about fear only serve to make his later writings about fear and pain, including *A Grief Observed* (1961), all the more compelling.

Yet it would be a mistake for me to leave the impression that *Volume II* is riddled with fear and angst. It contains many passages reflecting Lewis's characteristic humor, one being a self-effacing account of having left the Kilns one day, only to find that he had on mismatched shoes compounded by the fact one was old and the other new: "As it was impossible to clean the dirty one, I decided that the only way of making myself look less ridiculous was to *dirty* the clean one. Now wd. you have believed that this is an impossible operation? You can of course get some mud on it—but it remains obviously a clean shoe that has had an accident and won't look in the least like a shoe that you have been for a walk in" (April 21, 1940; 400 and emphasis Lewis). Readers will also be delighted to read letters revealing his wide reading; his gratitude to those who sent him "care" packages after World War II during the strictest rationing period in England; how his relationship with Charles Williams came about; his disaffection for the poetry of T. S. Eliot (as well as his letters to Eliot on a variety of literary subjects); his humorous correspondence in mock Tudor English with E. R. Eddison (whose *The Worm Ouroboros* [1922] Lewis greatly admired); his account of a meeting of the Inklings (April 28, 1940); his highly complimentary letter to J. R. R. Tolkien immediately following Lewis's reading of the typescript of *The Lord of the Rings* (October 27, 1949); and his delightful correspondence with Dorothy L. Sayers, Sister Penelope (Ruth Penelope Lawson), Mary Neylan, and poet, Ruth Pitter. Lewis's friendly, open, honest, and intellectually stimulating exchanges with these women may finally silence the oft-repeated but hollow charge that he was a misogynist. To one female correspondent, he says: "Who said I disliked women? I never liked or disliked any *generalization*" (April 8, 1948; 849 and emphasis Lewis).

Other letters show him anticipating his later books and essays. For example, on February 21, 1932, approximately a year after his conversion to Christ, he writes his brother about the efficacy of prayer: "The efficacy of prayer is, at any rate *no more* of a problem than the efficacy of *all* human acts. i.e. if you say 'It is useless to pray because Providence already knows what is best and will certainly do it,' then why is it not equally useless (and for the same reason) to try to alter the course of events in any way whatever—to ask for the salt or book your seat in a train?" (49; emphasis Lewis). A slightly altered version of this later appears in his essay, "The Efficacy of Prayer" (*The Atlantic Monthly*, 203 [January 1959]: 59–61, reprinted in *The World's Last Night* [1960]). Again to his brother on May 4, 1940 he writes: "There were three words in Gk. which covered most kinds of love (Eros=sexual love, Storge=family affection, Philia=friendship) but the N. T. word for 'love' or 'charity' is Agapë, wh. has hardly any use in classical Gk—i.e. it is a new word for a new thing" (408). Lewis later fleshes this out fully in his *The Four Loves* (1960). After attending communion at his local parish church, Holy Trinity, on July 20, 1940, he tells Warren: "Before the service was over—one cd. wish these things came more seasonably—I was struck by an idea for a book wh. I think might be both useful and entertaining. It wd. be called *As one Devil to Another* and would consist of letters from an elderly retired devil to a young devil who has just started work on his first 'patient.' The idea wd. be to give all the psychology of temptation from the other point of view" (426–27). This, of course, reveals the conception of Lewis's *The Screwtape Letters* (1942). To another correspondent he writes about temptation: "On the *general* problem of Our Lord's temptation the most helpful remark I know is Westcott's 'Only he who completely resists temptation knows its true strength'—i.e. if you give in at point X you never know how fierce it wd. have become an hour later. You only discover the strength of the German army by fighting it" (May 26, 1942; 521–22 and emphasis Lewis). This idea is later adapted in the seventh talk of the third series of BBC radio broadcasts, "Faith," delivered on November 1, 1942, and it also appears in *Christian Behaviour*, ch. 7, and *Mere Christianity*, Book III, ch. 11. The net result of seeing in the letters these "prequels" of important Lewisian ideas is that a certain mystery about Lewis's seemingly inexhaustible creative impulse is tempered by a more commonplace reality: great writers have great ideas that become great pieces of writing not on the spur of the moment but instead through persistent thinking, writing, and re-writing. Genius is not simply a matter of inspiration; it is tempered by hard work and practice.

By far the greatest number of letters reflect Lewis's own Christian maturation, including reflections upon hard times, God, evil, the sacraments, "high" versus "low" church, temptation, modernism, the Bible, and Catholicism; in addition, there are numerous letters where Lewis responds to requests for spiritual advice. There are so many rich examples that I will limit myself to Lewis's spiritual advice to New Zealander, Rhona Bodle, and then highlight his correspondence with many Catholic friends. Bodle writes Lewis in late 1947 about her difficultly in believing that Christ was God. In his reply of December 31, 1947, Lewis says:

> I think it possible that what is keeping you from belief in Christ's
> Divinity is your apparently strong desire to believe. If you don't think
> it true why do you *want* to believe it? If you do think it true, then you

believe it already. So I wd. recommend less anxiety about the whole question. You believe in God and trust Him. Well, you can trust him about this . . . I *don't* mean by this that you should cease to study and make enquiries: but that you shd. make them not with frantic desire but with cheerful curiosity and a humble readiness to accept whatever conclusions God may lead you to. (But always, all depends on the steady attempt to obey God all the time. 'He who *does* the will of the Father shall know of the doctrine.")." (823; emphasis Lewis)

After Bodle reports some success in following Lewis's advice, he replies on June 22, 1948: "Splendid! As long as you keep in your present way—holding fast to God, whether the Incarnation can be accepted or not—you can't go wrong. Because, you see, it is not really you who are holding fast to Him but He to you: and He will bring you to wherever He wants" (857). In this same letter he tells her that "I don't mind betting you will come to the Xtian belief [about Christ's Divinity] in the end." On February 10, 1949 he sees her moving ever closer to faith in Christ: "Adding to Pascal's 'if you had not found me you wd. not seek me' (a sentence I have long loved), the very obvious further step 'And if I had not drawn you, you wd. not have found me,' and seeing both in the light of Our Lord's words 'No man cometh to me unless the Father have drawn him'—well, it is pretty clear that you are being conducted" (915). Lewis, though no Calvinist, nonetheless urges Bodle to see the work of God in her life as irresistible grace. After she tells Lewis she has come to faith in Christ, Lewis's response is delightfully short and gracious: "Welcome home!" (June 24, 1949; 947). Other letters follow in which he responds to her queries about systematic spiritual reading and the like. In Lewis's correspondence with Bodle we see gentleness, kindness, insight, honesty, and, above all, grace. Having fully experienced God's grace himself after many years of agnosticism and atheism, Lewis was both awed and honored to be something of a spiritual midwife for Bodle and countless others.

Lewis's correspondence with many Catholic friends also illustrates his grace. His most dogmatic friend was Griffiths who aggressively attempted to proselytize Lewis: "You, in your charity, are anxious to convert me: but I am not in the least anxious to convert you. You think my specifically Protestant beliefs a tissue of damnable errors: I think your specifically Catholic beliefs a mass of comparatively harmless human tradition which may be fatal to certain souls under special conditions, but which I think suitable for you" (February 20, 1936; 178). He ends the letter by gently chiding Griffiths: "With other Catholics I find no difficulty in deriving much edification from religious talk on the common ground: but you refuse to show any interest except in differences." On May, 8, 1948 Lewis explains to another correspondent his views on Catholicism; the analogy he uses is so rich that I quote at length:

My position about the Churches can best be made plain by an imaginary example. Suppose I want to find out the correct interpretation of Plato's teaching. What I am most confident in accepting is that interpretation wh. is common to all the Platonists down all the centuries: what Aristotle and the Renaissance scholars and Paul Elmer More agree on I take to be true Platonism. Any purely modern views wh. claim to have discovered for the first time what P. meant, and say that everyone from Aristotle down has misunderstood him, I reject out of hand. But there is something else I wd. also reject. If there were an ancient Platonic Society still existing in Athens and claiming to be the exclusive trustees of P's meaning, I shd. approach them with great respect. But if I found that their teaching in many ways was curiously unlike his actual text and unlike what ancient interpreters said, and in some cases cd. not be traced back to within 1000 years of his time, I shd. reject these exclusive claims: while still ready, of course, to take any particular thing they taught on its merits. I do the same with Xtianity. What is most certain is the vast mass of doctrine wh. I find agreed on by Scripture, the Fathers, the Middle Ages, modern R.C.'s, modern Protestants. That is true "catholic" doctrine . . . . The Roman Church where it differs from this universal tradition and specially from apostolic Xtianity I reject. Thus their theology about the B[lessed] V[irgin] M[ary] I reject because it seems utterly foreign to the New Testament . . . . Their papalism seems equally foreign to the attitude of St. Paul towards St. Peter in the Epistles. The doctrine of Transubstantiation insists in defining in a way wh. the N.T. seems to me not to countenance. In a word, the whole set-up of modern Romanism seems to me to be as much a provincial or local *variation* from the central, ancient tradition as any particular Protestant sect

is. I must therefore reject their *claim*: tho' this does not mean rejecting particular things they say. (645–47; emphasis Lewis)

He ends the letter by advising his correspondent who has also asked about
books on Anglicanism to read Hooker's *Laws of Ecclesiastical Polity*. Then
he adds: "But the great point is that in one sense there's no such thing as
Anglicanism. What we are committed to believing is whatever can be proved
from Scripture. On that subject there is room for endless progress" (647).

In fact there were aspects of Roman Catholicism that Lewis respected,
including the idea of taking a spiritual director; beginning in November
1940 Lewis made regular confessions to an Anglican priest, Father Walter
Adams of the Society of St. John the Evangelist, until Adams died in 1952.
Moreover, Lewis shared a warm, loving correspondence with Catholic priest
Don Giovanni Calabria, founder of the Congregation of the Poor Servants of
Divine Providence near Verona. Deeply moved by reading an Italian translation of *The Screwtape Letters*, Calabria, who could not read or write English,
writes Lewis in Latin on September 1, 1947; Lewis, who could not read or write
Italian, replies in Latin on September 6 and there follows a charming correspondence lasting until Calabria's death in 1954.[13] Topics covered in the letters
include the troubles of the world, points of common ground between Catholics
and Protestants (although Calabria, like Griffiths, was hopeful Lewis would
become a Catholic), the possible union of the Churches, prayer, and the threat
of communism. Running through all of Lewis's letters to Calabria is genuine
affection for a fellow laborer in Christ. Although some have wondered whether
or not Lewis would have eventually converted to Roman Catholicism, his letters through *Volume II* do not indicate him entertaining such a shift. As he
did in *Volume I*, Hooper provides extensive footnotes in which he thoroughly
explains passing references to people, places, books, and ideas. Again, also
invaluable are a "Biographical Appendix" of seventy-one pages and another
exceptionally detailed index. *Volume II* is simply a must for those desiring a
more intimate look into Lewis's life.

The *Collected Letters: Volume III, Narnia, Cambridge and Joy, 1950–1963* is a
fitting final volume. It has a three-fold value: first, it largely supersedes earlier
smaller collections of Lewis's letters; second, it offers numerous examples of
Lewis's winsome ability to encourage others in the Christian faith; and third,

it offers critical insight into Lewis's relationship with the two most important women in his life—Mrs. Janie Moore and Joy Davidman.

Before Hooper started work on the collected letters, there were in print several volumes of letters, including *Letters of C. S Lewis* (1988 [1966]), *Letters to an American Lady* (1969), *They Stand Together: The Letters of C. S. Lewis to Arthur Greeves, 1914–1963* (1979), *Letters to Children* (1985), and *Letters of C. S. Lewis to Don Giovanni Calabria* (1989). There were also several works that included smaller collections of Lewis's letters, most notably Sheldon Vanauken's *A Severe Mercy* (1977). Of special note is *They Stand Together*; for readers interested in Lewis's literary, spiritual, intellectual, cultural, and social maturation as a young teenager, the letters to Greeves are required (and fascinating) reading. These collections are gold mines of information, but they are also fragmentary because they do not offer a comprehensive view of Lewis as a letter writer; instead, for the most part they offer parallel accounts of Lewis's close relationships with persons such as Greeves; his American pen friend, Mary Willis Shelburne; and his Roman Catholic priest acquaintance and spiritual confidant, Calabria. While the *Letters of C. S. Lewis* and *Letters to Children* provide a larger glimpse of Lewis as a correspondent, both are limited and incomplete.

There will always be a place for these smaller collections, especially if one is interested in tracing Lewis's relationships with particular correspondents. *Letters to Children* is charming and illustrates how warm and genuine Lewis was to the many children who wrote him about Narnia. For instance, he writes one girl who had been especially complementary about Reepicheep, the valiant fighting mouse in *The Voyage of the Dawn Treader*: "I love real mice. There are lots in my rooms in [Magdalen] College but I have never set a trap. When I sit up late working they poke their heads out from behind the curtains just as if they were saying, 'Hi! Time for you to go to bed. We want to come out and play!'" (*CL*, 3, 335). However, despite the enduring value of these previous collections, now that we have the three collected volumes we can for the first time "read" Lewis's life in a systematic and integrated fashion.

After the success of books such as *The Screwtape Letters*, *The Problem of Pain*, and *The Great Divorce*, as well as his World War II BBC radio broadcasts (later published as *Mere Christianity*), persons by the hundreds wrote Lewis seeking spiritual advice and counsel. Although Lewis actually disliked receiving mail (he once described an ideal day as one in which he would never hear "the postman's knock"), he felt called—as a spiritual duty—to answer every letter he received, albeit sometimes with the assistance of his brother, Warren. Simply to list by name these many correspondents in *Volume III* would take several paragraphs (Hooper estimates that Lewis probably wrote in excess of 10,000 letters during his lifetime), so rather than sampling these many correspondents, here I will focus upon a series of letters Lewis wrote to one correspondent, Mary Van Deusen.

On December 7, 1950 Lewis, while in sympathy with Van Deusen's dislike of public worship, cautions her: "If people like you and me find much that we don't naturally like in the public & corporate side of Christianity all the better for us: it will teach us humility and charity towards simple low-brow people who may be better Christians than ourselves. I naturally loathe nearly all hymns: the face, and life, of the charwoman in the next pew who revels in them, teach me that good taste in poetry or music are *not* necessary to salvation" (68–69; emphasis Lewis). In another letter he anticipates ideas that find later expression in *The Four Loves*: "Say there are two kinds of love: we love wise & kind & and beautiful people because we need them, but we love (or try to love) stupid & and disagreeable people because they need us. This second kind is the more divine, because that is how God loves us: not because we are lovable but because He is love, not because He needs to receive but because He delights to give" (May 25, 1951; 119). When she asks him about the controversy between low and high church advocates, he writes: "Whatever the merits of the dispute are, the 'heat' is simply and solely Sin, and I think parsons ought to preach on it from that angle" (May 5, 1952; 186).

Van Deusen also queries Lewis on various aspects of Roman Catholicism. To her question about Hail Marys, Lewis offers a gracious yet cautionary reply:

> Hail Marys raise a *doctrinal* question: whether it is lawful to address devotions to any *creature*, however holy. My own view would be that a *salute* to any saint (or angel) cannot in itself be wrong any more than taking off one's hat to a friend: but that there is always some danger lest such practices start one on the road to a state (sometimes found in R. C.'s) where the B[lessed]. V[irgin]. M[ary]. is treated really as a deity and even becomes the centre of the religion. I therefore think that such salutes are better avoided. And if the Blessed Virgin is as good as the best mothers I have known, she does not *want* any of the

attention which might have gone to her Son diverted to herself. (June 26, 1952; 209; emphasis Lewis)

When she writes him several letters about the value of confessing to a spiritual mentor, he replies: "Most of [us] have never really faced the facts about ourselves until we uttered them aloud in plain words, calling a spade a spade. I certainly feel I have profited enormously by the practice. At the same time I think we are quite right not to make it generally obligatory, which wd. force it on some who are not ready for it and might do harm" (April 6, 1953; 320). And Lewis confesses to Van Deusen his own struggles with forgiveness: "I had assented to the doctrine years earlier and would have said I believed it. Then, one blessed day, it suddenly became real to me and made what I had previously called 'belief' look absolutely unreal" (May 14, 1956; 751).

He also offers his thoughts on faith healing, discerning God's will, the person of Jesus Christ, the value of suffering for the Christian, the fate of unbelievers who never have the chance to hear about Christ, the value of set prayers and worship services, the potential help a Christian psychiatrist can be, free will vs. predestination, becoming active in a religious order, God's grace, how to endure incompetent parsons, the spiritual value of physical pleasures, his love of the Psalms, the Incarnation, Christian apologetics, existentialism, envy, glorification, and prayers for the dead. Throughout Lewis's lengthy correspondence with Van Deusen (his first letter to her was August 9, 1949, and his last was November 16, 1963—only one week before his death), Lewis is gracious, patient, sincere, and genuine; this comes through especially in his common way of closing his letters to her by assuring her that she and her family (Lewis also wrote a series of letters to Van Deusen's daughter who underwent many spiritual and personal crises) are daily in his prayers. He shared with Van Deusen his time, his mind, his spiritual insight, and his empathy, not as one superior to her, but as one Christian brother to a Christian sister. Such generosity is testimony to the depth of his soul and certainly worthy of emulation.

While Lewis's hundreds of letters to persons who asked him for spiritual counsel are powerful, those concerning Moore and Davidman are revelatory. *Volume III* supplements the little we know about Lewis's relationship with Mrs. Janie Moore, the woman he lived with from roughly the end of World War I until her death in January 1951. Lewis's well known pledge to Moore's son, Paddy, before the boys went off to the trenches in France (that if either of the boys survived the war and the other did not, the survivor would take care of the deceased's parent) was one he kept, much to the distress of Warren (who came to despise Moore), the consternation of Lewis biographers (who are desperate to know if Lewis and Moore were ever lovers), and the head-scratching wonder of general Lewis readers. This conundrum will probably never be settled this side of eternity, but Lewis offers a few hints about his relationship with Moore in the years before her death. For instance, on April 5, 1950 Lewis writes Greeves and puts off a visit to Ireland after Minto (one of Lewis's nicknames for Moore) has to enter a nursing home; although Lewis dreads the expense, he tells Greeves "in one way it will be an enormous liberation for me . . . . I hardly know how I feel—relief, pity, hope, terror, & bewilderment have me in a whirl" (28–29). On June 15, 1950 he tells Greeves that Moore seems to have adjusted to the nursing home, and then adds: "Remember that if you can get over to England the Kilns [his home] is *now* a house less horrible to stay in than I know it was before" (37–38; emphasis Lewis). To another correspondent he writes on July 26, 1950 that Moore is more at peace now than in previous years: "She was for many years of a worrying and, to speak frankly, a jealous, exacting, and angry disposition" (45).

To Jill Freud who had once been a favorite guest and helper at the Kilns Lewis is even more emphatic: "Minto continues much the same, some days recognizing us, some days not. It sounds horribly unChristian and callous, but I can't help wishing she would die. Can you imagine anything more horrible than lingering on in this state?" (September 29, 1950; 56). In other letters Lewis admits that Moore's removal to the nursing home has given him the freedom to plan his days and be freed from time-consuming domestic duties for the first time in fifteen years; in one case he also describes his life as now being "more physically comfortable and more psychologically harmonious." The end finally comes on January 12, 1951. To Van Deusen Lewis confides "that I have lived [most of my life] in a house wh. was hardly ever at peace for 24 hours, amidst senseless wranglings, lyings, backbitings, follies, and *scares*. I never went home without a feeling of terror as to what appalling situation might have developed in my absence" (April 18, 1951; 108; emphasis Lewis). And he writes his friend Sister Penelope (Ruth Penelope Lawson): "'Jane' died almost a year ago . . . . I beg you will often pray for her. She was an unbeliever and, in later years, very jealous, exacting, and irascible, but always tender to the poor and to animals" (January 10, 1952; 158). Clearly Lewis was relieved when Moore died, yet his pledge to care for her—and his keeping the pledge through so many adverse circumstances and in spite of Moore's unpleasant personality—is powerful testimony of his integrity and personal character.

With divine irony, just as God was removing Moore from Lewis's life, he replaced her with Joy Davidman, the woman who would become the love of his life, his wife, and his soul mate. After Davidman's well-known rejection of communism and after her conversion to Christianity in the late 1940s, in which the writings of Lewis played no small part, she decided to seek out a relationship with him. She began corresponding with Lewis in January 1950, and a lively correspondence developed, one enjoyed as much by Warren as by his brother.[14] By the fall of 1952 Davidman had sailed to England and invited Lewis to meet her at a luncheon in the Eastgate Hotel in Oxford. Lewis, who obviously enjoyed being with Davidman, reciprocated and invited her to luncheon at his rooms in Magdalen College; surprisingly, he then followed this up with the very unusual invitation that she spend Christmas at the Kilns.[15] Lewis was clearly overwhelmed by this visit. On December 19, 1952, Lewis writes his godson, Laurence Harwood, about Joy's visit: "I am completely 'circumvented' by a guest, asked for one week but staying for three, who talks from morning till night. I hope you'll all have a nicer Christmas than I. I can't write (write? I can hardly think or breathe. I can't believe it's all real)" (268).

After Davidman moves to England in 1953 with her two sons, David and Douglas Gresham, Lewis invites the three of them for a Christmas stay December 17–20, 1953. On December 21, 1953 Lewis writes Harwood: "We have had an American lady staying in the house with her two sons .... Whew! But you have younger brothers, so you know what it is like. We didn't: we do now. Very pleasant, but like surf bathing, leaves one rather breathless" (389). In other letters about this time, Lewis reveals both how tiring it was for him and Warren to try to keep up with Davidman and her boys, but also how much he enjoyed their company; by April 1954 Lewis and Warren have invited the three back. Lewis writes his former pupil and good friend George Sayer and apologizes for not being able to meet for dinner: "By bad luck Mrs. Gresham [Davidman] (our queer, Jewish, ex-Communist, American convert) and her two boys will be here all next week" (April 2, 1954). Lewis's slighting references to Davidman in this letter suggests he had yet to be attracted to her, although he and Warren meet with her in August of the same year, shortly after her divorce from American writer William Gresham.

There are no references again to Davidman until Lewis writes Dorothy L. Sayers on April 6, 1955, yet we know Lewis and Davidman were meeting on a regular basis since she was helping with the manuscript that eventually became *Till We Have Faces* (1956). Davidman and her boys move to Oxford (at the same time Lewis is in the midst of his academic move to Cambridge) in August 1955, but still there are only scattered references to her in Lewis's many letters between then and October 1955; why this is so is open for interpretation, but the most common supposition is that Lewis, now almost certainly romantically attracted to Davidman, was fighting his own feelings and was not interested in tipping his hand about his feelings in his letters to others. Moreover, since most of his friends seemed not to like Davidman—citing her abrasive personality and over-bearing nature (claims that I have not seen substantially documented)—Lewis may have wanted to avoid the inevitable controversy a public relationship with Davidman would have precipitated. Yet, he writes Greeves on October 30, 1955 and confirms that he is thinking of marrying Davidman in a civil ceremony in order to extend to her British citizenship: "The other affair remains where it did. I don't feel the point about a 'false position.' Everyone whom it concerned wd. be told. The 'reality' [of a marriage and sexual consummation] wd. be, from my point of view, adultery and therefore mustn't happen" (669). In fact, Lewis married Davidman in a civil ceremony on April 23, 1956, but he did not make the marriage public (other than to several close friends) until after her bone cancer threatened her life. Lewis writes Greeves on November 25, 1956: "It will be a great tragedy for me to lose her. In the meantime, if she gets over this bout and emerges from hospital, she will no longer be fit to live alone so she must come and live [at the Kilns]. That means (in order to avoid scandal) that our marriage must shortly be published" (812). The official announcement of their marriage appeared in *The Times* on December 24, 1956.

Letters throughout the early months of 1957 reveal Lewis's candid worries about his wife's health and their future together, but they also reflect his happiness as this excerpt from a letter to Chad Walsh illustrates: "You wd. hardly believe how much happiness, not to say *gaiety*, we have together—a honeymoon on a sinking ship" (February 13, 1957; 832 and emphasis Lewis). Indeed, Lewis often uses the word gaiety in letters of this period to describe his moments with his wife. *Volume III* also documents Lewis's "second" marriage to Davidman (on March 21, 1957) as well as the well-known service of healing performed by the man who married them, Peter Bide. Lewis's love for his wife did, in fact, surprise him. He tells Dorothy L. Sayers "my heart is breaking and I was never so happy before: at any rate there is more in life than I knew about" (June 25, 1957; 862). To another correspondent he positively gushes: "We are crazily in love" (July 9, 1957; 866).

For the next two and a half years Davidman's cancer goes into remission (while Lewis develops osteoporosis) and they enjoy what appears to be a happy and comfortable time together. Letters early in 1960 show that her cancer returns with a vengeance, and she dies on July 13, 1960. When he writes friends about her death, he is clearly saddened although he does not communicate the kind of anger that surfaces later in *A Grief Observed* (1961). For instance, he tells Bide: "I can't *understand* my loss yet and hardly (except for brief but terrible moments) feel more than a kind of bewilderment, almost a psychological paralysis. A bit like the first moments after being hit by a shell" (July 14, 1960; 1169 and emphasis Lewis). Later he confides to Walsh: "It was a wonderful marriage. Even after all hope was gone, even on the last night before her death, there were 'patins of bright gold.' Two of the last things she said were 'You have made me happy' and 'I am at peace with God' (October 18, 1960; 1199). Although many letters after this time mention his wife, Lewis does not dwell on her, perhaps because he pours his grief into *A Grief Observed*.

Volume III also contains a supplemental section that includes many letters that were missed by the first two volumes, including the "Great War" letters between Lewis and Owen Barfield (in which Lewis tried to dissuade Barfield from belief in anthroposophy). The supplement explains why *Volume III* is a third longer than the first two volumes; Hooper tried to get in every letter he could, but there are omissions, including several letters Lewis wrote to poet Ruth Pitter. For instance, he is particularly gracious to Pitter in his new year's remarks for 1952: "Congratulations on [*Urania*] being a Book of the Year for '51. Whenever I re-read your poems, I blame myself for not re-reading them oftener. . . . All blessings. I will drink to your health (not 'only with my eyes') at lunch time" (December 29, 1951).[16] In a project this big, such omissions are perhaps inevitable. Such lapses can be forgiven, particularly as Hooper provides extensive footnotes in which he thoroughly explains passing references to people, places, books, and ideas. Again, also invaluable are a "Biographical Appendix" of ninety pages and another exceptionally detailed index. All readers of Lewis owe Hooper a huge debt for his persistence and perseverance in completing his last great work of Lewis scholarship. I, for one, take my hat off to him.

A Review of Peter J. Schakel's
Imagination and the Arts in C. S. Lewis:
Journeying to Narnia and Other Worlds
(Columbia, MO: University of Missouri Press, 2002)[17]

Peter J. Schakel's fourth book on C. S. Lewis (following *Reading with the Heart: The Way into Narnia,* **1979;** *Reason and Imagination in C. S. Lewis: A Study of Till We Have Faces,* 1984, and *Word and Story in C. S. Lewis* [co-edited with Charles A. Huttar], 1991) is another welcomed addition to the growing list of scholarly books on Lewis. This distinction is significant; too many books on Lewis simply re-hash his ideas, stories, or apologetics. Frankly, I would rather read Lewis directly. The value of a book like *Imagination and the Arts* is that Schakel offers thoughtful, informed, and perceptive discussions that take us beyond the obvious and offer us new and penetrating insights; he brings a scholar's eye to Lewis's texts, particularly the Narnian Chronicles, and helps us draw deeper understandings and enjoyments from them.

Of central focus in *Imagination and the Arts* is Lewis's imagination and love of the arts (music, dance, drawing, painting, architecture, and clothing); in particular, Schakel attempts "to consider [Lewis's] different definitions of imagination and the way they relate to each other; to treat him as a contributor to what is now referred to as 'moral imagination' as well as artistic imagination; and to demonstrate the extent of Lewis's interest in the other arts and show how arts shape some of his deepest and most fundamental concepts about life and the universe" (ix). While the Narnian Chronicles take up the lion's share of his attention, Schakel also includes discussions of many other Lewis books.

In the first chapter, "'Feeding the Imagination': Lewis's Imaginative Theory and Practice," Schakel argues that "imagination, for Lewis, can be defined as the mental, but not intellectual, faculty that puts things into meaningful relationships to form unified wholes . . . . Imagination connects things that were previously unconnected, not through a logical or intellectual process but through association, intuition, or inspiration" (4–5). In the rest of the chapter Schakel traces Lewis's evolving ideas about the imagination in *Surprised by Joy*, his early letters to Arthur Greeves and Owen Barfield, *An Experiment in Criticism*, *The Discarded Image*, and *The Abolition of Man*. "In each [of these four books], the nourishing of the imagination can be considered a central theme" (11).

Chapters 2–5 focus in particular upon Lewis's ideas about the imagination and literary texts, beginning with his earliest delightful experiences as a reader and ending with a discussion of his impressive gifts as a storyteller. Schakel suggests that Lewis's imaginative life as a reader was holistic; while content, style, and text were important, equally important were "the look and feel of the book, and . . . the context in which the reader encounter[ed] the work" (23). For Lewis, "to experience books fully is to feel almost a personal relationship with them" (25). Because Lewis believed the historical context of each book is key to understanding it fully, Schakel spends a good deal of effort arguing that the "correct" order for reading Lewis's Narnian Chronicles is the order in which they were first published beginning with *The Lion, the Witch and the Wardrobe* and ending with *The Last Battle*. While some might believe Schakel is jousting with windmills, I for one am glad someone has finally articulated my own bias; those who believe (including the misguided publishers) the "best" way to read the Chronicles is to begin with *The Magician's Nephew* sacrifice dramatic effectiveness and literary excellence to chronological "correctness" and authorial intent (always shifting sand). As Schakel puts it: "To read one of the other books before *The Lion, the Witch and the Wardrobe* sacrifices strategies that Lewis used to lead readers into the world of Narnia and to help them share imaginatively in the experiences of Lucy, and later the other children, as they discover what that world is like" (45). Schakel is also helpful in his discussion of Lewis's ideas about story, noting especially the way Lewis relies upon the imaginative power of suspensefulness, "other worldliness," mythic resonance, and human longing. Moreover, his discussion of Lewis's own storytellers, including the narrator of the Chronicles, the narrator "Lewis" of the Ransom stories, and Ransom himself, explores the imaginative range of Lewis's storytelling voice: "All of this (directly addressing the reader, wit, humor, irony, satire) creates in the stories the impression of a genial, likeable storyteller whose tales are a pleasure to listen to" (87).

Subsequent chapters consider Lewis's interest in music, dance, art, architecture, and clothing. Schakel is best in his discussion of music, tracing via the Greeves letters Lewis's early love of music (and lifelong distaste for hymns) and illustrating in various places the role of music in his imaginative works. I thought Schakel was particularly sharp in picking up the significant role of music in Lewis's first two published works: *Spirits in Bondage* and *Dymer*, both volumes of poetry. I was less impressed with the chapter on dance. While Schakel rightly notes Lewis was no dancer himself, and thus uses the image of dance in his works for "its aesthetic and imaginative impact as an idea, or archetype" (112), I thought his discussion of the idea of the Great Dance, important not only in the Chronicles but also in *Perelandra*, was truncated and underdeveloped. He is better on the role of the visual arts, particularly drawing on Lewis's imaginative development, and he rightly notes the way Lewis used to include rudimentary drawings in letters to children later in life. While Lewis himself criticizes his drawings for lack of beauty, intent instead on communicating action, comedy, and invention, Schakel is on the mark in discussing how Lewis's early interest in the visual arts looms large in his creative imagination throughout his life: "All of the arts—story, music, dance, the visual arts, and architecture as well as the design and crafting of clothes—celebrate the nobility and value of humanity. Lewis held that all artists, whether Christians or non-Christians, as they use their imaginations to create works of beauty, reflect the beauty God embodied in the created universe and the sense of beauty God implanted in human beings" (162).

The last chapter, "Let the Pictures Tell Their Own Moral: Lewis and Moral Imagination," moves the book from its cataloguing of examples of the arts in Lewis's oeuvre to a thoughtful discussion of how Lewis may have put to service his imagination. Schakel observes that for Lewis imagination "is the organ of meaning. Imagination is needed in the moral realm, therefore, to give meaning to morality, to connect its principles to life, [and] to bridge the gap between theory and practice . . . . [The arts] are so important because Lewis believed that the artistic imagination could be used in the service of the moral imagination" (164). Schakel explores the outworking of this idea in Mark Studdock in *That Hideous Strength*, in the ill-advised educational theories Lewis attacks in *The Abolition of Man*, and in various characters of the Chronicles. Many readers will be stimulated by Schakel's discussion of Lewis's use of witches, evil characters, and magic in various stories and the connections he makes with contemporary author J. K. Rowling's popular Harry Potter stories. Schakel argues "Lewis would have enjoyed and commended the

Potter books, for their creativity in conceiving of a unique fantasy world, for their skill in adapting the traditional school story to a new and more positive use, and for the way in which they nurture the moral imagination by having characters and events affirm virtues Lewis valued highly" (187).

Imagination and the Arts is well-conceived, well-developed, and well-argued. While I admit I tired at times as example after example was given from the Chronicles, to be fair Schakel needed to provide ample illustrations to support his contentions. Also, I was unconvinced by his discussions of architecture and clothing. The Kilns, Lewis's primary adult residence, was a bit of a shambles and might have fallen in upon itself but for the partial renovation brought about by Joy Davidman (happily, the Kilns has now been completely restored by the C. S. Lewis Foundation). Unlike the elaborate architecture so central to Tolkien's *Lord of the Rings,* Lewis expends little energy on creating magnificent buildings or castles. And Lewis's penchant for ill-dress is legendary. His brother, Warren, captures this best: "His own clothes were a matter of complete indifference to him: he had the extraordinary knack of making a new suit look shabby the second time he wore it."[18] Indeed, the two most memorable Lewisian characters for me are the Green Lady of *Perelandra* and Puddleglum of *The Silver Chair;* she is naked and he is a shabbily attired Marshwiggle—a creature who is a cross between a human and a frog. It is not clothing (or lack thereof) that calls attention to them; it is instead the nobility of the former and the tenacious (if pessimistic) faith of the latter. Still, these are quibbles. *Imagination and the Arts* belongs on the bookcase of all readers of Lewis.

Enchanted: A Review of Alan Jacobs' *The Narnian: The Life and Imagination of C. S. Lewis*

(San Francisco: HarperSanFrancisco, 2005)[19]

With the flood of C. S. Lewis books timed to capitalize on Disney's December 2005 release of a feature-film version of *The Lion, the Witch and the Wardrobe,* readers awash in the deluge may be forgiven a certain amount of cynicism. While it may be hyperbole to call such marketing a Narnian frenzy, the truism "Lewis sells" is being eagerly exploited by publishers determined not to miss their chance to turn a profit. Thankfully

Alan Jacobs' *The Narnian: The Life and Imagination of C. S. Lewis* is one of the better offerings amid the flotsam, combining fine scholarship with winsome writing to produce what may be called a critical biography—that is, a careful reading of Lewis's works with an eye for how they comment upon his imaginative life. This is not hagiography nor a definitive biography (it never set out to be so), but it is an important contribution to Lewisian biography drawing extensively upon the massive work of Walter Hooper in the first two volumes of Lewis's *Collected Letters*. In addition, Jacobs cites from but does not depend upon Lewis's autobiography, *Surprised by Joy*, and the earlier biographies of A. N. Wilson, Walter Hooper and Roger L. Green, and George Sayer; some eyebrows will be raised by any use of the Wilson biography, but Jacobs rightly discerns when Wilson is worth citing and when he is patently ill-informed.

Jacobs' biography is guided by his "belief that Lewis's mind was above all characterized by a *willingness to be enchanted*, and it was this openness to enchantment that held together the various strands of his life: his delight in laughter, his willingness to accept a world made by a good and loving God, and (in some ways above all) his willingness to submit to the charms of a wonderful story—whether written by an Italian poet of the sixteenth century, or by Beatrix Potter, or by himself" (xxi; emphasis Jacobs). Because of this willingness to be enchanted, Jacobs argues "Lewis's imagination was a transforming one: he took the people he knew and loved, the great events he experienced, the books he read, and swept them all together into the great complicated manifold world of Narnia . . . . He was a Narnian long before he knew what name to give that country; it was his true homeland, the native ground to which he hoped, one day, to return" (xxv). At the same time, while Jacobs does discuss in specific ways how this plays itself out in the Narnian stories, his approach is not systematic—that is, he does not devote chapters to each of the Narnian books; instead he integrates discussions of Narnia into chapters offering a chronological telling of Lewis's life.

Likewise, he does not offer a systematic discussion of Lewis's imagination as illustrated in all his books; rather, he is judiciously selective. For instance, he is excellent in his discussions of *The Abolition of Man* and *That Hideous Strength*. He calls the former "the most profound of Lewis's cultural critiques" (174), noting that the educational theorists Lewis attacks in the book have unwittingly promoted an "infernal pedagogy: by insisting that our feelings are mere preferences—none of which can be greater or more valuable than another—they open the way for dark forces to conduct their own campaign of education in the values of Hell" (179–80). Jacobs then augments this discussion by showing how Lewis imaginatively uses the latter book to illustrate the literary application of such an infernal pedagogy, primarily through the character Mark Studdock who only at the last moment realizes he has become a "man without a chest" as a result of his manipulation by the National Institute of Coordinated Experiments (N.I.C.E.). When Jacobs applies this to Narnia, he exposes how Uncle Andrew's rhetoric from *The Magician's Nephew* is moral relativism, summed up by Digory who says: "All it means . . . is that he thinks he can do anything he likes to get anything he wants." In fact, along with his discussions of *The Pilgrim's Regress, The Problem of Pain, The Screwtape Letters,* and *English Literature in the Sixteenth Century (Excluding Drama),* Jacobs offers one of the best discussions of Lewis's critique of modernity that I have read.

Jacobs is also very perceptive in his discussion of the Inklings, particularly Lewis's relationship with Tolkien. While noting Lewis's spiritual debt to Tolkien—it was a long evening conversation with Tolkien and Hugo Dyson on September 19, 1931, that Lewis noted as key to his eventual movement to faith in Christ—Jacobs also highlights Tolkien's early affection for Lewis. For example, Tolkien confided in his diary: "Friendship with Lewis compensates for much, and besides giving constant pleasure and comfort has done me much good from the contact with a man at once honest, brave, intellectual—a scholar, a poet, and a philosopher—and a lover, at least after a long pilgrimage, of Our Lord" (151). Jacobs rightly points out how often and with what enthusiasm Lewis encouraged Tolkien to persevere in his writing of the books that eventually became *The Hobbit* and *The Lord of the Rings.* At the same time, Jacobs suggests the later cooling of Tolkien's affection toward Lewis had to do with the writing of the Narnian stories; Tolkien, ever the perfectionist, wrote and re-wrote his stories, intent on offering a coherent and integrated mythology. Accordingly, he found the hodge-podge collection of imaginative characters in Narnia—dryads, dwarves, werewolves, witches, and even Father Christmas—repugnant. Jacobs also suggests that the popular success of the Narnian stories may have led to jealousy on the part of Tolkien.

On the matter of Lewis's relationship with Mrs. Moore, the woman he lived with after his return from the trenches in World War I until her death in 1951, Jacobs, like earlier biographers, is limited by the dearth of primary documents regarding this relationship. Although he notes Lewis took seriously his pledge to Paddy Moore to care for his mother if he did not survive the war, and the fact she, like Lewis, was from Ireland, Jacobs, with one exception, adds little to the speculations of earlier biographers. Lewis himself precluded insight here, noting in *Surprised by Joy* about his return to Oxford in 1919: "But before I say anything of my life there I must warn the reader that one huge and complex episode will be omitted. I have no choice about this reticence . . . . Even were I free to tell the story, I doubt if it has much to do with the subject of the book" (*SJ*, 198). Jacobs' intriguing speculation is that Mrs. Moore may have served as the model for Orual, the domineering, possessive, self-deceived central character of Lewis's greatest work of fiction, *Till We Have Faces*. Jacobs also has little new to say about Lewis's late marriage to Joy Davidman although he does faithfully recount the genesis of their relationship and is sympathetic to Joy—something not universally shared by other biographers. His writing about their relationship, while brief, is poignant and captures well the tenderness, love, affliction, and grief Lewis experienced.

There are flaws in Jacobs' biography. One is a minor stylistic distraction—Jacobs frequently uses parenthetical expressions promising readers more detail later on the topic under discussion or longer parenthetical passages containing information that could either easily be included in the main text or assigned to footnotes. More troubling, however, is his failure to explore in depth the critical role Lewis's aspirations to be a poet had upon his imaginative life. Until Lewis was twenty six, his central literary passion was to become a poet. Owen Barfield said that if you knew Lewis in Oxford in the early 1920s, you knew him as someone who wanted to become a great poet. Moreover, while Jacobs does mention that Lewis's first two published works were volumes of poetry, *Spirits in Bondage* and *Dymer*, he expends little energy discussing them nor showing how Lewis's dedication to verse later contributes to his imaginative gifts as a prose writer.

The point here is not that Lewis was a great poet—although he was certainly much better than Jacobs credits him; instead, in a biography that claims to focus upon Lewis's imagination, it is a critical oversight to give such short shrift to Lewis's poetic aspirations. His early letters to his father, Albert, and his great friend, Arthur Greeves, are peppered with references not only to his reading great poets, including Homer, Virgil, Dante, Milton, Wordsworth, but also to his earnest efforts at writing both lyrical and narrative verse. In addition, he wrote and published poems until the last year of his life, a body of verse totaling over three hundred poems. This lifelong dedication to poetry finds wonderful expression in Lewis's prose, so much so that some of his best prose is marked by passages of poetic prose, including *Mere Christianity, The Problem of Pain, The Screwtape Letters, The Great Divorce, A Grief Observed,* and large portions of *Out of the Silent Planet, Perelandra,* and the Chronicles of Narnia. Indeed, while Lewis's imaginative success as a poet may have been constrained by his careful attention to poetic conventions—meter, rhyme, and stanziac patterns—his imagination was liberated by the relative form-lessness of prose.

Despite these flaws, *The Narnian: The Life and Imagination of C. S. Lewis* is a worthy addition to Lewisian biography. In addition to the strengths already cited, Jacobs' final chapter is a spirited exposé of the wooly-headed, specious, and mean-spirited attacks on Lewis by Philip Hensher—"Let us drop C. S. Lewis and his ghastly, priggish, half-witted, money-making drivel about Narnia down the nearest deep hole, as soon as conveniently possible" (306)—and Philip Pullman who wrote regarding Narnia: "Death is better than life; boys are better than girls; light-coloured people are better than dark-coloured people; and so on. There is no shortage of such nauseating drivel in Narnia, if you can face it" (307). As Jacobs deftly notes, it is not Lewis's limitation as a literary craftsman that irks Hensher and Pullman: "It is his insistence that people are immortal. It is Lewis's holding to—and more, emphasizing—the Christian promise of eternal life that makes Hensher accuse him of 'doctrinaire bullying' and Pullman to accuse him of believing that 'death is better than life'" (307).

Jacobs concludes the book by citing Kenneth Tynan, the flamboyant British dramatist, director, screenwriter, critic, and essayist, who had Lewis as his tutor at Magdalen. Tynan, who was not a believer, recounted in his diary occasions when Lewis befriended him as a student. During one crisis when Tynan was suicidal, he went to Lewis for counsel; Lewis reminded Tynan of how he had escaped certain death during a German bombing of his house in Birmingham, leading Tynan to write: "As I listened to him, my problems began to dwindle to their proper proportions; I had entered the room suicidal, and I left it exhilarated" (311). Toward the end of his life Tynan found himself turning again and again to Lewis's books; at his funeral in 1980 the last person to speak was thirteen-year-old Roxana Tynan who read three sentences from Lewis's great sermon, "The Weight of Glory": "The books or the music in which we thought the beauty was located will betray us if we trust to them; it was not *in* them, it only came *through* them, and what came through them was longing. These things—the beauty, the memory of our own past—are good images of what we really desire; but if they are mistaken for the thing itself, they turn into dumb idols, breaking the hearts of their worshippers. For they are not the thing itself; they are only the scent of a flower we have not found, the echo of a tune we have not heard, news from a country we have never yet visited" (314; emphasis Lewis). This is a most fitting conclusion to Jacobs' fine biography.

Gold Mining or Gold Digging?
The Selling of Narnia

A Review Essay[20]

Walking through the Wardrobe: A Devotional Quest into The Lion, the Witch and the Wardrobe. By Sarah Arthur. Wheaton, IL: Tyndale House, 2005.

Aslan's Call: Finding Our Way into Narnia. By Mark E. Smith. Downers Grove, IL: InterVarsity Press, 2005.

A Family Guide to Narnia: Biblical Truths in C. S. Lewis's the Chronicles of Narnia. By Christin Ditchfield. Wheaton, IL: Crossway Books, 2003.

The Way into Narnia: A Reader's Guide. By Peter J. Schakel. Grand Rapids, MI: Eerdmans, 2005.

Into the Wardrobe: C. S. Lewis and the Narnia Chronicles. By David C. Downing. San Francisco: Jossey-Bass, 2005.

Inside Narnia: A Guide to Exploring The Lion, the Witch and the Wardrobe. By Devin Brown. Grand Rapids, MI: Baker Books, 2005.

A Reader's Guide Through the Wardrobe: Exploring C. S. Lewis's Classic Story. By Leland Ryken and Marjorie Lamp Mead. Downers Grove, IL: InterVarsity Press, 2005.

Seeking the Secret Places: The Spiritual Formation of C. S. Lewis. By Lyle W. Dorsett. Grand Rapids, MI: Brazos Press, 2004.

The C. S. Lewis Chronicles: The Indispensable Biography of the Creator of Narnia, Full of Little-Known Facts, Events, and Miscellany. By Colin Duriez. New York: BlueBridge Books, 2005.

Mere Theology: A Guide to the Thought of C. S. Lewis. By Will Vaus. Downers
  Grove, IL: InterVarsity Press, 2004.
Beyond the Shadowlands: C. S. Lewis on Heaven & Hell. By Wayne Martindale.
  Wheaton, IL: Crossway Books, 2005.
Bareface: A Guide to C. S. Lewis's Last Novel. By Doris Myers. Columbia, MO:
  University of Missouri Press, 2004.
The Lion, the Witch and the Wardrobe. Directed by Andrew Adamson, Walden
  Media and Walt Disney Pictures, 2005.

As I write this review essay the Disney and Walden Media 150 million dollar film adaptation of C. S. Lewis's beloved *The Lion, the Witch and the Wardrobe* has been out for six months (see the end of this essay for a review of the film). Worldwide ticket sales long since passed 800 million dollars and already over 11 million copies of the DVD version have sold. Total revenue from ticket and DVD sales is approaching a billion dollars. That is a staggering reality, and one that prognosticators at numerous publishing houses anticipated well before the release of the movie. The prognosticators understood well one simple marketing fact: Lewis sells. This is especially true about books written by Lewis; sales of the Chronicles of Narnia alone top one million dollars annually. Books written about Lewis are less certain of turning a profit. Yet publishers eager to get on the Lewis train went into overdrive in the year leading up to the release of the movie; in fact, in the last twelve months I have received or seen twenty different books on or about C. S. Lewis. While the majority of these books are connected in some way with the Chronicles of Narnia, some are biographical and some are concerned with his other books. I wish I could say all these books were mining the gold of the master; in fact, some are simply gold-digging, seeking to capitalize on the release of the movie in order to turn a quick buck. While I suppose this is to be expected—publishers have to make money—it leaves me (and I suspect many other Lewis readers) weary and cynical. It is not for me to say that some of these books should not have been written; however, I do believe some of them did not need to be written.

Among the books that did not need to be written are Sarah Arthur's *Walking through the Wardrobe: A Devotional Quest into The Lion, the Witch and the Wardrobe* and Mark E. Smith's *Aslan's Call: Finding our Way into Narnia.*

On the one hand, I can appreciate writers like Arthur and Smith who owe Lewis a deep debt of gratitude as their spiritual mentor; Lewis is my spiritual mentor as well. On the other hand, Arthur and Smith do Lewis's Narnian books no particular favor by attempting to pull out the spiritual insights they see. Arthur says her book "is meant to be a devotional guide to help you grow in your faith" (xxv). While laudable, I do not find her comments all that helpful nor particularly insightful; like many writers who love Lewis, she makes the cardinal error of trying to re-state many of Lewis's important ideas as if her "translations" of Lewis are more effective than the original. A case in point is her application of Lewis's so-called trilemma from *Mere Christianity* where Lewis rejects those who want to accept Jesus as a great moral teacher but not as the son of God: "A man who was merely a man and said the sort of things Jesus said would not be a great moral teacher. He would either be a lunatic—on a level with the man who says he is a poached egg—or else he would be the Devil of Hell. You must make your choice. Either this man was, and is, the Son of God: or else a madman or something else" (*MC*, 41). Lewis makes his point rather succinctly—he uses seventy-two words. Arthur's application of this idea to *LWW* goes on for four pages. Are readers really so dense that they need a pony like this to ride?

Arthur is well-intentioned, perhaps only guilty of bringing coals to Newcastle. Smith, on the other hand, is operating with a hidden agenda that only becomes apparent at the end of his book. *Aslan's Call* offers a chapter of summary and commentary on each of the seven Narnian books. When I realized what Smith was doing, I admit I became quite impatient. I mean, really! Do we need Smith to retell us Lewis's wonderful stories interspersed with his pedestrian thoughts, reflections, and opinions? Wouldn't Smith have been wiser simply to have advised readers on a website to read the Narnian stories for themselves? Did he and his publisher really need to put together a book like this? I kept asking myself these questions until I got to the last chapter when all suddenly became clear—the entire book up until that point was an excuse for Smith to publish in the last chapter his own Narnia-inspired short story. Talk about shameless self-promotion. Shame on both Smith and the publisher.

Perhaps the most useful of the books drawing spiritual insights from the Narnian stories is Christin Ditchfield's *A Family Guide to Narnia: Biblical Truths in C. S. Lewis's the Chronicles of Narnia*. Ditchfield does not try to do too much in this book, and that makes it rise a notch above similar books. While she does cover all seven Narnian books, by limiting herself to a page or two of notes for each chapter and by focusing on biblical parallels, principles, and scriptural references, she invites readers to do the work of interpretation themselves. That is, she does not condescend and resort to trying to translate Lewis for us. My only quibble with Ditchfield is her decision to order her presentation by beginning with *The Magician's Nephew* instead of *The Lion, the Witch and the Wardrobe*; I suspect this may have been the publisher's decision since many of the new editions of the Narnian books follow this unwise ordering of the books.

The next group of books are by established Lewis scholars. Peter Schakel's *The Way into Narnia: A Reader's Guide* is a thoughtful, helpful overview of all seven Narnian books. While it includes some material from earlier books by Schakel—most notably excerpts from his *Imagination and the Arts in C. S. Lewis: Journeying to Narnia and Other Worlds* where he argues convincingly for the need to read the entire Narnian series in the order as originally published—this book offers an overview of fairy tale, fantasy, and myth, and a thematic discussion of each of the seven books. Schakel's discussions of each book are more than competent and his final chapter, "The Stories Told: Fairyland and Its Effects," ends with a nice evaluative summary: "The appeal of the Chronicles derives to a significant extent from the magic of Faerie evident everywhere in them: the 'elvish craft' of stories well told. Lewis as story maker proved to be a highly successful subcreator, bringing to life a series of fairy tales that relate exciting adventures in an enchantingly real world but also, through their mythical dimensions, offer readers a taste of Reality" (118). Another fine aspect of this book is an appendix that offers selective annotations to archaic words, allusions, parallels to other works by Lewis, and interpretive commentary on problematic passages throughout the seven books.

David Downing's *Into the Wardrobe: C. S. Lewis and the Narnia Chronicles* employs a different device to discuss the series; rather than a thematic overview of each book, Downing explores how Lewis drew upon his experiences as a child, as a medieval and Renaissance scholar, and as a literary artist in writing the books: "Lewis was . . . able to pour more of his whole self into his writing [the Chronicles], including his love of wonder and enchantment, his affection for animals and homespun things, his shrewd observations about human nature, his vast reading, and his robust humor, not to mention theological speculations, medieval scholarship, and arcane linguistic jokes" (xvi). Downing is particularly good in the chapter "Moral Psychology." For instance, he notes that "contemporary fiction, even children's fiction, often stresses moral ambiguity, cultural relativism, and the difficulty of discerning good and evil. But Lewis believed there is a broad consensus among religious traditions about basic right and wrong, about the value of honesty, courage, and compassion." Downing then adds: "But the crucible of character is not moral precepts but actual moral choices, situations where the right decision is not the easiest or the safest one. In the world of Narnia, all the major characters are faced with such choices, and readers are allowed to learn along with them" (91). Edmund from *The Lion, the Witch and the Wardrobe* is then carefully considered as a case in point.

In another chapter, "Classical and Medieval Elements," Downing deftly explores how Lewis's understanding of concepts such as hierarchy, chivalry, magic, and astrology impact the stories. Regarding magic, for instance, Downing rightly notes that Lewis generally thought of magic as something used "to describe anything marvelous or unexplained, from divine mysteries to diabolical sorcery" (120). While the magic associated with Aslan links to his mysterious workings—taking on "rich theological dimensions in the Deep Magic of law from the dawn of time and the Deeper Magic of redemption from before time began" (121)—Downing explains that Lewis believes human pre-occupation with magic is a matter of pride and power: "Apart from the intrinsic dangers of the occult, the practice of magic also suggests an underlying attitude of not accepting one's creatureliness, of trying to escape the inevitable vulnerability of being human. Though Aslan's magic is a mystery, it is a benign mystery. But when humans turn to magic, they too often succumb to the old temptation recorded in the book of Genesis: 'Ye shall be as gods'" (123–24). Downing's book includes copious notes and a thorough index.

The last two Narnia books discussed here are book-length studies of *The Lion, the Witch and the Wardrobe*. Devin Brown's *Inside Narnia: A Guide to Exploring The Lion, the Witch and the Wardrobe* is a thorough, well-researched, and articulate exploration of Lewis as a writer, noting in particular what may be called the "internal world" of Lewis's creativity. That is, Brown offers readers a detailed and delightful look at what influenced Lewis's writing of *The Lion, the Witch and the Wardrobe* —including borrowings, parallels, and allusions—as well as a wonderful discussion of how ideas, motifs, characters, and events in *The Lion, the Witch and the Wardrobe* are inter-related to the other six Narnian books. Equally helpful is the way Brown moves easily between the worlds of Narnia and J. R. R. Tolkien's Middle Earth, suggesting along the way how Lewis and Tolkien, who read portions of their stories out loud to each other as they were writing them, may have influenced the other's imaginary world. In brief, *Inside Narnia* should be on the shelf of all serious devotees of the Chronicles of Narnia.[21]

Like Brown's book, Leland Ryken's and Marjorie Lamp Mead's *A Reader's Guide through the Wardrobe: Exploring C. S. Lewis's Classic Story* is primarily a literary study; frankly these two books rise head and shoulders above the "devotional" books on Narnia discussed at the beginning of this essay. *A Reader's Guide* is perhaps the most mature work on a Narnian book yet published. This is in no small part because the authors decided to approach their subject "through lenses gathered from Lewis's literary criticism on the subject of literature and literary analyses" (10). Another strength of this book is that it treats *LWW* as a literary creation of Lewis's rich imagination—not as a religious tract with a hidden evangelistic purpose: "Too often readers assume that Lewis began writing his children's stories with an intentional Christian objective and *then* crafted a story to express his meaning. This was decidedly not the case. As Lewis recounted, when he wrote the Narnian stories 'everything began with images: a faun carrying an umbrella, a queen on a sledge, a magnificent lion. At first there wasn't even anything Christian about them; that element pushed itself in of its own accord.' In other words, the imaginative impulse definitely came first in Lewis's creative process" (11–12; emphasis Ryken and Mead).

After offering a review of how Lewis first got the idea for the Narnian stories, Ryken and Mead take us through each chapter in *LWW*. But rather than offer readers a summary of what happens in each chapter, they explore the literary dimensions of the chapter. For example, in their discussion of Chapter 1 of *LWW*, "Lucy Looks into a Wardrobe," they include commentary on how fairy tales "typically" begin, initiation motifs in literature, the gothic details of the Professor's house, and the journey to a strange world motif. These are very important matters and not likely to be touched upon elsewhere; for this reason, the authors do their readers a real service. Their discussions are crisp, literate, and expand our appreciation for what Lewis accomplishes in the opening chapter of the story. This pattern is followed throughout the book, as are other helpful aides such as photos of important places or objects relevant to matters under discussion, questions for individual or corporate reflection and discussion, and strategically placed sidebars.

For instance, they include this delightful recollection of Dorothy L. Sayers scholar Barbara Reynolds:

> I often saw [C. S. Lewis] from the windows of my flat in St. John's Street walking up Bridge Street from Magdalene College [Cambridge]. Once . . . as I opened my front door, he happened to be passing by. With me was my six-year-old daughter, to whom I had just then been reading *The Lion, the Witch and the Wardrobe*. A tender-minded child, she was very anxious about Edmund and had asked to go out for a walk as she was finding the story frightening. Lewis stopped to talk with me and I told him what we had been doing. He was most affable. He wore a shabby grey-green overcoat, a battered felt hat, and he carried a knobbly walking stick. His large face was ruddy and cheerful, like a countryman's. No one would have taken him for an academic. When he moved on, courteously raising his hat, I said to my daughter, who had looked at him intently and in silence all through the brief encounter, "There! That is the very man who wrote the book we've just been reading." She paused and then said thoughtfully, "Well, he looks as though he'd make it come all right." (69)

Another helpful sidebar in one chapter includes the following excerpt from Lewis's essay "Sometimes Fairy Stories May Say Best What's to be Said" explaining why he wrote the Narnian stories the way he did:

> I thought I saw how stories of this kind could steal past a certain inhibition which had paralysed much of my own religion in childhood. Why did one find it so hard to feel as one was told one ought to feel about God or about the sufferings of Christ? I thought the chief reason was that one was told one ought to. An obligation to feel can freeze feelings . . . . But supposing that by casting all these things into an imaginary world, stripping them of their stained-glass and Sunday School associations, one could make them for the first time appear in their real potency? Could one not thus steal past these watchful dragons? I thought one could." (97)

A Reader's Guide is the best of all the recent books published on the Chronicles of Narnia.

Two books considered here are primarily biographical. Lyle Dorsett's *Seeking the Secret Place: The Spiritual Formation of C. S. Lewis* is a long over-due biographical look at Lewis's spiritual development, particularly after his conversion to Christianity in 1931. Dorsett, former director of the Marion E. Wade Center at Wheaton College, is supremely well qualified for the task, having spent twenty-five years reading spiritual biographies and autobiographies as well as overseeing a seven-year oral history project on Lewis's life. Dorsett argues that after Lewis's conversion, almost every book he wrote, in one way or another, was designed "to point people to Jesus Christ" (20). I first heard Dorsett make this argument some fifteen years ago, and I admit that at the time I was not sure I agreed. However, in the intervening years as I have read Lewis more and more, I believe Dorsett's argument is "spot on." Admitting his own deep debt to Lewis as spiritual mentor, Dorsett shapes his book around imagining he could ask Lewis two questions: "Professor Lewis, what have been the foundational elements of your spiritual formation? Can you help me learn from what has encouraged you?" (23).

Drawing extensively on Lewis's letters, the book offers a thoughtful and systematic discussion of Lewis's spirituality, focusing in particular on Lewis's prayer life, scriptural understanding, faithfulness to Anglicanism, and reliance on spiritually informed friends and directors. On Lewis's understanding of Scripture, Dorsett begins by noting that Lewis as a child would have regularly heard the Word preached in the Irish Protestant church he attended with his parents; in addition, one of the last gifts his mother, Flora, gave him before her death in 1908 was a Bible. At the same time, throughout his teens and twenties Lewis was living the life of a functional atheist; he doubted the historical accuracy and spiritual authority of Scripture. Yet after his conversion he began to read Scripture with unfettered eyes, and he immersed himself in its rich truths. As Dorsett puts it: "The more Lewis prayed and steeped himself in the Bible, the more God shaped his spirit and soul to do the work He had prepared him to do . . . . Much of it . . . was writing letters to people who had read his books and wrote to him seeking spiritual counsel. Lewis's responses were increasingly filled with references to Scripture—especially quotations and paraphrases of the Master. In brief, the more C. S. Lewis imbibed the words of the Lord, the more scriptural wisdom flowed from his pen to the minds and hearts of those who sought his advice" (67). Dorsett's biography masterfully fills a heretofore chasm in our understanding of Lewis's life.

The second biographical work, Colin Duriez's *The C. S. Lewis Chronicles: The Indispensable Biography of the Creator of Narnia, Full of Little-Known Facts, Events and Miscellany* (has there ever been a more immodest subtitle?) is disappointing; it takes a year by year approach to Lewis's life, offering notes and comments on events in the life of Lewis and others who became his friends, including J. R. R. Tolkien, Owen Barfield, and Charles Williams. I found little that was new here, much that bordered on the trivial (do I really need to know what constitutes a "good" meal in the Chronicles of Narnia?), and some that was simply incorrect. For instance, in the entry for May 21, 1936, Duriez writes that Lewis's *The Allegory of Love* (1936) "wins the Hawthornden Prize" (171). It most certainly did not—the winner that year was Evelyn Waugh's *Edmund Campion*. In fact, Lewis never won the Hawthornden Prize. Readers looking for a similar year-by-year approach to Lewis's life would be better advised to purchase William Griffin's venerable *Clive Staples Lewis: A Dramatic Life* (San Francisco: Harper & Row, 1986).

Three books remain for discussion, all unrelated to the Narnian furor. Will Vaus' *Mere Theology: A Guide to the Thought of C. S. Lewis* attempts to survey the important theological ideas found in Lewis's books. Vaus notes that Lewis repeatedly claimed he was not a professional theologian, but then he shows the countless ways in which Lewis succeeded as an amateur theologian: "The goal of theology is practical. Lewis insists that there is no good in endlessly talking about God; God wants our talk about him to draw us into his life. That is the goal of theology and the goal of this book: to draw the reader more closely into the life of God, that life which Lewis, following St. Gregory of Nazianzus, called the Great Dance" (16). When Vaus turns to writing about Lewis's theological ideas, he does so in twenty-five short chapters covering topics such as the Trinity, faith and works, the church, the *Tao*, and the sacraments. Too often Vaus makes the same mistake others do when writing about Lewis—he summarizes what Lewis says as if we need his "translation" of Lewis's words. Yet a saving grace in the case of Vaus is that he does a nice job of finding related theological passages in many different places in Lewis's corpus. In addition, he offers informed and articulate commentary; a case in point is how he ends the chapter on the *Tao*: "[Lewis reminds] us that the Law exists to be transcended and that transcending the Law begins to occur when we move from following a set of rules to painting Christ's portrait in our lives by God's power. The use of the Law in the life of the Christian is a dynamic activity, not a static one, because Christ has fleshed out the Law for us in his life. Instead of merely obeying a rulebook, we must put on Christ if we are to transcend the *Tao*" (120–21).

Vaus is well-equipped to engage Lewis's theological ideas, and is no flunky; for instance, he is quick to disagree with Lewis over some points, though always respectfully and in the spirit of genuine debate and honest difference. Although there is clearly a Reformed theological perspective driving Vaus, he is not doctrinaire nor close-minded at the points where he and Lewis differ theologically. Perhaps the best examples of where Vaus finds Lewis's theological positions suspect concern his views of Scripture and Purgatory. Regarding the former, Vaus shows that Lewis did not believe the Bible is inerrant, noting in particular four facts: the distinction Paul makes in 1 Corinthians 7:10–12 between commands he gives from himself and those he gives from the Lord; the apparent inconsistencies between the genealogies in Matthew and Luke; Luke's account of how he got the content for his Gospel; and the ahistoricity of some biblical narratives including some of Christ's parables and possibly the stories of Jonah and Job (35). At the same time, Vaus shows Lewis had a high view of the authority of Scripture and held little regard for modern biblical criticism. Moreover, he points out that for Lewis the Bible is subservient to Christ: "It is Christ who is most truly the Word of God, and the Bible is a reliable witness to Christ as that true Word" (39). Vaus also praises Lewis's ability to judge the nature of biblical texts through the lens of a literary critic: "Though some might disagree with Lewis's conclusions, his insights as a literary critic are still valuable. And when it comes to analyzing the literary genre of the Gospels there are few, laymen especially, who have been more perceptive than Lewis in the history of twentieth-century biblical criticism" (41).

Regarding Lewis's views on Purgatory, Vaus discusses *The Great Divorce*, letters, passages from *Reflections on the Psalms* and *A Grief Observed*, and most pointedly *Letters to Malcolm, Chiefly on Prayer* where Lewis "states categorically . . . that he believes in Purgatory" (206). After reviewing the evidence upon which Lewis bases his view of Purgatory, Vaus admits "that I do not agree with all of [Lewis's] thinking in this regard" (207). Yet Vaus does point out what Lewis does and does not say about Purgatory: "He does not say that we can pay for our sins in Purgatory or that anything can be added to the sacrifice of

Christ. The purpose of Purgatory, to Lewis's mind, is entirely one of cleansing and purification . . . . Even the most ardent Protestant, while not agreeing with Lewis that our souls demand Purgatory, can agree that our souls demand purgation" (207). Vaus ends his disagreement with Lewis civilly: "So while I may not fully agree with Lewis's thinking on Purgatory, I am grateful for the way Lewis challenges and stretches my own thinking on this point. And reading Lewis makes me long for the purging of sin from my own soul that alone will prepare me for the joy of Heaven" (207). Surely Lewis would have enjoyed a wry smile at Vaus' compliment.

Wayne Martindale, an established Lewis scholar, gives us a wonderful book in *Beyond the Shadowlands: C. S. Lewis on Heaven and Hell.* By the neat device of demythologizing and then remythologizing both heaven and hell in Lewis's nonfiction and fiction, Martindale creates a useful rubric for discussing these most important Lewisian ideas. I was both charmed and disarmed by Martindale's opening: "I begin with a confession. I have not always wanted to go to Heaven" (15). I love confessions (they are, after all, good for the soul), and I love Martindale's honesty regarding heaven—his admission about heaven is one I, and I suspect many of his readers, share. Yet he takes us beyond this confession to sharing how reading Lewis's *The Great Divorce* "awakened in me an appetite . . . and aroused a longing to inherit what I was created for: that which would fulfill my utmost longings and engender new longings and fulfill those, too . . . . [*The Great Divorce*] awakened me to my spiritual anorexia. I was starving for heavenly food and didn't even know I was hungry" (15). Reading Lewis on heaven, says Martindale, helped him discover "that all desires are, at rock bottom, for Heaven. All of them" (16).

When Martindale begins writing about heaven and hell in Lewis, he lists what he calls "myths" about each; for instance, about heaven he lists the following myths: it will be boring, there will be no sex, at death we become ghost-like, we will lose our sense of self in heaven, we will sit around playing harps and wearing gold crowns, heaven is wishful thinking, and we will become useless on earth if we become too heavenly minded. In each section where he writes about these myths, Martindale does a nice job of making counter arguments using examples from Lewis for illustrations. For example, for those of us who fear the loss of human sexuality in heaven, Martindale cites a passage from *Miracles* where Lewis uses an analogy comparing our fear of losing sex in heaven to that of a little boy losing out on chocolate; in this passage the little boy is told that "the sexual act is the highest bodily pleasure." He then asks

> whether you [eat] chocolates at the same time. On receiving the answer "No," he might regard absence of chocolates as the chief characteristic of sexuality. In vain would you tell him the reason why lovers in their carnal raptures don't bother about chocolates is that they have something better to think of. The boy knows chocolate: he does not know the positive thing that excludes it. We are in the same position. We know the sexual life; we do not know, except in glimpses, the other thing which, in Heaven, will leave no room for it. Hence where fullness awaits us we anticipate fasting. (31)

Our problem is that we know sexual intimacy, but we don't know heaven, so we assume that heaven will mean the loss of an intimacy we are comfortable with. Lewis, says Martindale, tries to help us see that the reality in heaven may be that "our adult sexuality awaits a heavenly spring when it will blossom into something as different as a flower from a bud [and into] something [that] does not eliminate but engulfs and completes" us in a way we could never imagine on earth. Similarly Lewis says in "The Weight of Glory" that we are too easily pleased on earth—content with making mud pies and sex—when what awaits us in heaven are "the unblushing promises of reward."

When he turns to how Lewis remythologizes heaven, Martindale cites passages from *Out of the Silent Planet, Perelandra, The Great Divorce,* the Chronicles of Narnia, and *Till We Have Faces.* Perhaps my favorite is from *Out of the Silent Planet* when Ransom is traveling toward Malacandra in a primitive spaceship; heretofore he thought of space in nightmarish images, but once there he is struck by its beauty:

> The period spent in the space-ship ought to have been one of terror and anxiety for Ransom . . . . The odd thing was it did not very greatly disquiet him . . . . There was an endless night on one side of the ship and an endless day on the other: each was marvellous and he moved from the one to the other at his will, delighted. In the nights . . . Earth's disk was nowhere to be seen; the stars, thick as daisies on an uncut lawn, reigned perpetually with no cloud, no moon, no sunrise to dispute their sway. There were planets of unbelievable majesty,

and constellations undreamed of: there were celestial sapphires, rubies, emeralds and pin-pricks of burning gold; far out on the left of the picture hung a comet, tiny and remote . . . . But the days . . . were the best of all. Often he rose after only a few hours' sleep to return, drawn by an irresistible attraction, to the regions of light . . . . There, totally immersed in a bath of pure ethereal colour and of unrelenting though unwounding brightness, . . . he felt his body and mind daily rubbed and scoured and filled with new vitality.[22]

Indeed, throughout the Ransom Space trilogy Lewis does a marvelous job of "re-inventing" our notions of heaven—or at least the heavens—and this is all the more notable since he was writing well before actual space travel, giving proof once again of the power and reach of his imagination. Martindale is equally good on images of hell in Lewis, but I leave that for readers to discover on their own. *Beyond the Shadowlands* should be added to your Lewis bookshelf.

Doris Myers' *Bareface: A Guide to C. S. Lewis's Last Novel* is, as the title suggests, a close reading and discussion of *Till We Have Faces* (hereafter *TWHF*); *Bareface* was the original title of the manuscript that became *TWHF*. As such Myers' book is a nice supplement to Peter Schakel's *Reason and Imagination in C. S. Lewis* (Grand Rapids: Eerdmans, 1984), the only other book-length study of *TWHF*. Rather than considering the mythic details of the novel, Myers writes from the perspective of "emotional resonances of Orual's experience"; moreover, she treats the book as a realistic modern novel, one that can be read like Thomas Hardy's *Tess of the d'Urbervilles* or John Steinbeck's *Grapes of Wrath*. As such readers need to "tentatively accept the story as something that really happened in a specific time and place" (5). In order to help readers, Myers provides historical background and discussions linking the characters to modern psychology. She utilizes a threefold organizational technique for the book. First, she offers a chapter-by-chapter discussion emphasizing Lewis's art as a novelist, the historical and cultural context, the role of love, and finally the problem of faith raised in the chapter. Second, she provides brief articles on key topics. Third, she includes a glossary of dialectal and obsolete expressions.

Myers, another established Lewis scholar, is largely successful in this approach.[23] Some readers will no doubt benefit from the glossary since the novel is filled with odd sounding places, persons, and events. However, I was especially fascinated by her discussions of the possible influence of Jungian psychology on the character of Orual. For instance, Myers says the turning point in the novel is when Orual finds out from the priest about what happened to Psyche in exile: "Orual's surmise that the gods dropped the information 'into someone's mind, in a dream, or an oracle, or however they do such thing' shows that this is a message to her from the collective unconscious." Myers points out that this Jungian idea may have been in Lewis's mind as early as 1943 when, in *Broadcast Talks* writing about the pagan precursors of Christ, he wrote: "'[God] sent the human race what I call good dreams.'" She concludes this fine discussion by tying together the Jungian influence with her larger argument that *TWHF* is a realistic novel: "Without this context of Jungian psychology, the transmission of the Psyche myth might seem unlikely, a break in the literary realism that has dominated the novel to this point. But in a Jungian context, the priest's story simply adds psychological realism to what has gone before, showing that realism is more complicated than it originally seemed" (201). If there is a weakness to Myers' approach, it may be that we have less a unified scholarly book than a small, encyclopedic one. Still, it is a worthy addition to Lewisian scholarship.

After such a lengthy review essay covering so many books, I owe readers a brief summary of my final recommendations. Must buys are the books by Ryken and Mead, Brown, and Dorsett. Worth the money are those by Schakel, Downing, Martindale, and Myers. Honorable mention goes to Ditchfield and Vaus. With Arthur, Smith, and Duriez, save your gold; mine elsewhere.

But what of the film version of *The Lion, the Witch and the Wardrobe* that helped generate so many of the books discussed above? As I watched the credits screen by at the end of my initial viewing of the film I thought: "They got it!" Like many others in the theater, I was both smiling with delight and breathing a sigh of relief, buoyed by this latest attempt to translate Lewis's book to the screen. What I had most feared was that the makers of the movie would "dumb-down" Lewis's story into some kind of postmodern pabulum, effectively eviscerating Lewis's powerful tale of selfishness, love, sacrifice, and redemption. Certainly the temptation must have been there to sell out Lewis's intent; thankfully, however, the movie makers "got it." Specifically, here's what "they got." They "got" that squarely in middle of this wonderful tale of awe, wonder, and magic—what we feel with Lucy as she enters Narnia for the first time—is an accurate portrayal of the human heart. Edmund, angry, self-centered, proud, and mean-spirited, is actually Everyman or Everywoman, for whom among us fails to see in him our own self-love? Like him, we want the world to revolve around us—we want to be the smartest, the best-off, the one in control. And, like him, once bewitched by our own version of Turkish Delight, we'd willingly sell out even our own family in order to please our lofty visions of ourselves. The makers of the movie "got it" that Edmund's obsession with himself is the moral center of the story.

They also "got" that this is a story of love, poignantly portrayed by Lucy, Susan, and Peter. Yes, their brother is a bit of a brat and needs a good boxing of the ears. But he is also their brother, and once they learn he has betrayed them, they refuse to abandon him to the hands of the White Witch. This is more than "blood is thicker than water"—this is love for the lost, compassion for the unworthy, concern for the wretched. Again it is Lucy who best communicates this love, since who better to reject Edmund than she, especially after he lies to Peter and Susan about having been in Narnia with Lucy? His delight in making Lucy cry borders on the cruel, magnifying his egocentricity. The movie makers "got" this and did not pander to postmodern equivocation about good vs. evil—Edmund's actions are evil and shown to be that. Yet Lucy never despairs of her brother, and she is the first to embrace him when he finally comes to his senses.

But perhaps best of all the movie makers "got it" that Edmund's dark heart and even darker actions cannot be fobbed off as temperamental glitches in a basically good person. What he does is evil, plain and simple; what is not so plain and simple is what it takes to redeem Edmund and save all of Narnia from the consequences of Edmund's actions. Indeed, because of Edmund's betrayal, all of Narnia is at risk. The movie makers "got it" that waving a magic wand cannot trump the Deep Magic of Narnia—that the blood of all traitors is the rightful property of the White Witch. This is the hinge upon which the story turns, a key point the movie makers could have easily dumbed-down for fear of offending polite religious sensibilities, but they resisted such temptation and stayed true to Lewis's vision: evil can only be trumped by Deeper Magic, a magic that requires at its very core blood sacrifice and death. They "got it" that Lewis's story is more than a delightful tale of another world with talking animals, beautiful vistas, and heroic adventures—it is a story of sacrifice, death, and redemption that steals past tired old sermons and stained glass windows. And in their portrayal of Aslan they "got it." Any viewer not moved by the scene of Aslan and the White Witch at the Stone Table needs to have his or her pulse checked. Even more to the point, the movie makers "got it" that in the end it takes Aslan to complete the redemption of Narnia as he and his newly breathed upon and renewed followers show up at the last minute and destroy the White Witch, routing her army at the same time.

It is likely the movie will ignite renewed interest in and reading of other books by C. S. Lewis. Whether children's stories or literary criticism, Christian apologetics or social commentary, science fiction or theological romances, poetry or prose, there is something in Lewis's oeuvre that appeals to almost everyone. Why this is so is in part simple—Lewis knew how to write to a broad audience, and he rarely wrote for the specialist. The fact that the majority of his over forty books are still in print and selling briskly is evidence enough of his popular appeal. Another source of his appeal is his own wide, deep, and eclectic reading that reflects his passionate love of literature. Lewis is probably the best read Christian you will ever encounter. Given his photographic memory and visceral love of literature, it is not surprising that he easily draws deeply on the sources of his great reading and that he masterfully integrates them into his own writing. Also Lewis's success with readers illustrates his love of writing; he once said that "ink was a deadly drug." His addiction to writing is evidenced by his books, his over three hundred poems, his dozens and dozens of essays, not to mention the over 10,000 letters he wrote throughout his life.

But Lewis's continued popularity is more than the sum of what I have already said. More than anything else, his success rests upon what may be called his baptized imagination, a concept Lewis connected with his initial reading of George Macdonald's *Phantases*, a book he read well before he came to faith in Christ. Lewis's most amazing gift as a writer is his ability to make imaginative leaps forward when writing about a subject so that he takes us beyond the merely obvious, the mundane, the everyday. Instead, his writings make us jump imaginatively ahead towards the eternal, the lasting, the permanent, the ultimately significant. His baptized imagination helps him press forward into new vistas of imagination and thought. When he does this, we find ourselves almost breathless, waiting to see where he is going to take us. Yet because his pressing forward imaginatively seems so easy, so effortless, so comfortable, we find ourselves saying, "Of course, that's it. I've thought the same thing. . ."—when of course we could never quite do what Lewis does.

Lewis's gradual movement from atheism to agnosticism to theism to Christianity was not a matter of deciding that Christianity was somehow "good" for him and for other people. That something was good was no reason to stake one's whole life on it. Once Lewis believed Christianity was true, nothing else in the world was more important nor more worth pursuing. And, if it was true, all people should be challenged to consider its validity. While some would inevitably reject Christianity, for Lewis it was vital that they be honestly confronted with it so that they could make a decision about it. As Dorsett suggested above, it is no exaggeration to say that after his conversion to Christ, every book he wrote, albeit sometimes in an oblique or indirect fashion, had as one important intention the desire to move its readers "toward the light" of the Gospel.

If the new Narnian film rewards Hollywood (read "makes boatloads of money"), will Lewis survive the success? Will there be more Narnian movies? Not to worry, *Prince Caspian* is already in production. Will the moviemakers retain the Christian ideas implicit in the stories? That is a harder question to answer, but since the commercial success of Mel Gibson's *The Passion of the Christ*, Hollywood knows that religion sells. Accordingly, there will be more Narnian movies, and I think there is a good chance they will not dumb-down Lewis's theological motifs. In all likelihood Hollywood, although suckled on the breast of postmodernism, will continue to "get it."

A Review of Diana Glyer's
The Company They Keep: C. S. Lewis and J. R. R. Tolkien as Writers in Community
(Kent, Ohio: Kent State University Press, 2007)[24]

The Company They Keep is the latest in the small but steadily growing number of scholarly books focusing upon the Inklings. For example, while there are shelves of books focusing upon Lewis as an apologist, spiritual mentor, or children's writer, only a handful of books have appeared where scholars have shouldered the task of writing about Lewis in larger cultural, intellectual, literary, and scholarly contexts. Notable books in this regard are Bruce Edward's *The Taste of the Pineapple: Essays on*

C. S. Lewis as Reader, Critic, and Imaginative Writer (1988), Peter Schakel and Charles Huttar's *Word and Story in C. S. Lewis* (1991), Doris Myers's *C. S. Lewis in Context* (1994), and Wesley Kort's *C. S. Lewis: Then and Now* (2001). Diana Glyer's *The Company They Keep* is a welcomed addition to this group and offers a fascinating exploration of Lewis, Tolkien, and the other members of the Inklings as a writing group.

The essential argument Glyer makes contradicts what Lewis and his friends insisted upon: that they did not influence each other as writers. The most famous example is Lewis's declaration: "No one ever influenced Tolkien—you might as well try to influence a bandersnatch" (xvii). But Glyer also has to contend with the majority of Inkling scholars who up until now have accepted at face value similar disclaimers by Tolkien, Owen Barfield, and Robert E. Havard. However, based on her research of other writing "communities," including the Bloomsbury Group, the Brideshead Generation, and her own collaborative writing experiences, Glyer says that "common sense . . . suggests that the members of any long standing group are bound to change each other" (xiii). This leads to the primary focus of her book: "Did J. R. R. Tolkien, C. S. Lewis, . . . and the other Inklings influence each other? In what ways? To what extent? What is the evidence? And what are the larger implication for the study of creativity and community? That is the story I tell in these pages" (xix).

Chapter 1 explores how the friendship between Lewis and Tolkien developed, how Lewis in particular attracted a diverse group of men into the literary circle that has come to be known as the Inklings, and the eventual routine of their meetings on Thursday evenings in Lewis's rooms at Magdalen College and on Tuesday noon at the Eagle and Child pub. Glyer also lists, in addition to Lewis, Barfield, Havard, and Tolkien, the other fifteen men "in the standard list of the Inklings": J. A. W. Bennett, Lord David Cecil, Nevill Coghill, James Dundas-Grant, H. V. D. Dyson, Adam Fox, Colin Hardie, Warren Lewis, Gervase Matthew, R. B. McCallum, C. E. Stevens, Christopher Tolkien, John Wain, Charles Williams, and C. L. Wrenn (11). Chapter 2 traces the history of the Inklings, beginning somewhere in the early 1930s and ending in the late 1940s, and then offers insights into the overall impact of the group. By the end of the chapter, Glyer, relying upon the nomenclature of Karen Burke LeFevre's *Invention as a Social Act* (1987), introduces the "four specific roles that are common whenever writers work together. Writers in writing groups function as resonators, opponents, editors, and collaborators" (40).

Chapter 3 investigates the Inklings as resonators—as supporters, encouragers, and catalysts of each other as writers. As a notable example of a resonator, Glyer cites what Tolkien said about Lewis's response to reading and hearing drafts of what came to be *The Lord of the Rings*: "He was for long my only audience. Only from him did I ever get the idea that my 'stuff' could be more than a private hobby. But for his interest and unceasing eagerness for more I should never have brought it to a conclusion" (48). On the other hand, Chapter 4 considers the Inklings as opponents—that is, as friendly critics who would be quick "to challenge and criticize one another" (76). Glyer notes that often meetings of the Inklings were akin to mental and intellectual combat. Perhaps the best example of such intellectual warfare is the series of letters Lewis and Barfield wrote each other exploring their differences in ideas between orthodox Christianity and anthroposophy; known between the two men as the "Great War," these letters are now readily available in *C. S. Lewis, Collected Letters: Volume III, Narnia, Cambridge and Joy, 1950–1963* (2006).

How the Inklings functioned as editors for each other is the focus of Chapter 5. Glyer points out that "Warren Lewis read and corrected the proofs of *The Pilgrim's Regress*. C. S. Lewis read and corrected the proofs of Dyson's *Augustans and Romantics*. Williams did preliminary work on *The Allegory of Love* . . . . Owen Barfield read the manuscript of *Surprised by Joy*" (101). Of great interest to many will be the specific editorial changes Lewis suggested to Tolkien in what has come to be published as *The Lays of Beleriand*. Chapter 6 delves into how the Inklings worked as collaborators. Glyer cites examples of collaboration, including the two Lewis brothers in their youthful creation of the imaginative world of Boxen, collaborative verse by Barfield and Lewis ("Abecedarium Philosophicum") as well as their *Mark vs. Tristram*, Havard's assistance (he was a medical doctor) to Lewis as he was writing *The Problem of Pain* (1940), and several collections of essays. Glyer's book concludes with a chapter on how the Inklings also served as referents—that is, they wrote about each other—and a final chapter on how the Inklings were involved in other creative enterprises outside the context of their own writing community.

After reading the book and reflecting upon Glyer's central argument—that the Inklings, in spite of their insistence to the contrary, did in fact profoundly influence each other—I believe she is correct. She makes her case convincingly and offers multiple illustrations. Her final words in the book speak eloquently to the point: "Like filaments joined together in a web, writers work as members of larger communities. As they work, they influence and are influenced by the company they keep" (226). *The Company They Keep* is a significant contribution to scholarly work on the Inklings.

A Review of Michael Ward's
Planet Narnia: The Seven Heavens in the Imagination of C. S. Lewis
(Oxford: Oxford University Press, 2008)[25]

Brilliantly conceived. Intellectually provocative. Rhetorically convincing. A panegyric is not the usual way to begin a book review, but Michael Ward's *Planet Narnia: The Seven Heavens in the Imagination of C. S. Lewis* is worthy of such praise. I do not mean to suggest it is a perfect book, yet what Ward attempts—the first rigorously comprehensive reading of C. S. Lewis's Chronicles of Narnia—is magisterial and, in part for that reason, controversial. What he gives readers is a winsome example of the kind of passionate, informed scholarship that Lewis's books—especially his fiction—deserve. While there have been other worthwhile attempts to offer a comprehensive reading of the Chronicles, including Peter J. Schakel's *Imagination and the Arts: Journeying to Narnia and Other Worlds* (Columbia: University of Missouri Press, 2002) and David C. Downing's *Into the Wardrobe: C. S. Lewis and the Narnia Chronicles* (San Francisco: John Wiley & Sons, 2005), Ward goes several steps beyond them in his closely argued, richly supported, and unflinchingly determined critical study.

Ward says that the essential contention of his book—that Lewis secretly organized the seven Narnian stories around pre-Copernican cosmology and its model of seven planets (Sol, Luna, Venus, Mercury, Mars, Jupiter, Saturn)—came to him after thirty years of reading Lewis, ten years of teaching Lewis to undergraduates, three years of living in Lewis's home, the Kilns, and eighteen months of doctoral research. A series of events culminated one evening in his reading of Chapter 5, "The Heavens," of Lewis's *The Discarded Image: An Introduction to Medieval and Renaissance Literature* (Cambridge: Cambridge University Press, 1964) and Lewis's poem "The Planets" (a source Ward consistently references):

The phrase "winter passed / And guilt forgiven" sprang from the page, demanding attention. I had come across the passing of winter and the forgiving of guilt elsewhere in Lewis's writings: those things formed the centerpiece of his first Narnian tale. Could there be a link somehow between the poem and the Chronicle? That thought was the stray spark connecting Jupiter to *The Lion [the Witch and the Wardrobe]* in my mind, and one by one the other planet-to-book relationships began to be lit up in its train. (251)

Ward goes on to say: "I immediately and instinctively knew, though it took much longer to understand with clarity, that Lewis had cryptically designed the Chronicles so that the seven heavens spoke through them like a kind of language or song. He had translated the planets into plots, and the music of the spheres could be heard silently sounding (or tingling, as he would have said) in each work" (251). That Ward waits until the end of the book to reveal that his thesis was intuitively conceived is clever—on the one hand it is charming and compelling and on the other hand it is disarming and unpretentious.

Ward's seemingly encyclopedic knowledge of Lewis's writings ameliorates to some degree his provocative and controversial argument. For instance, in the chapters where he links a particular Chronicle to one of the planets, Ward is careful to discuss how the planet in question connects with other works by Lewis. Jupiter, says Ward, "has a long pedigree in Lewis's works; it shows strongly in his scholarship and poetry, makes a central contribution to the Ransom Space trilogy, and, most important, as I will argue, animates the imaginative vision of *The Lion, the Witch and the Wardrobe*. I will contend that this first Chronicle was deliberately designed to communicate the Jovial spirit" (42). In the remainder of the chapter Ward effectively surveys Lewis's scholarship, poetry, and Ransom trilogy and notes what he sees as Jupiter's influence; this survey lays the groundwork for the main argument of the chapter: "Aslan focuses and condenses (we might almost say, incarnates) that presiding [Jovial] spirit" (57). The chapters following this one demonstrate a similar wide angle lens with regard to the planet in question, offer an intellectually engaging and pertinent review of Lewis's corpus, and culminate in a thorough discussion of the planet's "influence" on the Narnian story under discussion. Although Ward often admits that he could have been even more thorough in his surveys, he rightly points out that too much of this kind of thing could be tiresome to the reader. Indeed, his thoughtful but balanced discussions of each planet and Chronicle advance his controversial thesis at an intellectually appropriate pace.

Rhetorically, *Planet Narnia* is stimulating and engaging. Certainly Ward's thesis is controversial—indeed many will find it over-reaching and some may be tempted to see hubris in Ward's contention. However, Ward is a master at anticipating objections, and he handles the arguments against his thesis with acuity and grace. For instance, he writes:

> What these arguments amount to is a large and bold claim, which is this: I think I have stumbled upon the secret imaginative key to the series. I know full well that finding secret codes is a favourite pastime for obsessives, conspiracy-theorists, charlatans with an eye to the main chance . . . [yet I believe I] have discovered a genuine literary secret, one that has lain open to view since the Chronicles were first published, but that, remarkably, no one has previously perceived. I am not claiming to have unearthed a hitherto unknown document in which Lewis divulged this secret, nor am I relying on the previously unpublished testimony from one of his friends or relatives. My case rests on an intellectual basis—that is, literally, a "reading between" basis. (5)

Another objection to Ward's thesis is that his assigning of one planet to one Narnian tale is arbitrary. For example, Ward links Mars with *Prince Caspian*; yet key scenes in the book take place at night under Luna, the moon; why not argue that Luna is the chief planetary influence in *Prince Caspian*? Ward, perhaps wisely, never tries to play this game; instead, once having conceived that Mars is the primary planetary influence in *Prince Caspian*, he marshals argument upon argument, evidence upon evidence, and draws conclusion upon conclusion with a kind of rapid fire discourse that is reminiscent of what G. K. Chesterton once attributed to Charles Dickens' creation of characters: "A Dickens character hits you first on the nose and then in the waistcoat, and then in the eye and then in the waistcoat again, with the blinding rapidity of some battering engine . . . . The thing about any figure of Dickens . . . is that he cannot be exhausted."

It remains to consider potential flaws in Ward's thesis. For many the main flaw in his argument is that Lewis "secretly" organized the Narnian stories around the seven planets. That Ward even makes the argument seems disingenuous for some. Once again, however, Ward demonstrates his rhetorical facility since the first chapter of the book is entitled "Silence" and therein he attempts to illustrate a number of instances where secrecy—most notably, the nature of his relationship with Mrs. Janie Moore and his concealed, private marriage to Joy Davidman—characterized Lewis's life. Moreover, he also explores in some detail Lewis's interest in literary secrets. Readers will, of course, draw their own conclusions about how successful Ward is in this regard. I, for one, do not see much connection between Lewis's desire for privacy with regard to the nature of his relationships with Moore and Davidman and the literary creation of Narnia.

A second potential flaw is a fact freely admitted by Ward—few critics, including Lewis's friends such as J. R. R. Tolkien (he thought the Chronicles so lacking in unity that he referred to them as a "hodge-podge"), have offered a comprehensive, unified reading of the tales. Again, Ward surveys those critics (including this reviewer) who have offered halting, incomplete, or undeveloped critical readings of the Chronicles, and he offers a fair but unsympathetic assessment: "This present work will not be making any attempt to challenge the various theories . . . . It would, in any case, be all but impossible to disprove some of them, so unspecific are they. It is enough to point out that none of them has been advanced in a fully serious way, nor has any one of them commanded general acceptance or even the support of a substantial minority of critics" (11). I think Ward is on target here, but it must be noted that several of Lewis's friends could have made the connection between the planets and the tales if there is one. In particular, Dorothy L. Sayers, who loved the Chronicles, was keenly aware of pre-Copernican cosmology as her notes on her translation of Dante's *Divine Comedy* and her copious letters reveal; in fact, during the last year of her life she was almost obsessive in her desire to defend Lucan's astronomical allusions in *Pharsalia* from Robert Graves who translated the latter for Penguin. That Sayers never makes a connection between the planets and Lewis's Chronicles proves nothing; at the same time, if the links that Ward sees are there, it is surprising that someone as insightful and perceptive as Sayers is with regard to pre-Copernican cosmology never notices them.

Yet I must partially contradict the argument I just made. Sayers wrote a letter on December 11, 1947 (well before the first Narnian tale appeared) in which she is discussing the elusive numerical symmetries of the *Inferno*: "But it is the very mark of great artistic skill, I think, that the formal structure of the thing *is* so elusive. Nothing leaps out at one; one just feels at first reading that some kind of masterly control has been exercised, but one doesn't see the hand manipulating the strings."[26] Clearly, as Sayers suggests, Ward may be completely correct in his contention—he may well have discovered how it was that Lewis manipulated the strings so that each Narnian tale is linked to one of the planets. In addition, Lewis himself was one of the first to uncover an important literary motif—that is, the notion of courtly love that he so eloquently discusses in his first and perhaps most enduring piece of literary criticism, *The Allegory of Love: A Study in Medieval Tradition.* So perhaps it is that Ward has uncovered the secret key to the Chronicles.

In conclusion it remains to ask the "so what" question. That is, what does it matter that Ward may have discovered the secret unifying principle of the Narnian stories? To the average reader of Lewis's tales, I do not think it matters. She reads the Chronicles not with a critical eye; instead, she reads the stories for their imaginative appeal, their delightful characters, their exciting adventures, and their spiritual depth. But for the literary critic Ward's argument is very important. What he has done is applied the kind of thoughtful, informed, perceptive, and rigorous literary analysis that the Chronicles deserve. That is, he has performed serious scholarly enquiry into Lewis's work as an artist—this is something every writer covets. Ward's work may well encourage others to apply the same kind of high quality literary analysis to Lewis's other imaginative works. In the end not all readers will buy Ward's argument; but every serious student of Lewis should buy *Planet Narnia.* In effect, it is the starting point from now forward for all serious scholarly discussions of the Chronicles of Narnia.

A Review of Mary Stewart Van Leeuwen's *A Sword between the Sexes? C. S. Lewis and the Gender Debates*

(Grand Rapids, MI: Brazos Press, 2010)[27]

A Sword between the Sexes? is a welcomed addition to the debate regarding Lewis and gender. While a handful of critical articles on this issue have been published, the only other book-length study,

Women Among the Inklings: Gender, C. S. Lewis, J. R. R. Tolkien, and Charles Williams (Westport, CT: Greenwood Press, 2001) by Candice Fredrick and Sam McBride, paints on too broad a canvas; moreover, it looks at the matter of gender primarily through the published works of Lewis, Tolkien, and Williams while eschewing their correspondence.[28] In addition, neither Fredrick (education) nor McBride (literature) has the academic training requisite to examine the issue of gender from a critically nuanced perspective. *A Sword between the Sexes* explores both Lewis's books and his correspondence in an effort to offer a comprehensive and chronological investigation of Lewis's views on gender, and Van Leeuwen's academic background in philosophy and the psychology of gender (including three other books on gender) well-equips her to write with a seasoned, informed, and perceptive eye on the multifaceted aspects of this issue.

Readers of *A Sword between the Sexes* will find much to admire, including Van Leeuwen's honest, engaging voice, her broad reading of Lewis's books, and her fresh insights. For instance, while Van Leeuwen offers a critical assessment of Lewis's early defense of "gender essentialism"—the idea that men and women are "faint and blurred reflections of masculine and feminine"—and "gender hierarchy"—the idea that but for our fall into sin "patriarchal monarchy would be the sole lawful form of government" (9)—she is fair-minded and has no personal axe to grind. In fact, she disarms readers in her opening chapter, "Surprised by Jack: An Ambivalent Journey," by noting how her own intellectual and spiritual development had paralleled Lewis's, noting in particular that like Lewis she acquiesced to being confirmed in her church as a young person, resigning "my agnostic self to going through the motions of confirmation" (17). In addition, when Van Leeuwen went to university, she regarded Lewis "as a positive model, an advocate for a robust Christianity whose scope included the life of the mind as well as piety and personal morality" (28). In spite of this debt to Lewis, she is honest enough to add:

> But now I need to point out that Lewis was at the same time a major stumbling block to my acceptance of Christianity. This was due to the mixed messages he sent about the nature (both actual and ideal) of women, men, and their relationships in books . . . such as *Mere Christianity, The Four Loves,* and *Surprised by Joy.* Moreover, much of what he said about these topics he claimed as part of

"mere" Christianity ("the belief that has been common to nearly all Christians at all times") and thus presumably not open to dispute by any who call themselves orthodox believers. (28)

However, because of her own life experiences as a young adult, she shares how she never really soured on Lewis; instead, she became curious about "separating what might rightly be called 'mere' Christianity in his writings, especially about gender, from conclusions rooted in other influences" (34).

Chapters 2–4—"A More Fundamental Reality than Sex? C. S. Lewis's Views on Gender"; "'Mere' Christianity? Sources and Results of Lewis's Views on Gender"; and "'Not the Only Fundamental Difference': The Edwardian World of C. S. Lewis and Dorothy L. Sayers"—offer a broad reading of Lewis's best known works wherein Van Leeuwen explores the issues noted in these chapter titles. Throughout these chapters readers will appreciate the careful research and detailed discussion of the issues she explores. Of special note is her comparison of the lives of Lewis and Sayers, and her suggestions that "Lewis's slowly changing views [on gender] owed much to the intellectual and Christian ties he forged with Dorothy L. Sayers, a woman of his own class and educational background" (107). For example, in a letter (Nov. 27, 1955) to Sayers he confessed "he had only 'dimly realized that the old-fashioned way (my Father did it exquisitely) of talking to all young women was v[ery] like an adult way of talking to young boys.' With his improved understanding of the origin and effects of such condescension, he added: 'It explains not only why some women grew up vapid but also why others grew up (if we may coin the word) *viricidal*'" (107; emphasis Lewis).

Chapter 5, "A Better Man that His Theories: C. S. Lewis as a Mentor and Colleague to Women," is one of the strongest in the book and has long needed to be written. Those who think that Lewis is misogynist are either wearing blinders or have not taken the time to do exactly as Van Leeuwen does in this chapter: investigate the facts about Lewis's relationships with women. There is no doubt, as Van Leeuwen points out, that early in his life Lewis said condescending things about women (as did many men of his time). Just after World War II Sayers wrote a friend about Lewis: "I do admit . . . that he is apt to write shocking nonsense about women and marriage. (That, however, is not because he is a bad theologian but because he is a rather frightened bachelor)" (109). Several years later Sayers added to another correspondent: "[I like

Lewis] very much, and always find him stimulating and amusing. One just has to accept the fact that there is a complete blank in his mind where women are concerned" (110). But Van Leeuwen is careful to point out that Lewis was not condescending in his actual relationship with women, including, Sayers, many female students (particularly Mary Shelley Neylan), Stella Aldwinckle (Chaplin to Women Students), other female students responsible for the creation of the Oxford Socratic Club (a legendary debate society), Sister Penelope Lawson, poetess Ruth Pitter, and Joy Davidman. Van Leeuwen surveys these relationships effectively in the chapter, quoting from a very important letter Lewis wrote to one of his postwar American correspondents: "Who said I disliked women? . . . I never liked or disliked any *generalization*" (127; emphasis Lewis). To this we can also add the host of female correspondents who wrote Lewis about their personal, spiritual, and even medical problems. Nor should we forget the grace, courtesy, and long-suffering he endured during the many years he took care of Mrs. Janie Moore, the mother of his World War I friend who was killed in action.

Chapters 6 and 7—"'You Can Only Get to Know Them': C. S. Lewis and the Social Sciences" and "Men Are from Earth, Women Are from Earth: The Psychology of Gender since C. S. Lewis"—offer Van Leeuwen the opportunity to bring to bear her scholarly expertise regarding psychology and gender upon Lewis's biased and perhaps ill-informed attitude toward the social sciences. She is very good in explaining Lewis's critical analysis of Freudian Psychoanalysis, his (according the Van Leeuwen) "theologically problematic affirmation of Platonic mind/body dualism" (151), and his seeming easy acceptance of Jungian psychology and archetypes. Van Leeuwen finds Lewis's position on the latter quite troubling:

> To the extent that the [Jungian] archetypes are seen as ideals to which people should aspire, one's conformity to them can be treated as either pathological or perverse. When Jung postulated the masculine Animus and its feminine counterpart Anima, he was engaging in yet another version of the nature/grace dualism. He was suggesting—as Lewis did for much of his life—that the "eternal forms" of masculinity and femininity were on a higher plane than shortsighted whining about the confines of gender roles, and that "healthy" people should set aside the latter and embrace the former. (163)

Her look at numerous gender studies (including charts and tables) may well tire some readers, but the empirical studies are interpreted clearly and go a long way toward supporting key arguments she makes throughout the book. The question of whether Lewis would have interpreted the data the same way Van Leeuwen does is a fascinating one; of one thing, however, I think we can be certain: he would have enjoyed debating the matter with so worthy an adversary.

Chapter 8 and 9—"'Nature Speaks Chiefly in Answer to Our Questions': C. S. Lewis and Some Neglected Issues in the Psychology of Gender" and "'True to the Kind of Things We Are': C. S. Lewis and Family"—argue that some of "Lewis's writings about gender relations had a prophetic edge to them, in the sense that they have steadily accumulated empirical support, even though they are treated as 'paradigmatically incorrect' by much of the secular academy" (193). Van Leeuwen focuses upon two issues specifically: Lewis's writings on divorce and parenting. Regarding the former, Van Leeuwen explores in some detail Lewis's late marriage to divorcee Joy Davidman. Those familiar with the story of Lewis and Davidman will not find much new here, but of note is Van Leeuwen's review of several research studies on the negative impact of divorce upon children. She ends the chapter by saying Lewis would not be surprised by this research: "His aversion to divorce was never just a case of adherence to an isolated divine command about lifelong marriage. He regarded marriage as a crucible for testing and refining an entire web of basic Christian—indeed, essentially human—virtues" (212).

Regarding the latter, Van Leeuwen traces Lewis's "informally recorded views about childrearing, beginning with his role as a godparent and ending with his step-parenting experiences with [Davidman's sons] David and Douglas Gresham" (217) Again, for those who know the story, there are no new revelations; yet Van Leeuwen gives a fresh perspective on this part of Lewis's life and believes that Lewis was in fact a very good step-parent to the Gresham boys.

The last chapter, "'Suppressed by Jack': The Two Sides of C. S. Lewis," neatly pulls together the threads of Lewis and gender that Van Leeuwen has woven throughout; in addition, she offers a final assessment in which she argues that Lewis came to realize that gender essentialism and gender hier-archy are not monolithic for the Christian. Men and women "are defined by the nature of their *activities*—writing, teaching, composing, etc.—not by the sex or class of the people who partake of them. This does not mean that every-one will be on a level playing field everywhere . . . . What is *does* mean is that authority is much more horizontally dispersed than was envisaged in the era of Lewis's 'discarded image' . . . . As Lewis was beginning to realize, the great vertical 'chain of being' represented by the discarded image is not chiseled in stone" (258–59; emphasis Van Leeuwen).

Perhaps the book's greatest strength is Van Leeuwen's exploration of how Lewis's public and private views on gender were in conflict; furthermore, her analysis of this conflict is penetrating, thought-provoking, and articulate. No book is without fault, although I suspect the main weakness of this book is the responsibility of the publisher: no bibliography is included. I think this is a serious oversight as it means readers find themselves constantly thumbing through the book looking at footnotes in order to find out more about the sources Van Leeuwen cites. That aside, *A Sword between the Sexes* is another very valuable addition to Lewis scholarship.

A Review Essay on Recent Books on C. S. Lewis

Narnia and the Fields of Arbol: The Environmental Vision of C. S. Lewis. By Matthew Dickerson and David O'Hara. Lexington, KY: University of Kentucky Press, 2009.

C. S. Lewis on the Final Frontier: Science and the Supernatural in the Space Trilogy. By Sanford Schwartz. New York: Oxford University Press, 2009.

The Rhetoric of Certitude: C. S. Lewis's Nonfiction Prose. By Gary L. Tandy. Kent, OH: Kent State University Press, 2009.

The Cambridge Companion to C. S. Lewis. Eds. Robert MacSwain and Michael Ward. Cambridge: Cambridge University Press, 2010.

In 2007 Diana Glyer and David Bratman published "C. S. Lewis's Scholarship: A Bibliographical Overview" in which they offered a fine review of the most important books written about Lewis in the last fifty years.[29] Accordingly, I confine this survey to a selection of important, recently published books on Lewis. The first book, *Narnia and the Fields of Arbol: The Environmental Vision of C. S. Lewis* by Matthew Dickerson and David O'Hara, partially fills a gaping hole in Lewis studies. In spite of the fact that Nature plays a significant role in Lewis's poetry and fiction, other than a handful of essays, little critical work has been done in this area.[30] Even a cursory glance at Lewis's oeuvre reveals how important Nature is, from the early nature poetry in *Spirits in Bondage*, through the Ransom space trilogy (Ransom's initial experience in the Perelandrian ocean is a sensuous riot of "natural" tastes, smells, and sights), in dozens of poems he published in magazines and journals from the mid-1930s onwards, and culminating spectacularly in the Chronicles of Narnia (recall, for instance, Aslan's singing into creation the natural world of Narnia, including its landscapes and animals). And in other places Lewis writes about Nature, including *The Four Loves*, *Studies in Words*, and many essays.[31]

When I read that neither Dickerson (environmental studies and computer science) or O'Hara (philosophy) had backgrounds in literary studies, I admit I was worried. Would the book simply be a polemic in support of "radical environmentalism" and a rant against Lewis's biblically informed view of Nature? Would they neglect a nuanced discussion of Lewis's ideas? Would they miss his imaginative reach, his creative mind, or his deep love of the natural world? I needn't have worried. From the beginning the authors eased my concerns, writing that "this book asks what . . . Lewis had to say, both directly and indirectly, about nature and ecology—about the world in which we live, and about our (human) relationships with that world and with our fellow inhabitants . . . . at its core, then, this is a work of literary exploration" (1). At the same time, however, they go on to say "we want to see how the works of C. S. Lewis may help shape our thinking so that we might live in ways that are ecologically more sound, that are healthier for the broad community that is the world as well as for the local communities we inhabit" (2). Part of what energizes their discussion is the way in which they see how Lewis's imagination—as expressed in the Chronicles of Narnia and the Ransom Space trilogy—may prompt readers into a deeper understanding of how Lewis's *environmental vision* (their emphasis) is one worthy of emulation.

After two introductory chapters, Dickerson and O'Hara discuss Lewis's environmental vision as it appears in Narnia—especially *The Magician's Nephew* and *The Last Battle*. They suggest that Narnia was very much an agrarian world when Aslan created it, but it was soon tainted by witchcraft (Jadis) and science (Uncle Andrew). I think their discussion of *The Last Battle* and how the Calormenes pillage Narnia's natural resources via deforestation, agribusiness, and human domination is quite powerful, and of course offers a telling parallel to what has often happened in our own world. Several chapters are then devoted to the Ransom Space trilogy. In their initial discussion of *Out of the Silent Planet* they note that while it is a story about space travel, "its setting is decidedly pastoral and earthbound," beginning "under the shelter of a tree in rural England" where we find Elwin Ransom, Cambridge professor of philology, "emerging from the branches of a large chestnut tree." Lewis, they point out, calls attention to the landscape, "pushing the beauty of the natural environment into the foreground of our imagination: 'Every tree and blade of grass was dripping, and the road shone like a river'" (153). When they turn to discuss human intervention on Malacandra (Mars)—which is destructive and abusive—they suggest Lewis wrote the book in part "in order to oppose a dehumanizing worldview—and one that pitted our species in violent and piti-less conflict with others" (157). While the humans on Malacandra other than Ransom—the scientist Weston and the adventurer Devine—want to exploit and control the creatures and resources of that world, the *hnau*—Lewis's term for the sentient creatures of Malacandra—in striking contrast offer hospi-tality and welcome. In addition, their discussions of Lewis's environmental vision as portrayed in *Perelandra* and *That Hideous Strength* are informed, articulate, and well-argued.

The final chapter of the book offers five summative principles Dickerson and O'Hara glean from Lewis's environmental vision. First, both the com-munity and the individual have great worth. Second, human activity should not do harm to the natural world without cause. Third, humans are obligated to improve other creatures and help them to "perfect their natures." Fourth, humans should be humble in the face of what they do not know or understand. Finally, stories are an important but largely missing element in ecological— and perhaps in all scientific—education (259). Lewis's stories, in particular, "offer us a vision of the world brimming with life and goodness, full of pur-pose, rich with value, every part enmeshed in deep and ethical relations with every other part." Moreover, they argue, "Lewis succeeded in enchanting, or rather *re-enchanting* nature" (260; their emphasis).

As is the case with every book, there are some deficiencies in *Narnia and the Fields of Arbol*. One concern is the authors' neglect of Lewis's poetry, espe-cially that written from the mid 1930s onwards, since a number of poems could have been brought in to support their arguments concerning Lewis's environmental vision. They do make brief reference to "Under Sentence" and "The Future of Forestry" but could have cited a dozen more. More egregious, however, is their error referring to "Eustace's betrayal of his siblings" (250), since it was Edmund who was guilty of this betrayal. One or other of the authors should have caught this gaffe (the error is even carried over into the index). Still, the overall value of the book is not diminished by these relatively minor blunders. While not all will agree with the reading of Lewis's environmental vision given by Dickerson and O'Hara, the arguments they make, the supporting evidence they offer, and the winsome way they engage the topic ensures that readers will give their book serious thought and reflection.

C. S. Lewis on the Final Frontier: Science and the Supernatural in the Space Trilogy by Sanford Schwartz is another welcomed scholarly treatment of Lewis as a writer, focusing particularly on the Ransom Space trilogy. Building on the work of three earlier studies—Martha C. Sammons's *A Guide through C. S. Lewis' Space Trilogy* (Westchester, IL: Cornerstone, 1980), David Downing's *Planets in Peril: A Critical Study of C. S. Lewis's Ransom Trilogy* (Amherst, MA: University of Massachusetts Press, 1992), and Jared Lobdell's *The Scientifiction Novels of C. S. Lewis: Space and Time in the Ransom Stories* (Jefferson, NC: McFarland, 2004)—Schwartz extends and broadens the discussion of the trilogy by concentrating on its structure, sequencing, and "world-building." By examining these three foci, Schwartz argues that we can see the trilogy as "a more integrated and systematically organized series that is generally assumed"; in addition, such an approach indicates "the Space Trilogy and its author are at once deeply engaged with the modern intellectual revolution and eager to explore some of the pioneering insights that arose in its wake" (8).

Schwartz's argument that there is a similar structure to the three books is fascinating, and, if true, does much to illustrate how Lewis was a careful craftsman of his fiction, thus countering the charge that there is lack of unity between the three books. He notes that while other scholars have long noticed a structural pattern in *Perelandra*, with the first seven chapters being "divided into three discrete sections, which proceed toward a climactic center—the temptation scene (chapters 8–10)—followed by another seven-chapter sequence (chapters 11–17) that mirrors the tripartite division of the first seven chapters" (8), a similar structural pattern may be seen in *Out of the Silent Planet* and *That Hideous Strength*. Although the structural pattern of each book is not an exact mirror of the other two, they all share what Schwartz calls "a compelling instance of . . . multivolume symmetry: at the identical point in all three novels the previously passive protagonist is placed in a situation that requires personal decision, a commitment to violent action, and a reckoning with the prospect of death" (9). This insight alone marks *C. S. Lewis on the Final Frontier* as a major step forward in studies of the trilogy.

Regarding the idea of sequence, Schwartz notes that while the three books can be read separately on their own, there is also a clear line of continuity seen in the conflict between Ransom and his two adversaries—the physicist Weston and the adventurer Devine. However, Schwartz believes what has been overlooked is the way Lewis sequences ideas about "evolutionary process," especially as espoused by Weston—from a kind of "materialist . . . orthodox Darwinism" (*OSP*) to "creative or emergent evolution" (*P*) and culminating in a kind of human directed evolution to bring about the self-transformation of man into "God almighty" (*THS*). As Schwartz puts it: "Strangely enough, as we progress through the Trilogy we are also progressing to seemingly higher forms of the evolutionary model itself as they ascend (and in a sense return) to the transcendent heights of the religious worldview that the new developmental cosmology had presumably left behind" (11–12). Following Schwartz's argument left me saying to myself, "Of course. That's right. I can see that, now." Although one reader's response to an argument may be overly subjective, I think Schwartz should be pleased that his thoughtful critique and penetrating insights regarding the idea of sequencing won me over—and I suspect it will win over others as well.

The third focusing lens Schwartz introduces in his analysis of the trilogy—"world building"—concerns "conceiving the conflict in these novels not as a clash between antithetical principles [religious versus naturalistic points of view] but as a relationship between 'archetype' and distorted 'copy.'" In the process Lewis reduces "the opposition to a parodic imitation, but at the same time his imagined archetypes bear witness to an irreducible element of receptivity to the very 'falsehoods' he is exposing." For instance, argues Schwartz:

> Lewis's Malacandra is not only an "unfallen" planet that reflects the traditional conception of the "heavens"; it is also a transfiguration of the evolutionary model into the site of a modern exploration of the means through which we establish the most basic distinctions

between ourselves and other beings—and in particular, the process that makes it possible for certain human beings to relegate other members of their own kind to inferior or subhuman status. (17)

He draws similar relevant examples from *Perelandra* and *That Hideous Strength*, positing that such a perspective may help readers see the Ransom Space trilogy "less as the irreconcilable struggle between an old-fashioned Christian humanism and a newfangled heresy and more of the effort of a modern Christian writer to sustain and enrich the former through critical engagement with the latter" (18).

I did not care for the appendix on "The Dark Tower." Even though many scholars believe Lewis may have written it as an intended continuation of *Out of the Silent Planet*, I could not see how including the appendix related to the central arguments of Schwartz's book. Still, *C. S. Lewis on the Final Frontier* is a major step forward in critical assessment of the Ransom Space trilogy, one that I would liken to Michael Ward's *Planet Narnia*; that is, just as Ward's book has advanced critical discussion of the Chronicles of Narnia, Schwartz's book does the same regarding *Out of the Silent Planet*, *Perelandra*, and *That Hideous Strength*.

The Rhetoric of Certitude: C. S. Lewis's Nonfiction Prose by Gary L. Tandy is a very different kind of book from *Narnia and the Fields of Arbol* and *C. S. Lewis on the Final Frontier* since it focuses not on Lewis's imaginative work but instead upon his nonfiction prose. He argues that "the most fruitful rhetorical analysis of Lewis's prose would be one that mediates between" (xi) an examination of the relationship between his religious prose and his literary criticism and a detailed analysis of his prose style. Tandy's working definition of rhetoric is all the "linguistic and literary choices a writer makes in order to communicate with his audience," and with regard to Lewis's nonfiction prose specifically, his definition of rhetoric is one that "will not ultimately concern itself with whether a writer's arguments are right or wrong. Rather it will ask, Why did the writer choose this particular method? And, Were these choices appropriate and effective in view of the writer's subject and audience?" (xii). In the five chapters following the introduction, Tandy looks at how Lewis's worldview often clashed with modernism, his rhetorical theory, the rhetoric of his arguments, his rhetorical style, and the unity of his nonfiction prose.

Tandy does a nice job of noting Lewis's squabbles with modernism—its elevation of personal opinion and taste over reason, its "chronological snobbery," its de facto acceptance of science as the sole arbiter of truth, its advocacy of political and social agendas, its casual rejection of religion, and especially its literary criticism. Concerning the latter, Tandy offers a brief yet thorough survey of the particular aspects of modern literary criticism that Lewis found objectionable. For instance, Tandy points out that chief among Lewis's "complaints against modern writers was that they tended to ignore their audience" (23); as a result, according to Lewis, readers "'are brow-beaten into appreciating . . . [not good work but] mere puddles of spilled sensibility or reflection'" (23). In his discussion of Lewis's rhetorical theory Tandy points out that it is Lewis's keen understanding of the three elements of any rhetorical situation—speaker, subject, and audience—that "generates the peculiar energy of Lewis's nonfiction prose" (26). In particular Tandy delves into Lewis's use of invention, arrangement, and style as argumentative strategies; and he rightly connects Lewis's love of argumentation with his first great teacher, William T. Kirkpatrick.

I found Tandy's exploration of the stylistic traits of Lewis's nonfiction prose to be most helpful. He suggests that Lewis's style can be best understood in terms of a "rhetoric of certitude," one that implies "'What I am talking about is quite true. I am convinced that I am right. I am not asking for discussion or debate. Take it or leave it'" (84–85). Drawing on the work of Winston Weathers, Tandy examines Lewis's rhetoric of certitude in terms of diction, negation, repetition, series, aphorism, and certitude. Regarding Lewis's diction, for example, Tandy shows how "Lewis often chooses words denoting the absolute, complete, or final" (88). He cites many examples, but I will let one from *Mere Christianity* suffice here: "But, *of course*, if you think some things *really* bad, and God *really* good, then you cannot talk like that. *You must believe* that God is separate from the world and that some of the things we see in it are contrary to His will" (89; emphasis Tandy). Lewis's use of repetition is illustrated by the following example from *Miracles*: "Nothing comes of it, nothing leads up to it, it establishes no body of doctrine, explains nothing, is connected with nothing" (97). Throughout Tandy's discussion of Lewis's stylistic traits he is on target, offering incisive insights into how Lewis's argumentative techniques "work."

The brief discussion in the last chapter on the unity of Lewis's rhetoric of certitude effectively pulls together the key points covered in the book and also suggests the need for a broader understanding of the value of Lewis's rhetoric: "Critics could find few writers whose works supply such a fertile field in which to test [the tools of rhetorical analysis] as do those of this literary historian and Christian apologist, who used every rhetorical device at his disposal to communicate his message to a diverse and demanding twentieth-century audience" (124). *The Rhetoric of Certitude* is a fine piece of scholarship that sheds light on a most under-examined and under-appreciated aspect of Lewis's writing. Tandy does a terrific job of making his case, and his book is the best treatment of the topic that I have seen.

The Cambridge Companion to C. S. Lewis is, curiously, a part of the Cambridge Companions to Religion series rather than the Cambridge Companions to Literature series—suggesting perhaps that Lewis has still not quite passed literary muster with the decision-makers at Cambridge University Press; it is nonetheless a valuable resource for those looking for competent, though brief, scholarly treatments of Lewis as scholar, thinker, and writer. Editors Robert MacSwain and Michael Ward organize the book into three sections: Lewis as scholar, Lewis as thinker, and Lewis as writer. In part one, "Lewis as Scholar," MacSwain and Ward offer essays on Lewis as a literary critic, literary theorist, intellectual historian, and classicist. Stephen Logan's "Literary Theorist" is the most compelling and intellectually nuanced piece in the first group of essays. After distinguishing between two understandings of literary theory—on the one hand, "the practice of reflecting philosophically on the nature and function of literature" (29) and on the other hand, "a matter of trying to say what literature is, how it differs from other kinds of writing (if it does), and how we form a sense of what a literary text means" (30)—Logan says that there is little doubt Lewis made a contribution as a literary theorist in the first "traditional" sense, but "that its application to Lewis becomes doubtful, even preposterous" (30) in the second "contemporary" sense. Logan goes on to point out that this second sense of literary theory only "assumed its distinctive forms in the period after Lewis's death in 1963 . . .being determined by the ideological tendencies of a group of European intellectuals between the late sixties and the turn of the millennium" (30). Moreover, Logan incisively notes that "the contrast between the traditional and contemporary forms of literary theory is ultimately moral and metaphysical" (30).

In "Lewis as Thinker," there are essays concerning Lewis's views on Scripture, theology, naturalism, moral knowledge, discernment, love, gender, power, violence, and suffering. One of the strongest essays in this section is Carol Simon's "On Love" where she looks primarily at Lewis's *The Four Loves* (1960) and correctly points out that Lewis's taxonomy of love, though seemingly ossified and limited to four categories (*agape, phileo, storge,* and *eros*), is actually much more robust since he discusses gift-love, need-love, love for the sub-personal vs. love for finite persons vs. love for God, natural love vs. supernatural love, need-love vs. gift-love vs. appreciative love, and affection vs. friendship vs. eros vs. charity. Simon is also on target when she explores the cultural contexts of Lewis's views on love, noting that while he was "a great scholar and gifted writer," he "was also a twentieth-century, British, middle-class, late-married male" (151). She wonders how seriously Lewis's views on love can be taken in the twenty-first century, concluding "that Lewis is better taken as a role model than as an oracle or final authority on the subject of love" (151). Although Simon suggests some of Lewis's ideas on love (and gender) are perhaps dated, she believes "much of what Lewis says on the subject of love *is* of lasting value, in no small part because of his ability to give clear and winsome articulation to the best intellectual products of a long tradition" (152; emphasis Simon). Other strong essays in part two are Charles Taliaferro's "On Naturalism," Stanley Hauerwas's "On Violence," and Michael Ward's "On Suffering."

Part three, "Lewis as Writer," is less successful than parts one and two, though this is not the fault of the essayists. Instead, the essayists are hamstrung by the limited amount of space they are given to discuss the works in question: *The Pilgrim's Regress, Surprised by Joy,* the Ransom trilogy, *The Great Divorce,* the Chronicles of Narnia, *Till We Have Faces,* and Lewis's poetry. For instance, eleven pages to discuss Lewis's *Out of the Silent Planet, Perelandra,* and *That Hideous Strength* is an impossible encumbrance, although T. A. Shippey soldiers on dutifully. Similarly, Alan Jacobs has thirteen pages to cover the Chronicles of Narnia; at best he can only offer a sweeping overview. The best essay in this section is Malcolm Guite's "On Poetry," although even here one wishes he had more space to develop his discussion of Lewis's poetry and "its place in the wider canon of twentieth-century verse: (1) [T. S.] Eliot and modernism; (2) [Lewis's] war poetry; (3) [W. B.] Yeats and Irish writing, (4) ecological consciousness and protest; and (5) the contemporary debate between reason and imagination as ways of knowing" (296).

In offering an overall assessment of the *Cambridge Companion to C. S. Lewis*, I note that its greatest weakness is typical of collections of this sort and already hinted at in my discussion of part three—it is overly ambitious; that is, it attempts to do too much in a limited amount of space. Since I have frequently used other *Cambridge Companions* in the undergraduate literature courses I teach (including, for example, the *Cambridge Companion to Milton*, the *Cambridge Companion to English Poetry: Donne to Marvell*, and the *Cambridge Companion to Modernism*), I am more than familiar with this limitation. Another (and perhaps related) weakness with the *Cambridge Companion to C. S. Lewis* is the topics of the essays included. For instance, why is there an essay on Lewis and gender but not one on Lewis and the church (after all, this book is in the Cambridge Companion to Religion series)? What about essays on Lewis and education, language, and myth? I believe that given the time, space, and editorial constraints of compiling such a volume, the editors did a commendable job in pulling together the essays they included. Moreover, in spite of these weaknesses, I believe this is a worthy collection of scholarly essays on Lewis. That it found a place in the Cambridge Companions to Religion series speaks to Lewis's on-going influence as a scholar, thinker, and writer. I plan on assigning the *Cambridge Companion to C. S. Lewis* to my students the next time I teach a senior seminar on Lewis.

As this brief review essay suggests, Lewis scholarship is thriving fifty years after his death. I conclude by noting two areas (there are certainly more) of Lewis studies that need additional scholarly attention. First, although *Narnia and the Fields of Arbol* touches on Lewis and Nature, it is largely focused upon Lewis's environmental vision; certainly more work could be done on how Lewis's early love of Nature influenced his poetry, fiction, and non-fiction. Beyond the obvious influence of the countrysides around Belfast and Surrey, work could be done exploring how the natural environ around Headington and Oxford impacts his work. And what about the scores of walking tours he took with his brother, Tolkien, Harwood, and others? Surely Lewis's work is imbued with these experiences. Beyond these experiential sources, additional work could be done exploring the literary sources of his interest in Nature, including Greek, Roman, and Norse influences. As far as I know, no one has offered a robust discussion of these matters. Second, scholars could explore more deliberately the ways in which Lewis's letters serve as "incubators" for ideas he develops later and more fully in his books. I think it would be fascinating to trace the ways in which his letter writing advances his thinking, offering him the opportunity to float new ideas, test out arguments, and follow trains of thought.

New areas of scholarly research aside, I believe that Lewis's success as a writer springs from his deeply held belief about the core values of civilized life, what he terms "stock responses." Tracing these back to the Greek and Roman writers he so admired—Homer, Virgil, and Ovid—as well as the towering figures of western literature—Dante, Chaucer, Shakespeare, Milton, Wordsworth, Shelley, Keats, and Yeats—Lewis infuses his work with passages promoting honor, courage, bravery, honesty, charity, respect, and related values. For example, *"Spartan Nactus,"* where he feigns being unable to understand the nuances of modern poetry, concludes by his claiming he is

> One whose doom
> Retains him always in the class of dunces,
> Compelled to offer Stock Responses,
> Making the poor best that I can
> Of dull things . . . peacocks, honey, the Great Wall, Aldebaran,
> Silver streams, cowslip wine, wave on the beach, bright gem,
> The shape of trees and women, thunder, Troy, Jerusalem (685).

With tongue-in-cheek, Lewis's self-effacing portrait of himself throws into ironic relief those subjects of poetry he genuinely admires. In his address upon assuming the Chair of Medieval and Renaissance English Literature at Cambridge University in 1955, Lewis puts the idea in a slightly different way: "It is my settled conviction that in order to read Old Western literature aright you must suspend most of the responses and unlearn most of the habits you have acquired in reading modern literature."[32] Throughout his writing Lewis never wavers from anchoring himself to stock responses; they are the common denominator, describing for him what it means to be fully human.

Will Lewis still be as popular in 2113 as he is in 2013? Which of his works will endure? Will literary scholars still be writing about Lewis? I leave those questions to the next several generations of Lewis scholars, but I doubt Lewis's influence will completely fade in the next hundred years. I can only affirm that I believe he may be remembered by future generations as a composite of John Milton, John Bunyan, and Dr. Samuel Johnson. Lofty comparisons, but deservedly so.

I conclude with a personal note.[33] In the fall of 1971 I was a sophomore at Virginia Tech. Like many others, I had a campus job— ten to fifteen hours a week washing dishes in one of the huge cafeterias on campus. One day at the end of my shift someone gave me a tattered copy of *The Lion, the Witch and the Wardrobe.* I suppose there is a chance I had heard of Lewis before then, but I doubt it. Since I was a literature major, I was always pretty hungry for something new to read, so I plunged into *LWW*; to say that I was overwhelmed by Lucy, Aslan, and Narnia would be an understatement. In spite of the fact that we were in the middle of final exams, I read the next six Narnia tales over the next day or two.

That was my introduction to Lewis. I was drawn to him through his imaginative books, but I kept discovering new books by him on wide-ranging topics. It seemed he had written a book that scratched all my itches. This was especially true with regard to literary studies. For instance, I was looking forward to a course on Milton that featured an extended study of *Paradise Lost.* I had heard *PL* was a distinctively "Christian" piece of literature, so I was primed for a rich literary experience, assuming that perhaps it would also be informed by Milton's Christian experience. I was not disappointed, and I was amazed that, once again, Lewis was there before me since a required supplemental text in the course was his *A Preface to Paradise Lost.* I still marvel at Lewis's insight on Milton's Satan:

> Set a hundred poets to tell the same story and in ninety of the resulting poems Satan will be the best character. In all but a few writers the "good" characters are the least successful, and every one who has tried to make even the humblest story ought to know why. To make a character worse than oneself it is only necessary to release imaginatively from control some of the bad passions which, in real life, are always straining at the leash . . . . But if you try to draw a character better than yourself, all you can do is to take the best moments you have had and to imagine them prolonged and more consistently embodied in action. But the real high virtues which we do not possess at all, we cannot depict except in a purely external fashion. We do not really know what it feels like to be a man much better than ourselves . . . . To project ourselves into a wicked character, we have only to stop doing something, and something that we are already

tired of doing; to project ourselves into a good one we have to do what we cannot and become what we are not.[34]

Here is a depth of literary and spiritual insight hard to find equaled elsewhere.

Without belaboring the point, Lewis has been the pivotal writer in my literary, intellectual, and spiritual life. Lewis combines literary excellence, hard-nosed thinking, and a winsome faith in Christ. It is no exaggeration to say he was the most articulate Christian writer of the twentieth century. Although I never met him, through his books he became my greatest teacher and most influential mentor.

Chapter Notes

1. A version of this review essay first appeared in *IIIS* 43 (April 1983): 28–29.

2. *The Lion of Judah in Never-Never Land* (Grand Rapids, MI: Eerdmans, 1973), 14.

3. "Education and Fantasy," *College English* 37 (November 1975), 286.

4. "On Three Ways of Writing for Children," in *Other Worlds: Essays and Stories*, ed. Walter Hooper (New York: Harcourt Brace Jovanovich, 1966), 30.

5. "On Fairy-Stories," in *The Monsters & the Critics and Other Essays* (London: HarperCollins, 1983), 156).

6. A version of this review first appeared in *World* 5 (May 19, 1990): 14–15.

7. *George MacDonald: An Anthology* (London: Geoffrey Bles, 1946), 10.

8. A version of this review first appeared in *World* (March 30, 1991): 14–15.

9. A version of this review first appeared in *World* 8 (January 15, 1994): 21.

10. A version of this review first appeared in the *Christian Scholar's Review* 27 (Fall 1997): 129–30.

11. A version of this review first appeared in *Christianity and Literature* 51 (Summer 2002): 679–82.

12. This review essay is a revision of the three following reviews: *C. S. Lewis, Collected Letters: Volume I, Family Letters, 1903–1931*, ed. Walter Hooper (London: HarperCollins, 2000), *Christianity and Literature* 50 (Summer 2001): 750–755; *C. S. Lewis, Collected Letters: Volume II, Books, Broadcasts, and War 1931–1949*, ed. Walter Hooper (London: HarperCollins, 2004), *Christianity and Literature* 54 (Autumn 2004): 128–133; and *C. S. Lewis, Collected Letters: Volume III, Narnia, Cambridge and Joy, 1950–1963*, ed. Walter Hooper (London: HarperCollins, 2006), *Christianity and Literature* 57 (Winter 2008): 329–36.

13. This correspondence was previously published as *The Latin Letters of C. S. Lewis*, ed. Martin Moynihan (South Bend, IN: St. Augustine Press, 1998).

14. See *Brothers and Friends: The Diaries of Major Warren Hamilton Lewis*, eds. Clyde S. Kilby and Marjorie Lamp Mead (San Francisco: Harper & Row, 1982). 232–251.

15. Davidman's biographer, Lyle Dorsett, writes about this in *And God Came In: The Extraordinary Story of Joy Davidman* (New York: Macmillan, 1983): "It is likely that Joy was already falling in love with C. S. Lewis. [Her cousin, Renee] believed that [Joy] had fallen in love with Lewis's mind during their extended period of correspondence, and since Joy's marriage was a shambles, it does not require an overly active imagination to believe this. Lewis perhaps was growing infatuated with Joy; at least he delighted in her company, or he never would have continued the round of luncheons" (86).

16. *HU*, 167.

17. A version of this review first appeared in the *Christian Scholar's Review* 32 (Spring 2003): 333–35.

18. *Letters of C. S. Lewis*. Ed. with a memoir by W. H. Lewis (London: Geoffrey Bles, 1966), 15.

19. A version of this review first appeared in *Books & Culture* 12, no. 1 (January/February 2006): 18, 20–21.

20. A version of this review essay first appeared in *Christianity and Literature* 55 (Summer 2006): 567–86.

21. In the spirit of full disclosure, I was a reader of this book in manuscript form.

22. *Out of the Silent Planet* (New York: Macmillan, 1947), 27–30.

23. See her *C. S. Lewis in Context* (Kent, OH: Kent State University Press, 1994).

24. A version of this review first appeared in the *Christian Scholar's Review* 37 (Winter 2008): 262–264.

25. A version of this review first appeared in *Christianity and Literature* 58 (Autumn 2008): 130–34.

26. *The Letters of Dorothy L. Sayers: Volume Three, 1944–1950, A Noble Daring* (Cambridge: Carole Green Publishing, 1998), 343; emphasis Sayers.

27. A version of this review first appeared in *Christianity and Literature* 60.4 (Summer 2011): 689–693.

28. For an extensive bibliography on Lewis and gender, see "C. S. Lewis and Gender: 'Positively Medieval?'" *Christian Scholar's Review* 36.4 (Summer 2007): 387–390; this entire issue is devoted to Lewis and gender with a lead article by Van Leeuwen.

29. "C. S. Lewis's Scholarship: A Bibliographical Overview," in *Scholar, Teacher, and Public Intellectual*, Volume 4 of *C. S. Lewis—Life, Works, and Legacy*, ed. Bruce Edwards (Westport, CT: Praeger, 2007). This essay was an updated version of Glyer's "A Reader's Guide to Books about C. S. Lewis, and Other Resources" published in *The Pilgrim's Guide: C. S. Lewis and the Art of Witness*, ed. David Mills (Grand Rapids: Eerdmans, 1998).

30. See Ed Chapman, "Towards a Sacramental Ecology: Technology, Nature, and Transcendence in C. S. Lewis's Ransom Trilogy," *Mythlore* 3 (June 1976): 10–17; Rhonda Herb, "C. S. Lewis and Nature: Bearers of God's Messages," *The Lamp-Post of the Southern California C. S. Lewis Society* 25.4 (Winter 2011): 3–13; and Kathryn Lindskoog, "Spoiled Goodness: Lewis's Concept of Nature," in her *The Lion of Judah in Never-Never Land:* 29–47.

31. See "Likings and Loves for the Sub-human" in *The Four Loves* (London: Geoffrey Bles, 1960), 19–41; "Nature," in *Studies in Words* (Cambridge: Cambridge University Press, 1960), 24–74; "Religion and Rocketry," in *The World's Last Night and Other Essays* (New York: Harcourt Brace Jovanovich, 1960), 83–92; and several essays in *God in the Dock: Essays on Theology and Ethics*, ed. Walter Hooper (Grand Rapids, MI: Eerdmans, 1970).

32. "*De Descriptione Temporum*," in *Selected Literary Essays*, ed. Walter Hooper (Cambridge: Cambridge University Press, 1969), 13.

33. Portions of the next three paragraphs appear in "A Writer We Can Read for the Rest of Our Lives," in *Mere Christians: Inspiring Stories of Encounter with C. S. Lewis*, eds. Mary Anne Phemister and Andrew Lazo (Grand Rapids, MI: Baker Books, 2009).

34. *A Preface to Paradise Lost* (London: Oxford University Press, 1942), 100–01.

Bibliography

Aaron, Daniel. *Writers on the Left*. New York: Harcourt, 1961.

Arthur, Sarah. *Walking through the Wardrobe: A Devotional Quest into The Lion, the Witch and the Wardrobe*. Wheaton, IL: Tyndale House, 2005.

Barfield, Owen. Address given at Wheaton College, Wheaton, IL, October 16, 1964.

Blake, William. "The Marriage of Heaven and Hell." In *Blake's Poetry and Designs*. Eds. Mary Lynn Johnson and John E. Grant. 2nd edition. New York: Norton, 2008.

Bloomfield, Morton W. *The Seven Deadly Sins: An Introduction to the History of a Religious Concept, with Special Reference to Medieval English Literature*. East Lansing, MI: Michigan State University, 1952.

Brown, Devin. *Inside Narnia: A Guide to Exploring The Lion, the Witch and the Wardrobe*. Grand Rapids, MI: Baker Books, 2005.

The Cambridge Companion to C. S. Lewis. Eds. Robert MacSwain and Michael Ward. Cambridge: Cambridge University Press, 2010.

Carnell, Corbin Scott. *Bright Shadow of Reality: C. S. Lewis and the Feeling Intellect*. Grand Rapids, MI: Eerdmans, 1974.

Concise Dictionary of Literary Terms. New York: McGraw-Hill, 1972.

Conrad, Joseph. *The Collected Letters of Joseph Conrad: Volume I, 1861–1897* Eds. Frederick Karl and Laurence Davies. Cambridge: Cambridge University Press, 1983.

Daniel, Jerry. "The Taste of the Pineapple: A Basis for Literary Criticism." In *The Taste of the Pineapple: Essays on C. S. Lewis as Reader, Critic, and Imaginative Writer*. Ed. Bruce L. Edwards. Bowling Green, OH: Bowling Green State University Popular Press, 1988.

Davidman, Joy. *Anya*. New York: Macmillan, 1940.

_____. "But the People Live" (movie review of *Hangmen Must Die*). *New Masses* 47 (May 4, 1943): 28–29.

_____. "Citizen Kane" (movie reviews of *Citizen Kane* and *The Sea Wolf*). *New Masses* 39 (May 13, 1941): 28–29.

_____. "Commandos Strike at Dawn" (movie reviews of *Commandos Strike at Dawn* and *China Girl*). *New Masses* 46 (February 9, 1943): 27–28.

_____. "Deaths and a Warning" (movie reviews of *The Ox-Bow Incident* and *Next of Kin*). *New Masses* 47 (May 18, 1943): 30–31.

_____. "Dinner Knives" (movie reviews of *The Man Who Came to Dinner* and *Louisiana Purchase*). *New Masses* 42 (January 20, 1942): 29–30.

_____. "Dutch Underground" (movie reviews of *One of Our Aircraft Is Missing, George Washington Slept Here, A Yank at Eton*, and *Iceland*). *New Masses* 45 (November 17, 1942): 29–31.

————. "False History" (movie review of *Young Mr. Pitt*). *New Masses* 46 (March 23, 1943): 30–31.

————. "Fantasy and Fun" (movie reviews of *Million Dollar Baby* and *Singapore Woman*). *New Masses* 40 (August 19, 1941): 30.

————. "Guerilla Brigade" (movie reviews of *Guerilla Brigade* and *The Ghost of Frankenstein*). *New Masses* 43 (April 21, 1942): 28–29.

————. "Heroes are Human Beings" (movie reviews of *In the Rear of the Enemy, Desperate Journey, Manilla Calling*, and *Tales of Manhattan*). *New Masses* 45 (October 13, 1942): 30–31.

————. "Huey Hooey" (movie reviews of *Meet John Doe* and *Rage in Heaven*). *New Masses* 39 (April 1, 1941): 30–31.

————. "Humdrum Cinema" (movie reviews of *Come Live with Me* and *So Ends Our Night*). *New Masses* 38 (March 18, 1941): 29–30.

————. "Kansas Poet" (book review of *The High Plains* by Kenneth Porter). *New Masses* 30 (February 7, 1939): 26–27.

————. "Keeper of the Flame" (movie reviews of *Keeper of the Flame, Chetniks*, and *Hitler's Children*). *New Masses* 46 (March 30, 1943): 28–29.

————. *Letter to a Comrade*. New Haven, CT: Yale University Press, 1938.

————. "Marxist Mania" (movie review of *Go West*). *New Masses* 38 (March 4, 1941): 27–28.

————. "Near Catalonia." *New Masses* 29 (October 18, 1938): 18. Rpt. in *Letter to a Comrade*, 67.

————. "Neptune's Pets" (movie reviews of *Washington Murderdrama, Power Dive*, and *Border Vigilantes*). *New Masses* 39 (June 10, 1941): 28–29.

————. "Other Movies" (movie reviews of *Dumbo, All That Money Can Buy*, and *Target for Tonight*). *New Masses* 41 (November 4, 1941): 27–28.

————. *Out of My Bone: The Letters of Joy Davidman*. Ed. Don W. King. Grand Rapids, MI: Eerdmans, 2009.

————. "Pacific Shore." *New Masses* 39 (March 25, 1941): 24.

————. "Perfect Landing" (movie reviews of *Wings of Victory* and *The Land is Bright*). *New Masses* 41 (November 25, 1941): 26–27 and 28–29.

————. "Peter the Plowman." *New Masses* 44 (September 15, 1942): 15.

————. "Prayer Against Indifference." *New Masses* 28 (August 9, 1938): 17. Rpt. in *Letter to a Comrade*, 31.

————. "Quack, Quack" (book review of *Hollywood: The Movie Colony—The Movie Makers* by Leo Rosten). *New Masses* 42 (February 10, 1942): 24.

————. "Rover Boys on Wings" (movie reviews of *I Wanted Wings* and *Topper Returns*). *New Masses* 39 (April 8, 1941): 28–29.

————. "Shining Screwballs" (movie reviews of *Love Crazy* and *Shining Victory*). *New Masses* 39 (June 17, 1941): 28.

————. *Smoke on the Mountain: An Interpretation of the Ten Commandments*. London: Hodder & Stoughton, 1953.

————. "Soviet Frontiers" (movie reviews of *Soviet Frontiers on the Danube* and *Underground*). *New Masses* 40 (July 15, 1941): 27–28.

————. "Soviet Love Story" (movie reviews of *The New Teacher* and *That Hamilton Woman*). *New Masses* 39 (April 22, 1941): 28–29.

_____. "Strength through Joy." *New Masses* 27 (April 5, 1938): 5.

_____. "The Face of China" (movie reviews of *Ku Kan* and *Out of the Fog*). *New Masses* 40 (July 8, 1941): 27, 29.

_____. "The Girl From Leningrad" (movie review of *The Girl From Leningrad*). *New Masses* 42 (January 6, 1942): 26–27.

_____. "The Longest Way Round." In *These Found the Way: Thirteen Converts to Protestant Christianity*. Ed. David Wesley Soper. Philadelphia: Westminster Press, 1951.

_____. "The Maltese Falcon" (movie reviews of *The Maltese Falcon, It Started With Eve,* and *The Man Who Seeks the Truth*). *New Masses* 41 (October 21, 1941): 28.

_____. "This Is the Enemy" (movie reviews of *This is the Enemy* and *Laugh, Town, Laugh*). *New Masses* 44 (July 7, 1942): 30–31.

_____. "Three Films" (movie reviews of *That Uncertain Feeling, The Flame of New Orleans,* and *Penny Serenade*). *New Masses* 39 (May 20, 1941): 30–31.

_____. "Under the Bombs" (movie reviews of *Mrs. Miniver, Nazi Agent,* and *Ring of Steel*). *New Masses* 43 (June 30, 1942): 29–30.

_____. "Volga-Volga" (movie review of *Volga-Volga*). *New Masses* 39 (May 27, 1941): 25.

_____. *Weeping Bay.* New York: Macmillan, 1950.

_____. "Women: Hollywood Style." *New Masses* 44 (July 14, 1942): 28–31.

Dickerson, Matthew and David O'Hara. *Narnia and the Fields of Arbol: The Environmental Vision of C. S. Lewis.* Lexington, KY: University of Kentucky Press, 2009.

Dickinson, Peter. "Ruth Pitter," *The Canadian C. S. Lewis Journal* 79 (Summer 1992): 1–3.

Ditchfield, Christin. *A Family Guide to Narnia: Biblical Truths in C. S. Lewis's the Chronicles of Narnia.* Wheaton, IL: Crossway Books, 2003.

Dorsett, Lyle. *And God Came In: The Extraordinary Story of Joy Davidman.* New York: Macmillan, 1983.

_____. *Seeking the Secret Places: The Spiritual Formation of C. S. Lewis.* Grand Rapids, MI: Brazos Press, 2004.

Downing, David. "'The Dungeon of His Soul': Lewis's Unfinished 'Quest of Bleheris.'" *SEVEN: An Anglo-American Literary Review* 15 (1998): 37–54.

_____. *Planets in Peril: A Critical Study of C. S. Lewis's Ransom Trilogy.* Amherst, MA: University of Massachusetts Press, 1992.

_____. *Into the Wardrobe: C. S. Lewis and the Narnia Chronicles.* San Francisco: Jossey-Bass, 2005.

Duriez, Colin. *The C. S. Lewis Chronicles: The Indispensable Biography of the Creator of Narnia, Full of Little-Known Facts, Events, and Miscellany.* New York: BlueBridge Books, 2005.

"Eight New Poets." *New Masses* 22 (February 16, 1937): 11–13.

Eliot, T. S. *Old Possum's Book of Practical Cats.* London: Faber and Faber, 1939.

Ferrari, Arthur C. "Proletarian Literature: A Case of Convergence of Political and Literary Radicalism." In *Cultural Politics: Radical Movements in Modern History.* Ed. Jerold M Starr. New York: Praeger, 1985.

Filmer, Kath. "The Polemic Image: The Role of Metaphor and Symbol in the Fiction of C. S. Lewis." *SEVEN: An Anglo-American Review* 7 (1986): 61–76.

Glyer, Diana. *The Company They Keep: C. S. Lewis and J. R. R. Tolkien as Writers in Community.* Kent, OH: Kent State University Press, 2007.

Gold, Mike. "Go Left, Young Writer." *New Masses* 4 (January 1929): 3–4. Rpt. in *Mike Gold: A Literary Anthology.* Ed. Michael Folsom. New York: International, 1972. 186–189.

―――. "Notes of the Month [on Proletarian Realism]." *New Masses* 5 (September 1930): 4–5. Rpt. in *Mike Gold: A Literary Anthology.* Ed. Michael Folsom. New York: International, 1972. 203–208.

Green, Roger Lancelyn and Walter Hooper. *C. S. Lewis: A Biography.* London: Collins, 1974.

A Handbook to Literature. Eds. William Thrall and Addison Hibbard. New York: Odyssey Press, 1960.

Hemingway, Ernest. "Fascism Is a Lie." *New Masses* 23 (June 22, 1937): 4.

Herbert, George. *The Poems of George Herbert.* London: Oxford University Press, 1961.

Hooper, Walter. *C. S. Lewis: A Companion and Guide.* London: HarperCollins, 1996.

Howard, Thomas. "*Poems*: A Review." *Christianity Today* 9 (June 18, 1965): 30.

Jacobs, Alan. *The Narnian: The Life and Imagination of C. S. Lewis.* San Francisco: HarperSanFrancisco, 2005.

King, Don W. *C. S. Lewis, Poet: The Legacy of His Poetic Impulse.* Kent, OH: Kent State University Press, 2001.

―――. *Hunting the Unicorn: A Critical Biography of Ruth Pitter.* Kent, OH: Kent State University Press, 2008.

Kort, Wesley. A. *C. S. Lewis: Then and Now.* Oxford: Oxford University Press, 2001.

Larkin, Philip. *Selected Letters of Philip Larkin.* Ed. Anthony Thwaite. London: Faber and Faber, 1992.

―――. *The Oxford Book of 20th Century English Verse.* Oxford: Oxford University Press, 1973.

Lewis, C. S. *The Abolition of Man.* New York: Macmillan, 1947.

―――. *The Allegory of Love: A Study in Medieval Tradition.* London: Oxford University Press, 1936.

―――. *The Collected Letters of C. S. Lewis, Volume 1: Family Letters 1905–1931.* Ed. Walter Hooper. London: Harper Collins, 2000.

―――. *The Collected Letters of C.S. Lewis, Volume 2: Books, Broadcasts and the War, 1931–1949.* Ed. Walter Hooper. London: Harper Collins, 2004.

―――. *The Collected Letters of C.S. Lewis, Volume 3: Narnia, Cambridge, and Joy, 1950–1963.* Ed. Walter Hooper. London: Harper Collins, 2006.

―――. *Dymer.* London: J. M. Dent, 1926. Under the pseudonym of Clive Hamilton.

―――. *An Experiment in Criticism.* Cambridge: Cambridge University Press, 1961.

―――. *A Grief Observed.* London: Faber and Faber, 1961. Originally published under the pseudonym of N. W. Clerk.

―――. *The Horse and His Boy.* London: Bles, 1954.

―――. *The Last Battle.* New York: Macmillan, 1956.

―――. *The Lion, the Witch and the Wardrobe.* New York: Macmillan, 1950.

―――. *The Magician's Nephew.* New York: Macmillan, 1955.

_____. *Mere Christianity.* New York: Macmillan, 1952.

_____. *Of Other Worlds: Essays and Stories.* Ed. Walter Hooper. New York: Harcourt, Brace, Jovanovich, 1966.

_____. *Perelandra.* New York: Macmillan, 1944.

_____ and E. M. W. Tillyard. *The Personal Heresy.* London: Oxford University Press, 1939.

_____. *Poems.* Ed. Walter Hooper. New York: Harcourt, Brace Jovanovich, 1964.

_____. *A Preface to Paradise Lost.* London: Oxford University Press, 1942.

_____. *Prince Caspian.* New York: Macmillan, 1951.

_____. *The Problem of Pain.* New York: Macmillan, 1943.

_____. *The Quest of Bleheris.* Bodleian Library, MS. Eng. Lett. C. 220/5. Fols. 5–43.

_____. *Reflections on the Psalms.* New York: Harcourt Brace and World, 1958.

_____. *The Screwtape Letters.* New York: Macmillan, 1943.

_____. *Selected Literary Essays.* Ed. Walter Hooper. Cambridge: Cambridge University Press, 1969.

_____. *The Silver Chair.* New York: Macmillan, 1953.

_____. "Spartan Nactus." *Punch 227* (December 1, 1954): 685.

_____. *Spirits in Bondage: A Cycle of Lyrics.* London: William Heinemann, 1919. Under the pseudonym of Clive Hamilton.

_____. *Surprised by Joy: The Shape of My Early Life.* New York: Harcourt, Brace & World, 1955.

_____. *The Voyage of the Dawn Treader.* London: Bles, 1952.

_____. *The Weight of Glory and Other Addresses.* Grand Rapids, MI: Eerdmans, 1965.

Lewis, Warren. *Brother and Friends: The Diaries of Major Warren Hamilton Lewis.* Eds. Clyde S. Kilby and Marjorie Lamp Mead. San Francisco: Harper & Row, 1982.

The Lion, the Witch and the Wardrobe. Directed by Andrew Adamson, Walden Media and Walt Disney Pictures, 2005.

MacDonald, George. *George MacDonald: An Anthology.* Ed. C. S. Lewis. London: Bles, 1946.

_____. *Creation in Christ: Unspoken Sermons.* Ed. Rolland Hein. Wheaton, IL: Harold Shaw, 1976.

_____. *The Gifts of the Child Christ.* Ed. Glenn Edward Sadler. 2 Volumes. Grand Rapids, MI: Eerdmans, 1973.

_____. *Phantastes and Lilith.* Grand Rapids, MI: Eerdmans, 1964.

_____. *The Princess and the Goblin.* London: Puffin, 1976.

Manlove, Colin. *Modern Fantasy: Five Studies.* Cambridge: Cambridge University Press, 1975.

Martindale, Wayne. *Beyond the Shadowlands: C. S. Lewis on Heaven & Hell.* Wheaton, IL: Crossway Books, 2005.

Milton, John. *Paradise Lost.* In *Complete Poems and Major Prose.* Ed. Merritt Y. Hughes. New York: Odyssey Press, 1957.

Murphy, James E. *The Proletarian Moment: The Controversy over Leftism in Literature.* Chicago: University of Illinois Press, 1991.

Murrin, Michael. "The Dialectic of Multiple Worlds: An Analysis of C. S. Lewis's Narnia Stories." *SEVEN: An Anglo-American Review* 3 (1982): 93–112.

Myers, Doris. *Bareface: A Guide to C. S. Lewis's Last Novel*. Columbia, MO: University of Missouri Press, 2004.

The New Princeton Encyclopedia of Poetry and Poetics. Eds. Alex Preminger and T. V. F. Brogan. Princeton: Princeton University Press, 1993.

Newton, Arvin. "A Letter on Proletarian Literature." *Partisan Review* (Feb. 1936): 12–14.

O'Brien, Kate. "Review of *Perelandra*." *The Spectator* 170 (May 14, 1943): 458.

Ong, Walter. "The Writer's Audience Is Always a Fiction." *PMLA* 90 (1975): 9–22.

Peters, Thomas. "The War of the Worldviews: H. G. Wells and Scientism and C. S. Lewis and Christianity." *Mission and Ministry* 11.4 and 12.1 (1998): 47.

Pilat, Oliver. "Girl Communist [Joy Davidman]." "An Intimate Story of Eight Years in the Party." *The New York Post* Oct. 31; Nov. 1; Nov. 2; Nov. 3; Nov. 4; Nov. 5; Nov. 7; Nov. 8; Nov. 9; Nov. 10; Nov. 11; Nov. 13, 1949.

Pitter, Ruth. *The Bridge: Poems 1939–1944*. London: Cresset Press, 1945.

———. *Collected Poems*. Petersfield: Enitharmon, 1990 (rev. 1996).

———. *End of the Drought*. London: Barrie & Jenkins, 1975.

———. *The Ermine: Poems 1942–1952*. London: Cresset Press, 1953 (winner of the Wm. Heinemann Award: Queen's Gold Medal for Poetry, 1955).

———. *First Poems*. London: Cecil Palmer, 1920.

———. *First and Second Poems*. London: Sheed & Ward, 1927.

———. *A Heaven to Find*. London: Enitharmon, 1987.

———. "Letter to C. S. Lewis." July 17, 1946. Marion E. Wade Center. CSL /L-Pitter/ 1a.

———. *A Mad Lady's Garland*. London: Cresset Press, 1934.

———. "Oral Interview." With Lyle Dorsett. July 23, 1985. Transcript available at the Marion E. Wade Center. Wheaton College, Wheaton IL.

———. *Persephone in Hades*. Privately printed, 1931.

———. *Pitter on Cats*. London: Cresset Press, 1946.

———. *Poems 1926–1966*. London: Barrie & Rockcliff/Cresset Press, 1968.

———. "Ruth Pitter Journal of Correspondence with C. S. Lewis." Bodleian Library, MS. Eng. lett. c. 220/3.

———. *The Rude Potato*. London: Cresset Press, 1941.

———. *The Spirit Watches*. London: Cresset Press, 1939.

———. *Still by Choice*. London: Cresset Press, 1966.

———. *A Trophy of Arms: Poems 1926–1935*. London: Cresset Press, 1936 (winner of the Hawthornden Prize in 1937).

———. Uncatalogued Papers of Ruth Pitter. Bodleian Library. See a holograph notebook beginning: "Transcribed 1970. All unpublished [poems], and of widely varying dates." "Passage from 'Perelandra'" is given first. In Bodleian MS Pitter Verse (uncatalogued), Box 28, 1–11.

———. *Urania* (selections from *A Trophy of Arms*, *The Spirit Watches*, and *The Bridge*). London: Cresset Press, 1950.

———. "We Cannot Take Less." BBC Radio. Feb. 17, 1961. Transcript available at the BBC Written Archives. Reading.

Rideout, Walter. *The Radical Novel in the United States, 1900–1954*. Cambridge, MA: Harvard University Press, 1956.

Ridler, Ann Margaret. "Capturing the Dance in Stillness." *The Guardian*, Mar. 3, 1992.

Russell, Bertrand. *The Conquest of Happiness*. London: Allen & Unwin, 1930.

_____. *Human Society in Ethics and Politics*. New York: Simon and Schuster, 1955.

_____. *Mysticism and Logic*. New York: Longmans, 1918.

_____. *Sceptical Essays*. New York: Norton, 1928.

_____. *Why I Am Not a Christian*. London: Allen and Unwin, 1957.

Ruth Pitter: Homage to a Poet. Ed. Arthur Russell. London: Rapp and Whiting, 1969.

"Ruth Pitter Obituary." *The Daily Telegraph*, Mar. 2, 1992.

"Ruth Pitter Obituary." *The [London] Times*, Mar. 3, 1992.

Ryken, Leland and Marjorie Lamp Mead. *A Reader's Guide Through the Wardrobe: Exploring C. S. Lewis's Classic Story*. Downers Grove, IL: InterVarsity Press, 2005.

Sayer, George. *Jack: C. S. Lewis and His Times*. San Francisco: Harper & Row, 1988.

Sayers, Dorothy L. *A Cat's Christmas Carol*. Marion E. Wade Center. Wheaton College, Wheaton, IL.

_____. "From the *Catalects of Pussius Catus I*." Marion E. Wade Center. Wheaton College, Wheaton, IL.

_____. *The Letters of Dorothy L. Sayers, Vol. 3, 1944–1950: A Noble Daring*. Ed. Barbara Reynolds. Cambridge: The Dorothy L. Sayers Society, 1998.

_____. *The Poetry of Dorothy L. Sayers*. Ed. Ralph E. Hone. Trowbridge, Wiltshire: The Dorothy L. Sayers Society, 1996.

_____. "Pussydise Lost." *Everybody's Weekly*, June 7, 1952.

Schakel, Peter J. *Imagination and the Arts in C. S. Lewis: Journeying to Narnia and Other Worlds*. Columbia, MO: University of Missouri Press, 2002.

_____. *The Way into Narnia: A Reader's Guide*. Grand Rapids, MI: Eerdmans, 2005.

Schwartz, Sanford. *C. S. Lewis on the Final Frontier: Science and the Supernatural in the Space Trilogy*. New York: Oxford University Press, 2009.

Shadowlands. Directed by Richard Attenborough. Savoy Pictures. 1993.

Smith, Mark E. *Aslan's Call: Finding Our Way into Narnia*. Downers Grove, IL: InterVarsity Press, 2005.

Tandy, Gary L. *The Rhetoric of Certitude: C. S. Lewis's Nonfiction Prose*. Kent, OH: Kent State University Press, 2009.

Tennyson, Alfred. *Poems of Tennyson*. Boston: Houghton Mifflin, 1958.

Tolkien, J. R. R. *The Tolkien Reader*. New York: Ballantine, 1972.

Van Leeuwen, Mary Stewart. *A Sword between the Sexes? C. S. Lewis and the Gender Debates*. Grand Rapids, MI: Brazos Press, 2010.

Vaus, Will. *Mere Theology: A Guide to the Thought of C. S. Lewis*. Downers Grove, IL: InterVarsity Press, 2004.

Walsh, Chad. *The Literary Legacy of C. S. Lewis*. New York: Harcourt, Brace, Jovanovich, 1979.

Ward. Michael. *Planet Narnia: The Seven Heavens in the Imagination of C. S. Lewis*. Oxford: Oxford University Press, 2008.

War Poems of the United Nations. Ed. Joy Davidman. New York: Dial Press, 1943.

Wilson, A. N. *C. S. Lewis: A Biography*. New York: Norton, 1990.

Word and Story in C. S. Lewis. Eds. Peter Schakel and Charles Huttar. Columbia, MO: University of Missouri Press.

Zinberg, Len. "Quiet and Safe." *New Masses* 28 (July 12, 1938): 152–153.

Index

CPSIA information can be obtained at www.ICGtesting.com
Printed in the USA
LVOW042253280113

317629LV00006B/9/P